ENVIRONMENTAL

CRIME

Published 1999 by Cameron May Ltd.

ISBN 1 874698 40 6

Printed by Biddles

The authors assert their moral right to be identified as the authors of this work.

You are advised that this book is merely a commentary on the authors' views of the environmental insurance industry and its likely legal impact on English law.

You should in no way whatsoever rely upon this text as legal advice or upon the accuracy of the text. Whilst every effort has been made to ensure accuracy, neither the authors, publishers nor anyone else connected with this book will in any way accept liability for the contents.

ENVIRONMENTAL CRIME

Fiona Darroch & Peter Harrison

CAMERON MAY
LONDON

Acknowledgements

The authors wish to express their thanks to the following for their assistance and advice:

Professor Michael G. Faure LLM
Institute for Transnational Legal Research
Maastricht University

Michael J. Penders
Special Counsel, US EPA

Mark Beard, Barrister
6 Pump Court

Researchers:
Dean Bialek
Leo Charalambides

Editorial Assistant:
Carrie Ann Berry

CONTENTS

Introduction

The proliferation of statutes and statutory instruments over the last few years, beginning with the Environment Act 1990 (EA 1990), has established a regulatory regime embodying a whole range of criminal sanctions available to the appropriate authorities when criminal enforcement is perceived to be the solution to a problem. Opinions vary as to the effects of the current levels and frequencies of prosecutions in the wider picture of environmental management; they also vary as to whether the appropriate fines are being levied. What is certain is that a framework of criminal sanctions is now in place to enable an appropriate authority to deal with most types of offences committed against the environment. There remain areas where criminal sanctions are not yet established as a means of enforcement, and areas where, although the framework is in place, criminal sanctions have yet to be used. Criminal sanctions are, correctly in the authors' views, used as a last resort: the extent to which they operate as a deterrent is probably increasing in proportion to the growth of public perception of the importance of both individual and corporate environmental responsibility.

The birth of the notion of Integrated Pollution Control (IPC) has marked the legal perception that environmental media can no longer be seen in spatial isolation from each other, any more than can forms of pollution which move between different media. This perception is slowly but surely growing at the international level, for example with the recent signing of the new European Environmental Crime Convention (EECC). Whilst the United Kingdom (UK) is not yet a signatory, it is likely that aspects of the Convention will pass into national legislation in the future.

An important aspect of this more holistic approach to the management of the national environment has been the establishment of the Environment Agency (EA), which in the UK is responsible for bringing the majority of prosecutions for environmental pollution and damage. The part which enforcement plays in management of the environment is part of the far wider role played by the EA, although current governmental opinion indicates that it considers enforcement to be an underused tool at the moment. Statistics indicate that, latterly, levels of prosecutions by the EA have not risen to the extent that some hoped. It remains to be seen, in the light of the new prosecution guidelines issued by the EA in November 1998, whether levels of prosecution will increase. Not only does there appear to be a funding shortage, but also a personnel shortage, leaving the EA challenged to comply with its licensing and enforcing duties in all the areas where it has a responsibility to do so. For example, implementation of the Groundwater Regulations, which generally concern the disposal of pesticide wastes and spent sheep-dip is far from comprehensive, although this will change with the arrival of guidelines.

There are also indications that the Government has higher expectations of local authorities in the consistent and thorough enforcement of Local Authority Pollution Control (LAPC), with emphases on consistency, proportionality and action where necessary.

Practitioners should also be aware of the Government's moves, in a draft Bill, towards the establishment of the Food Standards Agency (FSA). Enforcement of standards set by the FSA will be by local enforcement authorities, whose performance will be monitored by the FSA. The Bill currently includes powers for ministers to make regulations under the Food Safety Act 1990 (FSA 1990) in respect of the banning or regulating of the sale or use of substances in the regulating of pesticide control and releases of genetically modified organisms (GMOs). The ways in which the FSA will discharge its responsibility for consumer interests are as yet unclear.

The structure of this book is designed to give the practitioner speedy access to the parts of the statutes which contain the criminal offences. The book has been divided, for ease of reference, into the obvious discrete areas of regulation, although it is obvious that IPC, by definition, overarches the whole. The authors' intention has been to set out, by reference to that area of regulation, the elements of the related criminal offence, the defences available to a defendant charged under the statutes, and the powers of sentence which available to the Court, should the defendant either plead guilty to or be found guilty of the offence. The book is designed to be a relevant work for all those wishing to inform themselves of the regime of environmental offences, if only to avoid committing them. We include a simple procedural guide to assist those who may be unfamiliar with the criminal justice system.

Sentencing practices continue to change. In recent years, the maximum fine which a Magistrates Court can impose has risen generally to £20, 000, together with provisions for a custodial sentence. It is perceived to be a weakness in the system that sentences vary between Courts, however, particularly in view of the absence of specific sentencing guidelines. In a recent case brought against a company under the provisions of the Health and Safety at Work Act 1974 (HSWA 1974), the Court of Appeal laid down guidelines in respect of corporate offences which may in future apply to environmental offences. These are that the fine should reflect the degree to which the company in question has fallen short of the required legal standard, the degree to which any costcutting factor has resulted in that shortfall, the gravity of the offence itself and the defendant-means. A company wishing to submit that it was unable to pay a fine would be required to produce its annual accounts in order to prove this was the case. The recent *Sea Empress* case, in which a fine of £4 million was imposed for a no-fault, strict-liability offence under the provisions of the Water Resources Act 1991 (WRA 1991), indicates that some Courts are now seeking to impose fines which reflect increased public disquiet at substantial pollution damage. These levels of fines may begin to act primarily as a deterrent, although a cynic might suggest that until levels of fines across the board reflect the clean-up costs as well as a straightforward penalty for the offence, then possible fines for pollution offences may simply be factored into the company accounts as a reasonable economic price to pay, set against the risk of detection and the costs of changing a practice to ensure that the offence is not committed. However, there are now various provisions which allow either for a fine to be levied on a daily basis, in the event of the offence continuing, or for the fine to have regard to any consequential financial benefit which has accrued to the defendant through the commission of the offence. An added deterrent in some cases is the ignominy which attaches itself to a company through its acquisition of a criminal conviction.

At the time of writing, guidelines for implementation of legislation and enforcement are still awaited in various areas of the law (for example in respect of contaminated land), and therefore the book can make no claim to be a comprehensive work. New law is anticipated in a number of major areas and a practitioner looking for guidance in complex areas of litigation should simply regard this work as a starting point, generally providing signposts within the body of current legislation. Much of the recent law has appeared in domestic legislation in response to European Directives, and therefore practitioners should ensure that they have fully examined the current kaleidoscope of statutory instruments and sets of guidelines which address the relevant area of law, as well as the dates and consequences of implementation of certain crucial EC Directives. In particular, note the 1996 EC Directive on IPC. The British Government is attempting to implement the Directive through a Bill, currently at the Committee Stage, which will replace Part 1 of the Environment Act, in order to comply with the implementation deadline of October 30th, 1999. Draft regulations for implementation have already been issued, which will have far-reaching effects upon the entire pollution regime. Where relevant to them, practitioners should be also aware of the implications of the devolution legislation: although the responsibility for prosecutions will remain in the hands of the enforcing authorities as they currently are, there are European Union (EU) implications which may be reflected in other parts of the legislation. Practitioners and those who require their services should also take note of the definitional uncertainties which emerge from time to time (for example in respect of waste).

How to use this book

Our aim has been to provide quick access to information and the specific offence or area of control being considered.

Each chapter of the book covers a discrete topic such as water, waste, listed buildings or the investigation of offences. At the start of each chapter is a detailed list of points covered together with the appropriate heading number.

Once within the text, the numbered headings are designed both to provide a logical route through the information and to indicate precisely where a particular point is considered.

The index is based on key words and concepts rather than on a simple noun search.

CHAPTER 1

INLAND WATER POLLUTION

CONTENTS

CHAPTER 1

INLAND WATER POLLUTION

1.1 Introduction

Water supply, the control of pollution and the provision of sewerage services are the three principal areas of activity in the water industry which are subject to regulatory controls.

The pattern of regulation of water use is historically complex. That history has reflected the difficulties incumbent in any complex division of responsibility among regulatory bodies and the provision of a utility. The Water Act 1973 (WA 1973) established the 10 Regional Water Authorities and marked the first legislative move towards *integrating* the regulatory control of the water industry. Previously, the River Boards (established by the River Boards Act 1948 (RBA 1948)) and subsequently, the River Authorities (established by the Water Resources Act 1963 [WRA 1963]) were the bodies constituted for the regulation of sewage treatment, pollution control, water supply, land drainage and most other aspects of the management of watercourses. However, the RWAs reflected the dichotomy which emerged from vesting conflicting powers of authorisations 30th.

In 1986, the White Paper *Privatisation of Water Authorities in England and Wales* proposed the wholesale privatisation of water regulation, by the establishment of privately-owned water service public limited companies. The ensuing consultation revealed weaknesses in this plan. Firstly, conflict of commercial interest would be inevitable, with a private concern having regulatory power over another private concern. Second, the argument was made that 'poacher turned gamekeeper ' would render the scheme unjust. Thirdly, there was doubt as to whether the private water company would amount to the 'competent authority' that implementation of EC water legislation demanded.

In 1987, the Department of Environment (DoE) set out new proposals in a discussion paper: *The National Rivers Authority: the Government's Proposals for a Public Regulatory Body in a Privatised Water Industry*. This paper proposed a division of responsibility and power which would give the tasks of water supply and sewage treatment to the privately-owned companies, leaving the regulatory and environmental functions to be administered by a new body to be established, namely the National Rivers Authority (NRA).

The functions of the NRA were, *inter alia,* to set statutory standards and quality objectives, and to enforce the implementation of those standards, with powers to prosecute those whose acts or omissions resulted in a downward departure from those standards. The fundamental division of utility and regulatory responsibilities was achieved in the preamble to the Water Act 1989 (WA 1989).

The NRA was established by the WA 1989 s1(i). As its name suggests, it was an organisation which was homogenous in structure. Therefore, it was envisaged that to some extent there would be a degree of nationwide consistency in its enforcement policies.

However, in 1989, water law still derived from a number of different pieces of legislation and, to achieve a clearer water law regime, a consolidation process, under the powers of the Law Commission Act 1965 (LCA 1965), culminated in the passage of five new Acts in 1991. The two most significant of these were the Water Resources Act 1991 (WRA 1991) and the Water Industry Act 1991 (WIA 1991). (The other acts in this group of consolidating legislation were the Land Drainage Act 1991 (LDA 1991), the Statutory Water Companies Act 1991 (SWCA 1991) and the Water Consolidation (Consequential Provisions) Act 1991 (WCA 1991)).

1.2 The Legislation

1.2.1 Water Resources Act 1991 (WRA 1991)

Part I of this Act re-enacted the provisions which established the NRA, providing for the continuation of its functions. Part II of the Act legislates for the management of water resources. Part III addresses the control of pollution of those resources, defining offences The remaining parts of the Act deal with flood defence, control of fisheries, financial provisions in relation to the authority, lands and works powers, information provisions and the Schedules to the Act. This Act is now amended by the Environment Act 1995 (EA 1995).

1.2.2 Water Industry Act 1991 (WIA 1991)

Part I of this Act re-enacts the provisions for the appointment, by the Secretary of State, of a Director General of Water Services (DGWS). Part II provides for the establishment of companies whose business is the provision of water and treatment of sewage, and the powers of enforcement over such companies which are available to the Director and the Secretary of State. Part III outlines the general duties and the regulations and offences that flow from those duties. Part IV addresses the regulation of sewerage services. Part VI outlines an undertaker's powers and duties. Part VII legislates for the provision of information.

Governmental policy on environmental legislation had gained impetus (see *This Common Inheritance)*. In 1990, the Environmental Protection Act (EPA 1990) was passed. It legislated for the establishment of a system of Integrated Pollution Control (IPC). This amounted to control of pollution by means of authorisation and enforcement. The administration of IPC was by Her Majesty's Inspectorate of Pollution (HMIP). This authority was formed in 1987 to co-ordinate pollution control by amalgamating the tasks formerly performed by respective governmental inspectorates. HMIP was part of the Department of the Environment, operating on a regional basis. The IPC system is designed to address processes involving serious pollution, such processes being specifically prescribed by the Act.

The Environment Act 1995 (EA 1995) established the EA as the primary regulatory body in England and Wales, with a corresponding agency in Scotland. By s2 EA 1995, the powers formerly invested in the NRA were vested in the EA. These powers included the functions of the NRA under Parts II, III, IV, VII of the WRA 1991, the Land Drainage Act s136(8) and the WA 1989 (with Schedule 15 of that Act). The NRA's powers under various Acts relating to fisheries, and to its functions as navigation authority, harbour authority and conservation authority all passed to the EA, as did any other powers vested in the NRA by orders or agreement under Schedule 2 to the WRA 1991 — such as the powers of statutory consultancy, to agree exemption from charges due from an abstraction-licence holder in certain circumstances and to make and enforce bye-laws. General provisions for the EA's duties with respect to water are contained in s6 EA1995. These provisions reflect the duties imposed upon the NRA by ss2(2), 2(4), 2(5), 2(6), 19, 105(1), 114. By s2 EA 1995, the functions of HMIP were transferred to the EA, which now administers the IPC system. The EA's general functions with respect to pollution control are outlined at s5 EA 1995. Provisions with respect to water are to be found at s6 EA 1995.

The legacy of the NRA has been reflected to some extent in the degree to which the EA has been able to retain a nationwide consistency of approach in its enforcement policy in respect of water regulation. The regional nature of HMIP rendered such a consistency of approach more difficult to achieve.

1.3 Offences under WRA 1991

The principal groups of offences in respect of water legislation are to be found in WRA 1991 and WIA 1991. Offences arising out of IPC are found in EPA 1990. Other offences are contained within Salmon and Freshwater Fisheries Act 1975 (SFFA 1975) and the Land Drainage Act 1994 (LDA 1994).

1.3.1 Water Resources Act 1991

Part III of the WRA 1991 deals with control of pollution of water resources. Chapter 1 outlines the quality objectives of the Secretary of State's powers and duties in the achievement of those objectives. Chapter II contains the principal offences of the Act, defines the nature of certain types of discharges and outlines the defences to the principal offences in respect of authorised discharges and defences generally. Chapter III contains the provisions that enable governmental ministers to take precautionary action to control pollution.

WRA 1991: Chapter II: Pollution Offences

1.3.1.1 s85 WRA 1991: Offences of polluting controlled waters

s85(1) WRA 1991: *A person contravenes this section if he causes or knowingly permits any poisonous, noxious or polluting matter or any solid waste matter to enter any controlled waters.*

Definitions:

(1) *'controlled waters'*[1*]

These fall into four sub-categories:

(a) *'relevant territorial waters'* are those which stretch out to sea for three nautical miles from the baselines from which the breadth of the territorial sea adjacent to England and Wales is measured. The Secretary of State may order that any particular area of sea adjacent to England and Wales may be treated as if it were an area of territorial waters.[2]

(b) *'coastal waters'* are those extending landwards from the baselines as defined above, as far as the limit of the highest tide or, where appropriate, the freshwater limit of the watercourse or the river.[3] A watercourse includes

*Endnotes are given at page 61.

all rivers, streams, ditches, drains, cuts, culverts, dykes, sluices, sewers and passages where water flows through, other than the mains and other pipes which belong to a water undertaker or are used by one in the provision of a water supply to a premises.[4]

(c) *'inland freshwaters'* are defined as being the waters of a lake, pond, or river, or so much of the relevant river or watercourse as is above the freshwater limit[5]. 'Lake or pond' includes a reservoir of any description. 'Relevant lake or pond' means any lake or pond, whether artificial or natural, above or below ground which discharges into a relevant river or watercourse or into a relevant lake or pond.[6] 'Relevant river or watercourse' means any river or watercourse, including those underground, whether natural or artificial, which is neither a sewer or drains into a sewer.[7] By his powers under s104 WRA1991, the Secretary of State may order that any lake or pond which does not discharge into a relevant river or watercourse, or into a relevant lake or pond, is to be treated for those purposes as if it were a relevant lake or pond; likewise that a lake or pond which does discharge, and is of a description specified in the order, is to be treated for the purposes of the order as if it were not a relevant lake or pond.

(d) *'ground waters'* are defined as any waters contained in underground strata, including water that serves wells or boreholes.[8]

Notes

(1) *'Controlled waters'* include watercourses such as streams, ditches, drains, etc, irrespective of circumstances where they had overflowed, changed their course or dried up. See *R v Dovermoss Ltd* (1995) 159 JP 488, CA.
(2) The nature of the offence under s85(6) is held to include not only a discharge outside the condition of a consent, but an offence may also be committed where the defendant fails to comply with a condition of the consent. See *Taylor Woodrow Property Management Ltd v National Rivers Authority* (1994) 158 JP 1101.
(3) The fact that the defendant may not be either the owner or occupier of the land does not protect him from liability under s85(6) WRA1991. See also *Taylor Woodrow Property Management Ltd v National Rivers Authority.*

(2) *'causes or knowingly permits'*

The wording of this part of s85 WRA 1991 indicates two separate types of offence. The two are reflected in a large body of case-law, the majority of which is concerned with 'causes'.

(a) 'Causes'

It has now been held that this word should be given its commonsense meaning.[9] This meaning is to be question of fact and therefore not subject to elaborate redefinition of the word.[10] There is simply a requirement to show that there is a direct causational link between the defendant's act and the prohibited discharge. There is therefore no requirement to establish the *mens rea* of the defendant.

The issue of causation was explored extensively in the important case of *Alphacell v Woodward*, in which it was Lord Wilberforce's view that there was no place for the concept of *mens rea* where there had occurred a malfunction of a process for which a defendant was responsible, (even where no negligence had been proved), where the malfunction resulted in illegal pollution. The ruling in *Alphacell* was then followed in *Southern Water Authority v Pegrum and Pegrum*.[11] Here, an intervening act (in this instance blocked storm drains) caused water to flow into a lagoon where effluent from a pig farm was stored. The contents of the lagoon then began to seep into a stream and then into the River Medway. It was held that there was an unbroken chain of causation between the pig-effluence storage and the pollution.

For a prosecution under s85(1) WRA1991 to succeed, the chain of causation must be unbroken. If it is broken by the act of another, for example by the interference of a third party with plant or equipment, then a defendant may not be held liable.[12] However, even when vandals break the chain of causation, if such damage could have been reasonably foreseeable, then the chain does not necessarily break. In the *Impress (Worcester) Ltd v Rees* [1971] 2 All ER 357 QBD case, Lord Wilberforce commented that the act of a third person should not be assumed to break the chain of causation. He said: "The answer to such questions is one of degree and depends on a proper attribution of responsibility for the flow of polluting matter."[13]

The most recent significant case addressing the issue of causation where there is third-party involvement was decided in the House of Lords. In *Empress Car Company (Abertillery) Ltd v National Rivers Authority*, HL (5 February 1998), 1 All ER, the central facts of the case were that the tap on a diesel oil storage tank belonging to the defendant company had been opened, allowing the contents of the tank to flow out onto the yard and via the surface drains into the nearby river. It was perfectly possible that the tank was deliberately drained by a vandal. The Lords decided that the defendant company was liable for the pollution. When determining liability in a case brought under s85(1) WRA1991, a two-stage approach should be adopted. The Court should first determine whether the defendant has contributed by his own actions to the pollution that has occurred, even if such action has not been the immediate cause of the pollution. The threshold for the definition of 'action' is simply something more than absolute passivity. Lord Hoffman then defined the second stage of the approach as follows:

> if the defendant did something which produced a situation in which the polluting matter could escape but a necessary condition of the actual escape which happened was also the act of a third party or a natural event then the justices should consider whether that act or event should be regarded as a normal fact of life or something extraordinary. If it was in the general run of things as a matter of ordinary occurrence, it will not negative the causal effect of the defendant's acts even if it was not foreseeable that it would happen to that particular defendant or take that particular form. If it can be regarded as something extraordinary it will be open to the justices to hold that the defendant did not cause the pollution. The distinction between ordinary and extraordinary is one of fact and degree to which the justices must apply their common sense and knowledge of what happens in that area.

Three points emerge from this judgement:

(i) The *'polluter pays'* principle is now clearly reflected in environmental legislation.

(ii) The case-law indicates that this aspect of legislative policy is being construed strictly by the Courts.

(iii) Argument over ordinary and extraordinary and degree of foreseeability is likely to become one of the main issues in the whole question of liability.

An *extraordinary* degree of foreseeability is likely to be found in only a few cases where the prosecution will have to prove more than mere storage or use of the polluting matters on the land from which the polluting matter has flowed. Ordinary vandalism will not amount to this. This principle is confirmed by the decision in *CPC(UK) Ltd v National Rivers Authority* [1994] Env LR 131.

The case-law seems to have established that liability will generally fall where the direct, rather than indirect, responsibility for the pollution is held to lie, ie where a chain of causation can clearly be established between the defendant and the entry of the discharge.

In *Environment Agency v Brock* (ELM March 1998), an initial prosecution had been brought against the defendants for causing polluting matter to enter a watercourse contrary to s85(1) WRA 1991. The polluting matter was leachate from a landfill. On a routine inspection, the leachate had been found to have occurred at the point where two hoses were coupled together and a rubber seal had failed. The leachate had escaped into a ditch which had been dug by the defendants. This led eventually into a stream. At the trial, the magistrates found that since the ditch was man-made, it did not constitute controlled water within the meaning of the WRA 1991. They also found that the rubber seal had not failed as a result of the defendants' negligence. The EA appealed, because clarification was required as to whether the defendant's conduct amounted to negligence. The case was heard in the Divisional Court and Lord Hoffmann's test was applied – was the failure of the seal so 'extraordinary' that the strict-liability offence had not occurred? The failure of the seal was found to be 'normal' and, because the ditch flowed into a stream, this was 'controlled' water for the purposes of the offence.

Commentators have suggested that the man-made ditch flowing into the stream making the ditch a controlled water for the purpose of the offence is a ruling of some significance for future prosecutions. The comments include:

(i) A landlord does not 'cause' a discharge into controlled waters where the discharge has resulted from the activities of his tenant.[14]

(ii) Offences under s85 WRA 1991 are of strict liability. A company is vicariously liable for the acts of its employees, generally. It is not necessary to show that a company officer was involved. The acts of its employees alone will be sufficient to establish liability.[15]

(iii) It has been held by the Court of Appeal that where an offence is committed by more than one defendant, then where each had performed separate acts which contributed to the chain of causation, then each could be held liable for the offence.[16] The reasoning in this case echoed part of the judgment in the case of *National Rivers Authority v Yorkshire Water Services Ltd*,[17] where it was held that the defendant had inevitably caused the discharge of a pollutant by dint of the system it had established in its treatment plant. It should be noted that that particular defendant used a special defence available to sewerage undertakers under s87 WRA 1991.

(iv) There has been some question as to whether the offence of 'causing' requires a positive act. This question would now seem to be resolved when a positive act has been committed, although it is worth noting that in the case of *Wychavon District Council v National Rivers Authority*[18] there seemed to have been nothing done by the defendant to rectify matters after the discharge had been discovered, which may have amounted to negligence but that did not amount, so held Watkins LJ, to the discharge having being 'caused' within the meaning of the term. However, it was submitted in *National Rivers Authority v Yorkshire Water Services Ltd* that the case had been wrongly decided. Lord Mackay, for the House of Lords, took the view that a case should be decided on its own facts. Lord Taylor in the Court of Appeal suggested that the word 'causes' involved 'some active participation in the operation or chain of operations resulting in the pollution' and quoted Lord Widgery in *Price v Cromack*[19] 'mere tacit standing by and looking on' was not enough. However, in *Empress*, the whole question of causation was explored and the two-stage approach outlined above now gives clearer guidance on the nature of causation generally.[20]

(v) A separate offence is committed on the occasion of each discharge[21]

(b) 'Knowingly permits'

Here, the offence is committed where the defendant, having actual or constructive knowledge, fails to prevent the discharge into controlled waters. There is far less case-law here, because most prosecutions are based upon 'caused'.

(3) *'poisonous, noxious or polluting matter'*

This term is not defined in the Act. The case-law gives contrasting indications as to what may be considered poisonous, noxious or polluting:

(i) Surface water from a tarmac road, which contained tar acid, was held to be 'noxious',[22] although surface water conveyed by surface sewers to a watercourse was held not be so, although the surface water contained sand and silt.[23]

(ii) The timing of the assessment of the nature of the discharge appears to be the moment at which it enters the watercourse.[24] A 'noxious' discharge may be said to be so when the quality of the watercourse into which the discharge enters deteriorates as a consequence of the entry of that discharge.[25] It has been suggested that 'a tentative conclusion which may be drawn from these decisions is that 'poisonous' is a reference to an intrinsic quality of the mater discharged, whereas 'noxious' or 'polluting' refer to the effect of the matter upon the watercourse into which it is discharged.'[26]

(iii) 'Polluting' should be defined by reference to its ordinary dictionary meaning.

In *R v Dovermoss*, the *Oxford English Dictionary* was used to distinguish between the respective meanings of 'pollute', 'poisonous' and 'noxious'. Whether pollution had occurred was a question of fact and degree. It was not necessary to show that actual harm had occurred.

> s85(2) WRA 1991: A person contravenes this section if he causes or knowingly permits any matter, other than trade effluent or sewage effluent, to enter controlled waters by being discharged from a drain or sewer in contravention of a prohibition imposed under section 86 below.
>
> s85(3) WRA 1991: A person contravenes this section if he causes or knowingly permits any trade effluent or sewage effluent to be discharged -
>
> (a) into any controlled waters; or
> (b) from land in England and Wales, through a pipe, into the sea outside the seaward limits of controlled waters.
>
> s85(4) WRA 1991: A person contravenes this section if he causes or knowingly permits any trade effluent or sewage effluent to be discharged, in contravention of any prohibition imposed under section 86 below, from a building or from any fixed plant -
>
> (a) on to or into any land; or
> (b) into any waters or a lake or pond which are not inland freshwaters.
>
> s85(5) WRA 1991: A person contravenes this section if he causes or knowingly permits any matter whatever to enter any inland freshwaters so as to tend(either directly or in combination with other matter which he or another person causes or permits to enter those waters) to impede the proper flow of the waters in a manner leading, or likely to lead, to a substantial aggravation of-
>
> (a) pollution due to other causes; or
> (b) the consequences of such pollution

Definitions

'Effluent'

Effluent is interpreted at s221 WRA 1991 to mean any liquid which includes particles of matter and other *substances* in suspension of that liquid. *Substance* is to include microorganisms and any natural or artificial substance or other matter, either in solid or liquid form, or in the form of a gas or a vapour.

'Trade effluent'

The term trade effluent is to include any effluent discharged from premises used for carrying on any trade or industry, other than surface water and domestic sewage. This definition is, for the purposes of the Act, also to include any premises wholly or mainly used, whether for profit or not, for agricultural purposes or for the purposes of fish farming or for scientific research or experiment.

'Sewage effluent'

This term includes any effluent from sewage disposal, or from the sewerage works of a sewerage undertaker, other than surface water;

> s85(6) WRA 1991: Subject to the following provisions of this Chapter, a person who contravenes this section or the conditions of any consent given under this Chapter for the purposes of this section shall be guilty of an offence and liable
>
> (a) on summary conviction, to imprisonment for a term not exceeding three months or to a fine not exceeding £20,000 or to both;
> (b) on conviction on indictment, to imprisonment for a term not exceeding two years or to a fine or both.

Serious water pollution incidents have increased substantially in recent years. Water companies have regularly been fined substantial sums for offences under this section:

> In June, 1997, Welsh Water was prosecuted for allowing sewage works to discharge into the River Dee. The discharge had occurred during repairs to the works' aeration lanes. The company pleaded guilty to two charges of breaches of discharge

consent, contrary to s85(6) WRA 1991, and was fined £10,000 for each charge, with costs of £475. The same company was charged under s85(6) WRA 1991 for a similar offence in June 1997, when it was fined £4,000, with costs of £240.

In March, 1997, Southern Water pleaded guilty to a charge of causing polluting matter to enter the Herrings Stream — the result of which had been, *inter alia*, the death of fish downstream at Hickstead, because the ammonia concentrations downstream were four times those lethal to fish. The company was fined £5,000, with £580 costs.

In April, 1997, Wessex Water pleaded guilty to a charge under s85(1) WRA 1991 where a sewage burst polluted a Somerset stream near Weston-super-Mare. This was the fifth sewage leak since 1991. The company was fined £2,500 with £250 costs. In a further prosecution, in January, 1998, under s85(6) WRA 1991, the same company was fined for contravention of its discharge consent at a sewage disinfection plant. The contravention remained undiscovered until it was found the following morning. The discharge of sewage effluent led to bathing water falling below EC standards. The company was fined £10,000 and ordered to pay costs of £250.

In June, 1997, Anglian Water pleaded guilty to polluting a Lincolnshire watercourse with sewage. The company's Fenside pumping-station discharged raw sewage into the North Forty Foot Drain. No warning was given of the fault and 400 fish died. Anglian Water was fined £2,500 with costs of £1,395.

Pollution prosecutions have cost the water industry £1.3 million in fines and costs since privatisation of the water companies. Note that the largest single source of pollution is sewage. The next largest source of pollution is construction sources. The third largest source is the industrial sector. The EA has prosecuted six food firms recently, under s85(1) WRA 1991. Fines for significant amounts of pollution ranged from £4,000 to £10,000.

Until recently, there has been a perceptible fall in the level of fines, and a decline in the number of prosecutions. This is mainly due to a fall in the number of prosecutions for radioactive substances and partly to a decline in prosecutions under IPC.

However, the trend in fines is now clearly rising. The *Sea Empress*, an oil-tanker, ran aground off Milford Haven in February, 1996. More than 72,000 tonnes of oil was lost from the vessel before it was finally brought into the port six days later. In January 1999, Milford Haven Port Authority was fined a record £4 million, and ordered to pay £825,000 towards the EA's costs, for the offence of causing polluting matter to enter controlled waters in breach of s85(1) WRA 1991. The fine was imposed in order to emphasise the need 'for the highest possible standards on the part of the port authority', to address the 'grave threat' posed to the community environment by the spillage and to reflect the enormous cost of the response to the disaster, as well as the financial impact which it had upon tourism and commercial fisheries. At the time of writing, it is not known whether the Port Authority will appeal against the fine but it is worth noting that the fine imposed took account of the fact that the Authority is less well endowed than a major oil or manufacturing company whom the judge said would have been fined more severly in a case of this public significance.

What is particularly significant in this case, in addition to the record penalties which have been imposed, is that the judgment follows the reasoning in the *Empress Car* decision, indicating that Courts will construe 'causing' as a matter of strict liability. The Authority's 'causing' was to be found in three areas: the inadeqate navigation of the pilot who was not sufficiently qualified to bring in a vessel of the size of the *Sea Empress* (a very large crude carrier (VLCC)), the tardiness of the Port Authority's modification of the classification of incoming vessels; and the inadequacy of the procedures for entry into the harbour for VLCCs.

1.3.1.2 s86 WRA 1991: Offences arising out of prohibited discharges

s86(i) WRA 1991: A discharge amounts to an offence for the purposes of s85 WRA 1991 where the discharge has taken place in contravention of a notice, served by the EA, prohibiting the person concerned from either making or continuing the discharge, either unless specific conditions are observed, or at all. A notice period must be defined and expire for the notice to be valid and the period may be no less than three months beginning from the day when the notice is served, except where the EA is satisfied that there is an emergency. Where an application or an appeal is made, the period of notice is deemed not to expire until a result of an application is known or until an appeal is withdrawn or determined (ss4-6 WRA 1991).

s86(ii) WRA 1991: A discharge also amounts to an offence under s85 WRA 1991 where the effluent or matter discharged contains either a prescribed substance or concentration thereof, or derives from a prescribed process or from a process which involves the use of prescribed substances, or the use of substances in quantities which exceed the prescribed amounts. Note that radioactivity possessed by any substance or article, or existing in part of the premises, is excluded from these provisions (s40 Radioactive Substances Act 1993 (RSA 1993)).

Vessels are excluded from these provisions. (Vessels are defined at s221[1] WRA 1991.)

1.3.1.3 s87: Discharges into and from public sewers etc

This section deals with the determination of liability where sewage is being discharged, as defined by s85 WRA 1991. The liability of the discharging sewage undertaker extends past 'cause or knowingly permit' for the undertaker is deemed to have caused the discharge if

(a) matter included in the discharge was received by it (the undertaker) into the discharging sewer, or works vested in it,
(b) or if it was bound to receive that matter into that sewer or works.

There are circumstances when the liability passes from the discharging undertaker. For example, in an agreement between the discharging undertaker and the sending undertaker, under s110 WIA 1991, where the sewage effluent was, before being discharged from the discharging sewer, discharged through a main connection into that sewer, or into any other sewer or works vested in the discharging undertaker by another sewerage undertaker, the 'sending undertaker'. The sending undertaker may then be liable, by the same token as the discharging undertaker at (a) or (b) above.

1.3.1.4 Defences to charges brought under s87 WRA 1991

1. A sewerage undertaker shall not be guilty of an offence simply because it contravenes a condition of a discharge, if another was responsible for the discharge being made or permitted to be made.

2. The undertaker does not commit an offence if it was not bound to receive the discharge, or was bound to receive it but subject to certain conditions which were not observed.

3. The undertaker may also use the defence that it could not reasonably have been expected to prevent the discharge into the sewer or works.

4. If it is available to it, the undertaker may use the defence, when charged under s85 WRA 1991, that it was bound to receive the discharge, either unconditionally or subject to conditions which were observed.

Defences to principal charges of offences under s85 WRA 1991 are to be found at s88 and s89 WRA 1991.

1.3.1.5 s88: Defences to charges brought under s85 WRA 1991

These are based on the notion that the discharge has prior consent and that it has been made in accordance with the relevant consents or authorisations:

(i) A *consent* issued by the EA under the WRA 1991 (or one issued similarly under Part II of the Control of Pollution Act 1974 [COPA 1974] which makes the same provisions for Scotland). The provisions for this type of consent may be found in Chapter II (85-91), Part III WRA 1991.

Note that provisions for the modification of such consents, their giving and revocation, are to be found at s88(2) WRA 1991, which gives effect to Schedule 10. See s190(1)(b)(c) 2, 3, WRA 1991 for registration of the applications and conditions of such consents.

(ii) An *authorisation* for a prescribed process granted by the EA under the IPC provisions of the EPA 1990. The Act provides that no prescribed process may be operated without an authorisation from the relevant enforcing authority. The requirements for obtaining such an authorisation are set out in the Environmental Protection (Applications, etc) Regulations 1991.

(iii) A *licence* for waste management or disposal.

A *waste-management licence* means a licence granted under the provisions of Part II EPA, 1990.

A *disposal licence* is defined as a licence issued in pursuance of s5 COPA 1974. Provisions for the rules and procedures governing the issue of these licences are to be found in Schedule 10 and in the Control of Pollution (Applications, Appeals and Registers) Regulations 1996. A disposal licence may not be treated as authorising any entry or discharge which is described in s85(2-4) WRA 1991, or any act or omission which results in such an entry or discharge.

(iv) A *licence* granted under Part II of the Food and Environment Protection Act 1985 (FEPA 1985) (for dumping at sea).

(v) A *licence* granted under s163,165, WIA 1991 (discharges for works purposes).

(vi) A discharge made in accordance with a statute or statutory order. A statutory order means any order under s168 WRA 1991 or s167 WIA 1991 (which refer to compulsory works orders). It also means "any order, bye-law, scheme or award made under any other enactment, including an order or scheme confirmed by Parliament or brought into operation in accordance with special parliamentary procedure" (s88[4][b] WRA 1991).

1.3.1.6 s89 WRA 1991: Defences (Other defences to principal offences)

This group of defences is a miscellany under s89(1) WRA 1991:

(a) A person is not guilty of an offence if the entry has been caused or permitted, or the discharge made in an emergency, in order to avoid danger to life and health. An emergency is considered to be a set of circumstances which are beyond the defendants' control. This excludes the defendants' failure to maintain his equipment.[27]

(b) If a person can show that they have taken all reasonably practical steps in the circumstances to minimise the extent of the discharge or entry, and its polluting effects, then they will not be guilty of an offence.

(c) A person will not be guilty of an offence if they provide details of the entry or discharge to the Agency as soon as reasonably practical after the entry occurs.

Under s89(2) WRA 1991, a person is not guilty of an offence if the discharge of trade or sewage effluent occurs from a vessel.

Mines and quarries s89(3)(4) WRA 1991

A person is not guilty of an offence under s85 WRA 1991 if the discharge is of water from an abandoned mine entering controlled waters s85(3) WRA 1991. There are other mine and quarry circumstances where a person shall not be guilty of an offence under s85 WRA 1991. When solid refuse which amounts to poisonous, noxious or polluting matter, from a mine or quarry is deposited on land so that it falls or is carried into inland freshwater, the defences are that the person had the consent of the Agency, or that no other site was reasonably practicable, or that the person took all reasonably practicable steps to prevent the refuse from entering the inland freshwater s85(4) WRA 1991. 'Mine' and 'quarry' have the same meanings as in the Mines and Quarries Act 1954 (MQA 1954).

Highways under s89(5) WRA 1991

A highway authority (defined at s1-3 of Highways Act 1980 [HA 1980]) or other person entitled to keep open a drain (s100 HA 1980) shall not be guilty of an offence under s85 WRA 1991 when a discharge is made from that open drain, unless the discharge is made in contravention of a prohibition under s86 WRA 1991.

1.3.1.7 s90 WRA 1991: Offences in connection with deposits and vegetation in rivers

A person is guilty of an offence under s90(i) WRA 1991 when he removes a deposit which has accumulated from the existence of a dam, weir or sluice which holds water and the deposit is then carried away in suspension in the water.

A person is guilty of an offence under s90(ii) WRA 1991 if, without the consent of the EA (who may impose conditions on a consent), he cuts or uproots a substantial amount of vegetation either in an inland freshwater, or so near that it falls in, and then fails to take all reasonable steps to remove the vegetation from those waters. Excluded from these provisions are any actions taken for the purposes of land drainage, flood prevention or navigation. Inland waters may include reference to prescribed coastal waters (s90[6] WRA 1991).

s90(3) WRA 1991: A person guilty of an offence under this section shall be liable, on summary conviction, to a fine not exceeding level four on the standard scale.

1.3.1.8 Consents, Enforcement notices and Appeals in respect of consents

s90(A) WRA 1991: Requirements for applications for consents under s89, 90 WRA 1991

The requirements are that the application is made on the correct form and advertised properly unless an exemption from doing so is specified. An applicant for a consent must provide the EA with any information which it reasonably requires and any which is prescribed by the State. Further information may be requested and the granting of an application may depend upon the provision of that information.

s90(B) WRA 1991: Enforcement notices

These are issued by the EA when it is felt that the holder of a relevant consent is contravening a condition of that consent. The valid notice will specify the nature of the contravention, and the steps which must be taken to remedy the contravention or to remedy matters which are likely to produce the contravention. The period within which the steps are to be taken must be specified. The EA may apply to the High Court to secure a holder's compliance with an enforcement notice, if it considers that proceedings under this section would fail to effect compliance. The Secretary of State is empowered to give directions to the EA as to how it should exercise its powers under this section.

> s90(3) WRA 1991: A person who fails to comply with any requirement imposed by an enforcement notice shall be guilty of an offence and liable to:
>
> (a) on summary conviction, to imprisonment for a term not exceeding three months, or to a fine not exceeding £20,000, or to both.
> (b) on conviction on indictment, to imprisonment for a term not exceeding two years or to a fine, or both.

Definitions

Under s90(6) WRA 1991:

'relevant consent' means a consent for the purposes of s89(4)(a) WRA 1991 or s90(1) or (2) WRA 1991, or a discharge consent, as in s91 WRA 1991.

'the holder' is the person who has the consent in question.

1.3.1.9 s91 WRA 1991: Appeals in respect of consents under Chapter II

This section deals with the grounds on which a person may appeal against the refusal or revocation of a consent, the imposition of conditions upon a consent, or for the variation of conditions attached to a consent. An appeal may also be made pursuant to the service of an enforcement notice. Note that where an appeal is brought under this section against an enforcement notice, the effect of the appeal will not be to suspend the operation of the notice. Also note that 'discharge consent' means consent which has been applied for under s88(1)(a) WRA 1991, or under paragraph [6] of Schedule 10 to the Act, where such an application has not been made.

1.3.1.10 Mines s91 A WRA 1991: Abandoned mines

s91(A) WRA 1991 defines *abandonment*, which includes discontinuance of operations for the removal of water from the mine, and cessation of working any vein or seam of the mine, or similar discontinuance or cessation in the case of a mine where activities other than mining are carried on. It does not include disclaimers by the Official Receiver acting in a compulsory capacity under s178 or s315 of the Insolvency Act 1986 (IA 1986) (liquidators' powers or powers of a trustee of a bankrupt's estate, to disclaim onerous property). 'Compulsory capacity' is defined at s91(A)(2) WRA 1991.

'*Abandonment*' also excludes the abandonment of any rights, interests or liabilities by the Accountant in Bankruptcy acting as permanent or interim trustee in a sequestration (within the meaning of the Bankruptcy [Scotland] Act 1985 [B(S)A 1985]).

'*Mine*' is defined in the Mines and Quarries Act 1954 (MQA 1954). Other definitions are at s91(A)(2) WRA 1991.

s91(B) WRA 1991: Notice of proposed abandonment

The operator of a mine is now obliged by this section to give the EA at least six months' notice of the proposed abandonment of a mine. The EA has a duty to inform the local authority, if it considers that any land is, or is likely to become, contaminated within the meaning of Part IIA, EPA 1990, as a consequence of the abandonment. The notice served by the operator should contain prescribed information which may include the operator's opinion of the consequences of abandonment. Local advertising is required.

> s91(B)(3) WRA 1991: A person who fails to give the notice required . . . shall be guilty of an offence and liable:
>
> (a) on summary conviction, to a fine not exceeding the statutory maximum
> (b) on conviction on indictment, to a fine.

1.3.1.11 Defences

If the abandonment is in an emergency, to avoid danger to life or health, or if notice is given as soon as reasonably practicable after the abandonment has happened, then the operator will not be guilty of an offence.

Where the operator of a mine is either the Official Receiver acting in an official capacity, or the Accountant in Bankruptcy, then he will not be guilty of a failure to give notice, if the notice of abandonment is served on the EA as soon as reasonably practicable, whether before or after abandonment.

Chapter III WRA 1991: Powers to Prevent and Control Pollution

1.3.2 Powers

1.3.2.1 s92 WRA 1991: Powers of the Secretary of State

Under s92(1) WRA 1991 the Secretary of State is empowered to make provisions prohibiting a person from having custody or control of any poisonous, noxious or polluting matter unless prescribed works and prescribed precautions have been carried out or taken, to prevent or control the entry of matter into any controlled waters, or to require a person already having custody or control of any such substance to take such steps. Radioactive substances are excluded from these provisions.

Under s92(2) WRA 1991 powers are conferred on the EA to enable it to determine the circumstances in which steps would be taken, and to determine by notice what those steps should be. Provisions are made for an appeal to the Secretary of State against the service of such notice, subject to s114 EA 1995.

> s92(2)(c) WRA 1991: A contravention of the regulations shall be an offence the maximum penalties for which shall not exceed the penalties specified in s85(6) WRA 1991 above.

1.3.2.2 s93 WRA 1991: Water-protection zones

Under s93(1-3) WRA 1991, where the Secretary of State is satisfied that it is appropriate to do so, he has provision by this section to designate an area as a water-protection zone, which is with a view to preventing or controlling the entry of any poisonous, noxious or polluting matter into controlled waters, or to restricting the carrying on in that area of activities which he considers likely to result in the pollution of such waters. This provision excludes the entry of nitrate into controlled waters as a result of land use for agricultural purposes. The powers of the Secretary of State are exercisable by statutory instrument and only exercisable on the application of the Agency, in accordance with Schedule 11 to this Act.

Under s93(4) WRA 1991, powers may be conferred on the EA to enable it to determine the circumstances in which activity is prohibited or restricted, and to enable it to apply prohibitions or restrictions to activities which are prohibited or restricted.

Under s93(4)(c) WRA 1991, a contravention of a prohibition or restriction contained in the order of or a condition of a consent given for the purposes of any such prohibition or restriction shall be an offence the maximum penalties for which shall not exceed the penalties specified in s85(6) WRA 1991 above (see page 27 of this book).

1.3.2.3 s94 WRA 1991: Nitrate sensitive areas

Under s94(1-3) WRA 1991, where the relevant minister thinks it appropriate to do so, this subsection makes provision for the designation of land as a nitrate-sensitive area, with a view to preventing or controlling the entry of nitrate into controlled waters as a result of the use of that land for agricultural purposes. The designation may result in the imposition of requirements, prohibitions or restrictions upon activities specified in an order under this subsection.

> Under s94(4)(d) WRA 1991, a contravention of a requirement, prohibition or restriction contained in the order or in a condition of a consent given in relation to or for the purposes of any such requirement, prohibition or restriction shall be an offence the maximum penalties for which shall not exceed the penalties specified in s85(6) WRA 1991 above (see page 27 of this book).

No order has been made under this section at the time of writing, although 32 areas have been designated for voluntary participation, under EC Council Regulation 2078/92 OJ L 215, not under s94 WRA 1991.

Limitation

Note that under s101 WRA 1991, summary proceedings may be brought under Part III if the the information is laid not more than 12 months after the commission of the offence.

1.3.2.4 s161 WRA 1991: Anti-pollution works and operations

This section of the Act deals with the EA's powers to carry out works and operations for the removal or disposal of poisonous, noxious or polluting matter. Note that, under s161(5) WRA 1991, nothing derogates from any right of action or other remedy (whether civil or criminal) in proceedings instituted otherwise than under this section. The EA may recover expenses reasonably incurred in such works or operations, other than in certain circumstances. Again, no account is to be taken here of any radioactivity possessed by any substance or article or by any part of any premises.

s161 WRA 1991: Works Notices

Under s161 A WRA 1991 provision is made for service of a works notice on a person by the EA, where it appears likely that any poisonous, noxious or polluting matter or any solid waste is likely to enter or be present (or have been present) in any controlled waters. The works notice must specify the periods within which the person on whom the notice is served must do the things which are specified in the notice. The serving of such a notice should follow reasonable attempts at consultation, although this is not a condition of the validity of the notice. The Secretary of State is empowered by this section to make provisions in respect of works notices. Note that the EA is entitled to recover costs or reasonably-incurred expenses in carrying out its duties under this section.

s161(B) WRA 1991: Grant of and compensation for, rights of entry, etc

A person on whom a works notice has been served may have to carry out works in relation to land over which he has no right to carry out such works. His compliance with the terms of a works notice may require the appropriate person to grant him such rights in relation to works and operations. The grantor of such rights may apply within a prescribed period for compensation of an amount which may be determined in a prescribed manner. Again, consultation by the EA must be reasonably endeavoured, although again, the works notice will not be invalid for want of such consultation.

Under s161 C WRA 1991 appeals against works notices may be made to the Secretary of State within a 21 day period from the date when the notice is served.

s161 D WRA 1991: Consequences of not complying with a works notice

Under s161 D (1) WRA 1991: if a person on whom the EA serves a works notice fails to comply with any of the requirements of the notice, he shall be guilty of an offence.

Under s161(2) WRA 1991, a person who commits an offence under subsection (1) above shall be liable -

(a) on summary conviction, to imprisonment for a term not exceeding three months or to a fine not exceeding £20,000, or to both;
(b) on conviction on indictment to imprisonment for a term not exceeding two years or to a fine or both.

Under s161(3) WRA 1991, when a person has failed to comply with the requirements of the works notice, the EA may do what that person was required to do and recover from him the costs of doing so.

Under s161(4) WRA 1991, the EA has powers to take proceedings in the High Court against the person who has not complied with the works notice, to secure compliance with that notice.

1.3.2.5 s169 WRA 1991: Powers of entry

Powers of entry under s169(1) WRA 1991 are conferred on any person designated by the Minister or the EA to enter a premises or a vessel to make investigations for the purpose of establishing whether a provision of the Act is being contravened. The investigations may include inspections, measurements or tests, on premises or of articles found on premises, and authorise the removal of samples. Powers to carry out experimental borings and other works and to install and keep monitoring apparatus on the premises are similarly conferred. However, the powers conferred under this section do not have effect for the purposes of the EA's pollution-control functions.

The wide range of powers which are conferred upon the EA to enable it to carry out its function of pollution control are found in s108 EA 1995, and dealt with elsewhere in this chapter.

Impersonation

Under s174(2) WRA 1991, a person who is not designated or authorised by the EA but who purports to be entitled to enter a premises or vessel shall be guilty of an offence and liable:

(a) on summary conviction, to a fine not exceeding the statutory maximum;
(b) on conviction on indictment, to a fine or to imprisonment for a term not exceeding two years or both.

For the purposes of this offence, it is immaterial that the power of entry did not exist, or was not exercisable, even if the impersonating person had been designated or authorised.

By Schedule 20 to the Act, supplementary provisions with respect to powers of entry to premises or a vessel are granted to the EA:

(1) Seven days' notice of entry must be given, other than in an emergency.

(2) A warrant may be obtained from a justice of the peace in certain circumstances, and entry made by a designated person, taking with him such people or equipment as may be necessary. (The premises or vessel must be left by the designated person as secured against trespassers as they were when he entered.)

Schedule 20, Para. 7

A person who intentionally obstructs another person acting in the exercise of any power to which this Schedule applies shall be guilty of an offence and liable

(a) on summary conviction, to a fine not exceeding the statutory maximum;
(b) on conviction on indictment, to a fine or to imprisonment for a term not exceeding two years or both.

1.3.2.6 s190 WRA 1991: Pollution-control register

The EA has a duty to maintain registers which contain notices, applications for consents and variations of those consents, consents given, information arising out of sampling, steps taken on the basis of that information, enforcement notices, revocations of discharge consents, appeals, ministerial directions, convictions for offences under Part III of this Act, works notices, appeals and convictions in respect of works notices, and 'any other matters relating to the quality of water or pollution of water as may be prescribed by the Secretary of State'. Where information is excluded, its existence should nevertheless be indicated by a statement in the register. Information may be excluded on the grounds of national security and commercial confidentiality(see 191 A, B WRA 1991).

The EA has a duty to ensure that the registers are available for inspection by the public and that copies of entries are made available at reasonable charge. Note that the EA and ministers have powers to require a person, on notice, to furnish such information as is reasonably required by the EA or ministers for the purpose of carrying out its functions in respect of water pollution.

Under s202(4) WRA 1991, a person who fails without reasonable excuse to comply with the requirements of a notice served on him under this section shall be guilty of an offence and liable

(a) on summary conviction, to a fine not exceeding the statutory maximum;

(b) on conviction on indictment, to a fine or to imprisonment for a term not exceeding two years, or to both.

At s204 WRA 1991, the restrictions on disclosure of information are listed. They are subject to a list of exclusions found at s204(2) WRA 1991. There is nothing in this subsection which limits matters which may form part of reports by environmental authorities under other statutes.

Under s204(6) WRA 1991: A person who discloses any information in contravention of the preceding provisions of this section shall be guilty of an offence and liable

(a) on summary conviction, to a fine not exceeding the statutory maximum;
(b) on conviction on indictment, to imprisonment for a term not exceeding two years or to a fine, or both.

1.3.3 Information

1.3.3.1 s206 WRA 1991: False statements

When a person makes a statement under the provisions of this Act (listed at s206[1] WRA 1991), if the statement contains a false material particular, or the person recklessly makes a statement which is false in a material particular, then he is guilty of an offence.

By s206(5) WRA 1991, a person who is guilty of an offence under this section shall be liable

(a) on summary conviction, to a fine not exceeding the statutory maximum;
(b) on conviction on indictment, to a fine

proceedings for an offence by virtue of subsection (1) shall not be instituted except by or with the consent of one of the ministers or the Director of Public Prosecutions (DPP).

Under s206(3) WRA 1991, a person is guilty of an offence if he wilfully alters or interferes with a meter, gauge or device being used in connection with the provisions of this Act.

By s206(6) WRA 1991, a person who is guilty of an offence under this section ... shall be liable

(a) on summary conviction, to imprisonment for a term not exceeding three months or to a fine not exceeding the statutory maximum or both;
(b) on conviction on indictment, to imprisonment for a term not exceeding two years or to a fine, or both.

By s206(4) WRA 1991, if a person makes a statement in a record or journal which is false in a material particular, either knowingly or recklessly, then he is guilty of an offence. By s206(7) WRA 1991, a person who is guilty of an offence under this section . . . shall be liable

(a) on summary conviction, to imprisonment for a term not exceeding three months or to a fine not exceeding the statutory maximum or to both;
(b) on conviction on indictment, to imprisonment for a term not exceeding three months or to a fine or both.

1.3.3.2 s210 WRA 1991: Bye-law making powers of the EA

The powers of the EA to make bye-laws are conferred by this section through Schedule 25 to WRA 1991. These bye-law-making powers are in respect of controlling certain forms of pollution and for flood-defence and drainage purposes.

s211(3) WRA 1991: A person who contravenes any bye-laws made by virtue of paragraph 4 of Schedule 25 to this Act shall be guilty of an offence and liable, on summary conviction, to a fine not exceeding level four on the standard scale or, in the case of bye-laws made by virtue of paragraph 4, such smaller sum as may be specified in the bye-laws.

s211(4) WRA 1991: If any person acts in contravention of any bye-law made by virtue of paragraph 5 of that Schedule he shall be guilty of an offence and liable, on summary conviction

(a) to a fine not exceeding level five on the standard scale; and
(b) if the contravention is continued after conviction, to a further fine not exceeding £40 for each day on which it is so continued.

In a recent case brought under these provisions, *Environment Agency v Giles* (Env LR, November, 1998), the defendant had been prosecuted for contravention of Bye-law No 5(d)(iv)(e) of the Environment Agency (Welsh Region) Commercial Fishery Bye-laws. It was alleged that he shot or paid out a seine net, (a kind of long drag net) in the River Teifi Estuary from a point within 91 metres from the point at which another seine net had been fully drawn in and landed within the previous 15 minutes. The river was 150 metres in width at the relevant point and the nets were shot and drawn in from both sides of the bank. The issue referred to the High Court was whether or not the bye-law applied to a case where nets were shot from both banks, or only one. The Court took the view that the bye-law referred to the point at which the boats were. It could be assumed from the evidence that the second boat had come within 91 metres of the point from which the second net had been shot from the opposite bank, so the appeal was allowed and the case remitted.

1.4 Offences under WIA 1991

Part III of WIA 1991 is concerned with the general duties of water undertakers. Chapter I legislates for the general duty to maintain the water supply system, standards of performance in connection with the water supply, information with respect to levels of performance, the procedural requirements in respect of the regulations for the maintenance of those standards and the requirement for information to be available to customers about the overall performance of the water undertaker.[28] Chapter III, legislates for the quality and sufficiency of supplies.

1.4.1 Standards of wholesomeness

1.4.1.1 s67 WIA 1991

By this section, the Secretary of State is empowered to regulate for the standards of wholesomeness of the water supply. General and specific requirements are determinable, in respect of the purposes for which the water is being supplied, in respect of substances and concentrations thereof to be included or excluded in the water. Other characteristics of the supply may also be regulated, all by reference to sampling, if prescribed.

1.4.1.2 s68 WIA 1991

By this section, the water undertaker has a duty, with respect to water quality, to supply to premises for domestic or food production purposes only water which is wholesome at the time of supply. Time of supply is defined as the time when it leaves the undertaker's pipes. He also has a duty to ensure, as far as is reasonably practicable, that there is, in general, no deterioration in the quality of the water. There are two sets of circumstances in which water which would have been regarded as wholesome at the time of supply is regarded as unwholesome[29]: (1) When the wholesome water which has left the undertaker's pipes has ceased to be wholesome thereafter, whilst in a pipe subject to pressure from a water main (or which would have been so but for the closing of a valve). (2) When that water has ceased to be wholesome after leaving the undertaker's pipes because the undertaker has failed to take the prescribed steps to eliminate the risk of that happening. The provisions of this section apply to any water supplied by an undertaker, not just the water he is required to supply under this Act.

1.4.1.3 Definitions

'Food production purposes' embraces the whole spectrum of food production: manufacturing, processing, preserving or marketing of food or drink, including food-production premises where food or drink is prepared for consumption elsewhere.[30]

'Wholesome' is a standard determined by the Secretary of State.[31] The steps which an undertaker must take to comply with his duty to supply wholesome water are to be found in the Water Supply (Water Quality) Regulations 1989. These Regulations reflect the requirements of the 1980 EEC Directive on the Quality of Water Intended for Human Consumption.

'Domestic purposes' refer to the drinking, washing, cooking, central heating and sanitary purposes for which water is supplied to premises. Where the premises are partly or wholly occupied as a house (ie occupied as a dwelling house), then 'domestic purposes' also includes a profession being practised on the premises and the washing of vehicles and watering of gardens supplied by water from a tap within the house. Note that the use of a hose-pipe is excluded from this definition.

The following categories of use are excluded from this definition:

(i) the use of a bath with a capacity greater than230 litres;
(ii) the business of a laundry;
(iii) the purpose of a business of preparing food or drink for consumption other than on the premises.[32]

'Prescribed' means prescribed in regulations by the Secretary of State.[33]

'Water main' or *'trunk main'* means a water main which is or is to be used by a water undertaker for the purposes of conveying water:

(a) from a source of supply to a filter, or
(b) from one filter or reservoir to another filter or reservoir; or
(c) wheter in the course of taking a supply of water in bulk or otherwise between different places outside the area of the undertaker, from such a place to any part of that area or from one part of that area to another part of that area.[34]

'Pipe' is defined to include, within references to a main, a drain or a sewer, references to a tunnel or a conduit which is to serve as a pipe and to any accessories for the pipe. References to the laying of pipe therefore include constructions of tunnels and conduits, accessories and connections between pipes.[35]

1.4.1.4 s69 WIA 1991: Regulations for preserving water quality

In this section, the general power of the Secretary of State to impose obligations upon water undertakers is found in s69(1) WIA 1991. The more specific ambits of the groups of regulations are as follows:

s69(2) WIA 1991 may oblige an undertaker to monitor and record the wholesomeness of the water supply to a premises, from any source or combination of sources where the supply is or will be taken from. The undertaker may not be allowed to use the water until the quality of the water has been established. Records of monitoring must be kept and regulations adhered to in respect of analysis of water samples. The specific requirements are to be found in the Water Supply (Water Quality) Regulations 1989. These Regulations determine, by reference to Tables annexed to the Regulations, the precise nature of standards of 'wholesomeness'.[36] These Regulations govern the determination of sampling points and the frequency of sampling, the authorisation of supply points, and other matters concerning the water undertakers' obligations to monitor the wholesomeness of the water supply.[37]

s69(3), (4) WIA 1991 give authority to the Regulations in respect of forbidding the use of processes, substances and products which have not been approved, because all of those must conform to the standards to be found in the Regulations. This section also legislates for the giving, refusal and revocation of such approval, as well as for the conditions upon which such approval may be given. Obligations exist to provide a 'prescribed person' with information. A prescribed person may be a 'technical assessor' appointed by the Secretary of State for the purpose. Information must be provided to the prescribed person, either free or subject to payment. There is a requirement that it should be published in a prescribed manner.[38]

1.4.2 Offences under s69 WIA 1991

s69(4)(f) WIA 1991 provides 'for a contravention of the regulations' which constitutes

> (i) a summary offence punishable, on summary conviction, by a fine not exceeding level five on the standard scale or such smaller sum as may be prescribed; or
>
> (ii) an offence triable either way and punishable, on summary conviction, by a fine not exceeding the statutory maximum and, on conviction on indictment, by a fine;

Note that s28 *Water Supply (Water Quality) Regulations* 1989 outlines specific offences against the Regulations to which s69(4)(f) WIA 1991 refers:

28(1) A water undertaker which applies or introduces any substance in contravention of regulation 25(1) [application and introduction of substances and products] or

> in contravention of a notice given under Reg. 25(4) [prohibition of the application or introduction or a substance or product for a specified period];
>
> or uses any process in contravention of a prohibition imposed under Reg. 26(1) [application for approval of, or prohibition of, use of a process]
>
> or without complying with a condition imposed by virtue of regulation 26(2) [refusal of, or application of conditions to an approval]

shall be guilty of any offence and liable

> (a) on summary conviction, to a fine not exceeding the statutory maximum;
> (b) on conviction on indictment, to a fine.

28(3) If any person, in furnishing any information or making any application under Reg. 25 or 26 makes any statement which is false in a material particular, he shall be guilty of an offence, and liable

(a) on summary conviction, to a fine not exceeding the statutory maximum;

(b) on conviction on indictment, to a fine.

Proceedings under Reg. 28(3) may only be brought with the consent of either the Secretary of State or the DPP.[39]

It is a defence to a charge brought against a water undertaker under this regulation to show that it took all reasonable steps and exercised all due diligence to avoid the commission of the offence.

1.4.2.2 s70 WIA 1991: Offence of supplying water unfit for human consumption

This is perhaps the principal offence with which a water undertaker may be charged under this Act. There is no definition of *'unfit for human consumption'*. Water may be unfit for human consumption notwithstanding that it poses no risk to human health and cannot be described as *'unwholesome'* within the requirements of the 1989 Regulations. For example, the water may taste or smell repugnant but still be wholesome to drink.[40]

The offence is committed where drinking water is unfit by reason of its objectionable taste, appearance and smell. The prosecution, which will be brought on the recommendation of the Drinking Water Inspectorate (DWI), does not need to prove that the water was harmful to health.

Cases:

In October, 1998, Severn Trent, Northumbrian and Sutton and East Surrey water companies were all prosecuted under the provisions of this section.

In the case against Severn Water, it was alleged that the water was brown and contained sludge. The supply of water had been interrupted by a repair of a watermain in a street, damaged by other works going on. The company pleaded guilty and was fined £8,000 with £3,680 costs.

In the case against Northumbrian Water, a similar set of circumstances led to a similar unfit condition of the water supply but of a far greater magnitude, with hundreds of homes affected. The company was fined £6,000 on four charges, with costs of £3,776.

In the case against Sutton and East Surrey Water, a deposit had occurred in the water supply shortly after Sutton and East Surrey had merged. The deposit (chalk) was harmless, but complaints were received. The company was fined £1,000 on each of the five charges and ordered to pay costs of £2,971.

An employee of a water undertaker may be liable as well as the authority where it can be shown that the offence is attributable to the employee's negligence.

Under s70(1) WIA 1991, where a water undertaker supplies by means of pipes to any premises and that water is unfit for human consumption, the undertaker shall be guilty of an offence and liable

(a) on summary conviction, to a fine not exceeding the statutory maximum;
(b) on conviction on indictment, to a fine

Under s70 (2) WIA 1991, the penalty on conviction on indictment for an offence under this section shall be deemed to include imprisonment (in addition to or instead of a fine) for a term not exceeding two years.

Proceedings under this section may only be brought by either the Secretary of State or the DPP.

1.4.2.3 Defences to charges brought under s70 WIA 1991

Two defences are available to these charges: That the defendant:

had no reasonable grounds for suspecting that the water would be used for human consumption (s70[3][a] WIA 1991);

took all reasonable steps and exercised all due diligence for securing that the water was fit for human consumption on leaving its pipes or was not used for human consumption (s70[3][b] WIA 1991).

The three following sections of the Act are concerned with offences connected with wastage, contamination and the misuse of a water supply.

1.4.2.4 s71 WIA 1991: Waste from water sources

s71(1) WIA 1991: An offence is committed:

(a) when a person causes or allows water to run to waste, from a well, borehole or any other work, or

(b) when he abstracts from the well, borehole or other work, water in excess of his reasonable requirements.

s71(4) WIA 1991: A person who is guilty of an offence under this section shall be liable, on summary conviction, to a fine not exceeding level three on the standard scale.

Note that after a conviction has been brought under this section, the Court may order that the well, borehole or other work in question may be effectively sealed and any other appropriate orders made. Failure to comply with such an order, notwithstanding any issue of contempt of court, may result in the EA making an application and being authorised by the court to execute any order of the Court, and reclaim any expenses incurred as a civil debt.

1.4.2.5 Defences to charges brought under s71(1) WIA 1991

Two sets of defences are available to such charges:

s71(2) WIA 1991: If a person was doing something for the purpose of

(a) testing the extent or quality of the supply, or
(b) cleaning, sterilising, examining or repairing the well, borehole or other work.

s71(3) WIA 1991: [where underground works are being undertaken which are threatened by underground water]. . . it shall not be an offence under this section, if no other method of disposing of the water is reasonably practicable [to allow water to run to waste to an extent far enough to enable the works to be done].

1.4.2.6 s72 WIA 1991: Contamination of water sources

This section is concerned with the act or neglect by a person which results in the pollution of water in waterworks which is used or likely to be used either for human consumption or domestic purposes (s72[1][a] WIA 1991) or in the manufacture of food or drink for human consumption1 (s72[1][b] WIA 1991).

Definition

'Waterworks' include any spring, well, adit, borehole, service reservoir or tank; also, any main, other pipe or conduit of a water undertaker.

The two ensuing subsections provide the two sets of circumstances in which a restriction or prohibition of this sort will not apply:

> s72(2) WIA 1991 permits methods of cultivation which are commensurate with good husbandry,
>
> s72(3) WIA 1991 permits the reasonable use of oil or tar on any highway maintained at public expense. The highway authority must take all reasonable steps to prevent the oil or tar from polluting water in the waterworks.

s72(4) WIA 1991: A person who is guilty of an offence under s72 WIA 1991 shall be liable

> (a) on summary conviction, to a fine not exceeding the statutory maximum and, in the case of a continuing offence, to a further fine not exceeding £50.00 for every day during which the offence is continued after conviction;
> (b) on conviction on indictment, to imprisonment for a term not exceeding two years or to a fine, or both.

1.4.2.7 s73 WIA 1991: Offences of contaminating, wasting and misusing water

s73(1) WIA 1991: This offence can be committed by the owner or occupier of a premises who negligently causes or suffers any water fitting for which he is responsible to be rendered either out of order, in need of repair, or so constructed or adapted that water:

(a) in a water main or other pipe of a water undertaker, or in a pipe connected with such a watermain or pipe connected with such a water main or pipe, is, or is likely to be contaminated by the return of any substance from those premises to that main or pipe

(b) which has been supplied by the undertaker to those premises is or is likely to be contaminated before it is used or

(c) so supplied is or is likely to be wasted, or having regard to the purposes for which it is supplied, misused or unduly consumed.

That person shall be guilty of an offence and liable, on summary conviction, to a fine not exceeding level three on the standard scale.

1.4.3 Powers

1.4.3.1 s74 WIA 1991: Regulations for preventing contamination, waste, etc, and with respect to water fittings

This section lists the purposes for which the Secretary of State may make regulations. These regulations encompass the securing of water within the pipes, the installation, connection and use of water fittings, the imposition of duties upon water authorities and local undertakers to enforce any regulations, or to remedy contraventions of those regulations. Rights of entry into any premises for the purposes of determining whether regulations are being complied with may be conferred upon any person designated in writing. As yet, no regulations have been made under this section, although at

> s74(3)(e) WIA 1991: A contravention of a regulation may constitute a summary offence, punishable, on summary conviction, by a fine not exceeding level five on the standard scale, or such smaller sum as may be prescribed.

1.4.3.2 s75 WIA 1991: Power to prevent damage and to take steps to prevent contamination, waste, etc

This is the section of the Act from which a water undertaker derives its powers to take steps to prevent pollution and contamination, in certain defined circumstances. These circumstances are either in the case of an emergency generally, or in circumstances where the undertaker may serve notice on a consumer, requiring him to take steps to ensure that damage, contamination, waste, misuse or undue consumption do not occur. Once the supply has been disconnected in the exercise of power available in an emergency, the undertaker is bound to serve a notice outlining the steps which must be taken before supply will be restored. The steps must be specified and

> if the undertaker does not serve a notice without reasonable excuse, then he will be guilty of an offence and liable on summary conviction to a fine not exceeding level three on the standard scale.

Notice requirements

(1) Where a supply has been cut off for reasons of an emergency nature and the undertaker serves a notice, the notice must specify which steps

must be taken to ensure that the damage, pollution, etc, would not recur on re-connection of the supply.

(2) Where a notice is to ensure that pollution and contamination, etc, does not occur, the notice must specify the period within which the steps must be taken, to ensure that the adverse circumstances will not occur. If those steps are not taken within the specified period, and the premises appear to be unoccupied, then the water taker may disconnect the service pipe and cut the supply of water to the premises.

Where notice requirements are other than those imposed in an emergency or upon what appear to be unoccupied premises, then the undertaker is permitted to take those steps itself and to recover the expenses for doing so thereafter.

It is an offence to disconnect a service pipe to any premises, or otherwise to cut off a supply of water to any premises, where there is no power to do so under this section.

1.4.3.3 s85 WIA 1991: Local Authority power to obtain information

This section empowers the local authority (LA) to serve on *any person* a notice requiring him to furnish to the LA such information as it might reasonably require to enable it to exercise its power or perform its duties under s85 and ss 77-83 WIA 1991. These powers and duties are:

• 77: To take appropriate steps to keep itself informed about the wholesomeness and sufficiency of water supplies to premises in its area, which includes every private supply to such premises. This section also gives the Secretary of State power to determine what the LA's duties and powers are to be.

•78: To notify an undertaker of water to premises for food or domestic purposes that a supply is, or is in danger of becoming unwholesome or insufficient.

• 79: To provide a supply to a premises in certain circumstances where:

(a) there is insufficiency or unwholesomeness of supply causing a danger to life or health; or
(b) where it is practical to do so, for domestic purposes; or
(c) where the undertaker notifies that a supply is necessary other than in pipes.

• 80: These are similar provisions in respect of LA's powers and duties in relation to private supplies, with notice requirements specified as being the particulars, the specific steps to be taken, the period of time during which they are to be taken. The notice may be served on *the private supplier or any relevant person*. It is described as a *private supply notice*.

The *'relevant person'* is one of the following:

> (a) the owners or occupiers of the premises;
> (b) the owners or occupiers of the premises where the source is located;
> (c) any person who exercises powers of management or control in relation to the source.

Reasonable expenses incurred by taking those steps may be paid by the person or the LA, other than in circumstances where there is no house on the premises, in which case the LA should not be required to bear any of the expenses.

• 81: Private supply notices must be submitted, at the end of a period for representations and objections to the Secretary of State, and may be confirmed by him with or without modifications, with a public local inquiry if he decides it is necessary, if he is satisfied that the notice is properly served.

• 82: This section deals with the LA's powers in relation to the powers of recovery of expenses. Also, it deals with the apportionment of expenses reasonably incurred and excludes from the Act any right of action in respect of any loss or damage sustained by a person as a consequence of another's failure to take any step specified in a private-supply notice. This section also deals with the consequences of the variation of a period defined in the notice, or the discharge, postponement or abatement of payment to the LA.

• 83: This section gives powers to the LA to act in the capacity of water undertaker. It also gives powers to the LA to purchase land, compulsorily or otherwise, for the purpose of ensuring that private supplies of water to premises are both wholesome and sufficient for domestic purposes for the houses in that area. This section gives wide-ranging powers of entry to the LA: it must be read in conjunction with Schedule 6 to the Act.

• On presentation of duly-authenticated documents showing his authority, *any person* has a right, at all reasonable hours, to enter *any premises* for the purposes of assessing whether there has been or is any contravention of the provisions of s72 WIA 1991 (see above, page 50).

The designated person has powers to carry out inspections, measurements and tests on fittings and any other articles, and to take away samples.

• The same provisions were also put in place in respect of the parts of the Act which define the LA's powers and duties with regard to undertakers.

1.4.3.5 Schedule 6

It is important to note that a person thus designated by the LA is bound by Part II and not Part I of Schedule 6 to the Act. The person thus designated may not, by the provisions of this Act, have access to business premises (meaning any factory or any place in which people are employed otherwise than in domestic service):

(a) without giving 24 hours' notice; or
(b) on a warrant, and by force if necessary.

This warrant may only be issued on reasonable grounds, on the basis of which a warrant may be issued by a justice of the peace who is satisfied by the sworn information which forms the substance of the request for the warrant. The sworn information must indicate that one or more of the conditions described in Para. 2, subssection 2 of the Schedule has been satisfied. (See Annex WIA 1991.) A warrant will not be issued unless the justice of the peace is satisfied that certain other requirements are satisfied. These are detailed in Para. 3 of Schedule 6. (See Annex WIA 1991):

The warrant will continue in force until the purpose of the entry for which it has been granted has been fulfilled.
A person entering these premises will leave them as secure against trespassers as when he entered.

1.4.3.6 s85 WIA 1991: Local authority's power to obtain information

When a notice has been served requiring any person to provide information to a LA, then a failure to comply with a term of that notice without reasonable excuse will render that person liable to conviction and a fine not exceeding level five on the standard scale.

1.4.3.7 s86 WIA 1991: Assessors

This section empowers the Secretary of State to appoint technical assessors in relation to his powers. Such an assessor is appointed to investigate and report on any contravention of his powers under this Act.

> Any water undertaker who fails to comply with the assessor in giving assistance or providing information under the provisions of this Act may be guilty of an offence and liable on conviction to a fine not exceeding level five on the standard scale.

1.4.4 Consents

1.4.4.1 s118 WIA 1991: Consent required for discharge of trade effluent into public sewer

Definition

'Trade effluent'

This is defined at s141(1)(a) WIA 1991 and means any liquid, either with or without particles of matter in suspension in the liquid, which is wholly or partly produced in the course of any trade or industry carried on at a trade premises. It also means any liquid which is produced in the course of any trade or industry carried on at the premises but *does not include domestic sewage*. *'Trade premises'* include any land or premises used or intended for use (in whole or in part and whether or not for profit) for agricultural or horticultural purposes, or fish-farming, or for scientific research or experiment. *'Trade effluent'* includes the same categories for purposes of references in this section.

This section makes it a requirement for the discharge, by an occupier of trade premises, of trade effluent from those premises into an undertaker's public sewer, to obtain that undertaker's consent.

> If the occupier of the trade premises discharges without such consent, or other authorisation, then he will be guilty of an offence and liable on summary conviction to a fine not exceeding the statutory minimum, or on indictment to a fine.

Note that this section does not apply to any radioactive substance or article, which is dealt with by s40 RSA 1993.

1.4.4.2 s120 WIA 1991: Applications for the discharge of special category effluent

Definitions

'Special category effluent'

The definition of special category effluent is set out in full at s138 WIA 1991. (See Annex WIA 1991.) Note the distinctions between trade effluent and SCE.

When an application is made for a consent or authorisation to a sewerage undertaker in respect of a special category effluent, the undertaker must refer questions which arise out of the application to the EA. These questions are whether the discharge should be prohibited, or subject to conditions. This reference must take place within the two months which follow the notice containing the application. The sewage undertaker may refuse permission within that two-month period and in those circumstances a reference is not obligatory. By the same token, when a reference has been made to the EA, an undertaker may not give a consent, or enter into an agreement over the discharge until the EA has determined the reference.

> If the undertaker fails to make a reference to the Agency when he had a duty to do so, then he will be guilty of an offence, and liable, on summary conviction, to a fine not exceeding the statutory maximum, and on conviction on indictment to a fine.

1.4.4.3 s121 WIA 1991: Conditions of consent

These are listed in this section (see Annex WIA 1991).

A contravention of a condition which has been imposed upon a trade premises may render the occupier of the trade premises liable to

> (1) summary conviction and to a fine not exceeding the statutory maximum; or
> (2) conviction on indictment and a fine.

Subsequent sections of WIA 1991 (s122-s127) deal with appeals and variations in respect of discharge consents, variations of the time limit, appeals in respect of variations of consent and the review by the Secretary of State of consents. Applications for variation of time for discharge are legislated for by s128 WIA 1991, and agreements with respect to the disposal of trade effluent by s129 WIA 1991.

1.4.4.4 s130: Reference to the Secretary of State of SCE agreements

Where a sewerage undertaker and the owner or occupier of a trade premises propose to enter into an agreement under s129, then the undertaker is under a duty to refer to the EA questions concerning the discharge (whether it is prohibited or not and whether the agreement should be subject to conditions).

If the undertaker fails to make such a reference, he may be guilty of an offence and liable

(1) on summary conviction, to a fine not exceeding the statutory maximum;
(2) on conviction on indictment, to a fine.

ss131, 132 WIA 1991 deal with the Secretary of State's powers to review agreements and define those powers. A notice, which does not restrict the EA's power to specify conditions which appertain to the agreement, may be served upon the sewerage undertaker and the owner or occupier of the business premises.

1.4.4.5 s133 WIA 1991: Effect of determination on reference or review

A sewerage undertaker remains unrestricted in his power to impose a condition specified under s132 WIA 1991.

If the sewage undertaker fails to secure compliance with the terms of the notice, then he will be liable:

(1) on summary conviction, to a fine not exceeding the statutory maximum;
(2) on conviction on indictment, to a fine.

1.4.5 Information

1.4.5.1 s135 A WIA 1991: EA's power to acquire information for the purpose of its functions in relation to special category effluent

This section empowers the EA a power to serve a notice on *any person*, requiring them to provide to the EA any such information as the EA may reasonably require, in such form and within a period which the EA must specify.

If that person fails to comply with the terms of the notice, without reasonably excuse, or makes a statement which he knows to be false or misleading in a material particular, then he will be guilty of an offence, and liable:

(1) on summary conviction, to a fine not exceeding the statutory maximum; or
(2) on conviction on indictment, to a fine or to imprisonment for a term not exceeding two years, or both.

Part VI WIA 1991 gives the powers which undertakers have to deal with foul water and pollution on land (s161 WIA 1991).

It also contains the provisions for an undertakers rights of entry. These are supplemented by Schedule 6 to the Act which may be found in Annex WIA 1991.

1.4.5.2 Rights of entry

s168 WIA 1991:

(1) *'to enter land for works purposes.'*

This power may be devolved to any person designated in writing by the undertaker to enter for specific purposes. The purposes are specified at s168(3) WIA 1991. The exercise of the rights and powers for this section is by reference to Part II of Schedule 6 to WIA 1991.

s170 WIA 1991:

(2) *'to enter land for other purposes.'*

This wide-ranging power may be exercised by any person designated in writing for the purpose by the undertaker. The designated person may enter at any reasonable hour, to make surveys, conduct tests, take samples, monitor and record the supply of water for domestic purposes, ascertain whether there is a breach or contravention of any provision of this Act in respect of water fittings, or the waste or misuse of water, and determine whether it is appropriate in the circumstances for the water supply to be cut off, or a pipe disconnected. (See Annex WIA 1991 to distinguish between the subsections to which Parts I and II of Schedule 6 to the Act apply.)

s171 WIA 1991:

(3) *'to enter for sewerage purposes.'*

This power may be devolved to any person designated in writing by the undertaker to enter for specific purposes which arise from the exercise of his functions under the relevant sewerage provisions of WIA 1991. The powers which are conferred by this section are exercisable according to Part 1 of Schedule 6 to WIA 1991.

1.4.5.3 s173 WIA 1991: Impersonation of persons entitled to entry

> A person who purports to be entitled to enter any premises or vessel to exercise any of the powers under the Act without designation or authorisation shall be guilty of an offence. He will be liable on summary conviction to a fine not exceeding level four on the standard scale.

1.4.5.4 Schedule 6 to WIA 1991

This Schedule, which lists the supplementary provisions relating to rights of entry, is included in full in Annex WIA.

Schedule 6 Part I lists the rights which require notice for entry into non-business premises. The list includes provisions for notice of entry, warrants to exercise the right of entry and supplementary powers conferred on the person making an entry.

> The consequences of obstructing a person exercising his right of entry, which is an offence, render that person liable, on summary conviction, to a fine not exceeding level three on the standard scale.
>
> It is the duty of a person exercising his right of entry to maintain commercial confidentiality. Failure to do so may render that person liable
>
> (1) on summary conviction, to a term of imprisonment not exceeding three months, or to a fine not exceeding the statutory maximum, or to both.
> (2) on conviction on indictment, to imprisonment for a term not exceeding three months, or to a fine, or to both.

Schedule 6 Part II lists other rights of entry, and related powers. These include the requirements for notice, obtaining a warrant to exercise the right of entry and the manner in which that right must be exercised, the supplementary power available to the person making an entry, his duty to secure the premises on his departure and the duty to compensate where a person has sustained loss or damage by reason of the exercise of that right.

> It is an offence to obstruct a person in the exercise of his right of entry, leading on summary conviction to a fine not exceeding level three on the standard scale.

1.4.5.5 s204 WIA 1991: Provision of information to sewerage undertakers with respect to trade effluent discharges

The owner or occupier of land on or under which a sewer, drain, pipe, channel or outlet is situated and used or intended to be used for a discharge of trade effluent into the sewer of a sewerage undertaker must provide, when required to do so by the undertaker, plans of the sewer, drain, pipe, channel or outlet and any other information which he can reasonably be expected to supply.

A person who fails to comply with this requirement may be guilty of an offence and liable on summary conviction to a fine not exceeding level three on the standard scale.

1.5 Other offences

1.5.1 Public Health Act 1936 (PHA 1936)

1.5.1.1 s141 PHA 1936: Power to deal with insanitary cisterns, etc

By this section, an insanitary cistern, well, tank or waterbutt used for the supply of water for domestic purposes which is positioned in such a way as to render the water therein contaminated will amount to a statutory nuisance, for the purposes of Part III EPA 1990. (See below)

1.5.1.2 s259 PHA 1936: Nuisances in connection with watercourses, ditches, ponds, etc

This section lists the following matters as being statutory nuisances for the purposes of Part III, EPA 1990.

s259(1)(a) PHA 1936: Any pond, pool, ditch, gutter or watercourse which has become so foul or fallen into such a state that it is prejudicial to health, or a nuisance.

s259(1)(b) PHA 1936: Any part of a watercourse (not being a part ordinarily navigated by vessels employed in the carriage of goods by water, which is so choked or silted up as to obstruct or impede the proper flow of water, and thereby cause a nuisance, or give rise to conditions prejudicial to health).

Liability is imposed solely upon the person by whose act or default the nuisance arises or continues.

Note:

A problem may arise over the use of the word 'default.' In *Neath RDC v Williams,*[41] because the riparian owner was not liable to maintain the watercourse, he could not be found guilty of default if he failed to clear obstructions which had arisen naturally. Therefore, a nuisance abatement could not properly be served upon him. If the obstruction arises for other than natural causes, however, and the riparian owner either is or ought to be aware in all the circumstances of the existence of the nuisance, then liability will attach to the riparian owner, extending to damages caused thereby. See *Sedley Denfield v Callaghan*[42] from which it is possible to argue that the riparian owner may be in default where the obstruction is not the result of natural causes.

1.6 Bye-laws

1.6.1 Water Act 1945 (WA 1945)

1.6.1.1 s18 WA 1945: Byelaws to prevent pollution by water undertakers

This section of this Act gives powers to a statutory water undertaker to define an area which becomes subject to bye-laws and in which they deem it necessary to prohibit or regulate activity specified in the bye-laws. If the owner or occupier of that area fails to comply with the requirement which is made of him by the bye-law, then he shall be liable, on summary conviction, to the same penalties as if he had committed an act prohibited by the bye-laws.

1.6.2 Rivers (Prevention of Pollution) Act 1951 (R[PP]A 1951)

1.6.2.1 s5 R(PP)A 1951: Bye-laws

This section of this Act gives powers to a river authority to make byelaws in respect of any stream or part of a stream as seems to the authority expedient for prohibiting or regulating the keeping or use on the stream of vessels provided with sanitary appliances, from which polluting matter passes or can pass into the stream.

> A person who contravenes such bye-laws shall be liable on summary conviction to a fine not exceeding level three on the standard scale and if the contravention continues, the fine will continue at a rate of £5.00 for each day that it does so.

1.7 Damage to fish

A considerable number of prosecutions are brought under the SFFA 1975 for this offence. It is an alternative to prosecution under s85 WRA 1991.

1.7.1 Salmon and Freshwater Fisheries Act 1975 (SFFA 1975)

1.7.1.1 s4 SFFA 1975: Poisonous matter and polluting effluent

Offence

> s4(1) SFFA 1975, makes it an offence for any person who causes or knowingly permits to flow, or puts or knowingly permits to be put, into any waters containing fish or into any tributaries of waters containing fish, any liquid or solid matter to such an extent as to cause the waters to be poisonous or injurious to fish or the spawning grounds, spawn or food of fish.

A person who is prosecuted for this offence is liable

> (1) on summary conviction, to a fine not exceeding £2000,00, with a further fine of £40.00 per day for each day thereafter that the offence continued;
> (2) on indictment, to a term of not more than two years' imprisonment or a fine, or both.

s4(3) SFFA 1975 requires that proceedings under s4(1) SFFA 1975 may only be brought by the water authority or by a person who has obtained a certificate from the minister that he has a material interest in the waters alleged to be affected.

Definitions:

'Causes or knowingly permits' is defined at s85WRA 1991 above.

1.7.2 Defence to s4 SFFA 1975 offence

> s4(2) SFFA 1975: A person shall not be guilty of this offence if he can prove that he is by law exercising a right to which he is entitled by law, or continuing to use a method in connection with the premises which was established thus before July 18th, 1923.

For this defence to succeed, the person must be able to satisfy the court that he has used the best practical means, within reasonable cost, to prevent such matter from doing injury to the fish, spawning rounds, spawn or food or fish.

1.8 Other statutory provisions in respect of water pollution related to Scotland are summarised below

1.8.1 Sewerage (Scotland) Act 1988 (S[S]A 1988)

This Act contains provisions for dealing with sewerage in Scotland which generally reflect the offences which are to be found in WIA 1991.

They are listed here for reference:

s12 S(S)A 1988: Rights of owners and occupiers to connect with and drain into public sewers.

> s12(8) S(S)A 1988: Any person who connects a drain or sewer to the sewers or a works of a public authority or alters a drain or sewer without permission granted under this section shall be guilty of an offence and liable to a fine of £20,000, and the local authority may recover the costs of removal or rectification.
>
> s14(6) S(S)A 1988: It is an offence to construct a drain, sewer or sewerage treatment works in a particular manner other

than in accordance with the terms of a direction from an authority. The summary offence will attract a fine, level four on the standard scale.

s24(2) S(S)A 1988: It is an offence to discharge trade effluent into the sewers or sewerage treatment works without the consent of the authority, or contrary to any direction or condition imposed under the Act. The maximum sentence on summary conviction is £20,000, with a further fine for each day on which the offence continues after conviction.

s46(2) It is an offence for a person to pass, or permit to be passed into, or into a drain connected with a public sewer or treatment works, any matter or substance which . . . is likely to injure the sewer or works, or to affect prejudicially the treatment or disposal of their contents or to be prejudicial to health.

It will be a defence to prove that at the time of the relevant act he did not know, and could not be reasonably expected to know, that it would be likely to have the aforementioned effects.

Sentence on summary conviction may be a fine not exceeding £20,000, and a further fine of £50 for each day on which the offence continues after conviction; on indictment, up to two years' imprisonment, a fine, or both.

s50(1) S(S)A 1988: It is an offence for a person, admitted to land in compliance with the Act's provisions or by warrant, to make use of or disclose any information obtained with regard to a manufacturing process or trade secret, unless use or disclosure was made in the performance of his duty or unless the disclosure is made with the consent of the person by whom the information was furnished, in connection with the Act's execution, or for purposes of criminal proceedings,, whether arising out of the Act or not.

The sentence on summary conviction may be a fine, level five, or three months' imprisonment, or both.

1.8.2 Water (Scotland) Act 1980 (W[S]A 1980)65

s75 (1) W(S)A 1980: It is an offence to commit any act or neglect whereby any spring, well or adit, the water of which is used or likely to be used for human consumption, domestic purposes or manufacturing food or drink for human consumption, is polluted or likely to be polluted.

[This section largely reflects s72 WIA 1991, save that the 'domestic purposes' capacity makes provision for water used for central heating greater: 100gallons.]

Exclusions from this section are (i) methods of cultivation or land use in accordance with principles of good husbandry and (ii) the reasonable use of oil or tar on public roads, so long as the road authority takes all reasonable steps to prevent pollution of such spring, well or adit.

Sentence, on summary conviction, is a fine not exceeding the 'prescribed limit'; on indictment, a fine or imprisonment for a term not exceeding two years.

1.8.3 See also

Orders Relating to Water Undertakings, for provisions in respect of waste and meters.
Detergent (Composition) Regulations 1978
Water Supply(Water Quality) Regulations 1989
Control of Pollution (Silage) Regulations 1991

Notes

[1] s104(1) WRA 1991.
[2] s104(4)(a) WRA 1991.
[3] s104(1)(b) WRA 1991.
[4] s221(1) WRA 1991.
[5] s104(1)(c) WRA 1991.
[6] s104(3) WRA 1991.
[7] s104(3) WRA 1991.
[8] s 104(1)(d) and s221(1) WRA 1991.
[9] *Alphacell and Woodward* [1972] AC 24, 834, per Lord Wilberforce.
[10] *A-G's Reference* (No. 1 of 1994)[1995] 1 WLR 599 CA, per Lord Taylor.
[11] *(1989 153 JP 581 QBD).*
[12] *Impress (Worcester)Ltd v Rees* [1971] 2 All ER 357 QBD.
[13] *ibid* p835.
[14] *National Rivers Authority v Welsh Development Agency* (1992) 158 JP 506 QBD.

[15] *National Rivers Authority v Alfred McAlpines Homes East Ltd* [1994] 4 All ER 286 QBD.
[16] *AG's Reference* (No. 1 of 1994) [1995] 1 WLR 599.
[17] [1994] 3 WLR 1202,1210,HL.
[18] [1993] 2 All ER 440 QBD.
[19] [1975] 1 WLR 988,993 QBD.
[20] [1991]JPL B 89; [1997] Env LR 227 QBD.
[21] *Severn Trent Water Authority v Express Foods Group Ltd* (1988) 153 JP 126, DC.
[22] *Dell v Chesham UDC* (1921) 85 J.P.186.
[23] *Durrent v Branksome* UDC[1872] 2 Ch 291.
[24] *R v Justices of Antrim* (1906) 2 I.R.298.
[25] *Schulmans Inc. v National Rivers Authority* (1992) 4 Land Management and Env LR, 3 Water Law 72 Div Ct.
[26] *Wisdom's Law of Watercourses,* ed. William Howarth, pub. Shaw and Sons, 1992.
[27] (1992) 4 Land Management and Env LR 131.
[28] ss37-39A WIA 1991.
[29] s68(ss3a,3b).
[30] s93(ss1) WIA 1991.
[31] s67 WIA 1991.
[32] s218 WIA 1991.
[33] s219 WIA 1991.
[34] s219(1) WIA 1991.
[35] s219(2) WIA 1991.
[36] Water Supply(Water Quality) Regulations 1989 Part II.
[37] Water Supply (Water Quality) Regulations 1989 Part IV.
[38] Water Supply (Water Quality) Regulations 1989 Part VII.
[39] Water Supply (Water Quality) Regulations 1989 Part VI (Para 28(4)).
[40] *Drinking Water Inspectorate and Secretary of State v Severn Trent* (1995) Independent April 25th, 1995.
[41] *Neath RDC v Williams* [1951] 1KB 115, [1950] 2 All ER 625.
[42] *Sedley Denfield v Callaghan* [1940] AC 880, [1940] 3 All ER 349.

CHAPTER 2

POLLUTION OF THE SEA

CONTENTS

CHAPTER 2

POLLUTION OF THE SEA

2.1 Introduction

The law in respect of criminal offences committed through acts of pollution at sea is contained in three Statutes and a body of Regulations. These statutes — the Prevention of Oil Pollution Act 1971 (POPA 1971), Food and Environment Protection Act (FEPA 1985), the Merchant of Shipping Act 1995 (MSA 1995) — and several sets of regulations reflect the international law which generally governs pollution of the sea. An analysis of the international law from which the body of domestic legislation derives is outside the scope of this work and it is proposed in this section to deal solely with the main offences which can be tried in British courts. Note that the Crown has power, by s128 MSA 1995, to act by Order in Council to take the appropriate steps to give effect to any of the treaties on marine pollution listed in it or any other treaties. A list of treaties to which the UK is a party is in the Annex to this Act.

2.2 Legislation

2.2.1 Prevention of Oil Pollution Act 1971 (POPA 1971)

This Act contains two criminal offences which address oil pollution. Prosecutions are generally brought by harbour authorities. Most prosecutions have been in connection with discharges of oil into harbour waters.

The offence which formerly arose out of s1(2) POPA 1955 is now at Reg. 12 and 13 of the *Merchant Shipping (Prevention of Oil Pollution) Regulations 1996*. Part IX contains the detailed and complex provisions for the enforcement of the Regulations. Reg. 36 provides for the prosecution of the offence. Breach of a regulation leading to a summary conviction carries a potentially extremely high penalty: a fine not exceeding £250,000 (Reg. 36). The 'due diligence' defence is available to an owner or master charged under this Regulation. Third parties may also be charged where it is appropriate to do so, irrespective of whether the first person is proceeded against. Note that where a foreign company is charged with an offence under these Regulations, the company will be considered as having been served when the document is served on the master of the ship. Any person serving such a document has a legal right to board the ship to do so. At Reg. 37(3) there are detailed provisions which address the rights of the owner and master in the situation where the ship has been detained under the power of Reg. 34.

2.2.1.1. s1(2) POPA 1971

This section encompasses crude oil, fuel oil, heavy diesel oil and any other description of oil determined as such by the Secretary of State including vegetable oil.

[See the MSA 1995 for offences arising out of the discharge of oil from ships. See also the Merchant Shipping (Prevention of Oil Pollution) Regulations 1996 generally].

Note that where a discharge is authorised under Part I EPA 1990, then the following sections will not apply.

2.2.1.2 s2 POPA 1971: Discharge of oil into United Kingdom waters

2.2.1.3 Offence

> s2(1) POPA 1971: If any oil or mixture containing oil is discharged as mentioned in the following paragraphs into waters to which this section applies, then ... the following shall be guilty of an offence:
>
> (c) if the discharge is from a place on land, the occupier of that place, unless he proves that the discharge was caused as mentioned in paragraph (d) of this subsection;
>
> (d) if the discharge is from a place on land and is caused by the act of a person who is in that place without the permission (express or implied) of the occupier, that person;
>
> (e) if the discharge takes place otherwise than as mentioned in the preceding paragraphs and is the result of any operations for the exploration of the seabed or subsoil or the exploitation of their natural resources, the person carrying on the operation.

This section applies to the whole of the sea within the seaward limits of the territorial waters of the United Kingdom and all other inland waters within those limits which are navigable by seagoing ships. This will include waters in dry dock other than when there are no waters to receive a discharge.

2.2.1.4 Defences

The owner or master of the vehicle may use as a defence his proof that a discharge was for the purpose of securing the safety of the vessel, preventing damage to any vessel or cargo, or of saving life, subject to the Court taking the same view of the discharge.

Where the defendant can prove that all reasonable steps had been taken to minimise the discharge where it has occurred in damage to the vessel, then this will be a defence.

It will also be a defence to prove that the discharge occurred through leakage which did not occur through negligence and was stopped as soon as possible.

2.2.1.5 Sentence

A person convicted of an offence under this section is liable to a fine not exceeding £250,000. Clean-up costs may be deducted from the fine.

2.2.1.6 s3 POPA 1971: Discharge of certain oils from pipelines or as the result of exploration, etc, in designated areas

2.2.1.7 Offence

> s3(1) POPA 1971: If any oil to which section 1 of this Act applies, or any mixture containing such oil, is discharged into any part of the sea-
>
> (a) from a pipeline
>
> (b) (otherwise than from a ship) as the result of any operation for the exploration of the seabed and subsoil or the exploration of their natural resources in a designated area, then, subject to the following provisions of this Act, the owner of the pipeline or, as the case may be, the person carrying on the operations shall be guilty of an offence unless the discharge is from a place in his occupation and he proves that it was due to the act of a person who was there without his permission (express or implied).

'Designated area' means an area designated made by an Order under s1 of the Continental Shelf Act 1964 (CSA 1964).

Vessels of less than 80 tons gross tonnage are excluded from the provisions of this section.

Sentence

> s3(3) POPA 1971: A person guilty of an offence under this section shall be liable on summary conviction to a fine not exceeding £50,000 or on conviction on indictment to a fine.

2.2.1.8 Defences

It will be a defence to a charge under either s2 or s3 POPA 1971 to prove that the escape of oil or mixture containing oil or delay in the discovery of the escape occurred not through want of reasonable care and that all reasonable steps were taken after its discovery.

It will also be a defence to prove, subject to s6(3) POPA 1971,

(a) that the oil was contained in an effluent produced by operations for the refining of oil;
(b) that it was not reasonably practicable to dispose of the effluent otherwise than by discharging it into waters to which that section applies; and
(c) that all reasonably practicable steps had been taken for eliminating oil from the effluent.

Where the surface of the water or the land is fouled by oil, then the defences in the previous paragraph will not be available, unless the court is satisfied that the fouling was caused other than by the discharge with which the offence is concerned.

2.2.1.9 s11 POPA 1971: Duty to report discharge of oil into waters of harbours

> s11 POPA 1971: If any oil or mixture containing oil . . . is found to be escaping or to have escaped into any such waters from a place on land . . . the occupier of the place on land shall forthwith report the occurrence to the harbour master, or, if the harbour has no harbour master, then to the harbour authority.

2.2.1.10 Offence

> s11(3) POPA 1971: If a person fails to make a report as required by this section he shall be liable on summary conviction to a fine not exceeding level five on the standard scale.

2.2.1.11 s18 POPA 1971: Powers of Inspection

This section provides extensive powers of inspection which may be used by harbour masters or any person appointed by the Secretary of State. These include power to board a vessel and to conduct a comprehensive inspection of the vessel and its records.

2.2.1.12 Offence

> s18(8) POPA 1971: If any person fails to comply with any requirement duly made in pursuance of [powers to inspect apparatus for transferring oil, to copy entries and require certification of those copies], he shall be liable on summary conviction to a fine not exceeding [level three on the standard scale]; if any person wilfully obstructs a person acting in the exercise of any power conferred by virtue of this section . . . he shall be liable [note s28 provisions] on summary conviction to a fine not exceeding level four on the standard scale.

2.2.2 Food and Environment Protection Act 1985 (FEPA 1985)

Part II of this Act implemented the requirements which flowed from the UK ratifications of the 1972 Oslo Convention and the London Dumping Convention. The Act creates a licensing system for deposits at sea, scuttling or associated operation, in which conditions may be attached to the licence, and breaches of the licence amount to a criminal offence.

2.2.2.1 Requirement for a licence

In ss5, 6 FEPA 1985, the circumstances are laid out in which a licence is needed. No distinction is drawn between public and private vessels. The circumstances are:

(1) A licence is required for the deposit of substances or articles either in the sea or under the seabed, within UK territorial waters, from a vehicle, vessel, aircraft, hovercraft or marine structure, floating container, or structure on land constructed or adapted wholly or mainly for the purpose of depositing solids in the sea; likewise, a licence is required by any British vessel, etc, for a deposit anywhere at sea or under the seabed.

(2) A licence is required for the scuttling of vessels, either in UK-controlled waters or *anywhere* at sea, if the scuttling is controlled by a British vessel, aircraft, hovercraft or marine structure. A licence for towing or propelling a vessel for the purpose of scuttling it is also required.

(3) A licence is required for the loading of a vessel, etc, in the UK or UK waters with substances or articles for deposit *anywhere* at sea or under the seabed. A licence is required for a vehicle being loaded for a similar purpose.

(4) A licence is also required for the incineration of substances or articles on a vessel or marine structure, either in UK-controlled waters or anywhere at sea on British vessel.

2.2.2.2 Licence authorisations

By s8 FEPA 1971, the licensing authority must take account of a number of factors when granting a licence: the need 'to protect the marine environment, the living resources which it supports and human health'; and the need 'to prevent interference with legitimate uses of the sea', and include provisions within the licence which address these objectives. The licence may include limitations for its use, requirements of information and fees to be paid. There are provisions for the variation and revocation of a licence, either because the authorities have perceived a breach of the licence, or because the environmental circumstances themselves or the state of knowledge have altered.

Schedule 3 to this Act provides for appeals against the licence's terms.

See also *Urban Water Treatment (England and Wales) Regulations* 1994, which concerns the specific regime for the dumping of toxic materials.

2.2.2.3 Offence

> s9(1) FEPA 1971: Subject to subsections (3) to (7) below, a person who-
>
> (a) except in pursuance of a licence and in accordance with its provisions, does anything for which a licence is needed; or
> (b) causes or permits any other person to do any such thing except in pursuance of a licence and in accordance with its provisions,
>
> shall be guilty of an offence.
>
> S9(2) FEPA 1971: A person who for the purpose of procuring the issue of a licence, or in purporting to carry out any duty imposed on him by provisions of a licence-

(a) makes a statement which he knows to be false in a material particular;
(b) recklessly makes a statement which is false in a material particular; or
(c) intentionally fails to disclose any material particular,

shall be guilty of an offence.

2.2.2.4 Defences

If the accused can show that the unlicensed action he took was to secure the safety of a vessel, aircraft, hovercraft or marine structure, or to save life, and that he notified the ministers of the operation, this will amount to a defence. This defence will not succeed if the operation was not necessary for those purposes, or it was not a reasonable step to take in the circumstances, or that it the defendant's fault that it *was* necessary.

If the accused can show that the unlicensed action he took was taken within the territorial waters of, or within, a Convention State, where authorisation had been issued by the responsible authority, then this will be a defence.

2.2.3 Merchant Shipping Act 1995 (MSA 1995)

The offences within this Act deal primarily with discharges of oil or oil mixture from ships into UK waters. However, the Act also creates the improvement or prohibition notice: the former may be served upon a person who appears to be in breach of oil-pollution provisions within the Act or the relevant regulations; the latter may be served on a person who appears to be engaging in an activity which may result in 'serious pollution of any navigable waters'.

Full definitions of the terms used in the Act are at Part XIII.

The jurisdictional powers in respect of offences committed under this Act are to be found in ss279-284 MSA 1971.

s100(C) MSA 1971 empowers the Secretary of State to require the removal of a nonUK ship from within UK territorial waters when it appears not to be exercising either the right of innocent passage, or the right of transit passage through straits used for international navigation. The section provides that the owner or master of the ship may be required either to move or not to move the vessel.

2.2.3.1 Offence

> s100(D)(1) MSA 1995: If a person to whom a direction is duly given under s100C contravenes, or fails to comply with, any requirement of the direction, he shall be guilty of an offence.
>
> s100D(2): If a person intentionally obstructs any person who is
>
> (a) acting on behalf of the Secretary of State in connection with the giving or service of a direction under s100C MSA 1995;
> (b) acting in compliance with a direction under that section; or
> (c) acting under s100C(6) or (7) MSA 1971
> (the exercise of further powers of the Secretary of State)
>
> he shall be guilty of an offence.

2.2.3.2 Defence

The defences which are available to a charge under s100(D)(1) POPA 1995 are that the accused may prove that he used all due diligence to ensure compliance with the direction, or that he had reasonable cause to believe that compliance with the direction would have involved serious risk to human life.

2.2.3.3 Sentence

A person convicted of an offence under this section shall be liable

> (a) on summary conviction, to a fine not exceeding £50,000
> (b) on conviction on indictment, to a fine.

2.2.3.4 Waste-reception facilities at harbours

s130 MSA 1995 gives powers, *as yet not used*, to the Secretary of State to regulate the transfers between ships in UK territorial waters. These transfers may include cargo, stores, bunker fuel or ballast. The regulations may prohibit the transfer of specified things, or regulate the transfer of such things, in respect of the design of and standards to be met by ships and equipment, as well as the manning of the ship, including the qualifications and experience both of those employed on board and those controlling the transfer operation. The regulations may provide for records and information about the procedure to be compiled and kept.

Provision may be made for the offence of contravening the regulations, for which the penalties on summary conviction may be a fine not exceeding

£25,000, and on conviction on indictment, imprisonment for a term not exceeding two years, or a fine, or both.

Under s130(A-D)MSA 1995, the Secretary of State is empowered to regulate for waste-reception facilities at harbours. The *Merchant Shipping (Port Waste Receptions Facilities) Regulations* 1997 were made under these subsections and they contain sanctions for contravention. A summary conviction will render a person liable to a fine not exceeding the statutory maximum and on conviction on indictment to imprisonment for a term not exceeding two years, or to a fine or both.

2.2.3.5 Oil Pollution

Proceedings for the offences within this part of the Act (at ss131, 135,136 and 142 MSA 1995) may only be brought with the consent of, or by the Attorney-General, or the harbour master or authority, or by direction from the Secretary of State in respect of s135,136 or 142 MSA 1995.

2.2.3.6 s131 MSA 1971: Discharge of oil from ships into certain UK waters

This section creates the offence of discharging oil into UK waters navigable by seagoing ships.

2.2.3.7 Offence

> s131(1) MSA 1995: The following shall be guilty of an offence, that is to say
>
> (a) if the discharge is from a ship, the owner or master of the ship, unless he proves that the discharge took place and was caused as mentioned in para. (b) below;
> (b) if the discharge is from a ship but takes place in the course of a transfer of oil to or from another ship or a place on land and is caused by the act or omission of any person in charge of any apparatus in that other ship or that place, the owner or master of that other ship or, as the case may be, the occupier of that place.

This offence is not applicable where the discharge is made into the sea (that is to include any estuary or arm of the sea) and according to prescribed regulations. (No such regulations have yet been made.)

If the harbour master has reason to believe that an offence under this section has been committed he may detain the ship by the powers found in s144 MSA 1995. Note the limits to the length of time that the vessel may be detained.

2.2.3.8 Defences

It will be a defence to a charge against an owner or master under this section to prove that the discharge was made to secure the safety of any ship, to prevent damage to any ship or cargo, or to save life. The defence will not succeed if the Court takes the view that the discharge was not necessary for any of those purposes, or that it was not reasonable in the circumstances.
It will be a defence to a charge against an owner or master under this section to prove that the discharge was an escape which occurred as a consequence of damage to the ship, and that all reasonable steps were taken thereafter to minimise the escape, or that the discharge was an escape which occurred through leakage, which was negligent, and which, after discovery, was stopped or reduced by all reasonable steps being taken.

The same 'due diligence' defence is available to occupiers charged with an offence under s131 MSA 1995. Note that there is a presumption that harbour masters charged under the provisions of this section shall not be convicted unless they can be shown to have failed 'to take such steps as were reasonable in the circumstances for preventing, stopping or reducing the discharge'. This defence extends to cover actions taken whilst removing obstructions to dockyard ports (s13 Dockyards Ports Regulations Act 1865 [DPRA 1865]).

2.2.3.9 Sentence

A person convicted of an offence under this section shall be liable:

(a) on summary conviction, to a fine not exceeding £250,000;
(b) on conviction on indictment, to a fine.

Where expenses have been incurred in removing the pollution or repairing damage, then all or part of the fine may be used to defray those expenses.

2.2.3.10 Other offences

By s135 MSA 1995, no oil may be transferred between sunrise and sunset to or from a ship in any UK harbour, unless notice has been given, or the transfer is for the purposes of a fire brigade. A contravention of this section is a summary offence and will render a convicted person liable to a fine not exceeding level three on the standard scale.

By s136 MSA 1995, failure to report the discharge of oil or oil mixture to the harbour master or authority is an offence and the convicted person is liable to a fine note exceeding level five on the standard scale.

By s137 MSA 1995, where there has been a shipping casualty, the Secretary of State has powers to give directions to the owner or any person in possession of the ship (the master or the salvor). It is an offence to disobey the orders or to obstruct the execution of a direction which is given within the British pollution-control zone. Outside that zone, such directions may only be given to UK citizens or companies. Note that, through the powers added in 1997 by s138 A POPA 1971, this section now applies to forms of pollution other than oil, prescribed by the Secretary of State, pursuant to the requirements of the 1969 Intervention Convention, para. 1. The 'due diligence' defence is available to a person charged under s137 POPA 1971, as is the defence that he had reasonable cause for believing that compliance with a direction would have involved serious risk to human life. A person guilty of an offence under this section will be liable on summary conviction to a fine not exceeding £50,000; on conviction on indictment, the fine is unlimited.

2.2.3.11 s142 MSA 1995: Oil records

This section legislates for the keeping of comprehensive records of all operations which relate to oil cargoes. The regulations which have effect, by virtue of the Interpretation Act, are the *Oil in Navigable Waters (Records) Regulations* 1972, and the *Oil in Navigable Waters (Transfer Records) Regulations* 1957. Failure to carry an oil record book or to fail to comply with other requirements under this section is a summary offence, rendering the person convicted liable to a fine not exceeding level five on the standard scale. Note that a person committing the offence of entering information which is, to his knowledge, either false or misleading in any material particular, is liable, on summary conviction, to a fine not exceeding the statutory maximum, or imprisonment for a term not exceeding six months. On conviction on indictment, he is liable to a term of imprisonment not exceeding two years, or a fine, or both.

2.2.3.12 International Oil Pollution Compensation Fund

Contributions are payable to this Fund by importers and otherwise by the person receiving the oil. Provision has been made for regulations imposing obligations on persons who are liable or who may be liable to make contributions, to give security for payment. However, those regulations have not yet been made. Under s174 MSA 1995, a person liable to make contributions to this Fund must disclose information concerning his dealings in oil. Failure to disclose such information or giving false information will be an offence for which the penalty on summary conviction may be a fine not exceeding level four on the standard scale. On indictment, the penalties may be imprisonment for a term not exceeding 12 months, or a fine, or both.

2.2.3.13 Enforcement

s256 MSA 1995 gives the Secretary of State powers to appoint inspectors; an inspector may serve the person with an improvement notice or a prohibition notice where there has been a contravention of a statutory provision. Any dispute arising out of an improvement notice may be referred to arbitration.

s257 MSA 1995 creates the powers by which production of ships documents may be required:

> failure to produce a logbook without reasonable excuse will amount to a summary offence, for which a person may be liable to a fine not exceeding level three on the standard scale. Refusal to produce the logbook is also an offence (with liability of a fine not exceeding level five on the standard scale).

s258 MSA 1995 contains the powers by which inspectors may board and inspect a ship and its equipment.

s259 MSA 1995 gives powers to the inspector *inter alia* to board a ship or enter premises at any time, if he believes he has good reason to do so. Other powers under this section are comprehensive and wideranging.

> A person who either obstructs an inspector or does not comply with a requirement, without reasonable excuse, or makes a false statement in purported compliance shall be liable on summary conviction to a fine not exceeding the statutory maximum. On indictment, he will be liable to imprisonment for a term not exceeding two years, or to a fine, or both.

s266 MSA 1995 creates the offence of contravening a requirement imposed by an improvement notice. On summary conviction, a person may be liable to a fine not exceeding the statutory maximum, and on indictment to a fine. It also creates the offence of contravening a prohibition for which the penalties are, on summary conviction, a fine not exceeding the statutory maximum and on indictment, to imprisonment for a term not exceeding two years or a fine or both. The 'due diligence' offence is available to a person charged with any offence in respect of a notice.

Note that the proceedings for a *summary* offence must be commenced within six months of the offence being committed or where the defendant is out of the UK at the time of the commission of the alleged offence, within two months after he arrives back in the UK but before the expiration of three years from the date of the offence.

Also note that by s277, directors and managers of a company may be held personally liable, in addition to their corporate liability. A person aiding and or abetting the commission of an offence under this Act may be dealt with as though he were a principal offender.

2.2.4 Merchant Shipping (Prevention of Oil Pollution) Regulations 1996

These regulations implement the 1973 London Convention for the Prevention of Pollution from Ships (MARPOL) and the 1978 Protocol to that Convention. Noncompliance with the regulations renders the owner and master criminally liable, although a defence to a charge under these regulations will be that the defendant acted with due diligence, taking all reasonable precautions to avoid the commission of the offence.

In July, 1998, a Danish-registered container ship was observed discharging oil five miles off the Cornish coast. The slick which appeared was about six miles long and 30 metres wide. Proceedings were brought by the Maritime and Coastguard Agency under the Merchant Shipping (Prevention of Oil Pollution) Regulations 1996. The owners were fined the maximum penalty of £250,000 with costs of £1,243.

CHAPTER 3

AIR POLLUTION

CONTENTS

CHAPTER 3

AIR POLLUTION

3.1 Introduction

The regime for the control of pollution in the atmosphere and air pollution can be broadly divided into two parts:

(1) The system of prior-approval authorisations, in which Integrated Pollution Control (IPC),mainly concerned with the management of emissions from major industrial installations, is complemented by the role which the local authority plays in granting authorisations for part B processes, which is known as Local Authority Air Pollution Control (LAAPC).

(2) Statutory controls and enforcement provisions deriving from the Clean Air Act 1993 (CAA 1993) and further sections of the Environmental Protection Act 1990 (EPA 1990). The former provides a lower level of control, over combustion plants and the operation of furnaces which are not sufficiently pollutant by their nature to be caught by IPC or LAAPC.The latter provides a more general framework for the offence of statutory nuisance.

At the time of writing, although the Government has placed itself under a duty to produce a national air-quality strategy, that strategy is not yet entirely in place.Whilst that strategy is awaited, this chapter confines itself to a pragmatic approach, examining the offences for which people can be changed, available defences and sentencing practices.

3.2 Integrated Pollution Control (IPC)

3.2.1 Introduction

The genesis of the concept of Integrated Pollution Control (IPC) occurred over a period, following the *Fifth Report* produced by the *Royal Commission on Environmental Pollution* in 1976.What lay at the heart of the *Fifth Report* was a recognition that environmental media could no longer be considered as intrinsically separate units.In practical terms, where an industrial process was to be used, then the polluting implications, for example in respect of emissions to atmosphere, must be assessed by the controlling authority in combination with the implications of wastes disposed on land or discharged into water. The Report also addressed the 'transferability of pollution': the problem of close linkage between the three principal forms of pollution (air, water and land) which it seemed impossible to address in the absence of systematic coordination between the various authorities who were then responsible for pollution control.The Report recommended that a crossmedia approach should be established,to ensure that pollution was not simply being shifted from one medium to another, causing repeating pollution. In 1987, Her Majesty's Inspectorate of Pollution (HMIP) was established, to coordinate the management of pollution with a view to minimising or preventing it altogether. The principle which underlay this coordinated approach was to determine the 'Best Practicable Environmental Option'. (BPEO) A subsequent consultation paper entitled *Integrated Pollution Control* combined the idea of BPEO with the introduction of a system of pollution control designed to manage the pollution which resulted from the operation of certain types of industrial processes.The process technology, methods of operation and levels of discharge into each environmental media would be scheduled and subject to authorisation. The key differences in approach now appeared to be acknowledgments that (i) pollutants discharged into one medium were not confined in their effects to that medium alone and (ii) minimising environmental damage did not necessarily amount to confining a discharge to one medium. In its *Twelfth Report* produced in 1988, the Royal Commission defined BPEO thus:

> The selection of BPEO requires a systematic approach to decision-taking in which the practicability of all reasonable options is examined and in which environmental impact is a major factor in the final choice.

BPEO is defined as being the achievement of the option which offers the greatest protection for environment. In any application for an authorisation under IPC, an applicant must submit an assessment of the environmental effects of the release he is seeking to authorise.Although BPEO is not legally defined, and therefore occasionally somewhat indistinct in its application,a number of Environment Agency (EA) publications will assist operators:

(1) *BPEO Assessment for Integrated Pollution Control, Technical Guidance Note E1*

(2) *BPEO Assessment for IPC Vol. 1: Principles and Methodology; Vol. II Technical date (for consultation) 1997.*

(3) *Process Guidance Notes*. These detail requirements of the Secretary of State, environmental quality standards, EC directives and other obligations under international law. They also contain notes on abatement technologies and monitoring techniques.

The system of IPC was established in Part 1 of the EPA 1990.It is a centralised system in which the enforcing authority is the EA. The system is designed to apply to the most potentially-polluting or technologically-complex industrial processes in England and Wales.

Its main objectives are to:

(1) prevent or minimise the release of prescribed substances and to render harmless any such substances which are released; and
(2) ensure consideration of releases from industrial processes to all media in the context of the effect on the environment as a whole [cite : *IPC a Practical Guide*, DoE, March, 1996].

3.2.2 IPC prescribed processes and substances

IPC applies to all processes falling within any description or process prescribed in the Regulations compiled by the Secretary of State. In the *Environmental Protection (Prescribed Processes and Substances) Regulations* 1991 [SI 1991/472, as amended, Schedule 1 contains the descriptions of the process to which the controls apply].

3.2.2.1 Schedule 1

This is divided into Part A and Part B:

Part A processes

These are prescribed for IPC, that is to say the processes with the greatest potential for serious pollution to the three environmental media.

Part B processes

These processes are subject to Local Authority Air Pollution Control (LAAPC).

3.2.2.2 Regulation 4

This Regulation excludes certain processes from control even though they may be on the Schedule.These exclusions are, for example, where the prescribed substance is released in a sufficiently small quantity to be regarded as insignificant. In *Tandridge District Council v P & S Civil Engineering Ltd and Others* [1995] Env LR, the question of where the burden of proof lay in respect of these exceptions went to appeal to the Divisional Court by way of case stated. It was held that the burden of proving the exception lay upon the defendant, s101 Magistrates' Courts Act 1980 (MCA 1980) applying.

3.2.2.3 Schedule 2

This Schedule clarifies the nature of what forms the prescribed process listed in Schedule 1. Note that all related parts of the process become subject to control, 'providing that they are at the same location, carried on by the same person and do not warrant authorisation in their own right'. The Regulations also provide a timetable by which processes will be brought under IPC.

3.2.2.4 Prescribed substances

The Regulations also list the substances which when released into any of the three media could be most harmful or potentially polluting.The use of Best Available Techniques Not Entailing Excessive Cost (BATNEEC) is required, either to prevent their release at all, or, if that is not possible, then to minimise the release and render it harmless.

The concept of BATNEEC is derived from EC legislation, in particular the Air Framework Directive.

Full guidance on what will constitute BATNEEC can be found in the *Practical Guide* (see 3.2.1. above). The four basic elements are:

(i) *'availability'* meaning that which is generally accessible to the operator of the process. This includes piloted techniques, or techniques which are unavailable inside the UK.

(ii) *'techniques'* including the concept and design of the process, its components and the relationships between all parts of the process.This includes the entire personnel team, as well as the design, construction, layout and maintenance of the building where the process will occur.

(iii) *'best'* in terms of the EPA 1990 means quite simply what is most efficient. This may include, where there is more than one process being used, an assessment of the relative costings, ie 'not entailing excessive cost'.

(iv) *'excessive cost'* is not determined by reference to the economic condition of the business making an application *in respect of a new process* but by reference to the costs to that part of an industry as a whole. However, assessing excessive cost *in respect of an existing process* should be done by reference to Art. 13 of the *EC Air Framework Directive.* This requires the following to be taken into account:

(a) technical characteristics of the plant;

(b) its rate of utilisation and length of life remaining;

(c) the nature and volume of polluting emissions and,

(d) a consideration of the commercial implications of costs involved.

There are three lists of prescribed substances, according to whether the substance being controlled would otherwise be released into the following media:

(i) Schedule 4 (Air);

(ii) Schedule 5 (Water) and;

(iii) Schedule 6 (Land).

3.2.2.5 Application procedures

These are governed by the *Environmental Protection (Applications, Appeals and Registers) Regulations* 1991(SI 1991/507), as amended. All applications for IPC authorisations are made to the EA.

3.2.2.6 Local Authority Air Pollution Control (LAAPC)

Authorisations for Part B processes (that is the less-polluting ones, resulting from air alone), are given by the local authority (LA), the district, London and metropolitan boroughs and port health authorities.The principle of BATNEEC applies here as well. Three kinds of guidance notes have been compiled to assist operators and LAs in establishing LAAPC.The General Guidance notes, which are occasionally revised, emphasise the need for consistency among LA's approaches.

There is a substantial number of Process Guidance notes providing information on standards for emission limits, and other standards, such as for monitoring, sampling, chimney heights, operational controls. They are regularly revised.

One Up-grading Guidance Note has been produced to date. Note that the DoE has a Briefing Note on LAAPC on the Internet, which is regularly up-dated.

3.2.2.7 Part 1, EPA 1990: Definitions for IPC and APC

s1 EPA 1990 contains the definitions upon which both the IPC and air pollution control (APC) systems are based. Some of these are included below for the purposes of clarification:

> s1(2): *'Environment'* consists of all, or any of the following media, namely the air, water and land; and the medium of air includes the air within buildings and the air within other natural or man-made structures above or below ground.
>
> s1(3): *'Pollution of the environment'* means pollution of the environment due to the release (into any environmental medium) from any process of substances which are capable of causing harm to man or any other living organisms supported by the environment.
>
> s1(4): *'Harm'* means harm to the health of living organisms or other interference with the ecological systems of which they form part and, in the case of man, includes offence caused to any of his senses or harm to his property; and harmless has a corresponding meaning.
>
> s1(5): *'Process'* means any activities carried on in Great Britain, whether on premises or *by means of mobile plant*, which are capable of causing pollution of the environment and *'prescribed process'* means a process prescribed under s2(1) EPA 1990 below.

Note that 'process' may be interpreted widely to include any activities which are capable of causing pollution of the environment. In *HMIP v Safety Kleen UK Ltd*, the company was prosecuted by HMIP after an incident in which a large quantity of solvent-based fuel escaped from a tanker which was parked overnight on company premises. The fuel ended up released into controlled waters. The IPC authorisation which the company had forbade such a release. In Court, the company argued that the storage of the fuel in the tanker was not part of the prescribed process and therefore it had not breached the conditions of its authorisations. The Court took the view that the prescribed process did indeed include storage and the company was therefore breaching a condition of its authorisation.

s1(6) EPA 1990: Definitions for the purposes of s1(5) EPA 1990

'Activities' are very widely defined to include activities of any sort, as well as the passive keeping of substances.

Great Britain's territoriality is relevant here specifically for the avoidance of doubt in the location of the process. Territorial waters are defined at s104(1)(a) WRA 1991.

'Mobile plant' is a plant *designed* to move or be moved, whether on roads or otherwise. There is ambiguity about the word *'designed'*.

s1(7, 9, 10) EPA 1990: Other definitions

s1(7) EPA 1990: The *'enforcing authority'* in relation to England and Wales, is the EA or the LA. Note that in Scotland, SEPA is the local enforcing authority for LAAPC as well as IPC.

s1(9) EPA 1990: *'Authorisation'* means an authorisation for a process (whether on premises or by means of mobile plant) granted under s6 EPA 1990. A reference to a condition of an authorisation is a reference to the conditions subject to which at any time the authorisation has effect.

s1(10) EPA 1990: *'Release'* includes, whether within or outside Great Britain, in relation to:

> (a) air, any emission of the substance into the air;
> (b) water, any entry (including any discharge) of the substance into water;
> (c) land, any deposit, keeping or disposal of the substance in or on land.

s1(11) EPA 1990: This subsection provides the rules by which the medium into which a substance is released can be determined.

3.2.2.8 s2 EPA 1990

This section gives to the Secretary of State his power to regulate, prescribing processes which may not be carried out after a certain date without authorisation, under ss6 and 7 of the Act. By s2, he may prescribe substances and regulate which processes should be subject to central control, and which to the control of the LA. The *Environmental Protection (Prescribed*

Processes and Substances) Regulations are the regulations made under this section.

3.2.2.9 s3 EPA 1990

This section gives to the Secretary of State power to regulate to establish standards, objectives or requirements in relation to prescribed processes or substances.It is the basis both of a nationwide strategy of pollution reduction and the means of compliance by the UK with its international obligations (such as in the reduction of emissions of SO_2 and NO_2) and in respect of its obligations under EC law, such as in emission limits, quality objectives and quality standards.

3.2.2.10 s4 EPA 1990

The purpose of this book is to deal with criminal offences and so, a detailed assessment of the scope and discharge of the functions of the respective authorities belongs elsewhere. One subsection from s4 EPA 1990 is important to observe, however: s4(9) EPA 1990 requires the enforcing authority to keep up to date with developments in relevant techniques and technologies. This duty, which is either identical to or very closely related to BATNEEC, has implications which run through the remainder of the Act.

3.2.2.11 s6 EPA 1990

This section legislates for the authorisations to be made which form the basis of the system of IPC. It requires an application to be made for an authorisation, if necessary subject to conditions, for a prescribed process to be 'carried on' after the prescribed date.

It also legislates for the circumstances in which such an authorisation may not be made. These circumstances exist, it seems, where there appears to be a lack of competence in the history of the management of the operation which could not be addressed by the imposition of conditions.

Note that 'carry on' has been the subject of argument.It would seem that a repetition or series of acts is necessary and that the person who carries on the process must have control and direction over it, although cases brought under EPA 1990 do not help to decide this point.

There may also be transitional arrangements for authorisations to be put in place and conditional authorisations may be subject to review, after four years, by the Secretary of State.

Note that the procedure governing the granting of an authorisation is found at Schedule 1, Part I of this Act. Generally, applications will be determined within four months of receipt by the enforcing authority.Failure to determine the application within that time, or the agreed period, may be deemed to be a refusal.

3.2.2.12 s7 EPA 1990

This section legislates for the circumstances in which appropriate conditions may be placed upon authorisations by the enforcing authority.Those circumstances include ensuring that BATNEEC is used in carrying on a prescribed process, either for preventing a release, or reducing the release to a minimum, and rendering that minimum release harmless, as well as rendering harmless any other substances which might, if released, cause environmental harm.Note that where a process, designated for central control, is likely to release into more than one environmental medium, then the BATNEEC is to be used to minimise the pollutant effects *taken as a whole.*

The circumstances may also include a range of other compliance requirements such as:

(i) compliance with any Community Treaty obligations or international law;

(ii) compliance with any limits or requirements and achievement of any quality standards or quality objectives prescribed by the Secretary of State under any of the relevant enactments.These 'relevant enactments' are listed at s7(12) EPA 1990. They are:

(a) s2 Clean Air Act 1968 (CAA 1968)
(b) s2 European Communities Act 1972 (ECA 1972)
(c) Part I of Health and Safety at Work etc Act 1974 (HSWA 1974)
(d) Parts II, III or IV of the Control of Pollution Act 1974 (COPA 1974)
(e) WRA 1991
(f) s3 EPA 1990
(g) s87 EA 1995

The Secretary of State may also direct an enforcing authority to include conditions within an authorisation. These directions may apply to all authorisations, specified descriptions of them, or individual authorisations, but the BATNEEC requirement remains a condition from which there can be no derogation or supplementation. There is much written about what BATNEEC amounts to and what constitutes BPEO but the offences with which the EPA is concerned are, in general, about breaches of original authorisations and the conditions accruing to those authorisations.

s8 EPA 1990 concerns the fees and charges for authorisations and applications for variations of authorisations:

s9 EPA 1990 concerns the transfer of authorisations and the requirement under s9(2) EPA 1990 for notice of the transfer to be given to the enforcing authority. *Note the criminal offence at s23(1)(b) EPA 1990 below, which is committed where this section is not complied with.*

ss11 and 12 EPA 1990 provide the regulations which govern the enforcing authority's capacities in respect of variations and revocations of authorisations.

3.2.2.13 s13 EPA 1990: Enforcement notices

This section provides for the service of enforcement notices.Where the enforcement authority takes the view that a person is contravening a condition of an authorisation, or is likely to contravene such a condition, then the authority may serve on that person an enforcement notice. s13(2) EPA 1990 outlines the requirements of that notice. In brief, these are that the enforcing authority holds the opinion that it does, the matters giving rise to the notice are specified, the steps which amount to a remedy are taken and the period within which those steps should be taken is defined.

It is an offence to fail to comply with the enforcement notice (see below at s23[1][c] EPA 1990).

3.2.2.14 s14 EPA 1990: Prohibition notices

This section legislates for the service of prohibition notices. s14(1) EPA 1990 legislates for the enforcing authority to serve a prohibition notice on the operator of an authorised prescribed process, relating to any aspect of the process, if, in the opinion of the enforcing authority, the continuation of the process will amount to a risk of serious pollution of the environment. Note that this sort of notice has much in common with an enforcement notice served under the Town and Country Planning Acts. The effect of the prohibition is to suspend the authorisation, (unless otherwise directed, in line with conditions already established).

It is a criminal offence to fail to comply with the terms of the prohibition notices (see below, at s23[1][c] EPA 1990).

3.2.2.15 s15 EPA 1990

This section of the Act concerns appeals, in respect of refusal of authorisations, or conditions attached thereto, variations, enforcement and prohibition notices.

3.2.2.16 ss19-22 EPA 1990

These sections concern the obtaining of information, keeping public registers of information and the exclusion from registers of information which affects national security or which is confidential.

3.2.3 Offences

3.2.3.1 s23 EPA 1990

This section creates the main criminal offences under Part 1, EPA 1990.

> s23(1) It is an offence for a person:
>
> (a) to contravene section 6(1) above . . .

The s23(1)(a) offence, the carrying on of a prescribed process either without an authorisation or not in accordance with the conditions attached to the authorisation, can result in substantial penalties being imposed. The offence appears to be one of strict liability, for which ignorance will provide a defence or a 'reasonable excuse'. It also appears that the offence can be committed on an intermittent basis, over a period of time (see *Hodgetts v Chiltern District Council* [1983] 2 AC 120).

On summary conviction, a defendant may be fined up to £20,000 and/or imprisoned for a period not exceeding three months. On conviction on indictment, the defendant may receive an unlimited fine, and/or a term of imprisonment, not exceeding two years.

Note that by s23(2) EPA 1990, similar penalties may be imposed in respect of s23(1)(c) EPA 1990 and s23(1)(l) EPA 1990 (see below).

> (b) to fail to give the notice required by s9(2) EPA 1990 above;
>
> (c) to fail to comply with or contravene any requirement or prohibition imposed by an enforcement notice or a prohibition notice;

(g) to fail, without reasonable excuse, to comply with any requirement imposed by a notice under s19(2) EPA 1990 above, which is the requirement to furnish to the authority such information as the authority has reasonably considered to be necessary, and then specified in the notice, to be furnished within a specified period following the service of the notice;'

(h) to make a statement which he knows to be false or misleading in a material particular, or recklessly to make a statement which is false or misleading in a material particular, where the statement is made -

(i) in purported compliance with a requirement to furnish any information imposed by or under any provision of this Part: or
(ii) for the purpose of obtaining the grant of an authorisation to himself or any other person or the variation of an authorisation;

(i) intentionally to make a false entry in any record required to be kept under s7 EPA 1990 above;

(j) with intent to deceive, to forge or use a document issued or authorised to be issued under s7 EPA 1990 above, or required for any purpose thereunder or to make or have in his possession a document so close resembling any such document as to be likely to deceive;

(l) to fail to comply with an order made by a court under s26 EPA 1990.

By s23(3) EPA 1990, a person guilty of an offence under s23(1)(b), (g), (h), (i) or (j) EPA 1990, shall be liable on summary conviction to a fine not exceeding the statutory maximum, or on conviction, on indictment to a fine, or to imprisonment for a term not exceeding two years, or to both.

Offences under s110 EA 1995

s110 EA 1995 replaced parts of s23 EPA 1990, creating the offences which are committed when a person intentionally obstructs an authorised person in the exercise or performance of his duties. Comprehensive powers of entry and investigation are given to the enforcing authority under the two preceding sections.

s110 EA 1995 provides that the following acts or omissions amount to offences:

- intentional obstruction of an authorised person in the exercise or performance of their duties;
- failure to comply with any requirement imposed under s108 EA 1995 *without reasonable excuse;*
- failure to provide facilities, assistance or information, and failure to permit inspection by an authorised person;
- preventing another from appearing before an authorised person, or from answering questions from that authorised person;
- impersonation of an authorised person.

3.2.3.2 s24 EPA 1990

This section provides what may be viewed as an alternative enforcement provision to proceedings under s23 EPA 1990.In circumstances where a person has failed to comply with the requirements of an enforcement notice or a prohibition notice, and where the enforcing authority has concluded that proceedings under s23(1)(c) will be ineffectual, then they may take proceedings in the High Court (or in Scotland, in any court of competent jurisdiction), for the purpose of securing compliance with the notice.Proceedings may result in an injunction (or interdict, in Scotland), with which failure to comply may result either in imprisonment, or sequestration of assets for contempt of court.

In *Tameside Metropolitan Borough Council v Smith Brothers (Hyde) Ltd* October 4 1995 QBD, Ends Reports 250, s24 proceedings were taken by the LA against an animal by-product rendering business. An authorisation under Part I, EPA 1990 had originally been refused. The LA took the view that s23 EPA 1990 proceedings would be ineffectual and therefore it applied for an injunction. This application was unsuccessful, for the reason that the principles established in *City of London Corporation v Bovis Construction* (1988) 86 L.G.R. were held to apply. These were:

(i) that civil injunctions should be used sparingly as an aid to enforcing criminal law and should be confined to situations where 'nothing short of an injunction will be effective to restrain', per Bingham LJ; and

(ii) the principles in *American Cyanimid Co v Ethicon Ltd* [1975] AC 396 HL applied, two of those being that there must be a serious issue to be tried and that the balance of convenience should favour the plaintiffs.

In *Tameside*, the defendants had grounds for arguing that the enforcement notice served upon them was invalid and that the requirements for commencing s24 EPA 1990 proceedings had not been met. There was an indication that an injunction might put the defendants out of business, which, coupled with the LA's refusal to give an undertaking in damages, indicated that it was not certain that they would win at trial.Finally, the Court took the view that the LA had not taken advantage of the remedy offered by s26 EPA 1990 (see below).

3.2.3.3 s25 EPA 1990: Burden of proof

This section, which deals with the onus of proof in respect of techniques and evidence, places upon the defendants to s23(1)(a) EPA 1990 proceedings the burden of proving that in failing to comply with the general condition implied in authorisations under s7(4) EPA 1990 above, there was no BATNEEC other than that used by them, to satisfy the condition.

Where an entry, required in respect of the observance of a condition or authorisation has not been made, then that shall be admissible as evidence that the condition has not been met. Note that similar provisions in respect of a licence are dealt with at s111 of the EA 1995.

3.2.3.4 s26 EPA 1990: Remediation

This section gives the Court a power, where there has been a conviction under s23(1)(a) or (c) EPA 1990, or indeed wherever the Court takes the view that a defendant has the power to remedy a matter, to order a defendant, in addition to, or instead of imposing a punishment, to take steps, within a specified time to remedy matters. If the defendant needs an extension of time, he must make application for an extension of time before the original time, or original extension has expired. While that time is passing, the defendant will not be subject to further penalties under s23 EPA 1990 for the offence.

If the defendant fails to comply, he may be found guilty of an offence under s23(1)(1) EPA 1990 and he becomes liable to penalties set out at s23(2) EPA 1990.

3.2.3.5 s27 EPA 1990: Remedial powers of EA/SEPA

This section gives further remedial powers to the EA (or SEPA), to arrange for any reasonable steps to be taken to remedy harm which has amounted to an offence under s23(1) EPA 1990, as well as to recover the costs of taking those steps from the person convicted of the offence. On occasions when the harm is substantial and significant, then the costs may be in addition to the fines levied under s23(2) EPA 1990. The powers may only be used with the written approval of the Secretary of State.

In March, 1998, ICI Chemicals and Polymers Limited were found guilty of IPC offences following a prosecution under s23(1)(a) and s23(2) EPA 1990 (as well as offences under WRA 1991). The facts were that some 147 tonnes of chloroform was spilled from a pipeline at an ICI facility in Runcorn. Of the escaped substance, 20 tonnes would have evaporated into the air, 3 tonnes were recovered and 1 tonne is estimated to have leaked into Weston Canal. The rest — 123 tonnes — remains in the ground. Charges were brought for breaches of authorisation, under s6(1)EPA 1990. The company pleaded guilty, was fined £300,000 and ordered to pay costs of £50,000 to the EA.

3.2.4 Clean Air Act 1993 (CAA 1993)

Parts I-III of this Act are concerned with emissions of smoke from chimneys and certain open sites. This Act generally does not apply in circumstances where either an IPC or APC authorisation has been granted or refused.

In Scotland, the corresponding provisions of the Alkali etc Works Regulation Act 1906 (AWRA 1906), and s5 HSWA 1974, are gradually being replaced by the provisions of Part I, EPA 1990. Applications for authorisations have generally been dealt with, and when all have been dealt with, then, in Scotland, the 1906 Act and the 1974 Act will cease to apply.

The CAA 1993 does not apply to many industrial processes which are legislated for in the 1990 Act (or the 1906 Act in Scotland). Nevertheless, a large number of smaller industrial processes remain which are regulated by Parts I and II of the CAA. These processes, found in small factories or foundries, with minor combustion plants, are subject to 'dark smoke', and smoke, grit, dust and fumes controls.

3.2.4.1 Part 1 Dark Smoke

Offences

s1(1), (2) CAA 1993

It is prohibited for dark smoke to be emitted from a chimney of any building, or a chimney which serves a furnace of a fixed boiler or industrial plant. If such smoke is emitted, then the occupier of the building shall be guilty of an offence, likewise the person in possession of the boiler or plant.

This does not apply where the emission has been prescribed and or limited by the Secretary of State, solely during the period which has been prescribed.

Definitions

'Dark smoke' is defined at s3 CAA 1993 as being equivalent to smoke as dark as or darker than shade 2 on the Ringelmann Chart, a chart in use when the 1956 Clean Air Act (CCA 1956) was passed. The method by which the smoke is defined as dark or not is not confined to the use of the chart and the Secretary of State may prescribe the method by which dark smoke can be ascertained. [No such method has as yet been prescribed.]

s64 CAA 1993 contains many of the definitions used in the CAA 1956. This list is not comprehensive:

'Smoke' is defined as including soot, ash, grit and gritty particles emitted in smoke.

'Fumes' means any airborne solid matter smaller than dust.

'Chimney' includes structures and openings of any kind from or through which smoke, grit, dust or fumes may be emitted, and, in particular, includes flues, and references to a chimney of a building include references to a chimney which serves the whole or a part of a building but is structurally separate from the building.

'Fixed boiler or industrial plant' means any boiler or industrial plant attached to a building or for the time being fixed to or installed on any land.

'Practicable' means reasonably practicable having regard, among other things, to local conditions and circumstances, to the financial implications and to the current state of technical knowledge, and *'practical means'* includes the provision and maintenance of plant and its proper use.

'Occupier of a building' is defined at s64(2) CAA 1993 as referring to the occupier or other person in control of the part of the building in which the relevant fireplace is situated.

'Building' is not defined but appears to be an immovable structure capable of containing something.

Defences

A defence to a charge under this section will be to prove that the emission was solely due to the lighting up of a cold furnace and that all practicable steps had been taken to prevent or minimise the emission of dark smoke.

It will also be a defence to prove that the emission was due to some failure of a furnace, or of apparatus used in connection with a furnace, provided that the failure could not reasonably have been foreseen, or if foreseen, could not reasonably have been provided against; and that the emission could not reasonably have been prevented by action taken after the failure occurred.

It will also be a defence to prove that the emission was solely due to the use of unsuitable fuel,that suitable fuel was not available, that the least unsuitable available fuel was used and that all practicable steps had been taken to prevent or minimise the emission which was the result of using that fuel.

A defence may comprise of a combination of these conditions.

A person guilty of an offence under this section shall be liable on summary conviction, in respect of a private chimney, to a fine not exceeding level three onthe standard scale, and, in respect of any other offence, to a fine not exceeding level five on the standard scale.

s2(1) CAA 1993

Dark smoke may not be emitted from any industrial or trade premises.If dark smoke is so emitted, then the occupier of the premises, and any person who causes or permits the emission, shall be guilty of an offence. This section does not apply to any premises to which s1 CAA 1993 applies, or to the emission of dark smoke caused by materials already prescribed in the Secretary of State's regulations. By s2(3) CAA 1993, there is assumed to have been an emission of dark smoke from industrial or trade premises in any case where material is burned on the premises, and the circumstances are such that such burning would give rise to the emission of dark smoke, unless the occupier or permitting person can show that no dark smoke was emitted.

Definitions

By s2(6) CAA 1993: *'Industrial or trade premises'* means premises used for any industrial or trade premises or premises not so used on which matter is burnt in connection with any industrial or trade process.

'Premises' here includes a vacant demolition site, with no requirement for a building, as in s1 CCA 1993.

In *Sheffield City Council v ADH Demolition* (1983) 82 LGR 177.DC, it was asserted and accepted that dark smoke was emitted from this site and it was suggested that there is a test for liability which is stricter than in 'knowingly causes or permits'.

'Process' has been decided as having its *Shorter Oxford Dictionary* meaning, ie 'a continuous and regular action or succession of actions, taking place or carried on in a definite manner; a continuous (natural or artificial) operation or series of operations.'

Defences

It is a defence to a charge under this section to prove that the emission was inadvertent notwithstanding that all practicable steps had been taken and to prevent or minimise the emission of dark smoke.

A person guilty of an offence under this section shall be liable on summary conviction to a fine not exceeding £20,000.

3.2.4.2 Part II CAA 1993: Smoke, grit, dust and fumes

s4 CAA 1993: Installation of furnaces

Notice must be given to the LA of any proposal to install a furnace in a building or in any fixed boiler or in an industrial plant.Failure to give notice of such a proposal will give rise to an offence.The notice must be in writing.

The furnace should be capable of being operated, so far as is practicable, smokelessly, when burning the kind of fuel for which the furnace was designed.

Any furnace installed in accordance with plans submitted to and approved by the local authority shall be treated as complying with the requirements of this section. The plans have to be expressly approved for the purpose, not simply as a matter of compliance with Building Regulations. There is no right of appeal against the LA's refusal to grant authorisation.

Offence

If a person installs a furnace, or instructs another to do so (other than a domestic furnace) in contravention of these requirements, then he commits an offence.In respect of failure to notify, he may be liable to a fine not exceeding level three on the standard scale. In respect of liability for emissions, then the fine may not exceed level five on the standard scale.

s5 CAA 1993: Emission of grit and dust from furnaces

This section applies to any furnace other than a domestic furnace. The Secretary of State may regulate the limits on the rates of emission of grit and dust for the chimneys of furnaces under this section. In fact, in the absence of regulations, the *Clean Air (Emissions of Grit and Dust from Furnaces) Regulations*, SI 1971/162 apply (as does the corresponding SI in Scotland).

Offence

If the level of grit and dust emitted from a chimney serving a furnace exceeds the limit prescribed, then the occupier of any building where the furnace is situated 'shall be guilty of an offence'.The defendant shall be liable, on summary conviction, to a fine not exceeding level five on the standard scale.

Defences

It is a defence to a charge under this section to prove that the best practicable means have been used for minimising the alleged emission, either where the emissions from the furnace are regulated, or where they are not.

s6 CAA 1993: Arrestment plant requirements for new, nondomestic furnaces

> By this section, a furnace may not burn fuel -
>
> (a) which is pulverised; or
>
> (b) at a rate of 45.4 kilograms or more an hour, any other solid matter; or
>
> (c) at a rate equivalent to 366.4 kilowatts or more, any liquid or gaseous matter, unless the furnace has been provided with a plant, approved of by the LA, for arresting grit and dust.The plant must be properly maintained and used.

Note that this section applies to outdoor furnaces also.

Offence

If a furnace is used in contravention of these requirements, then the occupier of the building where the furnace is housed shall be guilty of an offence and liable on summary conviction to a fine not exceeding level five on the standard scale. Contravention attracts a daily fine, in case of a continuing default.

s7 CAA 1993: Exemptions

The LA may exempt a furnace from compliance with the requirement for an arrestment plan, when the LA is satisfied that the chimney serving the furnace will not be prejudicial to health, or a nuisance, if the furnace is used.

It is a requirement for the LA to determine an application for an exemption either within eight weeks of the application or within such period as has been agreed between the LA and the applicant. If the LA fails to determine and give written notice of its decision, within either period, then the furnace shall be treated as having been given an exemption from the arrestment plant requirement, so long as it is used for the purpose which has been specified in the application. Note that here there *is* a right of appeal to the Secretary of State against the LA's refusal to grant an exemption. The right of appeal must be exercised within 28 days of the applicant's receipt of notification of refusal. The Secretary of State must give written reasons for his decision.

Offence

If a furnace which has an exemption from an arrestment plant requirement is used, at any stage, for a purpose which has not been prescribed, or which is not otherwise exempt, then the occupier of the building shall be guilty of an offence, and liable, on summary conviction, to a fine not exceeding level five on the standard scale.

s8 CAA 1993: Arrestment plant requirements for burning solid fuel

By this section, a *domestic* furnace may not burn fuel -

(a) which is pulverised; or

(b) at a rate of 1.02 tonnes an hour or more, either solid fuel or solid waste, unless the furnace has been provided with a plant, approved of by the LA, for arresting grit and dust. The plant must be properly maintained and used. Note that this section also applies to outdoor furnaces.

Offence

> If a furnace is used in contravention of these requirements, then the occupier of the building where the furnace is housed shall be guilty of an offence and liable on summary conviction to a fine not exceeding level five on the standard scale.

s10 CAA 1993 Measurement of grit, dust and fumes

Where a furnace is used to burn -

(a) pulverised fuel; or
(b) at a rate of 45.4 kilograms or more an hour, any other solid matter; or
(c) at a rate equivalent to 366.4 kilowatts or more, any liquid or gaseous matter,

then the LA may, by this section, require by notice in writing that the occupier must comply with any of the following requirements, where prescribed:

> (i) measuring and recording grit, dust and fumes emitted from the furnace;.
> (ii) adapting the chimney for that purpose;
> (iii)providing and maintaining measuring and recording apparatus;
> (iv)informing the LA of the results of the measurements.

The occupier is obliged to permit the local authority to be represented during the measuring and recording processes.The LA may also alter the directions it gives by notice in writing.

Offence

> Where an occupier fails to comply with such requirements as have been made of him, then he shall be guilty of an offence and liable on summary conviction -
>
> (a) to a fine not exceeding level five on the standard scale; or
> (b) to cumulative penalties.

This is in accordance with s50 CAA 1993 which provides for cumulative penalties where certain offences continue.

s12 CAA 1993: Information about furnaces and fuels consumed

By this section, the LA may, by notice and in writing, require an occupier of a building to furnish it, within 14 days or time specified by the notice, with information about the furnaces in the building and the fuel or waste burned therein.

Offence

Where an occupier fails to comply with the terms of the notice, within the time which is stated in the notice, or where he furnishes his reply with information which he knows to be false in a material particular, then he shall be guilty of an offence and liable on summary conviction to a fine not exceeding level five on the standard scale.

s14 CAA 1993: Height of chimneys for furnaces

This section applies to any furnace served by a chimney, other than those served by a chimney whose construction was begun, or whose plans for construction were approved before 1st April, 1969.

s14(2) CAA 1993: The occupier of a building shall not knowingly cause or permit a furnace to be used in the building to burn-

(a) pulverised fuel;

(b) at the rate of 45.4 kilograms or more an hour, any other solid matter or

(c) at a rate equivalent to 366.4 kilowatts or more, any liquid or gaseous matter,

unless the height of the chimney serving the furnace has been approved of for the purposes of this section and any conditions subject to which the approval was granted have been complied with.

Offence

If the occupier of a building contravenes this subsection, then he commits an offence. Likewise, a person having possession of any fixed boiler or industrial plant other than an exempted boiler or plant shall not knowingly cause or permit a furnace of that boiler or plant to be used as defined in s14(2) CAA 1993, unless the height of the chimney has been similarly approved of.

Offence

If a person having possession of any boiler or industrial plant contravenes this subsection, then he shall be guilty of an offence.

Persons guilty of offences under this section shall be liable on summary conviction to a fine not exceeding level five on the standard scale.

3.2.4.3 Part III CAA 1993: Smoke control areas

s18 CAA 1993: Declaration of a smoke control area bylocal authority

By the powers of this section, the LA may declare the whole or part of a district of the authority to be a smoke control area.Any order made under this section is referred to as a 'smoke control order.' See Schedule 1 to the Act.

A smoke control order may make different provisions for different parts of the smoke control area, or limit the operation of the prohibitive powers of s20 CAA 1993 [see below], or exempt buildings, classes of buildings, including specified or specified classes of fixed boiler or industrial plant, specified fireplaces or classes of fireplaces.

A smoke control order may be revoked or varied by subsequent order.

s19 CAA 1993: This section empowers the Secretary of State to require the creation of smoke control areas, after consultation with the LA.

s20 CAA 1993: Prohibition on smoke emission in a smoke control area

Offences

s20(1) CAA 1993 If, on any day, smoke is emitted from a chimney of any building within a smoke control area, the occupier of the building shall be guilty of an offence.

s20(2) CAA 1993: If, on any day, smoke is emitted from a chimney (not being a chimney of a building) which serves the furnace of any fixed boiler or industrial plan within a smoke control area, the person having possession of the boiler or plant shall be guilty of an offence.

s20(3) CAA 1993 Subsections (1) and (2) have effect -

(a) subject to any exemptions for the time being in force under ss18, 21 or 22;
(b) subject to s51 CAA 1993 (duty to notify offences to occupier or other person liable).

Definitions

'Authorised fuel' means a fuel declared by regulations of the Secretary of State to be an authorised fuel for the purposes of this Part [Smoke Control Area (Authorised Fuels) Regulations 1991 SI 1991/1282].

Defence

It is a defence in proceedings brought for an offence under this section to prove that the alleged emission was caused by no other fuel than an authorised fuel. The burden of proof here lies upon the defendant.

A person guilty of an offence under this section shall be liable on summary conviction to a fine not exceeding level three on the standard scale. The offences will incur daily, continuing fines.

s23 CAA 1993: Dealings with unauthorised fuel

This section creates offences connected with the acquisition and sale of unauthorised fuel.

s23(1) CAA 1993: Any person who -

(a) acquires any solid fuel for use in a building in a smoke control area otherwise than in a building or fireplace exempted from the operation of section 20 (prohibition of smoke emissions in smoke control area);
(b) acquires any solid fuel for use in any fixed boiler or industrial plan in a smoke control area, not being a boiler or plant so exempted; or

(c) sells by retail any solid fuel for delivery by him or on his behalf to-

(i) a building in a smoke control area; or
(ii)premises in such an area in which there is any fixed boiler or industrial plant,

shall be guilty of an offence and liable on summary conviction to a fine not exceeding level three on the standard scale.

These offences are subject to certain qualifications:

(a) s23(3) CAA 1993: the limitations of a smoke control order to specified classes of buildings, boilers or plants;
(b) s23(4) CAA 1993: whole or partial suspension of operation of this subsection, in part or all of the smoke control areas.

Definitions

'Solid fuel' means any solid fuel other than an authorised fuel.

Defences

It will be a defence to the charge of the sale of fuel for delivery to a building or premises for the accused to prove that he believed, or had reasonable grounds for believing -

(a) that the building was exempted from the operation of s20 CAA 1993, or that the building did not belong to the specified class of building where section 20 was operating;
(b) that the fuel was acquired for use in a fireplace, boiler or plant exempted, or for use in a boiler or plant not of the specified exempted class.

The test of the validity of the grounds alleged as a defence is an objective one.

s24 CAA 1993: Adaptation of fireplaces in private dwellings

By this section, the LA may, by notice and in writing, require the owner of a private dwelling within a smoke control area to make adaptations to avoid contravention of s20 CAA 1993.

s290(6) PHA 1936 provides that in the event of noncompliance with the notice, the LA may make the adaptations and a proportion of the expenses reasonably incurred may be recovered from the owner.If the owner does not comply with the notice, then the owner may be liable to a fine not exceeding level four on the standard scale and to a further fine of £2 per day, for continuing the offence after conviction.

3.2.4.4 Part IV CAA 1993: Control of certain forms of air pollution

s30 CAA 1993: Regulations about motor fuel

This section legislates for the imposition of requirements as to composition and contents of motor fuel, for the purpose of limiting or reducing air pollution.

s31 CAA 1993: Regulations about sulphur content of oil fuel for furnaces or engines

This section legislates for the imposition of limits on the sulphur content of oil fuel used in furnaces or engines.

s32 CAA 1993: Supplementary provisions to ss30 and 31

This section authorises the Secretary of State to make exemptions to the regulations made under ss30 and 31.

Offence

> A person who contravenes or fails to comply with any provision of regulations under ss30 or 31 CCA 1993 shall be guilty of an offence, and liable -
>
> (a) on conviction on indictment, to a fine; and
> (b) on summary conviction, to a fine not exceeding the statutory maximum.

But the regulations may in any case exclude liability to conviction on indictment, or reduce the maximum fine on summary conviction.

s33 CAA 1993: Cable burning

Offence

(i) A person who burns insulation from a cable with a view to recovering metal from the cable shall be guilty of an offence, unless the burning is part of a process subject to Part I, EPA 1990.

(ii) A person guilty of an offence under this section shall be liable on summary conviction to a fine not exceeding level five on the standard scale.

3.2.4.5. Part V, CAA 1993: Information about air pollution

LAs are empowered to obtain information about the emission of pollutants and other substances into the air. They can do this by issuing notices under s36 CAA 1993, or by measuring and recording emissions after entering the premises either by agreement or by exercise of their powers under s56 CAA 1993, or by entering into arrangements by which occupiers of premises measure and record emissions on behalf of the LA. ('Premises' here do not include private dwellings or caravans.)

The authority may only exercise its power of entry in circumstances where (i) the occupier has been served with a notice in writing indicating the measurements it intends to make and that it proposes to make an entry unless the occupier requests a notice to be served under s36 CAA 1993 and (ii) a period of 21 days from the service of the notice has expired. If the occupier requests the service of a s36 CAA 1993 notice, then the right of entry may not be exercised.If the authority wishes to investigate a process subject to Part I, EPA 1990, then it may not do so other than by issuing a s36 CAA 1993 notice, or by exercising its powers under s34(1)(a) CAA 1993.

Subsections 4,5 and 6 legislate for the LA's obligation to consult the relevant persons about the extent and manner of the exercise of its powers. Such consultations should occur not less than twice in each financial year.

s36 CAA 1993: Notices requiring information about air pollution

The LA may serve a notice in writing, under the provisions of this section, requiring an occupier of a premises to furnish information and estimates by way of periodical returns, or other means, in respect of the emission of pollutants and other substances into the air from the premises (this does not include a private dwelling or a caravan). The periodical returns shall not be made at intervals of less than three months and the notice applies for no more than 12 months.

> **s36(3) CAA 1993:** If the notice relates to a process which is subject to Part 1, EPA 1990, the person on whom the notice is served is not obliged to supply any information which, as certified by an inspector appointed under that Part, is not of a kind which is being supplied to the inspector for the purposes of that Part.

The person on whom the notice is served has six weeks from the date of service to comply with the terms of the notice. This period may be longer.

Offence

s36(8) CAA 1992: A person who -

> (a) fails without reasonable excuse to comply with the requirements of a notice served on him in pursuance of this section; or
> (b) in furnishing any estimate or other information in compliance with a notice under this section, makes any statement which he knows to be false in a material particular or recklessly makes any statement which is false in a material particular
>
> shall be guilty of an offence and liable on summary conviction to a fine not exceeding level five on the standard scale.

Definitions

s40 CAA 1993: *'Emissions'* of substances into the atmosphere are to be construed as applying to substances in a gaseous or liquid or solid state, or any combination of those.

'Measurement' includes the taking of samples.

s37 CCA 1993: Appeals

A person who is served with a s36 CCA 1993 notice may appeal to the Secretary of State; the grounds are listed in this section, being that disclosure to the LA or to the public would be unreasonably prejudicial, or contrary to the public interest. The Secretary of State is under a duty to consult, before he regulates for Appeals, as he is empowered to do.

3.2.4.6 Part VI CAA 1993: Special Cases

s42 CAA 1993: Colliery spoilbanks

This section applies to any mine or quarry from which coal or shale has been, is being or is to be got.

Offence

The owner of the mine or quarry is under a duty to employ all practical means -

> (a) for preventing combustion of refuse deposited from the mine or quarry; or
> (b) for preventing or minimising the emission of smoke and fumes from the refuse.
>
> If he fails to do so, he shall be guilty of an offence.
>
> A person guilty of an offence under this subsection shall be liable on summary conviction to -
>
> (a) a fine not exceeding level five on the standard scale; or
> (b) cumulative penalties on continuance (s50 CAA 1993).

s43 CAA 1993: Railway engines

The provisions of s1 CAA 1993 in respect of emissions of dark smoke apply to railway engines likewise.

A reference to an occupier of a building is substituted by a reference to the owner of the engine.

Offence

s43(3) CAA 1993 -

> The owner of any railway locomotive engine shall use any practicable means there may be for minimising the emission of smoke from the chimney on the engine and, if he fails to do so, he shall, if smoke is emitted from that chimney, be guilty of an offence.

A person guilty of an offence under subsection(3) shall be liable on summary conviction to -

(a) a fine not exceeding level 5 on the standard scale; or
(b) cumulative penalties on continuance (s50 CAA 1993).

Note that the provisions relating to the discharge of dark smoke alone apply to railway engines.

s44: Vessels

This section provides similar s1 legislation in respect of vessels.The reference to occupier of a building is substituted by a reference to the owner of, and the master or other officer or person in charge of the vessel.

Offence

A person guilty of an offence under that section [1] in relation to a vessel shall be liable on summary conviction to a fine not exceeding level five on the standard scale.

Note that the vessel in any waters will be deemed to be within the district of the LA whose district includes that point on land which is nearest to the spot where the vessel is.

s44(4) CAA 1993 -

The waters to which the section applies are -

(a) all waters not navigable by seagoing ships; and

(b) all waters navigable by seagoing ships within the seaward limits of the territorial waters of the UK, and are contained within any port, harbour, river, estuary, haven, dock, canal or other place so long as a person or body or persons is empowered by or under any Act to make charges in respect of vessels entering it or using facilities in it.

(Note 'charges' exclude light dues, local light dues and charges in respect of lighthouses, buoys, beacons and pilotage charges.)

This section does not apply to ships belonging to the Royal Navy, or governmental ships.

s45 CAA 1993 provides for exemptions for the purposes of investigations and research, to be granted by the LA to an applicant.

3.2.4.6 Part VII ss49: 52 CAA 1993: Powers of administration and enforcement

s49 CAA 1993: Disclosures of information

Offence

s49(1) CAA 1993 -

> If a person discloses any information relating to any trade secret used in carrying on any particular undertaking which has been given to him or obtained by him by virtue of this Act, he shall, subject to subsection (2), be guilty of an offence and liable on summary conviction to a fine not exceeding level five on the standard scale.

Defence

s49(2) CAA 1993 -

> A person shall not be guilty of an offence under subsection (1) by reason of the disclosure of any information if the disclosure is made -
>
> (a) in the performance of his duty;
>
> (b) in pursuance of s34(1)(b) CAA 1993 [research and publicity];
>
> (c) with the consent of a person having a right to disclose the information.

s50 CAA 1993: Cumulative penalties on continuance of certain offences

The purpose of this section is to give the courts enhanced powers to deal with persistent offenders in certain areas of polluting emissions.

References have been made to this section at s10(3)(b), 42(3) and 43(4) CAA 1993 above, where sentencing may include the application of cumulative penalties for continuing offences.

s50(1) CAA 1993 -

Where

(a) a person is convicted of an offence which is subject to cumulative penalties on continuance in accordance with this section; and

(b) it is shown to the satisfaction of the court that the offence was substantially a repetition or continuation of an earlier offence by him after he had been convicted of an earlier offence

then the penalty provided by s50(2) CAA 1993 shall apply instead of the penalty otherwise specified for the offence.

s50(2) -

Where this subsection applies, the person convicted shall be liable on summary conviction to a fine not exceeding -

(a) level five on the standard scale; or
(b) £50 for every day on which the earlier offence has been so repeated or continued by him within the three months next following his conviction of that offence.

s50(3) -

Where an offence is subject to cumulative penalties in accordance with this section -

(a) the court by which a person is convicted of the original offence may fix a reasonably period from the date of conviction for compliance by the defendant with any directions given by the court; and

(b) where a court has fixed such a period, the daily penalty referred to in subsection (2) is not recoverable in respect of any day before the end of that period.

s51 CAA 1993 -

Where an officer of the LA takes the view that an offence has been committed under the provisions prohibiting certain emissions of smoke (that is, under ss1, 2 and 20 CAA 1993). The notification must be made to the occupier of the premises, the person who has possession of the boiler or plant, the owner of the railway locomotive engine or the person in charge of the vessel. This notification should, if in writing, be made four days after the offence was noticed. Note that it is a defence, in proceedings brought under ss1, 2 or 20 CAA 1993, to prove that provisions of s51(1) CAA 1993 have not been complied with.

s52 CAA 1993: Corporate body liability

This section corresponds to s157 EPA 1990. When an offence has been committed by a corporate body, either with the consent or connivance of, or attributable to neglect of a director, manager, secretary (or other officer), then the officer is also guilty of the offence and liable to the same charge and penalties. See *Tesco Supermarkets Ltd v Nattrass* [1972] AC 153, [1971] 2 All ER 127 HL.

s53 CAA 1993 - This section corresponds to s158 EPA 1990. Where someone has committed an offence, but due to someone else's act or default, then the other person will be guilty of the offence. Proceedings being brought against one person do not depend upon proceedings being brought against another.

s56 CAA 1993 - Rights of inspection are defined within this section. A person authorised by the LA may enter land or vessels, to perform their functions and to carry out their inspections, measurements and tests, as well as remove samples or articles.

Entry may be made by force, if a warrant has been issued by a justice of the peace. To issue such a warrant, the justice must be satisfied that seven days' notice of the intended entry has been given, that entry would otherwise be refused, that the land or vessel is unoccupied, or that an application for admission to the land or vessel would 'defeat the object of the entry'.

Offences

> A person who obstructs someone exercising their powers under s56 CAA 1993 shall be guilty of an offence, and liable on summary conviction to a fine not exceeding level three on the standard scale.
>
> A person who either fails (without reasonable excuse) to comply with the requirements of a notice or who makes a statement recklessly, or which he knows to be false in a material particular shall be guilty of an offence and liable on summary conviction to a fine not exceeding level five on the standard scale.

CHAPTER 4

WASTE

CONTENTS

CHAPTER 4

WASTE

4.1 Introduction

Until EPA1990, waste management and waste disposal were regulated by COPA 1974. The changes in regulation which took place under Part II, EPA 1990 were wide ranging and conceptually fundamentally different. COPA 1974 had been the first legislative attempt to deal with waste in a comprehensive manner. Within COPA 1974 lay the introduction of a licensing system to control the deposit of waste (household, commercial and industrial) upon designated sites. There was also a requirement, for the first time, for a local authority in its role as a Waste Disposal Authority (WDA), to compile plans for the disposal of waste within its area. The plan was to be produced after consultation with other regulatory bodies, such as the water authorities in the area. It was to include large amounts of information about quantities, sites, methods of disposal and cost of disposal, as well as projections about future requirements. The plan was to be the subject of public consultation.

COPA 1974 marked a radical departure from the piecemeal approach to waste management which had grown out of the Public Health Acts which foreran it. The legislation was passed as a response to public concerns over the proliferation of waste, which has now become one of the major environmental problems. However, as a piece of pioneering legislation, COPA had some basic limitations: these centred on the inadequacy of the licensing provisions, both in the ambit and enforceability of the conditions of a licence and on the extent of the responsibility which lay upon a licensee in his administration of the disposal site. A licensee could simply surrender his licence and with it the obligations and liabilities which had arisen out of his use of the site. The other fundamental flaw was the conflict of interest that could arise from the regulatory body's dual roles of responsibility for both regulation and disposal of waste.

Part II, EPA 1990 heralded a new approach to the management and disposal of waste. What underlies the new regime is that whilst the legislation continues to operate a licence system, the management of waste is a process which tracks a substance from its creation, throughout its existence, to its final disposal. The definition of what constitutes waste lies at the heart of the legislation. This, coupled with the duty of care which is statutorily defined in respect of waste, changes the whole axis of the statutory regulation of waste management. In Part II, EPA 1990, fundamental changes have been brought about in the licensing system, as well as a complete reorganisation of the structure and distribution of the duties and responsibilities of the respective authorities which regulate and enforce.

There are implications in the long-term objectives for waste management reflected, for example, in a National Waste Strategy, and in IPC, analyses of which are outside the scope of a work strictly concerned with current criminal liability. The National Waste Strategy has not yet been produced, because the collection of data upon which it will be based has yet to be completed. Whilst figures on municipal waste have now been compiled, a survey has yet to be completed of industrial and commercial waste producers.

It is worth remarking that the concept of waste itself has undergone radical transformation in recent years. New and complex issues of definition, information, recycling and packaging are emerging which present considerable legislative challenges.

Accurate statistics about waste remain elusive. For example, with the advent of the landfill tax and deregulation some landfill operators maintain that a huge tonnage of inert waste simply went missing: there is limited evidence either to support or refute this claim. The landfill tax, through returns received by Customs and Excise, has generated the first collection of reliable data on the amount of waste sent to landfill. It would appear that the diversion of inert waste away from landfill has been to other projects, such as golf courses, landscaping and amenity bunds. Flytipping *may* have increased, but, similarly, lack of evidence makes the substantiation of such a claim difficult. Note that the EA is said to be pressing for stricter controls upon the operation of sites which are currently exempt from the requirement for a waste licence and that the Government is intending a general review of the exemptions from waste licensing, after specific examination of exemptions granted in construction and land reclamation projects.

Waste Regulation Authorities (WRAs) were established by EPA 1990. There are two in the UK, the Environment Agency (EA) and the other being the Scottish Environmental Protection Agency (SEPA). The functions of the two agencies are to administer the licensing system and to ensure compliance with the duty of care imposed in s34EPA 1990. They are responsible for compiling and maintaining registers of waste brokers and they must inspect land for health risks and pollution. They also have powers and duties to deal with the removal of unlawfully-deposited waste. Moving powers of regulation from the county and local councils to these centralised administrative bodies was intended to effect a separation of the functions of regulation and disposal and to produce a more uniform (and therefore fair) regime.

Waste Disposal Authorities (WDAs) comprise LAs. Their functions under EPA 1990 centre on the organisation of the disposal of controlled waste. The WDA may involve itself directly in the actual business of disposal only, through the operation of a LA waste disposal company (LAWDC), through which the WDA may be indirectly connected to the practical business of disposal. The WDA provides sites for the disposal of household waste. The EA has begun to produce regional waste-management assessments which will be used to assist LAs in their planning.

Waste Collection Authorities (WCAs) comprise London borough councils and district councils. It is their duty to provide receptacles for waste and to collect household and commercial waste.

4.2 Offences under Environmental Protection Act 1990 (EPA 1990)

s33 EPA 1990 established a set of offences which amount to the means of enforcement of the waste-management licensing system. s33 EPA 1990 creates three main *and separate* offences which cover the keeping, treatment and disposal of controlled waste.

4.2.1 Definitions

1. *Waste*

At the root of the new regime established by this legislation is the definition of waste. Waste was originally defined at s75 EPA 1990. This definition has since been amended, because it had become inadequate for the purposes of implementation of the *EC Waste Framework Directive.*

s75 EPA 1990: Meaning of *'waste'* and *'household'*, *'commercial'* and *'industrial'* waste and *'special'* waste.

S75(2) EPA 1990 *'Waste'* includes -

> (a) any substance which constitutes a scrap material or an effluent or other unwanted surplus substance arising from the application of any process:

(b) any substance or article which requires to be disposed of as being broken, worn out, contaminated or otherwise spoiled

but does not include a substance which is an explosive within the meaning of the Explosives Act 1875 (EA 1875).

This definition has been modified, through the *Waste Management Licensing Regulations* 1994, para. 9, which reads:

"Any reference to waste shall include a reference to Directive waste."

The Directive referred to is the 1975 *EC Framework Directive on Waste;' 'waste'* is defined (Reg. 1[3]) as:

> Any substance or object in the categories set out in Part II of Schedule 4 which the producer or the person in possession of it discards or intends or is required to discard but with the exception of anything excluded from the scope of the Directive by Article 2 of the Directive.

(The categories of waste *excluded* by Art. 2 are 'gaseous effluents emitted into the atmosphere' and those five categories of waste for which legislation is already in place: radioactive waste, waste resulting from mineral and quarry working, animal carcasses and certain other types of agricultural waste, waste waters and decommissioned explosives.)

What emerges from the Directive as a central point in the discussion on the nature of waste is that waste is defined thus *at the moment* when the person discards it, irrespective of the value it may go on to assume in the hands of another. This principle was established in the cases which were prosecuted under COPA 1974. For example, in *Kent County Council v Queensborough Rolling Mills Ltd* (1990) 154, JP 530, DC, it was held that the material moved from one site to another was viewed as being waste, notwithstanding that the waste was to be sorted and deposited for a useful purpose at another site. In that case, the waste had been removed from a porcelain factory and was due to be used as ballast in infill. The ruling here was that the waste was perceived as a substance which was being discarded, not recycled, which might have changed the complexion of the case. As such, it was therefore *'controlled waste'* within the meaning of s75 EPA 1990 and therefore subject to the regulatory controls of the Act which meant there was a requirement for a licence.

In *R v Rotherham Metropolitan Borough Council, ex p Rankin* {1990] JPL, it was decided that *'waste'* should be given its ordinary meaning.

The approach to the *point* at which waste assumes its status was confirmed in the European Court. The Joined Cases C 206/88 and C-207/88 (*Vesso and Zanetti* [1990] 2 LMELR 133) had been referred to the Court by Italy for a ruling on the interpretation of Art. 1 of Directive 75/442/EEC and Directive 78/319/EEC on toxic and dangerous waste. The cases were referred to the ECJ to settle questions of the compatibility of Italian waste legislation with EC law. In the 1982 the definition in Italian law which was to implement the 1975 Directive, waste was defined as *'any substance or object deriving from human activity or natural cycles which is abandoned or destined to be abandoned'*. Subsequent decree-laws introduced further provisions for waste, some of which distinguished between *'waste'* and *'residue'*. The cases involved olive oil residues, marble rubble and debris from a marble factory and the defendants argued that because these were 'residues' no offence had been committed. The Court took the view that where national legislation excludes from the definition of waste objects or substances which are capable of reutilisation, then that national legislation is not compatible with the 1975 Directive as originally drafted, nor as amended by the 1991 amendments. The judgment included these words:

> The concept of waste, within the meaning of Art. 1 of Directive 74/442/EEC and Art. 1 of Directive 78/319/EEC, is not to be understood as excluding substances and objects which are capable of economic reutilisation. The concept does not presume that the holder disposing of a substance or an object intends to exclude all economic reutilisation of the substance or object by others.

The important issue in this case therefore was whether the definition of waste could be held to exclude objects or substances which were capable of economic reuse. The Court took the inclusive view that the 1975 Directive as amended was 'intended to cover all objects and substances discarded by their owners even if they have a commercial value and are collected on a commercial basis for recycling, reclamation or reuse'.

In *Environment Agency v Short* (ELM Report, September, 1998) Divisional Court, July 13th, 1998, the respondent was carrying out demolition work when he was asked by the site owner for hard core material, said to be necessary for building works. The respondent delivered the hard core to the site owner. Whilst at the site, the site owner allowed the respondent to leave certain other waste, namely timber from the demolition work, on the site. The site owner said that this waste could be burnt on the site, and further stated that no waste-management licence was required, because the site had exempt status. On these assurances the respondent acted and completed a waste transfer note. The respondent was then charged by the Environment Agency with offences under s33(1)(c) EPA1990 and s34(1)(a) and (c) of the EPA 1990, in failing to take reasonable measures to secure the transfer of waste to an authorised person. The magistrates dismissed the information laid by the Agency on the grounds that the hard core fell outside the definition of controlled waste, as it was not an unwanted surplus within the meaning of s75(2)(a) EPA 1990 and was also exempt from under Schedule 3, para. 19 of the Waste Management Licensing Regulations 1994. In addition, the respondent had taken the reasonable precautions which amount to due diligence, providing a defence to the charges under s33 EPA 1990. An appeal was lodged in the Divisional Court by way of case stated.

The Divisional Court took the view that the definition of 'controlled waste' in s75 EPA 1990 *could* include industrial and commercial waste and that 'industrial waste' could include waste arising from construction or demolition works defined in the Controlled Waste Regulations 1992. This was therefore 'controlled' waste. The issue was whether or not it was exempt under Schedule 3 of the Waste Management Licensing Regulations 1994. The court held that para. 19 did allow an exemption for material to be recycled and put to further use. However, whilst such an exemption might cover the hard core, it could not be said to cover the timber which was left on site to be burned. The respondent had left the timber as a consequence of reassurance given to him by the site owner but had not pursued his enquiries into the nature of the exemption of the site. It was the court's view that the respondent had not taken all reasonable measures to secure the transfer of waste to an authorised person and that the justices had reached the wrong decision. The appeal was therefore allowed.

The case highlights the importance of careful use of the regulations when assessing whether the substance or object falls within the definition of controlled waste. It also raises the question of what will constitute a breach of the duty of care at s34 EPA 1990. (See below at 4.2.8.6.)

4.2.2 Waste Management Licensing Regulations 1994

These Regulations introduced '*Directive Waste*'. They regulate the applications for the licence, for its transfer, or its surrender. They list the offences which will be relevant in considering such an application and the rules which govern an appeal against a refusal.

Schedule 1 to these Regulations deals with the requirements for an application for a licence, Schedule 2 with the requirements for an application for a transfer of a licence.

Schedule 3 lists activities which are exempt from the requirement for a licence.

Part 2 of Schedule 4 contains a list of 16 categories of waste which correspond to the categories of waste to be found in the Framework Directive. Note that the sixteenth category of waste amounts to a catch-all category which means that anything discarded as waste *per se* may be caught by EPA 1990, unless it falls into one of the categories of exceptions to be found in Art. 2 of the Directive.

Schedule 5 to the Regulations addresses the requirements for the registration of a broker. This schedule sets out the WRA's to keep a register of brokers of controlled waste, the requirements for an application for registration and the appeals procedure.

4.2.3 Controlled waste

The regulatory provisions of EPA apply generally to *'controlled waste'*, which is defined at s75(4) EPA 1990 as *'household, industrial and commercial waste'*. Only such waste is subject to the licensing system and the enforcement provisions of EPA 1990. Note that waste which is not 'controlled' within the meaning of the Act is nevertheless subject to the provision of s63 EPA 1990, for which see below. Further substance is given to the definition of controlled waste in the *Controlled Waste Regulations* 1992, and these regulations are expanded upon in the *DoE Circular* 14/92.

4.2.4 Household waste

s75(5) EPA 1990 *'household waste'* means waste from

- domestic property, that is to say, a building or self-contained part of a building which is used wholly for the purposes of living accommodation;

- a caravan;

- a residential home;

- premises forming part of a university or school or other educational establishment;

• premises forming part of a hospital or nursing home.

Note that in Regulation 2(1) and Schedule 1 to the Controlled Waste Regulations 1992 a number of additional categories of waste are listed as to be treated as 'household' waste. Certain exceptions found at Regulation 2 (2), 'namely waste arising from works of construction or demolition, including waste arising from work preparatory thereto and septic tank sludge', are to be treated as household waste only for the purposes of the 'duty of care' provisions at s34 EPA 1990.

In *Environment Agency v B&B Builders* (ELM July 1998), the defendant, Mr Baker, trading as B&B Builders, of Heacham, Norfolk had been contracted to remove waste which included a wooden car port, a large static caravan and other general household rubbish from a property in the Gayton area. However, later the same day, a report was received of two piles of waste being seen, which also included asbestos. Among the waste were items giving the address at which Mr Baker was working. He was fined £3,000 and ordered to pay costs of £580 after pleading guilty, to the illegal disposal of controlled waste on unlicensed land.

4.2.5 Industrial waste

s75(6) EPA 1990 *'Industrial waste'* means waste from any of the following premises:

(1) any factory

Factory is defined at s175(1) Factories Act 1961 [FA 1961] as being

> . . . any premises in which, or within the close or curtilage or precincts of which, persons are employed in manual labour in any process for or incidental to any of the following purposes:
>
> (1) the making of any article or of part of any article; or
> (2) the altering, repairing, ornamenting, finishing, cleaning, or washing or the breaking up of demolition of any article; or
> (3) the adapting for sale of any article; or
> (4) the slaughtering of cattle, sheep, swine, goats, horses, asses or mules; or
> (5) the confinement of such animals as aforesaid while awaiting slaughter at other premises, in a case where the place of confinement is available in connection with premises, in a case where the place of confinement is available in connection with

those other premises, is not maintained primarily for agricultural purposes within the meaning of the Agriculture Act 1947 (or Agriculture [Scotland] Act 1948), and does not form part of premises used for the holding of a market in respect of such animals;being premises in which, or within the close or curtilage or precincts of which, the work is carried on by way of trade or for purposes of gain and to or over which the employer of the persons employed therein has the right of access or control.

Under s175(2) FA 1961, the expression 'factory' also includes the following premises in which persons are employed in manual labour (whether or not they are factories by virtue of s175(1), that is to say:

(a) any yard or dry dock (including the precincts thereof) in which ships or vessels are constructed, reconstructed, repaired, refitted, finished or broken up;
(b) any premises in which the business of sorting any articles is carried on as a preliminary to the work carried on in any factory or incidentally to the purposes of any factory;
(c) any premises in which the business of washing or filling bottles or containers or packing articles is carried on incidentally to the purposes of any factory;
(d) any premises in which the business of holing, plaiting, lapping, making-up or packing of yarn or cloth is carried on;
(e) any laundry carried on as ancillary to another business, or incidentally to the purposes of any public institution;
(f) any premises in which the construction, reconstruction or repair of locomotives, vehicles or other plant for use for transport purposes is carried on as ancillary to a transport undertaking or other industrial or commercial undertaking;
(g) any premises in which printing by letterpress, lithography, photogravure, or other similar process, or bookbinding is carried on by way of trade or for purposes of gain or incidentally to another business so carried on;
(h) any premises in which the making, adaptation or repair of dresses, scenery or properties is carried on incidentally to the production, exhibition or presentation by way of trade or for purposes of gain of cinematograph films or theatrical performances, not being a stage or dressing-room of a theatre in which only occasional adaptations or repairs are being made;
(j) any premises in which the business of making or mending nets is carried on incidentally to the fishing industry;

(k) any premises in which mechanical power is used in connection with the making or repair of articles of metal or wood incidentally to any business carried on by way of trade or for purposes of gain;
(l) any premises in which the production of cinematographic films is carried on by way of trade or for purposes of gain, so, however, that the employment at any such premises of theatrical performers within the meaning of the Theatrical Employers Registration Act 1925 and of attendants on such theatrical performers shall not be deemed to be employment in a factory;
(m) any premises in which articles are made or prepared incidentally to the carrying on of building operations or works of engineering construction, not being premises in which such operations or works are being carried on;
(n) any premises used for the storage of gas in a gasholder having a storage capacity of not less than [140 cubic] metres.

s175(3) FA 1961: Any line or siding (not being part of a railway or tramway) which is used in connection with and for the purposes of a factory, shall be deemed to be part of the factory; and if any such line or siding is used in connection with more than one factory belonging to different occupiers, the line or siding shall be deemed to be a separate factory.

s175(4) FA 1961: a part of a factory may, with the approval in writing of the chief inspector, be taken to be a separate factory and two or more factories may, with the like approval, be taken to be a single factory.

s175(5) FA 1961: Any workplace in which, with the permission of or under agreement with the owner or occupier, two or more persons carry on any work which would constitute the workplace a factory if the persons working therein were in the employment of the owner or occupier, shall be deemed to be a factory for the purposes of this Act, and, in the case of any such workplace not being a tenement factory or part of a tenement factory, the provisions of this Act shall apply as if the owner or occupier of the workplace were the occupier of the factory and the persons working therein were persons employed in the factory.

s175(6) FA 1961: Where a place situate within the close, curtilage, or precincts forming a factory is solely used for some purpose other than the processes carried on in the factory, that place shall not be deemed to form part of the factory for the purposes of this Act, but shall, if otherwise it would be a factory, be deemed to be a separate factory.

s175(7) FA 1961: Premises shall not be excluded from the definition of a factory by reason only that they are open-air premises.

s175(8) FA 1961: Where the minister by regulations so directs as respects all or any purposes of this Act, different branches or departments of work carried on in the same factory shall be deemed to be different factories

s175(9) FA 1961: Any premises belonging to or in occupation of the Crown or any municipal or public authority shall not be deemed not to be a factory, and building operations or works of engineering construction undertaken by or on behalf of the Crown or any such authority shall not be excluded from the operation of this Act, by reason only that the work carried on thereat is not carried on by way of trade or for purposes of gain.

s175(10) FA 1961: Premises used for the purpose of housing locomotives or vehicles where only cleaning, washing, running repairs or minor adjustments are carried out shall not be deemed to be a factory by reason only of para (f) of ss2 of this section , unless they are premises used for the purposes of a railway undertaking where running repairs to locomotives are carried out.

(2) any premises used for the purposes of, or in connection with, the provision to the public of (a) transport services by land, water or air; (b) the supply to the public of gas, water or electricity or the provision of sewerage services; or (c) provision to the public of postal or telecommunications services.

Note that in Regulation 2(5) and Schedule 3 to the *Controlled Waste Regulations* 1992 further categories are added to the list of substances to be considered as industrial waste. These are:

(1) waste from premises used for maintaining vehicles, vessels or aircraft, not being waste from a private garage which falls under domestic waste by virtue of Schedule 1;

(2) waste from a laboratory.
(3) Waste from a workshop or similar premises not being a factory within the meaning of s175 FA 1961 because the people working there are not employees or because the work there is not carried on by way of trade or purposes of gain, excluding premises at which the principal activities are computer operations or the copying of documents by photographic or lithographic means.

(4) Waste from premises occupied by a scientific research association approved by the Secretary of State under s508 Income and Corporation Taxes Act 1988 (ICTA 1988).

(5) Waste from dredging operations.

(6) Waste from tunnelling on any other excavation.

(7) Waste from sewage not falling within a description in Reg. 7 which

(a) is treated, kept on disposed of in or on land, other than by means of a privy, cesspool or septic tank;
(b) is treated, kept on disposal of by means of mobile plant; or
(c) has been removed from a privy or cesspool.

(8) Clinical waste other than:

(a) clinical waste from a domestic property, caravan, residential home or from a moored vessel used wholly for the purposes of living accommodation;
(b) waste collected under s22(3) of COPA 1974; or
(c) waste collected under s89 EPA 1990 (LA's duty to keep land and highways clear of litter), s92(9) EPA 1990 (waste collected by a LA after a failure by any person to obey a litter-abatement notice) or s93 EPA 1990 (power to serve street-litter control notices).

(9) waste arising from any aircraft, vehicle or vessel which is not occupied for domestic purposes.

(10) waste which has previously formed part of any aircraft, vehicle or vessel and which is not household waste.

(11) Waste removed from land on which it has previously been deposited and any soil with which such waste has been in contact, other than waste collected under:

(a) section 22(3) COPA 1974 or
(b) sections 89,92(9),93 COPA 1974.

(12) Leachate from a deposit of waste.

(13) Poisonous or noxious waste arising from any of the following processes undertaken on premises used for the purposes of a trade or business:

(a) mixing or selling paints;
(b) sign writing;
(c) laundering or dry cleaning;
(d) developing photographic film or making photographic prints;
(e) selling petrol, diesel fuel, paraffin, kerosene, heating oil or similar substances; or
(f) selling pesticides, herbicides or fungicides.

(14) Waste from premises used for the purposes of breeding, boarding, stabling or exhibiting animals.

(15) Waste oil, waste solvent or (subject to regulation 7[2]) scrap metal, other than

(a) waste from a domestic property, caravan or residential home;
(b) waste falling within paras 3 to 6 of Schedule 1.

In this paragraph -
'waste oil' means mineral or synthetic oil which is contaminated, spoiled or otherwise unfit for its original purpose; and 'waste solvent' means solvent which is contaminated, spoiled or otherwise unfit for its original purpose.

(16) Waste arising from the discharge by the Secretary of State of his duty under s89(2) EPA 1990 (duty to keep clean any trunk road which is a special road and relevant highways or roads for which he is responsible).

(17) Waste imported into Great Britain.

(18) Tank washings and garbage landed in Great Britain.

4.2.6 Commercial waste

s75(7) EPA 1990 *'Commercial waste'* means waste from premises used wholly or mainly for the purposes of a trade or business or the purposes of sport, recreation or entertainment excluding:

(1) household waste;

(2) industrial waste;

(3) waste from any mine or quarry and waste from premises used for agriculture;

(4) waste of any other description prescribed by regulations made by the Secretary of State for the purposes of this paragraph.

Note that Schedule 4 to the *Controlled Waste Regulations* 1992 contains a detailed list of substances which should be considered as commercial waste. These are:

(1) Waste from an office or showroom.

(2) Waste from a hotel within the meaning of:

(a) in England and Wales, section 1(3) of the Hotel Proprietors Act 1956 (HPA 1956);
(b) in Scotland, section 139(1) of the Licensing (Scotland) Act 1976 (L(S)A 1976).

(3) Waste from any part of a composite hereditament, or, in Scotland, of part-residential subjects, which is used for the purposes of a trade or business.

(4) Waste from a private garage which either has a floor area exceeding 25 square metres or is not used wholly or mainly for the accommodation of a private motor vehicle.

(5) Waste from premises occupied by a club, society or any association of persons (whether incorporated or not) in which activities are conducted for the benefit of the members.

(6) Waste from premises (not being premises from which waste is by virtue of the Act or of any other provision of these Regulations to be treated as household waste or industrial waste) occupied by:

(a) a court;
(b) a government department;
(c) a local authority;
(d) a body corporate or an individual appointed by or under any enactment to discharge any public functions; or
(e) a body incorporated by a Royal Charter.

(7) Waste from a tent pitched on land other than a camp site

(8) Waste from a market or fair

(9) Waste collected under section 22(3) COPA 1974.

Note that scrap metal and waste motor vehicles are generally subject to the waste management licensing provisions in EPA 1990, although certain activities associated with them are exempt from the requirement for a licence. They remain registrable and subject to the duty of care. A scrapyard is subject to the requirement of registration, although not obliged to produce an environmental site assessment.

4.2.7 Special waste

s62 EPA 1990: *'Special waste'* is defined as controlled waste regarded by the Secretary of State as being so dangerous or difficult to treat, keep or dispose of that special provisions are required to deal with it. The regulations which govern management and disposal of special waste are the *Special Waste Regulations* 1996.

Special Waste Regulations 1996 (SWR 1996)

Schedule 2 to these Regulations contains lists of categories of substances to be regarded as special waste. Part 1 reproduces the list of hazardous waste annexed to Council Decision 94/904/EC, to which six-digit identifying code numbers have been assigned. Note that the consignment note must contain this identification.

Part 2 of the Schedule, which reproduces Annex III to the *Hazardous Waste Directive*, is a list of properties which will render an object or substance special waste for the purposes of this section. Some medicinal products are similarly defined and the Secretary of State is given powers to define certain radioactive substances as waste.

4.2.7.1 Offences

The regulations also list the requirements for consignment notes, registers and site records and set out the offences of failing to comply with the regulations, either intentionally or negligently. It is important to note that Reg. 17 creates the offence, in the absence of an exemption or an authorisation, of mixing special waste and other kinds of waste. It is also an offence to mix different categories of special waste. It is, however, a defence for a person charged under this regulation to prove that he was not reasonably able to comply with the provision in question, or to prove that he took all reasonably practical steps in the circumstances for:

(1) minimising any threat to the public or the environment
(2) ensuring that the provision in question was complied with as soon as reasonably practicable after the event.

In *Environment Agency v BBA Friction* (Ends Report, October 1997), the defendant, a brake pad manufacturer, whose landfill site at Swalesmoor in Halifax is an in-house operation, contracted to transport a consignment of waste to the site in breach of the conditions of its licence. The condition required the asbestos waste to be deposited in a segregated area, to avoid disturbing the asbestos in the event of an excavation. The firm was fined £4,000 for failing in its duty of care and £4,000 for failing to prevent an escape of waste under its control, but it was also fined a further £4,000 for failing to issue a consignment note for a load of asbestos, thus breaching the Special Waste Regulations 1996.

In *Environment Agency v Allum* (Ends Report, November 1997) a Suffolk scrap metal dealer, Frank Allum, had been contracted to remove copper pipes from the boiler room of a hospital in Stowmarket. In contravention of the hospital's instructions, he also removed and discarded the asbestos lagging, leaving asbestos fibres scattered around the site. The asbestos pollution was sufficient to cause the closure of an old folks' daycentre and the cost of cleaning up the asbestos amounted to tens of thousands of pounds. Mr Allum was found guilty of offences under s33(1)(c) EPA 1990 but he was also found guilty of offences under the Special Waste Regulations, having moved asbestos from the site without a consignment note. He was also in breach of the *Asbestos Licensing Regulations* 1983 and was sentenced for all of these offences to a term of imprisonment of three months.

In *Environment Agency v Chelsea and Westminster Healthcare Trust* (Ends Report, November 1997), the Trust, by a series of subcontracts, had been responsible for the mismanagement of the disposal of six drums of unwanted acid and 60-70 drums of waste oil. Some of the oil was tipped on common land in Surrey and other drums were deposited at a yard in Mitcham which operated as a waste-transfer station without a licence. The Trust was found guilty of offences under s34 EPA1990, (and fined £3,000) but it was also fined £3,000 for failing to raise a special waste- consignment note for the acid. The subcontracting company Kaledeal, responsible for transporting the waste to Mitcham, were charged with the same offences and fined £4,000.

In *Environment Agency v D&H Autos* (ELM Report, April 1998), the defendant, a scrap metal company, had been visited by an EA officer and advised that he would have to get a licence or register an exemption, having reduced his stock to 140 vehicles. He chose to register as exempt. A later routine visit revealed a stock of 282 vehicles, undrained, which caused fluids to contaminate the land. No sealed drainage system was in operation. A further 161 undrained vehicles were found outside the exempt area. Liam Hanlon, operating the defendant company, was charged under s33(1)(a) EPA 1990, fined £3,500 and ordered to pay costs of £1,685.82.

4.2.8 Waste other than controlled waste

s63 EPA 1990: By this section, the Secretary of State is empowered, after due consultation with the appropriate bodies, to regulate the management of waste from mines, quarries and agriculture. At s63(2) EPA 1990, the power is created by which waste not defined as controlled may be treated as though it were special waste, for the purposes of prosecuting an offence which would otherwise have been committed under s33 EPA 1990.

The purpose of this section is to establish a regime for management of waste not caught by other sections of the Act. Where the waste is dangerous or difficult to treat, then the controls are available as if the waste were special waste, ie waste of a kind which is or may be dangerous or difficult to dispose of. However, this section also creates the offence of disposing of such waste, for example by flytipping.

The DoE Circular, in Annex 2, gives guidance on the interpretation of the definition of waste, beginning with the assertion that whether or not a substance amounts to waste will depend upon the individual facts of the case. However, what is clear is that it is the holder of the substance who has the responsibility of determining whether the substance is or is not waste, although a view may also have to taken of the substance by the

WRA. The view expressed by the DoE is that waste should broadly be considered as 'those substances or objects which fall out of the commercial cycle or out of the chain of utility'. If a substance has not been discarded in such a way that it has done so, then it probably is not waste.

A twofold test for definition appears to emerge from the guidelines.

> For a substance or object to be waste, it must:
> (a) fall into one of the categories set out in Part II of Schedule 4 to the Regulations; and -
> (b) (i) be discarded, disposed of or got rid of by the holder; or
> (ii) be intended to be discarded, disposed of or got rid of by the holder; or
> (iii) be required to be discarded, disposed of or got rid of by the holder.

This is merely a statement of the first principle of waste definition. The Circular gives a good deal of guidance on the status of a substance or product. Broadly speaking, the guidance, set out in brief at paras 2.55 and 2.56 (excerpts set out below) suggests that the question to be posed is *"has the substance or object been discarded so that it is no longer part of the normal commercial cycle or chain of utility."*

If the answer is 'no' then the substance or object is unlikely to be waste. However, it should *not* be regarded as waste:

> (a) solely on the grounds that it falls into one of the categories listed in Part II of Schedule 4 to the Regulations;
> (b) solely on the grounds that it has been consigned to a recovery operation listed in Part IV of Schedule 4 to the Regulations;
> (c) if it is sold or given away and can be used in its present form (albeit after repair) or in the same way as any other raw material without being subjected to a *specialised recovery operation;*
> (d) if its producer puts it to beneficial use;
> (e) solely on the grounds that its producer would be unlikely to seek a substitute for it if it ceased to become available to him as, say, a by-product.

If the substance does appear to have been discarded, then it *should* be regarded as waste if it falls into one of the categories listed in Part II of the Schedule 4 to the Regulations and:

(a) it is consigned to a disposal operation listed in Part III of Schedule 4 to the Regulations;
(b) it can be used only after it has been consigned to a *specialised recovery operation;*
(c) the holder pays someone to provide him with a service and that service is the collection [and taking away] of a substance or object which the holder does not want and wishes to get rid of;
(d) the purpose of any [beneficial] use is wholly or mainly to relieve the holder of the burden of disposing of it and the user would be unlikely to seek a substitute for it if it ceased to become available to him as, say, a by-product;
(e) it is discarded or otherwise dealt with as if it were waste;
(f) if it is abandoned or dumped.

The interpretation of the term *'discard'* remains a subject of debate.

Further definitions for the purposes of Part II, EPA 1990 are to be found in the preliminaries at s29 EPA 1990. Whereas some terms coincide with those to be found in Part I, EPA, the definitions do not necessarily do so. For example:

s29(3) EPA 1990: *'Pollution of the environment'* is defined more widely and in more detail here than in Part I, applying to escapes as well as releases of substances both from land or a fixed plant.

s29(8) EPA 1990: *'Land'* is defined in a more limited way than in Part I, however, as being the seaward limit of the foreshore.

s29(11) EPA 1990: *'substance'* is defined more narrowly than for Part I (where it is defined at s1[13]) as being any natural or artificial substance, whether in solid or liquid form or in the form of a gas or vapour).

s29(6) EPA 1990: The *'disposal'* of waste includes its disposal by way of deposit in or on land. Waste is treated when it is subjected to any process, including making it reusable or reclaiming substances from it. 'Recycle' (and cognate expressions) shall be construed accordingly.

In *R v Metropolitan Stipendiary Magistrate, ex p London Waste Regulation Authority* [1993] 3 All ER 113,DC, Watkins LJ said:

an article may be regarded as disposed of it is destroyed or if it is passed from one person to another: the ordinary sense of the terms, certainly in a context such as that of this Act [COPA], rests on the notion of getting rid of something. It has, in our judgment, no more to do with finding a 'final resting' place than has the word 'deposit' in s3(1)a.

In *Thames Waste Management Ltd v Surrey County Council* [1997] Env LR 148, QBD 'deposit' was held to include a continuing state of affairs.

'knowingly causing or knowingly permitting'

may be interpreted in accordance with the meanings which these phrases have been given under WRA 1991. Whilst 'causing' does not require the *mens rea* to be present, some positive act is required for this offence to have been committed. 'Permitting' does not have the same requirement, however. In contrast to s85 WRA 1991, 'knowingly' has been expressly applied to both causing and permitting. (In s85 WRA 1991, it is only applied to permitting.) This has been strictly construed in case-law.

In *Shanks and McEwan (Teeside) Ltd v Environment Agency* [1997] 2 All ER 332 DC, the company was convicted of an offence under s33 EPA 1990. The facts of the case were that waste had been deposited from a tanker into a containment bund at a licensed site operated by Shanks. The site supervisor had complied with the licence conditions on the delivery of the waste. However, the tank for the planned offloading was altered and the site supervisor did not complete a new waste disposal form. This was a breach of the licence condition. The defendant company argued that it could not reasonably have known of this breach and the issue centred upon whether the site supervisor could be held to be of sufficient seniority to be part of the 'directing mind of the company'. There was an appeal by way of case stated.

The Divisional Court held that the term 'knowingly' qualified two of the three possible offences - 'knowingly cause' or 'knowingly permit'. It could not follow that the term qualified the second half of the definition, unless the licence authorised the deposit and the deposit was in accordance with its conditions. Therefore, it was unnecessary to prove knowledge on the part of the defendant company in respect of compliance with the licence. 'Knowledge' was to be construed as knowledge of the deposit, rather than knowledge of the breach of the condition of the licence.

4.2.8.1 s33 EPA 1990: Offences

s33(1) EPA 1990: Prohibition on unauthorised or harmful deposit, treatment or disposal, etc, of waste.

> Subject to ss(2) and (3) EPA 1990 [(2) being the exclusion category of household waste and (3) being the powers under which the Secretary of State may prescribe regulations or modify categories of exclusions] below and in relation to Scotland to s54 below, a person shall not-
>
> (a) deposit controlled waste, or knowingly cause or knowingly permit controlled waste to be deposited in or on any land unless a waste-management licence authorising the deposit is in force and the deposit is in accordance with the licence;
> (b) treat, keep or dispose of controlled waste, or knowingly cause or knowingly permit controlled waste to be treated, kept or disposed of-
>
> (i) in or on any land, or
> (ii) by means of any mobile plant,
> except under and in accordance with a waste-management licence;
> (3) treat, keep or dispose of controlled waste in a manner likely to cause pollution of the environment or harm to human health.

This is the central set of offences arising out of the controlled waste licensing management system which encompasses the management and disposal of all controlled waste. The person referred to in s33(1) EPA 1990 may be either the person who actually deposits the substance and/or the person who gives instructions that the deposit should be made, and/or who knowingly permits the deposit.

'In accordance with the licence' has been construed to mean that the relevant conditions of the licence are the only determinants for an offence to occur under this section.

In *Leigh Land Reclamation Ltd v Walsall Metropolitan Borough Council* [1991] JPL 867, DC, a case brought under s3 (1) COPA 1974, the deposit itself was not in breach of the conditions of the licence and although other aspects of of waste management on the site in question may have given rise to a breach of a condition of the licence, the deposit in question complied with the conditions so that there was no breach under this section of the Act.

Note that there are exceptions to the requirement for a licence which are to be found in the *Waste Management Licensing Regulations* 1994 (Schedule 4). For example, in certain circumstances, storage of waste does not carry the requirement for a licence.

In *North Yorkshire County Council v Boyne* [1997] Env LR 91, the defendant ran a skip hire business. His customers would fill the skips and the filled skips would be on his premises for a period before being taken by him to a landfill site. He was held not to be required to have a waste-disposal licence. Likewise, household waste from a domestic property is not subject to the requirement for a licence, although there are substances within this category, namely any mineral or synthetic oil or grease, asbestos and clinical waste which may not be treated as household waste for the purpose of the exception.

The offence at s33(1)(c) EPA 1990 may be committed even when there is no requirement for a waste-management licence, for example in the case of flytipping.

In *Environment Agency v M and W Maitchell* (Ends Report, February 1998), the defendants had represented to a Middlesbrough tyre manufacturer that they were certified toxic waste carriers, by using a borrowed certificate. They had then been paid to dispose of waste chemicals, including isocyanates. The 30 drums of chemicals, pickaxed to make them drain, were discovered by chance at a former Travellers site near Stockton. The clean-up cost came to £20,000. Before sentence, the two men fled the courtroom. They were sentenced to two years' imprisonment.

4.2.8.2 Flytipping

> s33(5) EPA 1990: Where controlled waste is carried in and deposited from a motor vehicle, the person who controls or is in a position to control the use of the vehicle shall, for the purposes of ss(1)(a) above, be treated as knowingly causing the waste to be deposited whether or not he gave any instructions for this to be done.

This is a special provision, aimed at the successful prosecution of a flytipper, where the case might otherwise be somewhat obscure and difficult to bring.

Control of Pollution (Amendment) Act 1989 (COPAA 1989)

Note that it is an offence under s1 COPAA 1989 for a person who is not a registered carrier to transport controlled waste to or from any place in Great Britain.

s1(4) COPAA 1989 contains the defences to such a charge, of which there are three:

> (a) that the waste was transported in an emergency (and notice was given as soon as practically possible after the event);
> (b) that the person did not know and had no reasonable grounds for suspecting that he was transporting controlled waste and had taken all reasonable steps to ascertain whether the substance was controlled waste; and
> (c) that he acted under instructions from his employer.
>
> s1(5) COPAA 1989: A person guilty of an offence under this section shall be liable to summary conviction to a fine not exceeding level five on the standard scale.

Under the *Controlled Waste (Registration of Carriers and Seizure of Vehicles) Regulations* (Nos 22, 22, 23), the vehicle may be seized and in certain circumstances subject to sale or destruction,

In a group of cases brought by the EA against two companies, reported in the Ends Report, February 1998, inert waste was being tipped at Moated Farm, a golf course development in Addlestone, to improve drainage. Suspicions developed that the waste being used was unsuitable and Surrey waste regulators were called in to inspect. Trial pits were subsequently dug by the EA, the results of which gave rise to a prosecution of the demolition contractor, BL Penwarden, for a 'duty of care' offence (s34 EPA 1990). The company had failed to complete transfer notes correctly, occasionally stating that the waste was 'muck-away' when this was not the case, because other materials were included. The EA also prosecuted Arlington Transport for keeping controlled waste on land without a licence. Arlington Transport, whose board shared a director with BL Penwarden, was fined £11,000 with £5,275 in costs.

4.2.8.3 s33(6) EPA 1990: A person who contravenes subsection (1) above or any condition of a waste-management licence commits an offence

A 'person' is generally both the licence-holder and the operator of the waste-disposal site. However, there are occasionally circumstances where this distinction is not as clear as this, for example when there is a complex corporate structure to the management of the site.

In *Shanks and McEwan (Midlands) Ltd v Wrexham Maelor Borough Council* (Divisional Court) March 18th, 1996, the company was the licence-holder but an associated firm, Shanks and McEwan (Northern)Ltd effectively operated the site. The company appealed against the conviction but, in the Divisional Court, Lord Leggatt concluded that the scheme of the Act was to render liable 'the person who is in actual occupation of the site' which in practice is the operator. It was held that 'a person' does not have to be a licence-holder, to fulfil the offence; he simply has to have breached a condition of the licence. The offence also prohibits the handling, processing or recycling of controlled waste, as well as instructing or knowingly permitting those activities, in or on land or through the use of a mobile plant.

It is important to note that by this subsection, a person may be prosecuted for *any* condition of a waste-management licence, not solely for a deposit. However, a prosecution can *only* be brought under this section for offences which arise out of breaches of licence conditions.

In *London Waste Regulation Authority v Drinkwater Sabey Ltd* [1997] Env LR 137, a prosecution was brought in respect of the defendant exceeding the amount of waste permitted to be brought daily to the site. However, although the waste exceeded the amount, an unquantified part of the amount that was measured to be in excess was in fact canal dredgings, therefore subject to an exemption under the Regulations and therefore not within the ambit of the offence.

4.2.8.4 Defences available to an offence charged under s33(6) EPA 1990

> s33(7) EPA 1990: It shall be a defence for a person charged with an offence under this section to prove:
>
> (a) that he took all reasonable precautions and exercised all due diligence to avoid the commission of the offence; or
> (b) that he acted under instructions from his employer and neither knew nor had reason to suppose that the acts done by him constituted a contravention of subsection(1); or
> (c) that the acts alleged to constitute the contravention were done in an emergency in order to avoid danger to human health in a case where
>
> > (i) he took all such steps as were reasonably practicable in the circumstances for minimising pollution of the environment and harm to human health; and
> > (ii) particulars of the acts were furnished to the waste regulation authority as soon as reasonably practicable after they were done.

'Reasonable precaution' and 'due diligence' defences succeed if they reach a certain standard.

In *Durham County Council v Peter Connors Industrial Services Ltd* [1992], a waste producer customarily left his waste in a skip for collection on a regular basis. On one occasion, the skip was found to contain special waste which was outside the terms of the licence. The defendant was convicted, because it was held to be his responsibility to be aware on each occasion what waste had been put into his skip. It has been suggested that due diligence amounts to the obligation to exercise reasonable care.

4.2.8.5 Sentencing provisions

s33(8) EPA 1990: Except in a case falling within subsection (9) below, a person who commits an offence under this section shall be liable:

> (a) on summary conviction, to imprisonment for a term not exceeding six months, or a fine not exceeding £20,000, or both; and
>
> (b) on conviction on indictment, to imprisonment for a term not exceeding two years, or a fine, or both.

s33(9) EPA 1990: A person who commits an offence under this section in relation to special waste shall be liable -

> (a) on summary conviction, to imprisonment for a term not exceeding six months, or a fine not exceeding £20,000, or both;
> (b) on conviction on indictment, to imprisonment for a term not exceeding five years, or a fine, or both.

There is an observable trend towards higher fines for waste offences. A survey of penalties by the National Association of Waste Regulation Officers showed that the average fine for offences of illegal disposal of waste under COPA 1974 was £399.00 in 1993/94. At the time, the statutory maximum available to magistrates was £5,000. For breach of the 'duty of care', the average fine amounted to £462.00, with a maximum of £3,000. In 1994, the maximum fine was raised to £20,000. For a résumé of current sentencing practice, see below.

4.2.8.6 s34 EPA 1990: Duty of care, etc, as respects waste

This section imposes a statutory duty of care upon anyone who produces, keeps, treats or disposes of controlled waste or, as a broker, has control of such waste. The duty of care is not exclusively imposed on the licence-holder or the operator of a site. It extends to all persons dealing with controlled waste, either depositing it or storing it on a site not licensed for the purpose.

> s34(1) EPA 1990: Subject to ss(2) [exclusion from the provisions of this section of the occupier of domestic property in respect of household waste], it shall be the duty of any person who imports, produces, carries, keeps, treats or disposes of controlled waste or, as a broker, has control of such waste, to take all such measures applicable to him in that capacity as are reasonable in the circumstances -
>
> (a) to prevent any contravention by any other person of s33 EPA 1990
> (b) to prevent the escape of the waste from his control or that of any other person; and
> (c) on the transfer of the waste, to secure -
>
> > (i) that the transfer is only to an authorised person or to a person for authorised transport purposes; and
> > (ii) that there is transferred such a written description of the waste as will enable other persons to avoid a contravention of that section and to comply with the duty under this subsection as respects the escape of waste.

s34(3) EPA 1990 lists the persons who are authorised for the purposes of s34(1)(c) EPA 1990 (waste collection authorities, holders of waste management licences, registered carriers of controlled waste); persons who are entitled, by s33 EPA 1990 or COPA (Amendment) Act 1989 [COPAAA 1989], to be excluded from the requirement of holding a waste-management licence and persons who are added by prescribed regulations through the Secretary of State's powers under s34(3A) EPA 1990.

s34(4) EPA 1990 lists the authorised transport purposes for the purposes of s34(1)(c). These are the transport of controlled waste (i) between different places within the same premises, or (ii) to a place in Great Britain from a country or territory outside Great Britain, not previously having been there, and (iii) from a place in Great Britain to outside Great Britain.

s34(4A) EPA 1990 defines the transfer of waste in stages. This is (i) when the first transfer takes place and (ii) when there is a series of transfers between the same parties of the same sort of waste, in that case the transfer occurs when the first in the series happens.

s34 (5) introduces the *Environmental Protection (Duty of Care) Regulations* 1991

4.2.8.7 Definitions

'Brokers' are those who have control of waste. Their *'duty of care'* may be said to reach to the extent of the control they exercise.

4.2.8.8 Offence

s34(6) EPA 1990: Any person who fails to comply with the duty imposed by s34(1) or with any requirement imposed under s34(5) above shall be liable:

> (a) on summary conviction, to a fine not exceeding the statutory maximum; and
> (b) on conviction on indictment, to a fine [unlimited].

Note that there is no penal sanction here, because the purpose of this section is to punish a company rather than the individual.

4.2.8.9 s175 Offences by bodies corporate

> (1) Where an offence under any provision of this Act committed by a body corporate is proved to have been committed with the consent or connivance of, or to have been attributable to any neglect on the part of, any director, manager, secretary or other similar officer of the body corporate or a person who was purporting to act in any such capacity, he as well as the body corporate shall be guilty of that offence and shall be liable to be proceeded against and punished accordingly.
>
> (2) Where the affairs of a body corporate are managed by its members, subsection (1) above shall apply in relation to the acts or defaults of a member in connection with his functions of management as if he were a director of the body corporate.

This important section gives effect to the extension of corporate criminal liability to include directors and officers of the company who have consented to or connived in the commission of an offence and it has effect not only for offences under EPA 1990 but also offences under the Waste Management Licensing Regulations 1994. In *Woodhouse v Walsall MBC* [1994] Env. LR, the question arose of the degree or existence of a manager's power or responsibility. The test appears to be whether the manager concerned has the power or responsibility to decided corporate policy and strategy. This will probably be a difficult test to satisfy below board level.

4.2.8.10 General note

Offences under Parts I,II,IV,VI, etc, due to others' fault

s158 EPA 1990: By this section, where a person commits an offence under Parts I,II,IV,VI or sections 140, 141, 142, due to the act or default of another, then that other person may be charged with and convicted of an offence, whether or not the first person has been charged.

4.2.8.11 Sentencing

In *Environment Agency v UK Waste Management* (Ends Report, January 1997), the defendant company picked up a consignment of waste which was described on the transfer note by the producer as 'dry solid waste and cleansing rags contaminated with solvent'. The consignment, later deposited at the Joint Stocks Quarry landfill, was found to have generated a large liquid spill. This contained viscous resins which had properties rendering them as special waste. The company pleaded guilty to breaching the 'duty of care', having failed to provide an accurate description of the waste. It was fined £1,000.

In *Environment Agency v K A Davies and Sons Ltd,* (ELM Report) July 1998, the defendant company, a waste landfill company, pleaded guilty to insufficient control of the dust generated by vehicles using their site, which was adjacent to a mobile home park and other dwellings. It also pleaded guilty to insufficient management of a well, designed to catch dangerous and polluting leachate from a landfill site, which was a breach of the conditions of its licence. It was fined a total of £4,000 and ordered to pay costs.

In *Environment Agency v Adair Construction* (ELM July 1998) the EA prosecuted both the company, Adair Construction, and one of its directors, Robert Simpkin, under s33(1)(a) and s44(1)(a) EPA1990. The company had contracted to excavate a basement on a housing development, removing 1,500 tonnes of chalk and depositing it on an an adjacent site, half burying a number of trees. The planning authority then issued an enforcement notice to restore the site to its original condition. Robert Simpkin then applied for an exemption under the Waste Management Licensing Regulations 1994, on the grounds that the excavation waste was to be used for the construction of the A16 Peaks Parkway Roadbuilding Scheme. An EA officer who attended the site found that a hole had been dug on the plot, the newly-excavated chalk was going to the rebuilding scheme and the hole was then being filled with the old excavation waste. The waste had become contaminated with soil and was therefore unsuitable for the scheme. The company was fined £3,000 and Mr Simpkin £1,500 at Caistor Magistrates Court in March, 1998.

In *Environment Agency v Premiere Environmental* (Ends Report, June 1998), the facts were that the defendant company, which treats waste using a distillation process, had deposited two lorry-loads of residue from the process at a landfill site in Sheffield. When a compactor drove into the material, a blue-tinged cloud appeared. This caused the driver of the lorry to suffer streaming eyes. When the company was tried, at Sheffield Crown Court, the judge ruled that whilst there was insufficient proof that the incident had caused pollution, the waste had been wrongly described, but the company pleaded guilty to two breaches of its 'duty of care' (s34 EPA1990) by wrongly describing the waste. Premiere Environmental was fined £1,500 for the first offence, £4,500 for the second, with £12,500 in costs.

4.3 Waste Management - The Duty of Care: A Code of Practice

The code of practice issued by the Secretary of State should be consulted in any impending proceedings. Whilst *Waste Management: the Duty of Care: a Code of Practice* is not legally binding, it is admissible in evidence and will be taken into account by the court. The duty of care is described therein as 'an essentially self-regulating system which is based on good business practice'. Sections in the Code deal with the identification and description of the controlled waste, keeping it safely, transferring it to the right person and receiving it. There are checklists for waste after transfer, after receipt and when there may be causes for concern. Advice is given on the circumstances when expert help may be required, in analysing, describing and handling waste, choosing a destination for the substance and getting help from the relevant authorities. At the end of the Code is a summary, if not exhaustive checklist of the main steps to be taken towards exercising the duty of care.

4.3.1 Section 7 of the Code: The duty of care and scrap metal

Scrap metal became a controlled waste substance for the purposes of the duty of care on October 1st, 1995. In *DoE Circular* 6/95/2 the Secretary of State indicated that WRAs should:

(a) have regard to the fact that scrap metal recovery and waste motor vehicle dismantling are a source of benefit to the environment and sustainable development;
(b) strike an appropriate balance between advice and encouragement and regulation and legal enforcement; and
(c) distinguish between and act proportionately in relation to (i) 'technical' breaches of the Regulations, the 1994 Regulations or Part II of the 1990 Act where there is no threat of pollution to the environment or harm to human health; and (ii) breaches which do give rise to such a threat. In the former case, the WRA's main aim should be to ensure that the person responsible is made aware of his legal responsibilities and that steps are taken by the authority or the person concerned to prevent the commission of any further 'technical' offences.

At the time of writing, a very high proportion of metal-recycling sites have registered neither as such nor for an exemption and a programme of renewed enforcement is anticipated.

4.3.2 Waste management licences

The detailed provisions which determine the circumstances in which a waste management licence is required are at s35 EPA 1990. Exceptions to this requirement are listed in the Waste Management Licensing Regulations, Schedule 3. It is outside the ambit of this chapter to discuss the provisions at length: it is the case that a waste-management licence is generally required for the treatment, keeping or disposal of controlled waste at a land site or by means of a mobile plant. Stringent conditions may be attached to the licence. A licence may only be granted to a person who is a fit and proper person.

4.3.2.1 Definition

s74 EPA 1990: Meaning of *'fit and proper person'*

An application for a waste management licence may be refused either (i) because planning permission has not been granted for that particular use of the landor (ii) on the grounds that the applicant is not a *fit and proper person* to hold the licence. The grounds on which the WRA may come to that conclusion are:

(1) s74(3)(a) EPA 1990: "that he or another relevant person has been convicted of a relevant offence."

The list of *'relevant offences'* is to be found in the Waste Management Licensing Regulations 1994, Reg.3. An offence under the Finance Act 1996 (FA 1996) Schedule 5 is also a 'relevant offence', although the circumstances of the case may be such that the WRA may still deem someone to be fit and proper, notwithstanding a conviction he may have. A *'relevant person'* in this context may be an employee of the applicant, or an employee, director, manager, secretary or officer of a company which has been convicted of a relevant offence.

(2) s74(3)(b) EPA 1990: "that the management of the activities will not be in the hands of a technically competent person."

The more specific licensing requirements of technical competence are set out in the Waste Management Regulations 1994, Reg. 4 and 5. These will include (a) a certificate of technical competence from the Waste Management Industry Training and Advisory Board (WAMITAB), and (b) for older people (55 years old or over, on 10th August 1994) a period of at least five years' experience in the past ten as the manager of a facility listed in Table 1 of the Regulations. *The five- year transitional period for this requirement concludes in August, 1999.* The present situation appears to be that very few people have applied for the WAMITAB certificate, which becomes an *obligatory requirement for a licence application from that date*. Where a site operator does not have a certificate of competence, then noncompliance may result in the partial suspension of the licence. A further requirement envisaged by the EA will be that a company employs a sufficient number of technically competent persons to operate the facility.

(3) s74(3)(c) EPA 1990: "the licence holder has no intention of making or is not in a position to make financial provision adequate to discharge the obligations arising from the licence."

Guidance on what constitutes adequate financial provision is to be found in 'Licensing of Waste Management Facilities', Waste Management Paper No. 4 (Chapter 3) produced by the DoE in 1994.

4.3.2.2 Offences concerning the provision of information

s35(7) EPA 1990: The Secretary of State may, as respects any licence for which an application is made to a WRA, give to the authority directions as to the terms and conditions which are, or are not, to be included in the licence; and it shall be the duty of the authority to give effect to the directions.

s35(7A) EPA 1990: In a case where:

(a) an entry is required under this subsection to be made in any record as to the observance of any condition of a licence, and
(b) the entry has not been made

that fact shall be admissible as evidence that that condition has not been observed.

s35(7B) EPA 1990: Any person who:

(a) intentionally makes a false entry in any record required to be kept under any condition of a licence or
(b) with intent to deceive, forges or uses a licence or makes or has in his possession a document so closely resembling a licence as to be likely to deceive,

shall be guilty of an offence.

s35(7C) EPA 1990: A person guilty of an offence under ss7B above shall be liable -

(a) on summary conviction, to a fine not exceeding the statutory maximum;
(b) on conviction on indictment, to a fine or to imprisonment for a term not exceeding two years, or to both.

(These sections were added to the Act by the EA 1995.)

4.3.2.3 Offences concerning the revocation and suspension of licences

s38 EPA 1990: Revocation and suspension of licences

This section gives the WRA the powers to revoke a licence in certain circumstances. It may be revoked entirely, or only in respect of certain processes. The nature and degree of the revocation depends upon the grounds on which the revocation is made.

s38(6) EPA 1990: Where a licence granted by a WRA is in force and it appears to the authority:

(a) that the holder of the licence has ceased to be a fit and proper person by reason of the management of the activities authorised by the licence having ceased to be in the hands of a technically competent person; or
(b) that serious pollution of the environment or serious harm to human health has resulted from, or is about to be caused by, the activities to which the licence relates or the happening or threatened happening of an event affecting those activities; and
(c) that the continuing to carry on those activities, or any of those activities, in the circumstances will continue or, as the case may be, cause serious pollution of the environment or serious harm to human health

the authority may suspend the licence so far as it authorises the carrying on of the activities specified in the licence or such of them as the authority specifies in suspending the licence.

s38(9) EPA 1990: Where a licence is suspended under s38(6), the authority, in suspending it or at any time while it is suspended, may require the holder of the licence to take such measures to deal with or avert the pollution or harm as the authority considers necessary.

s38(10) EPA 1990: A person who, without reasonable excuse, fails to comply with any requirement imposed under s38(9) above, otherwise than in relation to special waste, shall be liable:

(a) on summary conviction, to a fine of an amount not exceeding the statutory maximum; and
(b) on conviction on indictment, to imprisonment for a term not exceeding two years, or a fine, or both.

s38(11) EPA 1990: A person who, without reasonable excuse, fails to comply with any requirement imposed under s38(9) above in relation to special waste, shall be liable;

(a) on summary conviction, to imprisonment for a term not exceeding six months, or a fine not exceeding the statutory maximum, or both; and
(b) on conviction on indictment, to imprisonment for a term not exceeding five years, or a fine, or both.

In the *Environment Agency v K Collier* (Ends Report, September 1998), the defendant had persistently flouted his licence conditions, by tipping noninert, biodegradable wastes on the site, for which he had already been prosecuted a number of times during the 1980s. He had also exceeded the contours which had been defined in his planning consent. In 1990, his licence was revoked by Swansea City Council. The defendant continued to trade, however, under a variety of different names. The EA then conducted a surveillance operation which showed that in spite of the defendant's denials, business was still being done. His VAT returns also indicated that his business was active. The defendant was then charged with 61 offences in respect of illegal tipping between 1994-97. Having originally pleaded not guilty, he then pleaded guilty at Swansea Crown Court in September, 1998. He was sentenced to four months' imprisonment (suspended for two years) and fined £5,000. Other measures were imposed, under the Powers of Criminal Courts Act 1973 (PCCA 1973): Mr Collier's vehicle fleet was confiscated, as was the tracked machine used on the site. There are no plans to remove the waste, because the costs, estimated at £3m, would be prohibitive. However, the site will be monitored by the EA, to investigate leachate in the stream and to assess the need for remediation.

4.3.2.4 Disclaimer of licence

A recent case, *Environment Agency v Stout* (Ends Report, 30 April 1998) considered the question of whether a waste-management licence could not be disclaimed as 'property' under s178 Insolvency Act 1986 (IA 1986). This case has important ramifications where companies holding waste licences fall into receivership. The case concerned a company, Mineral Resources Ltd, which held a waste-management licence subject to conditions which related to control of leachate and gas, as well as ongoing monitoring following the capping of a landfill. A short lease on the site was followed by the company ceasing to trade. The insolvency practitioner Stout was appointed as liquidator of the company in September, 1997. As Stout sought to transfer the licence to other companies seeking a fresh lease of the site, it became clear that some parties thought that negotiation of the licence for the site might produce less onerous conditions, whereupon Stout sought to disclaim the licence under s178 IA 1986. The EA sought a declaration from the High Court that the liquidator had no power to disclaim the licence on the grounds that it did not constitute property for the purposes of the 1986 Act, or that if it did constitute property, its disclaimer was excluded by s35(11) EPA 1990. Mr Justice Neuberger ruled that a waste-management licence could constitute property under the definition of the 1986 Act. He held that a licence was transferable under s40 EPA 1990 and as such could be described as '*intangible property*' with a clear value. He preferred the definition under the EPA 1990, not only because it was the latest in time but also because the protection of the environment should prevail. If the licence were construed other than through the EPA, then the EA might be in difficulties proving 'loss or damage' according to s178(6) IA 1986, so as to rank as a creditor. This would have implications for clean-up costs under s42 EPA 1990, as well as potential implications for the personal liability of the directors of the company, under s157 EPA 1990 or the liquidator. Where the company has been wound up and there is a breach of the licence condition, it is not yet clear who would be liable.

There remains a certain inconsistency in the sentencing patterns which emerge in different parts of the country but the basis for a consistency of approach now exists.

Note that the convictions for offences in connection with special waste carry higher penalties than those in respect of controlled waste. Note also that in s38(13) EPA 1990, there are now provisions for enforcing compliance in the High Court where the WRA takes the view that criminal proceedings will be an ineffectual remedy.

4.3.2.5 s44 EPA 1990: Offences of making false statements

This section determines the penalties for convictions which arise out of making false statements in connection with licences.

> A person who, in an application for a licence, for a modification of the conditions of a licence or for the surrender or transfer of a licence, makes any statement which he knows to be false in a material particular or recklessly makes any statement which is false in a material particular shall be liable:
>
> (a) on summary conviction, to a fine not exceeding the statutory maximum, and
> (b) on conviction on indictment, to imprisonment for a term not exceeding two years, or to a fine, or both.

4.3.2.6 Collection of waste

ss46, 47 EPA 1990 legislate for the collection of household waste and commercial or industrial waste respectively, to be collected by the appropriate Waste Collection Authority (WCA). The WCA is entitled to require conditions to be met in respect of the provision of receptacles for the collection. If the requirement (which must be made on notice) is thought to be unreasonable, then it may be appealed in the Crown Court. However, a person's failure to comply with a requirement renders him liable to prosecution, under s46(6) or s47(6) EPA 1990, and summary conviction may lead to a fine not exceeding level three on the standard scale.

4.3.2.7 s57 EPA 1990: Secretary of State's power to require waste to be accepted, treated, disposed of or delivered

> s57(1) EPA 1990: The Secretary of State may, by notice in writing, direct the holder of any waste-management licence to accept and keep, or accept and treat or dispose of, controlled waste at specified places on specified terms.
>
> s57(2) EPA 1990: The Secretary of State may, by notice in writing, direct any person who is keeping controlled waste on any land to deliver the waste to a specified person on specified terms with a view to its being treated or disposed of by that other person.

4.3.2.8 Offence

> A person who fails, without reasonable excuse, to comply with a direction under this section shall be liable on summary conviction to a fine not exceeding level five on the standard scale.

Note that compliance with a direction under this section is a defence in a prosecution brought against a person under any other section of this Act.

4.3.2.9 s59 EPA 1990: Powers to require removal of waste unlawfully deposited

This section empowers both WRAs and WCAs to deal with the unlawful deposit of controlled waste. Note that the lodging of an appeal results in the suspension of the requirement which is the subject of the appeal.

> s59(1) EPA 1990: If any controlled waste is deposited in or on any land in the area of a WRA or WCA in contravention of section 33(1) above, the authority may, by notice served the occupier require him to do either or both of the following:
>
> (a) to remove the waste from the land within a specified period not less than a period of 21 days beginning with the service of the notice;

(b) to take within such a period specified steps with a view to eliminating or reducing the consequences of the deposit of the waste.

4.3.2.10 Offence

s59(5) EPA 1990:

> If a person on whom a requirement imposed under ss(1) above fails, without reasonable excuse, to comply with the requirement, he shall be liable, on summary conviction, to a fine not exceeding level five on the standard scale and to a further fine of an amount equal to one-tenth of level five on the standard scale for each day on which the failure continues after conviction of the offence and before the authority has begun to exercise its powers under s59(6) EPA 1990. [Powers of the authority to comply, in certain circumstances immediately, with the requirement, and to recover expenses for doing so.]

Note that, under 59(3) EPA 1990, the recipient of the requirement notice may appeal, on the grounds that he did not deposit the waste or that he did not knowingly cause or knowingly permit the deposit of waste.

He may also appeal on the grounds that the notice contains a material defect. In *Berridge Incinerators v Notts CC*, the conviction for failure to comply with a notice was overturned, on the grounds that the notice was unreasonable and unfair.

4.3.2.11 s60 EPA 1990: Interference with waste sites/receptacles

This section creates the offence of sorting or disturbing any waste deposited either at a site for deposit, or in a receptacle for waste, without the relevant consent. (It is a corresponding offence to do so in Scotland.)

4.3.2.12 Offence

s60(3) EPA 1990: A person who contravenes this section above shall be liable on summary conviction to a fine of an amount not exceeding level three on the standard scale.

4.3.2.13 s62 EPA 1990: Special provision with respect to certain dangerous or intractable waste

This section empowers the Secretary of State to regulate for the treatment, keeping or disposal of 'special waste'. The regulatory powers, outlined at s62(1), which are laid out in the Special Waste Regulations 1996 (SI 1996 No. 972), are wide-ranging. They include provision for the following:

4.3.2.14 Offence

s62(1)(g) EPA 1990:

> a contravention of the regulations shall be an offence and prescribing the maximum penalty for the offence, which shall not exceed, on summary conviction, a fine at level five on the standard scale and on conviction on indictment, imprisonment for a term of two years, or a fine, or both. (see above, on definition of 'special waste.')

4.3.2.15 s63 EPA 1990: Waste other than controlled waste

This section addresses the management of waste from mines, quarries and certain types of agricultural waste. The Secretary of State may regulate for the sort of controls to be exercised over this sort of waste which would be available if the waste had been classified as 'special waste' deposited without a licence.

4.3.2.16 Offences

s63(2) EPA 1990:

> A person who:
>
> (a) deposits any waste other than controlled waste, or
> (b) knowingly causes or knowingly permits the deposit of any waste other than controlled waste in a case where, if the waste were special waste and any waste-management licence were not in force, he would be guilty of an offence under section 33(9) above shall, subject to ss(3)below [being that the act was done in accordance with a consent, licence, approval or authority], be guilty of that offence and punishable accordingly.

4.3.2.17 s71 EPA 1990: Obtaining information from persons and authorities

Either the Secretary of State or the WRA is empowered by this section to request by notice in writing any information which they reasonably consider that they need, in a time specified by the notice.

4.3.2.18 Offence

s71(3) EPA 1990:

> A person who:
>
> (a) fails, without reasonable excuse, to comply with a requirement imposed under ss(2) . . .
> shall be liable
> (i) on summary conviction, to a fine not exceeding the statutory maximum,
> (ii)on conviction on indictment, to a fine, or to imprisonment for a term not exceeding two years, or to both.

4.4 Control of Pollution Act 1974 (COPA 1974)

Offences under COPA 1974 in respect of disposal of waste, (s3 COPA 1974) have generally been subsumed by the corresponding sections in EPA1990. The offences in COPA 1974 have been left on the statute book for the purpose of dealing with the exceptional or transitional situation. It is not proposed to deal with the relevant provisions of COPA 1974 in this section, because criminal proceedings in respect of waste offences are now generally commenced under EPA 1990. COPA 1974 will gradually cease to apply. At present, any outstanding application made for a disposal licence under COPA will become subject to the EPA 1990 licensing system as soon as the licence is granted. Where an appeal against a revocation of a COPA 1974 disposal licence is pending, the EPA 1990 will apply on the determination of the appeal, or its withdrawal, or when time runs out. The legislative provisions determining the transition of the waste-management licencing system from COPA to EPA are to be found in s77 EPA 1990.

CHAPTER 5

CONTAMINATED LAND

CONTENTS

CHAPTER 5

CONTAMINATED LAND

5.1 Introduction

The new regime for dealing with contaminated land was put in place by s57 EA 1995. The legislation has had a troubled passage through Parliament. At the outset, local authorities (LAs) were required to compile a register of sites they regarded as having been subjected to contaminative use. Concerns were then expressed that this sort of information would have a negative effect upon an already depressed property market. The proposal for registers was then dropped. The amendments to the proposed regime mitigated the effects of the regime which was originally planned, but there nevertheless remains a regime which amounts to strict and retroactive liability for previous or historic contamination. It contains complex issues of liability for the current landowner or occupier and for others. The questions of the extent and the apportionment of liability are to be the subject of government guidelines which have not yet been produced. There are a huge number of issues which remain to be resolved and which are generally outside the scope of this work. The sections of EPA 1990 which address this area of the law have not yet entered into force, other than to give the Secretary of State his powers to make regulations or orders, issue the appropriate guidelines, or make provisions with respect to the exercise of any of his powers.

Draft regulations and statutory guidance were circulated in late 1996 and generally approved by the Secretary of State a year later. The implications of costs implications which gave cause for concern to LAs have now been examined and the Government has announced that funds will be available for staffing, land remediation and Agency costs of implementation. Special site regulations will be introduced. The guidance will include definitions of contaminated land, information for a clean-up to a 'suitable-to -use standard', detailed consideration of the appropriate persons, available exemptions from liability, as well as guidance on remediation-costs, apportionment of the cost between parties and questions of cost-recovery for LAs including possible exemptions on hardship grounds.

It is expected that the regulations and statutory guidance will become law in July, 1999.

5.2 Definitions

s78 A EPA 1990 contains the definitions of the terms used in the ensuing sections, explicitly or by reference to those subsections in which the terms appear. Some of these are set out below.

s78A(2) 1990: *'Contaminated land'* is any land which appears to the LA in whose area it is situated to be in such condition, by reason of substances in, on or under the land that

(a) significant harm is being caused or there is a significant possibility of such harm being caused; or
(b) pollution of controlled waters is being, or is likely to be caused.

[The authority must then act in accordance with guidance issued by the Secretary of State with respect to the manner in which that determination is to be made.]

s78 A (3) EPA 1990: A *'special site'* is any contaminated land

(a) which has been designated as such by virtue of section 78C(7)or 78D(6) EPA 1990, and
(b) whose designation as such has not been terminated by the appropriate Agency.

s78(4) EPA 1990: *'Harm'* means harm to the health of living organisms or other interference with the ecological systems of which they form part and, in the case of man, includes harm to his property.

s78(5) EPA 1990: The questions

(a) what harm is to be regarded as *'significant'*;
(b) whether the possibility of significant harm being caused is *'significant'*
(c) whether pollution of controlled waters is being, or is likely to be caused

shall be determined in accordance with guidance issued for the purpose by the Secretary of State

[The scope within the guidelines is very wide for assessing the different degrees of importance to be assigned to descriptions of living organisms, ecosystems, places, harm to health or property or other interference, or degrees of varying significance.]

s78 A (7) EPA 1990: *'Remediation'* means:

(a) the doing of anything for the purpose of assessing the condition of:
   (i) the contaminated land in question
   (ii) any controlled waters affected by that land;
   (iii) any land adjoining or adjacent to that land;
(b) the doing of any works, the carrying out of any operations or the taking of any steps in relation to any such land or waters for the purpose:
   (i) of preventing or minimising, or remedying or mitigating the effects of any significant harm, or any pollution of controlled waters, by reason of which the contaminated land is such land; or
   (ii) of restoring the land or waters to their former state; or
(c) the making of subsequent inspections from time to time for the purpose of keeping under review the condition of the land or waters.

5.3 Identification

The first stage in the procedure for the management of contaminated land is to identify that the land in question is contaminated. s78 B EPA 1990 lays a duty upon the LA to inspect its area from time to time, to identify contaminated land and to determine whether it should be treated as a 'special site'.

5.4 Notification

If the LA concludes that a piece of land is indeed contaminated, it then has a duty to notify the appropriate agency, the owner of the land, any person who appears to the authority to be in occupation of the whole or part of the land and any person who appears to the authority to be appropriate. s78 C EPA 1990 further requires the LA to determine whether the site is a 'special site' and if it is so then to notify the relevant persons of that determination. This group of persons corresponds to the group at s78 B EPA 1990. Once designated as a 'special site', by reference to the regulations provided at s78 C (8) EPA 1990 (as yet not provided), the contaminated land then becomes the responsibility of the EA, which becomes the enforcing authority. s78 D EPA 1990 provides for an appeal to the Secretary of State where there is disagreement between the LA and the EA over the determination of the land.

5.5 Duty to require remediation

Where a LA has determined that land is contaminated, by virtue of s78(E) EPA 1990, it then has a duty to serve a remediation notice upon the appropriate person. The remediation notice may also be served upon different, appropriate persons and may require different things to be done by way of remediation. The notice must specify what must be done. Where more than one person is served with the notice in respect of the same requirements for remediation, the proportionate costs to be borne by the parties of the remediation must be set out. The methods of remediation must be 'reasonable'. What is reasonable is to be determined by reference to the costs which will be incurred and the seriousness of the harm or pollution of controlled waters which is in question. Once more, these issues will be the subject matter of guidance not yet forthcoming from the Secretary of State.

5.6 Determination of the appropriate person on whom notice should be served

The appropriate person is defined at s78 F EPA 1990 as being the person who *caused* or *knowingly permitted* the substances to contaminate the land. That person is only appropriate to the extent that the remediation relates to substances which he *caused or knowingly permitted* to contaminate the land. This is a complex issue, because there may be many different persons responsible for the compound contamination of a site. Where the identity of the person responsible for the contamination is unknown, then the onus for remediation falls upon the owner or occupier of the land in question. Guidance will be issued as to the method of determination of a person's appropriateness where more than one person is responsible for the contamination. This section lies at the heart of the difficulties that there have been in establishing the regulations and guidance for the management and remediation of contaminated land. Not surprisingly, the question of joint and several liability arising where there is historic contamination is a very complex one. At s78 F (10) EPA 1990, provision is made for remedial action to be taken by a person only in proportion to the contribution he has made to the contamination of the site and only by reference to the quantity of the substance which has caused the contamination. s78(G) EPA 1990 gives rights of entry where none previously existed for a person to enter on to the land and other rights which that person needs to exercise to effect remediation.

5.7 Consultation

The enforcing authority is under a duty from s78 H EPA 1990 to consult the appropriate persons when determining what remediation of contaminated land is to be effected. A period of three months must generally pass before a remediation notice may be served (eg. between the time of the identification of the contaminated land and three months after a notification of the determination has been served upon the appropriate persons). Where land has been determined as a 'special site', a remediation notice may not be served until three months after the date of notification, or, if appropriate, three months after the date when a dispute over the determination has been resolved by the Secretary of State. However, where the land is in a condition which poses imminent danger of serious harm or serious pollution of controlled waters, then the enforcing authority may serve a remediation notice which does not take account of this requirement.

There are circumstances in which the enforcing authority is precluded from serving a remediation notice, namely when there is nothing by way of remediation which could be specified in a notice, when the authority is satisfied that remediation is already being effected, when the authority would simply be serving a notice on itself, or when the authority has powers to effect remediation which are sufficient. In those circumstances, a 'remediation declaration may be produced by the authority, outlining what it would have specified in a remediation notice, and the grounds on which it has not served one. Where a remediation notice has been precluded, then the responsible person must produce a remediation statement, which will be a record of what remediation is being effected, by whom, and within what period. Failure to produce such a statement within a reasonable time after the notice entitles the authority to prepare and publish such a statement itself, and recover the costs of doing so.

5.8 Restrictions on liability relating to the pollution of controlled waters

According to s78 J EPA 1990, a remediation notice may only be served upon the owner of land or waters where the original polluter cannot be found on the basis of the general harm provisions contained within the definition of contamination. The owner may not be required to do anything which he could not have been required to do if the part of the definition of contamination referring to water pollution did not exist. A similar exemption exists in respect of a person who permits water from an abandoned mine to enter controlled waters. This exemption will cease to apply in future to owners of mines which became abandoned after December 31st 1999.

5.9 Liability in respect of escaping contaminated substances

By s78 K EPA 1990, liability attaches to the person who originally caused or knowingly permitted a substance to contaminate land and the same liability follows that person when the substance spills over onto other land. The owner of the other land will not be liable, or served with a remediation notice unless he himself is complicit, by either causing or knowingly permitting that substance to spill over. The interpretation of *'caused'* and *'knowingly permitted'* is likely to give rise to complications for the same reasons that apportionment of liability is a complex matter, a full discussion of which is outside the immediate ambit of criminal liability. Guidance on the issue of liability will be of considerable assistance in this area.

5.10 Appeals against remediation notices

The law governing an appeal against a remediation notice, at s78 L EPA 1990 determines that an appeal may be lodged within 21 days from the day when the notice was served. The appeal from a local authority is to the Magistrates Court, and from the Agency, to the Secretary of State. At present, the grounds of appeal have not been regulated for. Note that the regulations will make provision for an appeal on the grounds that the remediation notice should have been served on another person. It will also make, *inter alia,* provisions for the particulars to be included in a notice of appeal and provisions for different cases or classes of case.

5.11 Offence

> s78 M (1) EPA 1990: If a person on whom an enforcing authority serves a remediation notice fails, without reasonable excuse,to comply with any of the requirements of the notice, he shall be guilty of an offence.

> On summary conviction for this offence, the defendant is liable to a fine not exceeding level five on the standard scale, and to a further fine of an amount equal to one-tenth of level five on the standard scale for each day on which the failure continues after conviction of the offence and before the enforcing authority has begun to exercise its powers.

Note that the penalties for this offence when it concerns contaminated land which is an industrial, trade or business premises are far higher - not exceeding £20,000, or a greater sum if the Secretary of State has ordered, with a continuing penalty of one-tenth of the sum for each day that the failure continues after the conviction of the offence and before the authority has begun to exercise its own powers. There is also a provision at s78(M)(5) EPA 1990 for the enforcing authority to take recourse to the High Court to ensure compliance with the requirements of the remediation notice.

5.12 Defences

It will be sufficient for the defendant to prove that the only reason why he has not complied with the notice is that another defendant who was bearing a proportion of the costs of the requirements for remediation either refused or was unable to bear that share of the proportion of the costs. Commentators have suggested that lack of funds will not constitute reasonable excuse. Other defences, such as reliance upon the advice of an expert or access to land for remedial purposes, are not certain of success.

5.12.1 Special sites

Where a special site has been determined, then the Agency may adopt the remediation notice, if one has been served by the LA. The Agency will thus continue to inspect the site and subsequently redesignate it.

5.13 Recovery of costs

The Agency is entitled by s78 P EPA 1990, subject to any hardship it may cause, or to any guidance the Secretary of State may issue, to recover its costs of remediation, by serving on the appropriate person a charge notice, specifying the costs, with interest. The person may appeal against the notice to a County Court within 21 days. The Court may confirm, modify or nullify the notice.

Note that by s78 Y B EPA 1990, conflict between contaminated land regulations and other forms of environmental regulation is avoided. In respect of IPC and LAPC, contamination should be addressed under the powers of s27 EPA 1990 (the power of the enforcing authority to remedy harm).

In respect of Waste-management Licences, contaminated land regulations will only be used when the harm or pollution has been caused other than by a breach of licence conditions, or the activities which are licenced to carry on. The issue of joint liability may arise where the site is contaminated by a previous owner or occupier. Also, where a deposit has been made unlawfully, the appropriate powers to deal with the deposit will normally be found in s59 EPA 1990. Finally, a remediation notice may not include any requirement which would either restrict or prevent the making of a consented discharge to controlled waters.

See also:

> s59 EPA 1990
> s79 EPA 1990
> s215 TCPA 1990
> s161 WRA 1991.

CHAPTER 6

RADIOACTIVE SUBSTANCES

CONTENTS

CHAPTER 6

RADIOACTIVE SUBSTANCES

6.1 Introduction

The dangers and the longevity of effects associated with environmental exposure to radioactive materials have been the catalyst for the development of a comprehensive legislative and detailed regulatory regime. This level of coverage reflects concern over public health and safety, especially in the light of the well-publicised nuclear accidents at Chernobyl and of the global opposition to nuclear testing.

The domestic legislation promotes strict regulatory requirements and institutionalised supervision, primarily in the form of compulsory registration and authorisation for radioactive-associated activities.

6.2 Nuclear Installations Act 1965 (NIA 1965)

Beyond the criminal elements of this legislation, it is also important to note that civil liability[1*] for personal injury or property damage may ensue from breaches of duty owed by the licensee of a licensed site. Liability is strict and damage is such that results from the radioactive, toxic, explosive or hazardous properties of nuclear matter.[2] Further, the right to compensation in respect of a breach of duty and the bringing and satisfaction of a claim is dealt with in detail at Sections 10-16 NIA 1965.

6.2.1 Definitions per s26(1) NIA 1965

'the authority': UK Atomic Energy Authority (UKAEA)
'the Minister': in the UK, the Minister of Power; in Scotland, the Secretary of State.

6.2.1.1 s1 NIA 1965: Restriction of certain nuclear installations to licensed sites

> (1) . . . no person . . . shall use any site for the purpose of installing or operating :
>
> (a) any nuclear reactor (other than such a reactor comprised in a means of transport, whether by land, water or air); or

* Endnotes, see page 187.

(b) subject to subsection (2), any other installations of such class or description as may be prescribed, being an installation designed or adapted for:

(i) the production or use of atomic energy
(ii) the carrying out of any process . . . preparatory or ancillary to the production or use of atomic energy and which involves or is capable of the emission of ionising radiations; or
(iii) the storage, processing or disposal of nuclear fuel or of bulk quantities of other radioactive matter . . .
unless a licence . . . (nuclear site licence) has been granted in respect of that site by the Health and Safety Executive and is . . . in force

(3) Any person who contravenes subsection (1) . . . shall be guilty of an offence . . . and be liable:

(a) on summary conviction, to a fine not exceeding £500
(b) on conviction on indictment, to a fine not exceeding £500, or to imprisonment . . . not exceeding five years, or to both.

6.2.1.2 s2 NIA 1965: Prohibition of certain operations except under permit

(1) Notwithstanding that a nuclear site licence is . . . in force, no person other than the Authority shall use any site:

(a) for any treatment of irradiated matter which involves the extraction . . . of plutonium or uranium; or
(b) for any treatment of uranium such as to increase the proportion of isotope 235 contained therein;
except under, and in accordance with the terms of a permit in writing . . . granted by the Authority or a government department; and any fissile material produced under such a permit shall be disposed of only in such a manner as may be approved by the authority by whom the permit was granted:

(1A) A permit . . . unless granted by the Minister, shall not authorise the use of a site for purposes other than . . . research and development

(2) any person who contravenes subsection (1) shall be guilty of an offence . . . and be liable ;

(a) on summary conviction, to a fine not exceeding [the prescribed sum], or to imprisonment . . . not exceeding three months, or to both; or

(b) on conviction on indictment, to a fine not exceeding £500, or to imprisonment . . . not exceeding five years, or to both.

6.2.1.3 s4 NIA 1965: Attachment of conditions to licences

(1) The Health and Safety Executive, on granting any nuclear site licence, may from time to time thereafter, attach to the licence such conditions as may appear . . . necessary or desirable in the interests of safety . . .

(5) At all times while a nuclear licence remains in force, the licensee shall cause copies of any conditions . . . to be kept posted at the site . . . in such characters . . . and positions as to be conveniently read by persons having duties . . . which are or may be affected by those conditions.

(6) Any person who contravenes subsection (5) . . . and any contravention of any condition attached to a nuclear site licence . . . shall be guilty of an offence and be liable:

(a) on summary conviction, to a fine not exceeding £100, or to imprisonment . . . not exceeding three months, or to both; or

(b) on conviction on indictment, to a fine not exceeding £500, or to imprisonment . . . not exceeding five years, or to both;

and any person who without reasonable cause pulls down, injures or defaces any document posted in pursuance of . . . subsection (5) shall be guilty of an offence and be liable on summary conviction to a fine not exceeding level two on the standard scale.

6.2.1.4 s5 NIA 1965: Revocation and surrender of licences

Under this section, the licensee is obliged to comply with a request from the Health and Safety Executive (HSE) for the delivering up of the licence where a nuclear-site licence has been revoked or surrendered. Subsequent to such a revocation, the licensee may also find himself under other directions that the HSE "may think fit for preventing or giving warning of any risk of injury . . . or damage to property by ionising radiations . . ."[3]

A licensee found guilty of contravening such a direction is guilty of an offence and is liable:

(a) on summary conviction:
(i) in the case of a first offence under this subsection, to a fine not exceeding £50;
(ii) in the case of a second or subsequent offence . . . a fine not exceeding £100 and to imprisonment for a term not exceeding three months, or to both;
(b) on conviction on indictment, to a fine not exceeding £200, or to imprisonment for a term not exceeding one year, or to both.[4]

6.2.1.5 s19 NIA 1965: Special cover for licensee's liability

This section seeks to make available funds for the satisfaction of liabilities which arise under the Act's extensive civil liability provisions. The licensee is to make available, at all times, sufficient funds to ensure that any claims pursuant to the civil liability provisions are satisfied. This may take the form of insurance or 'some other means' as approved by the Minister with the consent of the Treasury.

A licensee who fails to comply with these requirements is guilty of an offence and therefore liable:

(a) on summary conviction, to a fine not exceeding the prescribed sum, or to imprisonment for a term not exceeding three months, or to both;
(b) on conviction on indictment, to a fine or to imprisonment for a term not exceeding two years, or to both.[5]

6.2.1.6 s22 NIA 1965: Reporting of and inquiries into dangerous substances

The licensee or a person with a duty with respect to the carriage of nuclear matter is responsible for informing the HSE on the occurrence of 'any such class or description as may be prescribed'[6] in regulations made by the Minister of Power and Secretary of State acting jointly.

If the occurrence is not reported, the licensee or aforementioned person is guilty of an offence and liable on summary conviction:

> (a) in the case of a first offence under this subsection, to a fine not exceeding £50;
> (b) in the case of a second or subsequent offence . . . a fine not exceeding £100 and to imprisonment for a term not exceeding three months, or to both.[7]

The reporting requirement is a necessary stage in the process by which dangerous events involving nuclear matter are investigated and made public. An inspector may be required to report on the incident and an inquiry may be initiated at the Minister's discretion.

6.2.1.7 s24 NIA 1965: Inspectors

s24(5) NIA 1965 provides a general offence for the disclosure of any information, without the Minister's consent, that is obtained in the *exercise of powers under this Act*. It carries liability:

> (a) on summary conviction to a fine not exceeding £50, or to imprisonment for a term not exceeding three months, or to both;
> (b) on conviction on indictment, to a fine not exceeding £100 or to imprisonment for a term not exceeding two years, or to both.[8]

6.2.1.8 s25 NIA 1965: General offences provision

s25(1) NIA 1965 lifts the "corporate veil". Where a body corporate is guilty of an offence that is proved to have been committed with the consent or due to the neglect of any director, manager, secretary, etc. who was purporting to act in such a capacity, that person shall be held to be guilty as well as the body corporate. This is an important provision in that s3(1) NIA 1965 of the Act provides that a "nuclear-site licence shall not be granted to any person other than a body corporate."

Further, with body-corporate convictions on indictment for offences under ss 1(3), 2(2), 4(6), 5(4) and 19(5) NIA 1965, maximum fine prescriptions do not apply and the body corporate shall be liable to a fine as the Court sees fit.

6.3 Radioactive Material (Road Transport) Act 1991 (RM[RT]A 1991)

The purpose of this legislation is to empower the Secretary of State for the making of such regulations, prohibitions, directions, investigations and enforcement notices as appear to be necessary and expedient for the prevention of harm caused by incidents arising out of the transport of radioactive material.

6.3.1 Definitions

'Radioactive material': any material having a specific activity in excess of

> "(a) 70 kilobecquerels per kilogram; or
> (b) such lesser activity as may be specified in an order made by the Secretary of State"[9]

'Transport' means transport by road."[10]

6.3.1.1 s2 RM(RT)A 1991: Regulations

The Secretary of State's power to make regulations is derived from this section and aims:

> (a) to prevent any injury to health, or any damage to property or to the environment, being caused by, or by any incident arising out of, the transport of radioactive material; and
> (b) to give effect to such international regulations . . . published by the International Atomic Energy Agency (IAEA).[11]

This power has been exercised in the form of the ***Radioactive Material (Road Transport) (GB) Regulations*** 1996 which provide detailed and strict guidance as to packaging, labelling, preparation, consignment, handling, keeping of records, placarding of vehicles, etc, for the transport of radioactive material.

Importantly, s2(4) RM(RT)A 1991 provides that 'any person who contravenes or fails to comply with any regulations under this section shall be guilty of an offence'. Liability is:

> (a) on conviction on indictment, to a fine or to imprisonment for a term not exceeding two years, or to both;
> (b) on summary conviction, to a fine not exceeding the statutory maximum, or to imprisonment for a term not exceeding two months, or to both.[12]

6.3.1.2 s3 RM(RT)A 1991: Prohibitions and directions

This section provides to an examiner or inspector the discretion to prohibit the driving of a vehicle if:

(i) it fails to comply with the *Radioactive Material (Road Transport) (GB) Regulations*, or
(ii) it has been involved in an accident, or
(iii) where the package being transported has been lost or stolen.[13]

The imposition of a prohibition may be accompanied by a written direction from the inspector or examiner for the removal of the vehicle to a place and subject to conditions as specified in the direction.[14]

Under s3(8) RM(RT)A 1991, any person who contravenes a prohibition or fails to comply with a direction shall be guilty of an offence, carrying the same liability as for a s2(4) RM(RT)A 1991 offence above.

6.3.1.3 s4 RM(RT)A 1991: Enforcement notices

Where an inspector believes that any person 'is failing or is likely to fail to comply' with the *Radioactive Material (Road Transport) (GB) Regulations* pertaining to the manufacture of packaging components, he may serve a notice under this section.

The notice will explain the inspector's belief, specify matters constituting, or likely to constitute a failure to comply with the regulations and should specify steps for the rectification of the situation.[15]

A failure to comply with this notice constitutes an offence[16] and conviction is the same as for a s2(4) RM(RT)A 1991 offence above.

6.3.1.4 s5 RM(RT)A 1991: Powers of entry

Under s5(5) RM(RT)A 1991, a person who 'intentionally obstructs any person exercising any power or warrant issued' under s5 is guilty of an offence. The penalty prescribed under s6(2) is a fine not exceeding level three on the standard scale.

The powers referred to here are set out in s5 RM(RT)A 1991 which gives the right to an inspector or examiner:

(a) to enter any vehicle used to transport radioactive packages for the purpose of ascertaining whether:
(i) the vehicle, or any radioactive package . . . being transported by it, fails to comply with the regulations under section 2;
(ii) the vehicle or . . . package . . . has been involved in an accident;
(iii) any radioactive package . . . or material . . . has been lost or stolen;
(b) to enter any premises for . . . ascertaining whether there is on the premises any vehicle used for transporting radioactive package, or any radioactive package or packaging component which fails to comply with regulations under section 2 . . . [17]

s5(2) RM(RT)A 1991 contemplates the issue of a warrant for such admission to vehicle or premises, including the use of reasonable force if necessary. Additionally, section 5(4) RM(RT)A 1991 provides for seizure of evidence based upon a reasonable belief that it is relates to an offence under section 2(4) RM(RT)A 1991.[18] An intentional obstruction of the use of these powers would constitute an offence under section 5(5) RM(RT)A 1991.

Section 5(6) RM(RT)A 1991 also creates an offence where manufacturing-process or trade-secret related information obtained through entry to vehicle or premises is disclosed, unless the disclosure was 'made in the performance of his duty'.[19] This offence carries liability under s6(3) RM(RT)A 1991:

(a) on conviction on indictment, to a fine or to imprisonment for a term not exceeding two years, or to both;
(b) on summary conviction, to a fine not exceeding the statutory maximum, or to imprisonment for a term not exceeding two months, or to both.

6.4 Radioactive Substances Act 1995 (RSA 1995)

This Act regulates the storage and use of radioactive material on premises in addition to provisions relating to the disposal and accumulation of radioactive waste. Generally, registration by the EA is necessary for the storage or use of radioactive material for commercial purposes by a person or company who believes on reasonable grounds that the material is radioactive.

6.4.1 Definitions

'Radioactive material': "a substance possessing radioactivity which is wholly or partly attributable to a process of nuclear fission or other process of subjecting a substance to bombardment by neutrons or to ionising radiations . . . "[20]

Alternatively, s1(2)(a) RSA 1995 provides for a definition that relies on the comparison of the proportion of becquerels to weight in the substance with numbers in Schedule 1 of the Act. The definition is satisfied by the requirements of either or both of s1(2)(a) and/or (b) RSA 1995.

'Radioactive waste': waste which consists wholly or partly of -

> (a) a substance or article which, if it were not waste, would be radioactive material; or
> (b) a substance or article which has been contaminated in the course of the production, keeping or use of radioactive material, or by contact with or proximity to other waste falling within paragraph (a) or this paragraph.[21]

'Mobile radioactive apparatus': any apparatus, equipment, appliance or thing which is radioactive material and:

> (a) is constructed or adapted for being transported from place to place, or
> (b) is portable and designed or intended to be used for releasing radioactive material into the environment or . . . organisms.[22]

6.4.2 Offences

The issue of criminal liability is dealt with in sections 32-38 (inclusive) of the Act. Each category of offence will be dealt with separately below.

6.4.3 s32 RSA 1995: Offences relating to registration or authorisation

The offences created by s32 RSA 1995 result in liability pursuant to subsection (2) RSA 1995:

> (a) on summary conviction, to a fine not exceeding £20,000 or to imprisonment for a term not exceeding six months, or both;
> (b) on conviction on indictment, to a fine or imprisonment for a term not exceeding five years, or both.

s32(1)(a) contravention of s6 RSA 1995:

No person shall, on any premises used by him for the purposes of an undertaking, cause or permit to be kept or used, radioactive material . . . knowing or having reasonable grounds for believing it to be radioactive material, unless

(a) he is registered. . . , or
(b) he is exempted from registration. . . , or
(c) the radioactive material. . . consists of mobile radioactive apparatus . . . registered under section 10 or is exempted from registration under that section.[23]

The wording of this section and the repetition of these terms in subsequent provisions of the Act give rise to a number of definitional considerations:

'Cause': the person 'causing' must be in a position of control over the subjectmatter.[24] This person will not be deemed to have "caused" the commission of an offence by influencing another's actions unless there is knowledge or deliberate ambivalence by the first as to the acts or omissions of the other.[25]

'Permit': permission may be expressed or implied; to permit the commission of an offence requires prior knowledge of the facts constituting the offence.[26] However, indifference as to whether an offence takes place or not is sufficient.[27] In a corporate context, this implies that someone exercising a 'directing mind over the company's affairs' had knowledge of the offence.[28]

'Knowing': this element is central to the prosecution's case. It seems to include shutting eyes to the obvious and perhaps even the failure to thoroughly investigate the matter.[29]

6.4.3.1

s32(1)(a) Contravention of s9 RSA 1995:

Where the use of a mobile radioactive apparatus involves the testing, measuring or investigating the characteristics of substances or articles or the release of radioactive material into the environment or introduction into organisms,[30] a person shall not

(a) keep, use, lend or let on hire mobile radioactive apparatus . . . , or
(b) cause mobile radioactive apparatus to be kept, used, lent or let on hire, unless registered under section 10 or exempt from registration. . .[31]

Exemptions from registration are granted by the Secretary of State under section 11 and may be subject to limitations or conditions specified in the order.

6.4.3.2

s32(1)(a) Contravention of s13(1),(2) or (3) RSA 1995:

> The disposal of radioactive waste, or causing or permitting any radioactive waste to be disposed of, if known or believed on reasonable grounds to be radioactive waste, can only be done by a person in accordance with an authorisation granted under section 16, where that waste arises from:
>
> (1) any premises used for the purposes of any undertaking carried on by him;
> (2) mobile radioactive apparatus kept by him;
> (3) the receipt of radioactive waste for the purpose of its being disposed by him.

6.4.3.3

s32(1)(a) Contravention of s14(1) RSA 1995:

> No person shall, except in accordance with an authorisation, accumulate any radioactive waste on any premises used for the purposes of an undertaking carried on by him, or cause or permit any radioactive waste to be accumulated if he knows or has reasonable grounds for believing it to be radioactive waste.

It is also important to note that under s.14(4), radioactive material produced, kept or used on any premises, and any substance arising from the production, keeping or use of that material accumulated and retained for at least three months, is presumed, unless disproved, to be radioactive waste and accumulated on the premises with a view to subsequent disposal.

6.4.4 Exemptions

(1) s14(1) RSA 1995 does not apply to the accumulation of radioactive waste on any premises situated on a nuclear site.[32]

(2) s14(1)RSA 1995 does not apply to the disposal or accumulation of radioactive waste arising from watches or clocks but will still apply

where that waste arises on or from premises on which clocks or watches are manufactured or repaired by processes involving the use of luminous material.[33]

(3) s32(1)(b) noncompliance with a limitation or condition subject to which he is registered or exempted

Registration and exemptions from registration are dealt with at ss 7 and 10 and ss. 8 and 11 s32 RSA 1995 respectively.

In August, 1998, Tyseley Waste Disposal was fined £120,000 for breaches of this section in that they had failed to fulfil conditions attached to a registration which required the appointment of a properly qualified radioactive substances expert, the prevention of a loss of the radioactive sources and the maintenance of legible records.

s32(1)(c) RSA 1995 Non-compliance with a limitation or condition subject to which an authorisation granted under section 13 or 14 has effect

These sections deal specifically with authorisations granted for the disposal and accumulation of radioactive waste.

6.4.4.3

s32(1)(d) RSA 1995 noncompliance with requirements of a notice served under ss 21 or 22 by a person registered under ss 7 or 10 or to whom an authorisation has been granted under ss 13 or 14.

6.4.5 s33 RSA 1995: Offences relating to ss 19 and 20

6.4.5.1

s 19:

> A person who fails to cause copies of certificates of registration or authorisation to be kept posted so as to be easily read by those affected by the matters set out in the certificate, is liable:
>
> (a) on summary conviction, to a fine not exceeding the statutory maximum;
> (b) on conviction on indictment, to a fine.[34]

Further, the removal or defacement of such certificates without reasonable cause will result in liability on summary conviction to a fine not exceeding level two on the standard scale.[35]

6.4.5.2

s 20:

A failure to comply with the requirements for the retention and production of site or disposal records is also an offence with liability:

(a) on summary conviction, to a fine not exceeding the statutory maximum, or to imprisonment for a term not exceeding three months, or both;
(b) on conviction on indictment, to a fine or to imprisonment for a term not exceeding two years, or both.[36]

6.4.6 s34 RSA 1995: Disclosure of trade secrets

This offence relates to the disclosure of information about a "relevant process[37] or trade secret", used by a particular undertaking, given or obtained under the Act or in its execution.

Under subsection (2) RSA 1995, this offence carries the same penalty as s33 RSA 1995:

(a) on summary conviction, to a fine not exceeding the statutory maximum, or to imprisonment for a term not exceeding three months, or both;
(b) on conviction on indictment, to a fine or to imprisonment for a term not exceeding two years, or both.[38]

6.4.6.1 Defences

A disclosure of this kind may be made in the following circumstances:

(a) with the consent of the person carrying on the undertaking, or
(b) in accordance with . . . directions given by the Secretary of State; or
(c) in connection with the execution of this Act, or
(d) for the purposes of any legal proceedings arising out of this Act.[39]

6.4.6.2 s34 A: Offences of making false and misleading statements, false entries

s34 A RSA 1995 provides that it is an offence to make a misleading statement or a false entry (ie false or misleading in a material particular, either knowingly or recklessly) either in compliance with a requirement to furbish information, or for the purpose of obtaining a registration.

The offence, on summary conviction, can be punished by a fine not exceeding statutory minimum. On conviction or indictment, the punishment may be a fine, or a term of imprisonment not exceeding two years.

6.4.7 s36 RSA 1995: Offences by bodies corporate

This section attaches liability to directors, managers, secretaries or other similar body-corporate officers where the body corporate is guilty of an offence under the Act and that offence is proved to have been "committed with the consent or connivance of, or attributable to any neglect on the part..." of those officers.

6.4.8 s37 RSA 1995: Offence due to another's fault

Where a person's offence is due to the act or default of another, that other may also be charged and convicted of the offence notwithstanding the proceedings against the first person.

6.5 Transfrontier Shipment of Radioactive Waste Regulations 1993 (TSRWR 1993)

These regulations are the UK's implementation of Council Directive 92/3/Euratom on the supervision and control of shipments of radioactive waste between Member-states and into and out of the Community. They entered into force on January 1, 1994.

The penalty for offences under these regulations is prescribed as liability on summary conviction to a fine not exceeding the statutory maximum, or on conviction on indictment to imprisonment for a term not exceeding two years, or a fine, or both.[40]

6.5.1 Definitions

'Competent authority': authority in the country, designated in accordance with Art. 17 of Council Directive 92/3/Euratom, empowered to implement the system of supervision and control defined in the Directive.[41]

'the Community': the European Atomic Energy Community (EAEC).

Under Reg.18(1), any person who fails to comply with any provision of reg. 6, 8(2), 9(2), 10, 15(1) or (2) commits an offence.

6.5.2 Part II RSA 1995 Offences: Shipments requiring authorisation by the competent authorities in the UK

Shipments requiring authorisation[42] under this Part are:

(a) radioactive waste from the UK to another country, whether a Community Member-State or a third country;
(b) waste import into the Community from a third country when the country of destination is the UK; and
(c) where such waste is to enter the Community from a third country and the country of destination is not a Member-State and the UK is the Member-State in whose territory the waste is first to enter the Community.

6.5.2.1 Reg. 6

No person shall carry out in the UK a shipment to which this part applies where the shipment is carried out under and in accordance with the conditions and requirements contained in an authorisation granted by the appropriate agency.

6.5.2.2 Reg. 8(2)

This regulation obliges the holder of an authorisation to take radioactive waste back if:

(a) the shipment cannot be completed;
(b) the conditions and requirements of the authorisation are not complied with.

6.5.2.3 Reg. 9(2)

Where the country of destination is a third country and this part applies under Regulation 5(a), the person who submitted the application for the particular shipment shall notify the chief inspector of its arrival in the third country within two weeks and shall indicate the last customs post in the Community through which the shipment passed.

6.5.3 Part III, RSA 1995: Offences: Shipments where the competent authorities in the UK are not responsible for giving authorisation

6.5.3.1 Reg. 10

No person shall carry out a shipment in the UK to which these regulations do not apply, except when carried out under and in accordance with the conditions and requirements of:

> an authorisation granted by the competent authorities of the Member-State competent to grant such authorisations under the Directive.[43]

6.5.3.2 Reg. 15(1)

No person shall carry out a shipment to which these Regulations apply within the UK unless accompanied by the application made under the Directive for authorisation, the necessary approvals for the shipment and the authorisation. Further, where a shipment is made by rail, those documents must be made available to the appropriate Agency.

6.5.3.3 Reg. 15(2)

In relation to shipments to which these regulations apply and where the UK is the country of destination, 'the consignee shall within 15 days of receipt of the radioactive waste send the appropriate Agency an acknowledgment of receipt using the appropriate standard document.'

6.5.3.4 Reg. 18(2)

This regulation creates the further offences of making a statement which a person

> knows to be false or misleading . . . or recklessly to make a statement which is false or misleading, where the statement is made:

(a) in purported compliance with a requirement to furnish any information imposed by or under the provisions of these Regulations; or

(b) for the purpose of obtaining the grant under these Regulations of any authorisation or approval . . .[44]

Notes

[1] A detailed examination of the civil liability provisions is beyond the ambit of this text.
[2] s 7 NIA 1965.
[3] ibid s6
[4] ibid s5(4)
[5] ibid, s19(5)
[6] ibid, s22(1)
[7] ibid, s22(2)
[8] ibid, s24(5)
[9] s1(1) RM(RT)A 1991. An order to vary this quantity measure had not been made at the time of writing.
[10] ibid, s1(2)
[11] ibid, s2(1)
[12] ibid, s6(3)
[13] ibid, s3(1)(a)-(c)
[14] ibid, s3(4)
[15] ibid, s4(2)(a)-(c)
[16] ibid, s4(3)
[17] ibid, s5(1)
[18] A breach of section 2 regulations ie: *Radioactive Material (Road Transport)(GB) Regulations.*
[19] ibid, s5(6)
[20] s1(2)(b) RSA 1995.
[21] ibid, s2
[22] ibid, s3
[23] ibid, s6
[24] *McLeod (or Houston) v Buchanan* [1940] 2 All ER 179 at 187, HL.
[25] *Ross Hillman Ltd v Bond* [1974] QB 435.
[26] supra, no 24
[27] *James & Son Ltd v Smee* [1955] 1 QB 78.
[28] *Tesco Supermarkets Ltd v Nattrass* [1972] AC 153, HL.
[29] *Knox v Boyd* 1941 JC 82 at 86.
[30] supra, no 20, s9(2).
[31] ibid, s9(1).

[32] ibid, s14(3).
[33] ibid, ss 8(4) and (5).
[34] ibid, s33(1).
[35] ibid, s33(2).
[36] ibid, s33(3).
[37] ibid, s34(3) defines *'relevant process'* as any process 'applied for the purposes of, or in connection with, the production or use of radioactive material'.
[38] ibid, s34(2).
[39] ibid, s34(1).
[40] *Transfrontier Shipment of Radioactive Waste Regulations* 1993, Reg. 18(7).
[41] ibid, Reg. 2.
[42] ibid, Reg. 5.
[43] Council Directive 92/3/EURATOM on the supervision and control of shipments of radioactive waste between member-states and into and out of the Community.
[44] ibid, Reg. 18(2).

CHAPTER 7

DANGEROUS OR HAZARDOUS SUBSTANCES

CONTENTS

CHAPTER 7

DANGEROUS OR HAZARDOUS SUBSTANCES

7.1 Introduction

These types of substances have been the subject of a number of EC Directives which have been transposed into domestic legislation through a number of sets of Regulations as well as the statutes. This is an area of the law which is subject to continual revision but the criminal offence generally occurs when a regulation is breached.

7.2 Major accident hazards: the 'Seveso' Directive

A Directive (82/501/EEC) was passed by the EEC in June, 1982 which addressed the prevention of major accidents which might result from major industrial activities. The Directive (commonly referred to as the *'Seveso' Directive*), refers to certain industrial activities which are defined at Annex I and Annex II. 'Dangerous substances' are defined by reference to criteria laid down in Annex IV. The Directive requires member-states to take the appropriate measures to enable them to deal with all the consequences of a disaster.

This Directive has been transposed into domestic law by the *Control of Industrial Major Hazards Regulations* 1984 (CIMHR 1984). Industrial activities are referred to at Reg 2(1) and set out at Schedule 4 (which reflects Annex 1 to the Directive). Reg. 4 requires the controller of an industrial activity to be aware of the potential dangers of that activity. Reg. 5 requires that where an accident occurs, the manufacturer is obliged to inform the Health and Safety Executive (HSE) of all the circumstances of that accident. On-site and off-site plans for an emergency are required by Reg. 10 and 11 to be provided by the manufacturer and the local authority (LA) respectively. It is the duty of the manufacturer to ensure that he keeps the HSE closely informed of any change. No criminal sanctions are contained within these regulations, because liability arising out this sort of disaster will be a civil matter.

Other Directives have dealt with the specific discharges of dangerous substances from industrial processes: mercury(82/176/EEC),(84/156/EEC); cadmium(83/513/EEC); lindane(84/491/EEC); and other dangerous substances(86/280/EEC),(92/3 EURTOM).

7.3 Transport of dangerous or hazardous substances

Reflecting similar Directives in respect of the Transport of Dangerous Goods by Road (94/55/EC) and the Control of Volatile Organic Compounds (resulting from the storage and distribution of petrol from terminals to service stations)(94/63/EC), stringent requirements are made of those who transport dangerous or hazardous substances.

In domestic legislation, these requirements are to be found in the *Carriage of Dangerous Goods by Road Regulations* 1996. These are detailed provisions, and divide into seven parts:

Part I deals with the interpretation and application of the terms used.

Part II outlines the Approved Document regime on which the regulations are based.

Part III specifies the mode of carriage which must be used for these purposes, and the means which must be used to examine and test the vehicle.

Part IV legislates for the provision of information by the consignors, of documentation by the operators, keeping of information by operators, and information which must be displayed on the vehicle

Part V regulates the loading and unloading of substances. *It is prohibited to carry certain loads.*

Part VI regulates emergencies and parking. Emergency equipment must be installed, steps must be planned for an accident and precautionary measures taken against fire or explosion.

Part VII deals with exemption certificates but also provides for the offence of breach of the Regulations: this offence will be brought under s36 HSWA 1974.

Defences to a charge brought under s36 HSWA 1974 are as follows:

> (i) where the defendant can prove that the offence was due to an act committed by another, *not* being one of his employees, and
> (ii) that he took all reasonable precautions and exercised all due diligence to avoid commission of the offence.

The leave of the Court is required to claim this defence, unless the defendant has notified the prosecutor seven days before the trial of the identity of the other person.

Certain types of vehicle may claim a transitional defence by reason of the goods in question having been carried before January, 1997.

Note that alternative compliance with international regulations is available to an operator.

A set of Regulations of a similar nature apply in the *Carriage of Dangerous Goods by Rail Regulations* 1996. The same structure has been imposed upon this activity, which therefore includes provisions for Approved Documents, mode of carriage, information, loading and unloading, security and emergency measures. An extra regulation provides the framework of requirements concerning the carriage of explosives.

A prosecution for an offence arising out of breach of these regulations may be brought under s36 HSWA 1974.

An identical set of defences is available to a defendant charged under these regulations.

7.4 Transboundary movement of hazardous waste

7.4.1 Council Regulation of 1 February 1993 on the supervision and control of shipments of waste, within, into and out of the European Community

These implement the EC Directives prohibiting the transboundary movement of hazardous waste, other than in accordance with contractual arrangements, prenotification of the consignment and approval of the consignment by acknowledgement of the prenotification on the part of the appropriate authority. Hazardous substances are described as being polychlorinated biphenyls (PCBs) and toxic and dangerous wastes (excluding chlorinated and organic solvents) which contain or are contaminated by any of the substances listed in the Council Directive on Hazardous Waste (91/689/EEC), and the European Waste Catalogue (Commission Decision 20 December 1993), in the form and to the extent that they constitute a risk to health or the environment. Documentation must be provided, by the holder, or consignee, in the form of 'consignment notes' or 'uniform documents'. A standard format for these is required by the Directives.

7.4.2 Control of Pollution (Special Waste) Regulations 1980

In UK law, these substances are the subject of the *Control of Pollution(Special Waste) Regulations*. Other member-states have implemented the Directives by reference to different definitions of 'hazardous substances' and where the substance of an import is not covered by the Regulations, then the disposal authority is advised nevertheless to use the Regulations procedure in respect of the import. Note that by Reg.9, a British 'holder' who exports a hazardous waste to a third state must, within six weeks of the consignment leaving the EC, notify the appropriate authority of the exit from the EC of the consignment and the arrival of the consignment at its destination. Part V of the Regulations contains the duties of the disposal authorities.

The Directives do not indicate what the procedure should be when a consignee refuses to accept the consignment, but guidance in *DoE Circular (16/89)* indicates that the foreign holder will be obliged to accept the return of the consignment. Contracts will need to contain provisions to deal with such an eventuality.

7.4.3 Offences

Reg.27 provides that a person (*'holder'*) who sends a consignment note which is false in a particular, or where he has been reckless as to whether it is false in a material particular, for the purpose of securing an acknowledgement, avoiding an objection or avoiding the imposition of conditions commits an offence.

Reg 28 sets out the penalties for infringing the regulations. Holders, consignees and carriers will be liable on summary conviction to a fine not exceeding £2,000, or on conviction on indictment, to a term of imprisonment not exceeding two years, or both. Infringement of regulations concerning the retention of documents carries a lesser penalty - on summary conviction, a fine, not exceeding £400.

7.4.4. Defences

The *'due diligence'* defence is available, as is the *'emergency'* defence. Where the offence is attributable to the action of a third party, that third party may be charged.

Note that the directors or managers of a company may be prosecuted for an offence, as well as the company itself.

See also:
Control of Pollution (Supply and Use of Injurious Substances) Regulations 1986;
Merchant Shipping (Chemical Tankers) Regulations 1986.

7.5 Food and Environment Protection Act 1985 (FEPA 1985)

7.5.1 Emergency order

Part I, s1 Food and Environment Protection Act 1985 (FEPA 1985) authorises the *designating authority* to make an emergency order when there has been an escape of 'substances' which may have the effect of contaminating food within a designated area. The order may prohibit the movement of potentially contaminated food; it may also prohibit agricultural activities, gathering of wild plants, slaughter of creatures, fishing and food processing.

It will be an offence to contravene an emergency prohibition, or to cause or permit any other person to do so. The available defence is to show that the contravention took place on foreign vessel, aircraft, hovercraft or marine structure and that nothing to which the prohibition related was landed from it in the UK. It will also be a defence to show that the contravention occurred with the consent of a Minister.

7.5.2 Ministers' power

s2 FEPA 1985 sets out the power of a Minister to give such a consent and creates the offence of noncompliance.

7.5.3 Investigating officers' power

s4 FEPA 1985 creates wide-ranging powers for investigating officers. These are powers of inspection and enforcement, with wide powers of entry. The full range of these powers is to be found at Schedule 2 to the Act.

7.5.4 Offences

7.5.4.1

It will be an offence intentionally to obstruct an officer in the performance of his functions under this Act. It will also be an offence not to comply with a requirement made by an officer, or, in providing information required by the officer, to make a statement which he knows to be false in a material particular, to make a statement reckless as to whether it is false in a particular or to make a statement which fails to disclose a particular.

On summary conviction, the defendant is liable to a fine, not exceeding level five on the standard scale.

7.5.4.2 s21 FEPA 1985

A person guilty of an offence under s1(6) or s2(4) FEPA 1985 shall be liable:

(a) on summary conviction, to a fine of an amount not exceeding the statutory maximum;
(b) on conviction on indictment, to a fine or imprisonment for a term not exceeding two years, or to both.

7.5.4.3 Directors' and managers' liability

s21(6) FEPA 1985 Where a company has been charged with an offence under this Act, the director or manager of a company may also be charged, if it can be proved that the offence occurred as a result of his consent, connivance, or negligence.

7.5.4.4 Company members

Note that by s21(7) FEPA 1985 'where the affairs of a body corporate are managed by its members, s21(6) FEPA 1985 above shall apply in relation to the acts and defaults of a member in connection with his functions of management as if he were a director of the body corporate.

7.5.5 Defences s22 FEPA 1985

Two groups of defences are available to charges brought under the provisions of this Act.

7.5.5.1

The *'due diligence'* defence is available to any of the charges - that is to say, that the defendant can prove that he took all reasonable precautions and exercised all due diligence to avoid the commission of the offence. There is a presumption that this has been established when he can prove that he acted under instructions given to him by his employer, or that he acted in reliance on information given to him by another, which he had no reason to suppose was either false or misleading. In either case, the defendant must be able to show that he took 'all such steps as were reasonably open to him to ensure that no offence would be committed'.

7.5.5.2

It is also open to the defendant to allege that the offence was committed by another person, other than by those set out above. For this defence to be effective, the defendant must, seven days before the hearing, furnish the prosecutor with information either identifying or assisting in the identification of the other person.

7.5.6. Pesticides

7.5.6.1 Definitions

'Pests' are defined as any organism harmful to plants or to wood or to other plant products, any undesired plant and any harmful creature (s16[15] FEPA 1985).

'Pesticide' means any substance, preparation or organism prepared or used for destroying any pest.

'Pesticide residue' means any substance resulting from the use of a pesticide including specified regulated derivatives of pesticides.

7.5.6.2.

s16[Part III] FEPA 1985 contains enabling provisions for the regulation and management of pesticides. The delegated legislation is to be found in the Control of Pesticides Regulations 1986 CPR 1986.

The express purposes of the Act are continuously to develop means

(a) (i) to protect the health of human beings, creatures and plants;
(ii) to safeguard the environment; and
(iii) to secure safe, efficient and humane methods of controlling pests and
(b) with a view to making information about pesticides available to the public;

There follow provisions for the powers of Ministers to regulate, by prohibition, by consent, by approvals and by prosecutions of breaches of regulations and powers of seizure and disposal. Ministers are also given powers to provide information to the public.

7.5.6.3 Enforcement powers

The local authority may authorise one of its officers to exercise powers of entry where he has reason to believe that an offence is being committed, and to request information

7.5.6.4 Offence

s16(12)(a) FEPA 1985 A person commits an offence who without reasonable excuse, contravenes, or causes or permits any other person to contravene

(i) any provision of regulations;
(ii) any conditions of approval of a pesticide; or
(iii) any requirement imposed by virtue of regulations

(b) in purporting to give information required by virtue of sub-section (11) above
(i) makes a statement which he knows to be false in a material particular
(ii) recklessly makes a statement which is false in a material particular or
(iii) intentionally fails to disclose any material particular shall be guilty of an offence.

'*Contravene*' here includes 'fails to comply with'.

7.5.6.5 Defences

A defence is available where a person can show that he placed poison or a poisonous substance on land, acting in accordance with an approval under:

(1) s8(b) Protection of Animals Act 1911 (PAA 1911)
(2) s7(b) Protection of Animals in Scotland Act 1912 (PAPSA 1912)
(3) s22(2)(b) Welfare of Animals Act (Northern Ireland) 1972 (WAA[NI]) 1972).

7.5.6.6 Penalties

A person guilty of an offence under s16(12) of the Act shall be liable:

(a) on summary conviction, to a fine not exceeding the statutory maximum; and

(b) on conviction on indictment, to a fine.

A person guilty of an offence under Schedule 2 to this Act (powers of enforcement), shall be liable on summary conviction to a fine of an amount not exceeding level five on the standard scale. (See also 7.5.4.3 and 7.5.4.4, FEPA 1985.)

7.6 Control of Pesticides Regulations 1986 (CPR 1986)

The Regulations start with a definition of their scope. This scope includes any pesticide or pesticide derivative. Reg.2 provides for the exceptions to the application of the Regulations, in an extensive list.

7.6.1 Prohibitions (Reg. 4)

7.6.1.1

Advertisement of a pesticide without provisional or full approval is prohibited: conditions in respect of advertising, attached to the approval, must have been met.

7.6.1.2

Sale of a pesticide is similarly prohibited

7.6.1.3

Storage of a pesticide is similarly prohibited

7.6.1.4

Use of a pesticide is similarly prohibited.

7.7 Approvals

Approvals, either full or provisional, are only granted after the requisite tests for safety and efficiency have been conducted by the Ministry of Agriculture, Fisheries and Food (MAAF). An approval may authorise the sale, storage or use of a pesticide, as well as its advertisement. The approval may be subject to conditions which may at any time be amended. The approval may be rescinded or suspended at any time. Where a Minister consents to the advertisement of pesticides (subject to Schedule 1 to the Regulations), or to the sale supply and storage of pesticides (subject to Schedule 2 to the Regulations), or to the use of pesticides by aerial application (subject to Schedule 4 to the Regulations), then that consent will be published.

7.8 Seizure and disposal

Where there has been a breach of a regulation in respect of a prohibition or a consent, there is a power to seize or dispose of the pesticide. There is also a power to require the holder of the approval to take remedial action to rectify the damage which has flowed from the breach. If the substance has been imported, then a notice may be served which requires the substance to be exported within a period determined as reasonable by the Minister.

7.9 s140 Environmental Protection Act 1985 (EPA 1985)

This section gives powers to the Secretary of State to prohibit the importation, use, supply and storage of injurious substances or articles. He may regulate under any Community instrument, or other enactment. Offences of breaches of any of the regulations are punishable with imprisonment for not more than two years, or on summary conviction with a fine not exceeding level five on the standard scale, and in the case of a continuing offence, a fine not exceeding one-tenth of the level on the standard scale specified as a maximum penalty for the original offence. These powers extend to articles, substances and control storage, as well as use and supply. Many sets of regulations made under COPA 1974 remain in force by this section.

Note the establishment of an Advisory Committee on Hazardous Substances (ACHS) by s149(5) EPA 1985. (The powers of the committee are set out at Schedule 12.)

CHAPTER 8

GENETICALLY-MODIFIED ORGANISMS (GMOs)

CONTENTS

CHAPTER 8

GENETICALLY-MODIFIED ORGANISMS (GMOs)

8.1 Introduction

Genetically-modified organisms (GMOs) present what is perhaps the greatest challenge to environmental management, both at the practical and legal levels. The GMO is beset by difficulties from the experimental stages onwards. The precautionary principle, which is the obvious principle to apply to the regulation and management of GMOs, lies uneasily next to the market economy which fuels the development of GMOs. The first regulatory consideration is obviously the containment of experimentation. Within the laboratory, working codes of practice have seen the diminution of concerns which were originally expressed over the possibility of escapes of organisms. The main concern has now been transferred to the issue of release of GMOs into the community. This concern is reflected in the 1990 *EC Directive*, which was introduced to regulate the risk assessment and authorisation of GMOs, when released into the environment, for research or as final products. Since the Directive came into force in 1991, more than 1,000 experimental ('Part B') releases have been notified to the various Member-State authorities. The notification procedure must include risk assessment and it is clear is that some harmonisation is required for the risk-assessment procedure, because conflict has arisen between Member-States over risk-assessment criteria. The Commission has now put forward proposals for common risk assessment principles, which must take into account information which 'may be necessary for evaluating any potential risks, whether immediate or delayed. By these proposals, a new product must be subjected to the scrutiny of a scientific committee before being put on the market, if there is any likelihood of the product having an effect upon human health or the environment. The Commission has also proposed that an application for notification should be accessible to the public, with the assessment report and the findings of the scientific committee being published. The Commission has also proposed mandatory monitoring of products after they are placed on the market, with the review of such monitoring becoming an integral part of the renewal of an authorisation.

One of the most controversial areas in GMO regulation is in the food and drink manufacturing sector. The major public concerns, replacing the laboratory control issue, have become the wide-ranging implications of releases of GMOs into the community. The biggest of these concerns is that GMOs will alter existing genetic balances in ways which cannot be anticipated at the time of their release.

Another concern regularly expressed is that GMOs will be introduced into food products with no indication of their presence. A voluntary system of labelling is in place in the UK. It is somewhat at odds with the labelling recommendations made by the Commission. Labelling is a requirement which will be modified by the Commission, with three kinds of food label - a compulsory label for products containing GMOs, a compulsory label for products which may contain GMOs and an optional label for products which are GMO free. The difficulty which lies at the heart of the labelling issue is how to harmonise the concept of 'substantial equivalence', the term used to reflect the point when the GMO is no longer distinguishable from the genetic nature of the product, such as in some soya oils. This difficulty reflects the absence of a generally accepted definition of GMOs.

8.2 Part VI, Environmental Protection Act 1990 (EPA 1990)

This legislation imposes a regulatory structure upon the import, acquisition, release and marketing of GMOs. Two sets of regulations were made under the Act, to increase the level of environmental protection:

(1) The Genetically Modified Organisms (Contained Use) Regulations 1992.
These regulations control the GMO within the laboratory and the factory.
(2) The Genetically Modified Organisms (Deliberate Release) Regulations 1992.
These regulations, which implement the *Deliberate Release Directive* (90/220/EEC), control the circumstances in which, and the procedure by which a consent for a release or marketing may be obtained.

Note that an Advisory Committee on Releases to the Environment (ACRE) was constituted by the Act advises the Secretary of State on granting of consents.

8.2.1 Purpose of the Act

s106 EPA 1990 defines the purpose and ambit of the provisions in the Act. The techniques which are subject to regulatory control are set out at s106(5) EPA 1990 and include any technique for the modification of any genes or other genetic material by the recombination, insertion or deletion of any parts of the genetic sequence. This subsection also includes provision for the control of any other technique which produces organisms which amount to genetic modification. There are certain exceptions to these groups, set out in the GMO (Deliberate Release) regulations 1992.

8.2.2 Definitions

s107 EPA 1990 contains the definitions of terms used in the Act.

'Damage to the environment' is defined at 107(3) EPA 1990 as being the presence in the environment of a GMO which is capable of causing harm to the living organisms supported by the environment. This definition in turn depends on the construction placed upon the concept of *'harm'*. This is defined, at s107(6) EPA 1990, as meaning "harm to the health of humans or other living organisms or other interference with the ecological systems of which they form part and, in the case of man, includes offence caused to any of his senses or harm to his property."

8.2.3 Risk assessment and notification

s108 EPA 1990 provides for the requirement of risk assessment and notification.

8.2.3.1

s108(1) EPA 1990 prohibits the release or marketing of any GMO without both of these, although where a consent is required or an exemption granted, this section does not apply.

8.2.3.2

s108(3) EPA 1990 requires a person who is keeping GMOs to carry out regular risk assessments and to notify the Secretary of State that he is doing so, providing any other information which he is required to do, by regulation. It is an offence to fail to comply with this provision.

8.2.3.3

s108(5) EPA 1990 requires a person to keep records of his assessments over a prescribed period (currently ten years). It is an offence to make a false entry in a record required under this subsection.

8.2.4 Duties

s109 EPA 1990 sets out the general duties of a person who deals at any stage with GMOs. This includes importation, acquisition, keeping, release or marketing of organisms. These duties do not apply where a consent has been granted under s108 EPA 1990.

8.2.5 s110 EPA 1990 Prohibition notices

These may be issued where a person proposes to use a GMO in a manner which the Secretary of State has reason to believe will constitute a threat of damage to the environment. The prohibition notice must state that the Secretary of State takes this view and it must specify what is to be prohibited by the notice and from what date.

It is an offence to contravene a prohibition notice.

8.2.6 s111 EPA 1990 Consents

This section of the Act sets out the framework for consents. It also requires the person making application for a consent to continue to provide the Secretary of State with specified information. There is a continuing obligation for the applicant to provide to the Secretary of State any new information which comes to light. This is a particularly important provision, in the light of the continual and rapid scientific progress in the field of biotechnology. Consents may be subject to conditions or limitations, or revoked. There is also provision for exemptions to be granted. The *Deliberate Release Regulations* contain the detailed provisions which govern the granting of a consent. Notice that one of the conditions attached to an application is that the application should be publicised in at least one newspaper. This is not an onerous requirement and some might say that it was an inadequate way of advertising a release with potentially enormous effects upon the environment.

8.2.7 s112 EPA 1990 Consents: conditions and limitations

This section provides for the attachment of conditions or limitations to a consent It requires the consent-holder to comply with any such conditions or limitations to such a consent and to use BATNEEC in doing so.

8.2.8 s115 EPA 1990 Powers of inspection

The powers of inspection and rights of entry which are given to inspectors in this subsection are wide-ranging. They are listed at s115(3) EPA 1990. *Inter alia*, they include powers to enter premises where the inspector thinks it is necessary to do so, to test, take samples and take possession of GMOs, in order to examine it or, to ensure that it remains inviolate for the purposes of examination or evidence at trial. He may also require of a person information, the production of records and assistance in respect of any matter under the person's control,

Where the inspector has removed a substance, he must leave a notice indicating the nature of what he has taken, sufficiently detailed to enable identification of the substance.

It is an offence to fail to comply with any of the provisions of this section.

8.2.9 s116 EPA 1990 Obtaining information

The Secretary of State may serve a notice on a person requiring that person to provide information which concerns any aspect of his activities in respect of GMOs. The notice will specify the information is required, the form and period in which it must be produced. It is an offence to fail to comply with a requirement of a notice.

8.2.10 s117 EPA 1990 Powers to deal with imminent danger

This section gives the inspector powers to seize a GMO and render it harmless. Before taking such action, if it is safe and practicable to do so, then he will take samples of the substance. He is obliged subsequently to make a report. Obstruction of an inspector in his exercise of these powers is an offence.

8.2.11 Offences

The offences which can be committed in respect the preceding sections are listed at s118(1) EPA 1990.

These are offences of contravention, non-compliance and obstruction. It is also an offence to make a statement which is knowingly false, or misleading in a material particular, where the statement is made for the purposes of compliance, or for the purpose of an application for the granting of a consent. It is an offence to falsify records, or, with intent, to deceive, forge or use a document purporting to be issued under the provisions of s111. It is also an offence to pretend falsely to be an inspector.

8.2.11.1 Defences

By s118(2) EPA 1990 the 'due diligence' defence is available to charges in respect of contraventions of s108(1)(a) EPA 1990, failure to comply under s108(3) EPA 1990, contraventions of s111 EPA 1990, failure to comply with the provisions of s109 EPA 1990, or contravention, under s115 EPA 1990, of a prohibition notice.

8.2.11.2 Sentence

s118(3) EPA 1990: A person guilty of an offence of contravention under s111, or failure to comply under s109 shall be liable:

> (a) on summary conviction, to a fine not exceeding £20,000 or to imprisonment for a term not exceeding six months, or to both;
> (b) on conviction on indictment, to a fine or to imprisonment for a term not exceeding five years, or to both

s118(4) EPA 1990: A person guilty of a contravention of a prohibition notice shall be liable:

> (a) on summary conviction, to a fine not exceeding £20,000 or to imprisonment, for a term not exceeding six months or to both;
> (b) on conviction on indictment, to a fine or to imprisonment for a term not exceeding two years, or to both

s118(5) EPA 1990: A person guilty of an offence of contravention or non-compliance under s108 shall be liable:

> (a) on summary conviction, to a fine not exceeding the statutory maximum, or to imprisonment for a term not exceeding six months, or to both;
> (b) on conviction on indictment, to a fine or to imprisonment for a term not exceeding five years, or to both.

s118(6) EPA 1990: A person guilty of an offence of failure to comply, or an offence of making a false statement, or offences of deception in the use of s111 documents, shall be liable:

> (a) on summary conviction, to a fine not exceeding the statutory maximum, or to a term of imprisonment not exceeding six months;
> (b) on conviction on indictment, to a fine or to imprisonment for a term not exceeding two years, or to both.

s118(7) EPA 1990: A person guilty of failing to comply with a requirement under s115, or of preventing another person from responding to questions from an inspector (s115[3] EPA 1990), or of obstructing an inspector in the performance of his duties or the exercise of his power, shall be liable:

> on summary conviction, to a fine not exceeding the statutory maximum, or to imprisonment for a term not exceeding three months, or to both.

s118(8) EPA 1990: A person guilty of the offence of falsely pretending to be an inspector shall be liable:

> on summary conviction to a fine not exceeding level five on the standard scale.

Note that where a person has been convicted of the offence of unauthorised keeping of a GMO, then where a contravention continues after the conviction this will be a further offence for which, on summary conviction the person will be fined one-fifth of level five on the standard scale for each day that the contravention continues.

Where a person is charged with 'failure-to-comply offences', then the burden of showing that he has complied with BATNEEC lies upon the person. Also, when an entry is required by a condition in a consent, as evidence of another condition being complied with, if the entry has not been made, that fact will be admissible as evidence that the other condition has not been observed.

The Court may order that a person convicted for certain offences be ordered to take steps to remedy matters.

8.2.12 Powers of the Secretary of State

This section gives powers of remediation to the Secretary of State, both to remedy the harm and to recover the costs of taking such steps from the person convicted of the offence.

He must obtain permission to take such steps from the person who owns the land in question where it is not the defendant. Commercial confidentiality must generally be preserved, although this may be the subject of representations to the Secretary of State.

8.2.13 Public register of information

These sections (ss122, 123 EPA 1990) legislate for the maintenance of a public register. The register contains notices under s108 EPA 1990, directions under s108 EPA 1990, prohibition notices, applications for consents, any other relevant information and any convictions under s118. The exact requirements are to be found in the *Deliberate Release Regulations.* There are provisions for the exclusion of information from the register, on the grounds of national security, potential damage to the environment, or commercial confidentiality.

8.2.14 Prosecutions

At the time of writing, the first prosecution for breach of a consent condition has taken place. The case concerned *Monsanto's* failure to observe the buffer zone around a site where trials of genetically-modified oilseed rape were taking place, thus breaching a condition of its consent and giving rise to the risk of crosspollination of crops. Monsanto was fined £17,000.

ACRE, DETR, HSE

The Advisory Committee on Releases to the Environment (ACRE) works in cooperation with the DETR and HSE and the observable trend is towards the strict enforcement of regulations. New measures are in view, in the wake of a report from the Cabinet Committee which is expected shortly.

CHAPTER 9

THE COMMON LAW OFFENCE OF PUBLIC NUISANCE

CONTENTS

CHAPTER 9

THE COMMON LAW OFFENCE OF PUBLIC NUISANCE

9.1 Introduction

Prior to the creation of statutory regimes for the prevention of pollution or the imposition of other environmental safeguards, the courts dealt with environmental problems such as the accumulation of rubbish on private land through a generic criminal offence. At common law it is an offence to cause a public nuisance.

The most frequently cited early example of a prosecution is that of Sir Charles Sidley in 1663 for standing naked on a balcony in Covent Garden and urinating on the crowd below. However, the offence is capable of covering pollution or environmental harm affecting the public at large. In 1975, the Court of Appeal confirmed that the offence still existed. Its flexibility and relevance are demonstrated by effective prosecutions of the organisers of illegal and environmentally-damaging rave/Acid-House parties. Charges have also been brought in major pollution incidents such as the oil spill from the tanker *Sea Empress*. The offence is triable in either the Magistrates or Crown Court.

9.2 What the prosecution must prove

The prosecution has to prove that:

(1) a public nuisance occurred because the defendant acted or failed to act;

(2) the defendant knew or ought to have known that his acting or failing to act would result in a public nuisance.

'Nuisance' will be interpreted as in the civil law. Authorities applying the definition of 'nuisance' under s79 EPA 1990 may be persuasive. Whether a particular set of circumstances amounts to a nuisance will be a matter of law, hence for the judge not the jury in a trial on indictment. There is no compendious definition but an act or state of affairs which is injurious to health or an unreasonable interference with the health, comfort or enjoyment of the public will probably be accepted as a working definition.

The nuisance will not be public unless it affects the public at large, as opposed to an individual property or small group of individuals. The boundary between public and private nuisance is not always clear. One definition is that of Lord Denning in *Attorney General v PYA Quarries Ltd* [1957] 2 QB 169.

He determined that a public nuisance is a nuisance which is so widespread in its range or so indiscriminate in its effect that it would not be reasonable to expect one person to take proceedings on his own to put a stop to it, but that it should be taken on the responsibility of the community at large. In *R v Madden* (1975) 61 Cr App rep 254, a hoax bomb threat led eight security guards to search premises and the police to trace the location of the call with the help of one telephone operator. The threat was held not to have had an affect on sufficient numbers of people to have constituted a public nuisance.

9.3 The defendant's state of mind

In *R v Peter Shorrocks* (1994) 98 Cr App R 67, the necessary mental element was held to be that the defendant should either have known that his actions or omissions would lead to a public nuisance or that he ought to have known. Mr Shorrocks owned farmland and let a field to the organiser of an Acid-House party. The party generated 275 complaints to the police and lasted from 10.30 pm on the Saturday to 1.20 pm the following lunchtime. The noise caused disturbance four miles away.

At trial, at the close of the prosecution case, the defence submitted there was no case to answer because the prosecution could not prove that the defendant actually knew that the Acid-House party was going to be held or that the consequence of it would be to cause a public nuisance. Mr Shorrocks' defence, in interview, was that he had let the land for £50 to a man who wanted to use it to raise money for a special school. He himself had, in fact, been miles away in Harrogate for the whole weekend. In a second interview, he accepted that he had, in fact, been paid £2,000 but said this was to compensate him for damage to the grass crop. The submission was rejected and the defendant then gave evidence that he had thought a disco was to be held to raise money for a wheelchair and that he had already planned a weekend to Harrogate with his wife. He said he had lied to the police about the amount he received because he was frightened. He had been forced to spend three days clearing up litter from the event.

The Judge directed the jury to be sure that the defendant either knew or ought to have known that when he left his farm there was a risk of a public nuisance such that the reasonable person would have been aware of the risk and guarded against it.

The Court of Appeal, after a general review of law relating to the offence of public nuisance, upheld the formulation that the defendant was guilty if either he knew or ought to have known, in the sense that the means of knowledge were available to him, that there was a real risk that the consequences of his actions or omissions would be to create the sort of public nuisance that in fact occurred.

9.4 Sentence

This being a common-law offence, sentence is at large. This means, in the Crown Court, a theoretical maximum of life imprisonment and/or an unlimited fine; and, at summary trial, statutory limits on sentences available to the magistrates. Historically, the court could also impose the sentence of 'prostration' or a requirement that the nuisance be abated if it is proved to be continuing. However, the last reported example of prostration appears to be in 1810. In the light of the current web of specific legislation, the criminal courts are unlikely to regard prostration as a sentencing option still open to them. In particular, the criminal courts would be unwilling to impose a sentence where clear difficulties could arise in determining whether or not the sentence had been complied with.

Appeals against sentence to the Court of Appeal provide some sentencing guidance:

R v David Ian Ruffell (1992) 13 Cr App R (S) 204

The defendant was a professional organiser of Acid-House raves. He knew of the necessity of proper sanitary facilities, fire cover, first aid and so forth. He had, in fact, arranged with a local council in Essex to hold an event but the council withdrew its consent and gained an injunction preventing the party going ahead as planned. The defendant was desperate to find another venue. He arranged for the party to go ahead on the date planned but at a site at Blindley Heath in Surrey.

It was estimated that the event was attended by a minimum of 3,000 people. There were no toilet facilities, no fire precautions and no medical facilities. There were 400 complaints to the police. Music was played from 11.00pm on the Saturday until 11.30am on the Sunday.

Human excrement made the surrounding woods a hazard to health for some weeks after the event.

The Court of Appeal indicated that, in principle, an immediate custodial sentence would have been appropriate. The Court indicated that the sentence of 12 months which was suspended could not be criticised.

A £7,000 fine was again not criticised, in principle, but was quashed after evidence that the appellant was penniless by the time his appeal came before the Court.

R v Jeremy John Alexander Taylor (1992) 13 Cr App R (S) 466

A £5,000 fine was upheld by the Court of Appeal but a suspended sentence of nine months' imprisonment quashed.

The defendant was a professional organiser of Acid-House parties. He organised one just off the M25 in Surrey. Specifically to prevent the party being detected and prevented, its exact location was revealed in stages only. The police became aware of the party but their roadblocks were removed by stewards acting for the defendant or by those trying to reach the event. Although the party was very noisy, the main element of nuisance appears to have been total saturation of the area by parked cars, obstructing any local residents and the emergency services. Toilet facilities were arranged but were inadequate for the numbers attending, put at 8,000 to 15,000. There does not appear to have been the spread of excrement and continuing risk to health present in the *Ruffell* case which was not cited to the Court.

The Court of Appeal noted that sentences of immediate imprisonment may be appropriate in such cases but determined the correct sentence to be £5,000, given the defendant's age of 23 and relatively good record.

CHAPTER 10

STATUTORY NUISANCE

CONTENTS

CHAPTER 10

STATUTORY NUISANCE

10.1 Introduction

Part III, Environmental Protection Act (EPA 1990) establishes the regime for statutory nuisance. Statutory nuisance augments the substantial body of public and private nuisance law. There is an upward trend in the number of complaints received from the public about noise and odour pollution. Opinions differ as to whether this is indicative of an increase in pollution of this sort, or simply an increased public awareness of these sorts of pollution. A local authority (LA) is under a duty to act against a statutory nuisance, even when the conduct complained of is subject to regulation by a consent system. In *R v Carrick District Council, ex p Shelley* [1996] JPL 857, the applicants were applying for judicial review of the LA's decision not to serve an abatement notice in respect of sewage-related debris. The LA took the view that the National Rivers Authority (NRA) had decided that screening should be a condition of the discharge consent (which decision was the subject of an appeal to the Secretary of State by South West Water), and an abatement notice would therefore be inappropriate. Carnwath J held that the existence of a statutory nuisance was a question of fact for the LA to decide; that decision should not be affected by the existence of a consent under the Water Resources Act 1991 (WRA 1991). The existence of a statutory nuisance was nevertheless a matter for the district council to address and the resolution not to issue an abatement notice was declared to be invalid. South West Water was then served with two abatement notices.

Note that this new statutory nuisance regime is a discrete code which contains criminal and other remedies: it cannot give rise to a civil cause of action for damages. In *Issa v Hackney London Borough Council* [1997] 1 All ER 999 CA, public housing provided for the plaintiffs had been the subject of statutory nuisance proceedings. The premises in question were severely affected by condensation and mould. The defendants were fined and a compensation order made against them. However, the plaintiff's claim for civil damages on the basis of the conviction did not succeed.

There is provision under s82 EPA 1990 for a private individual to institute summary proceedings on the grounds that he is aggrieved by a statutory nuisance. The Court in those proceedings may order that an abatement notice be served.

10.2 The New Regime

The LA, having established the existence of a statutory nuisance, may then serve an abatement notice on the person or persons who are responsible for the statutory nuisance. The recipient of the notice may appeal against that notice, on certain specified grounds. However, if a person served with an abatement notice fails to comply with one or more of the requirements set out in the notice, then he will be guilty of an offence.

The definitions of different types of statutory nuisance are found at s79 EPA 1990. (Note that statutory nuisances concerning watercourses, ditches ponds remain the concern of the PHA 1936.)

10.3 Definitions

s79(1) EPA 1990 : The following matters constitute 'statutory nuisances' for the purposes of this Part:

(a) Any premises in such a state as to be prejudicial to health or a nuisance

The test for nuisance contains two limbs:

(1) '*Prejudicial to health*' means injurious, or likely to cause injury, to health. It is not necessary to *show* that the activity is prejudicial to health for it to be classed as a statutory nuisance. In *Betts v Penge Urban District Council* [1942] 2 K.B. 154 (Div Ct), it was held to be sufficient to show that the premises interfere with personal comfort and by doing so, constitute a nuisance.

(2) '*A nuisance*' means, consistent with the common law definition, 'interference with reasonable enjoyment of the property'. Where this second limb is relied on, then the principles of common law apply and the test for reasonableness will concern itself with what would be acceptable or unacceptable to ordinary people.

In *Cunningham v Birmingham City Council* (*Times Law Report* June 9th, 1997), the facts were that the LA had offered to carry out remedial works to abate the nuisance but the occupier argued that these works were insufficient. One of her children was autistic and the occupier therefore relied on the first part of the definition, that the premises were prejudicial to the health of the very sensitive child. The Court ruled that an objective test should be applied to the first limb of the test, just as it was to the second. The magistrates had erred in relating the duty of the LA landlord to the specific health requirements of one of its occupiers.

(b) Smoke emitted from premises so as to be prejudicial to health or a nuisance

'Smoke' includes soot, ash, grit and gritty particles. There are certain exceptions to this subsection, to be found at s79(3) EPA 1990. These are: smoke emitted from a chimney of a private dwelling within a smoke-control area; dark smoke emitted from a chimney of a building, boiler furnace or industrial plant; smoke emitted from a railway locomotive steam engine; and dark smoke emitted from industrial or trade premises. (Note the additional exception in respect of certain military purposes.)

(c) Fumes or gases emitted from premises so as to be prejudicial to health or a nuisance

This category applies to fumes and gases from private dwellings.

(d) Any dust, steam, smell or other effluvia arising on industrial, trade or business premises and being prejudicial to health or a nuisance

'Dust' does not include chimney smoke. It seems that the general application of this provision will be restricted to effluvia which interfere with human comfort. In *Wivenhoe Port v Colchester Borough Council* [1985] J.P.L. 175 (Chelmsford Crown Court), where there was an alleged dust nuisance which arose from the handling of soya meal, Butler J said that to cross the threshold of statutory nuisance, the nuisance 'had to be one interfering materially with the personal comfort of the residents'.

(e) Any accumulation or deposit which is prejudicial to health or a nuisance

The *'accumulation or deposit'* has been held not to apply to inert substances which merely constitute a potential nuisance. In *Coventry City v Cartwright* [1975]1 WLR., the Divisional Court said that such an accumulation should effectively 'produce a threat to health in the sense of a threat of disease, vermin or the like.'

(f) Any animal kept in such a place or manner as to be prejudicial to health or a nuisance

(g) noise emitted from premises so as to be prejudicial to health or nuisance

> [(ga) noise that is prejudicial to health or a nuisance and is emitted from or caused by a vehicle, machinery or equipment in a street or, in Scotland, road]

This subsection concerns noise emitted from 'premises' which includes 'land'. The definition of noise, which includes vibration, has been extended by the Noise and Statutory Nuisance Act 1993 (NSNA 1993) to embrace street noise and the noise from machinery or equipment, including car alarms and generators. Aircraft noise is not included within the definition. Note that s10(7) Noise Act 1996 [NA 1996] empowers the LA to seize and remove the noise-making equipment.

In *Murdoch and another v Glacier Metal Co Ltd* (*Times Law Report* January 21st, 1998), a civil action had been brought in nuisance by plaintiffs who complained of a fluctuating low droning noise being emitted from the defendant's factory close by. The issue at trial in the first instance was whether or not the noise amounted to a nuisance in law. The courts will generally examine the character of the area and the consequent levels of noise which are considered to be reasonable. In this case, expert measurements revealed that the levels of noise were the same as or marginally above the World Health Organisation (WHO) levels recommended in its *Environmental Health Criteria*: 'Studies have indicated that the disturbance of sleep becomes increasingly apparent as ambient noise levels exceed about 35dBA'. The trial judge took the view that the measured noise levels did not amount to a nuisance. On appeal, the plaintiffs argued that the WHO recommendations had not been properly considered by the judge, particularly in respect of the importance of undisturbed sleep. However, in the Court of Appeal, Lord Justice Pill took the view that the trial judge had correctly taken account of the other factors in the case (few other complaints and a nearby bypass road) and rightly decided that there was no nuisance. The nature of the locality is a factor to be considered when the nuisance complained of, noise or smell in particular, causes general interference with quiet enjoyment. Where perceivable physical harm has ensued from the nuisance, then the nature of the locality does not have such a bearing on the status of the nuisance.

(h) Any other matter declared by any enactment to be a statutory nuisance

At present, this includes sections of the PHA 1936 - s141 (insanitary cisterns), s259 (nuisances associated with watercourses) s268 (nuisances relating to tents, vans, etc and s151 of the Mines and Quarries

Act 1954 (MQA 1954) (fencing of abandoned and disused mines and quarries).

10.4 Summary proceedings for statutory nuisance

> s80(1) EPA 1990: Where a LA is satisfied that a statutory nuisance exists, or is likely to occur or recur, in the area of the authority, the LA shall serve a notice (an 'abatement notice') imposing all or any of the following requirements:
>
> (a) the abatement of the nuisance of prohibiting or restricting its occurrence or recurrence;
> (b) the execution of such works and the taking of such other steps as may be necessary for any of those purposes.

The *abatement notice* is subject to certain requirements:

(1) If the abatement notice requires some positive action to be taken to abate the nuisance, then that action must be specified.

In *Kirklees Metropolitan Borough Council v Field* [1997] 45 LS Gaz R 28, a notice was served concerning a wall which was about to collapse. The abatement notice was held to be invalid, because it did not specify the steps to be taken.

(2) The abatement notice must also describe the facts which give rise to the nuisance, in addition to the steps which must be taken to abate it. However, the means by which the abatement is to be achieved need not be specified.

In *Myatt v Teignbridge District Council* [1994] Env LR 942, notice was served in respect of 17 dogs kept on the premises. The grounds of an appeal were that the action to be taken was not specified. However, the Court of Appeal took the view that what was required of the appellant in the circumstances of the case was perfectly clear and found against her. In cases of dogs barking, the notice specifying the requirement for abatement of the nuisance did not have to specify the steps that should be taken.

In *Budd v Colchester Borough Council* [1997] Env LR QBD, Schiemann LJ said that it was a matter for the owners to decide what steps should be taken to abate the nuisance.

(3) There is no requirement for a time limit to be specified on the notice. However, there is recent case law which concerns the date on which a statutory nuisance is to be assessed.

In *Surrey Free Inns v Gosport Borough Council* (*Times Law Report* February 13th, 1998) a noise-abatement notice had been served by Gosport Borough Council on premises known as Olivers Bar. It was subsequently quashed by Portsmouth Crown Court on the grounds that on the date of the hearing there was no statutory nuisance and it was unlikely that one would occur, on the facts. The Divisional Court decided that the justification for validity of an abatement notice had to be judged as at the date on which the abatement notice had been served. That decision has been confirmed in the Court of Appeal.

10.5 Offence

> s80(4) EPA 1990: If a person on whom an abatement notice is served, without reasonable excuse, contravenes or fails to comply with any requirement or prohibition imposed by the notice, he shall be guilty of an offence.
>
> S80(5) EPA 1990: A person who commits an offence . . . shall be liable on summary conviction to a fine not exceeding level five on the standard scale together with a further fine of an amount equal to one-tenth of that level for each day on which the offence continues after the conviction.

10.6 Defences

(1) Where the defendant can prove that he used the best practicable means either to prevent or to counteract the effects of the nuisance, in respect of nuisance as described at s79(1) (a), (d), (e), (f) or (g) EPA 1990, and the premises where the nuisance occurred is used either industrially, or for trade or business purposes, then this will be a defence. The defence is *not* available for nuisance under (c) or (h).

If the nuisance fell into the (ga) category, (noise emitted from a vehicle or machinery), then the same defence is available.

The same defence is again available in respect of (b), *except* when the smoke is being emitted from a chimney.

(2) Where the person has failed to comply with an abatement notice for a nuisance which falls into the (g) or (ga) categories, then it will be a defence to prove that the offence was covered by a notice served under s60 COPA 1974, or by a consent given under s61 or 65 COPA 1974.

(3) If the offence were committed when the premises were subject to a noise reduction notice, and the noise level being emitted did not exceed the required level, then this will be a defence, irrespective of whether an appeal is outstanding in respect of the notice.

(4) If the premises in question were new buildings subject to an abatement order and the noise level being emitted did not exceed the level fixed under s67 COPA 1974 then this will amount to a defence, irrespective of whether an appeal is outstanding in respect of the notice

Note that the penalties are far greater when the offence is committed on an industrial, trade or business premises. The person shall be liable on summary conviction to a fine not exceeding £20,000.

10.6.1 s80A EPA 1990: Abatement notice in respect of noise in the street

This section was added by the NSNA 1993. It provides for the service of abatement notices for statutory nuisance in the street. This section is designed to deal with car alarms, *inter alia,*: a person responsible for a noise of this kind may be served personally if he can be found within one hour. If he cannot be found, then the notice may be served by attaching it to the car. Otherwise, he may be served in person. Where the notice is not complied with, the LA may enter or open the vehicle, by force if necessary, or remove it to a secure place, having informed the police.

10.6.2 Offence

s80A(7) EPA 1990:

> A person who removes or interferes with a notice fixed to a vehicle, machinery or equipment . . . shall be guilty of an offence, unless he is the person responsible for the vehicle, machinery or equipment or he does so with the authority of that person.

10.6.3 Private prosecution

s82 EPA 1990 legislates for the private prosecution for statutory nuisance. These are criminal proceedings and compensation may therefore be made in certain respects, under the PCCA 1973. The complainant must prove that a criminal prosecution is more appropriate than a civil one would be. The complainant may institute proceedings for an abatement notice even though civil proceedings are progressing. The potential complainant must give notice to the defendant, 21 days, or three days in respect of a noise nuisance, before bringing proceedings under this section.

In *R v Dudley Metropolitan Borough Council ex parte Hollis* [1998] 1 All ER, statutory proceedings had been initiated against the LA. When it is proved that the nuisance existed at the date of the complaint, s82(12) EPA 1990 requires the magistrates to make an order for costs in favour of the complainant which amounts to compensation for costs 'properly incurred' in bringing the action. In this case, the magistrates had decided to disallow costs. At the appeal, the authority argued that the phrase 'properly incurred' allowed for excessive costs to be disallowed, or no costs to be awarded if the Court found that proceedings should not have been brought in the first place. The Divisional Court disagreed. No costs would be awarded if the nuisance had been abated before proceedings began, but otherwise an award for costs could be made in circumstances where the minimum period of notice had expired and the nuisance *had* existed at the time of the complaint. 'Properly incurred' meant just what it said, and the restriction placed on this requirement was only in respect of excessive costs. The ambit of 'expenses' which could be incorporated in the costs order was expanded by the Divisional Court to include those which were incurred in establishing the existence of a nuisance.

In a later case in the High Court, *Taylor v Walsall and District Property and Investment Company* (*Times Law Reports* February 5th, 1998), the Court held that advance notice of costs should be provided by a complainant in a statutory nuisance case. The defendant should indicate whether that sum was agreed. The Court also held that magistrates had a duty to investigate a claim for costs.

10.7 Defences

The main defence to a charge under s80(4) EPA 1990 is to be found at s80(7) EPA 1990, which is that the defendant used the best practicable means to prevent or to counteract the effects of the nuisance. This defence is not available other than as discussed at 'Defences' above.

10.8 Appeals

When a person is served with an abatement notice, he may appeal against the notice to a Magistrates Court within 21 days. The rules which govern appeals are to be found in the *Statutory Nuisance (Appeals) Regulations* 1995.

Whilst an appeal is pending, the abatement notice may be suspended, other than in circumstances where the nuisance is injurious to health, or where the nuisance is so limited in duration that the suspension of the notice would render it of no practical effect.

The grounds of appeal (Reg 2[2]) may be that the abatement notice was not justified; that there was a defect in the abatement notice; that the authority has unreasonably refused to accept alternative ways of compliance; that the specified time given for compliance was not reasonably sufficient for the purpose; that in the circumstances the best practicable means were used to prevent or counteract the effects of the nuisance; that the requirements of the notice exceeded the requirements which are currently in force in respect of noise in ss 60, 66, 61,65, or 67 COPA 1974, or the NSNA 1993; that the notice was served on the wrong person; or that the notice itself contained a material defect.

In consequence of the appeal, the notice may be quashed, or varied. The appeal may be dismissed. A variation shall have the same effect as if the LA had varied it.

In *Wyre Borough Council v North West Water and Bechtel Water Technology*, (Ends Report, March, 1997) the facts were that the water company had contracted with Bechtel to construct the Fylde Coastal Waters Improvement Scheme. This involved the construction of a sewage works and long sea outfall at Fleetwood, as well as extensive sewage works in the Blackpool area. A great deal of noise was generated and the complaints which ensued prompted the council into measuring the noise. The limits for a night-time operation were being breached by a substantial amount - about 30dBA. Proceedings were brought and both companies were fined £3,500 each, with costs of £3,200.

10.9 Litter

Part IV EPA 1990 contains the provisions which relate to the regulation, and the criminal offences which arise out of those regulations.

Note that a principal litter authority (PLA) is a county council, a county borough council, a district council, the London borough councils, the Common Council of the City of London and the Council of the Isles of Scilly.

10.9.2 s87 EPA 1990: Offence

> If any person throws down, drops or otherwise deposits in, into or from any place to which this section applies, and leaves, any thing whatsoever in such circumstances as to cause or contribute to, or tend to lead to, the defacement by litter of any place to which this section applies, he shall, subject to s87(2) be guilty of an offence. This section will include the public place, public place being defined as a place in the open air to which the public are entitled or permitted to have access without payment, or any covered place open to the air on at least one side, and available for public use (for example, railway stations or shopping precincts) shall be treated as a public open place. Trade or commercial refuse left out for collection is litter for the purposes of this Act, even if it is also commercial waste for the purposes of s35(1)EPA1990.

10.9.2.1 Sentence

"A person who is guilty of an offence under this section shall be liable on summary conviction to a fine not exceeding level four on the standard scale."

Provided the litter deposit was authorised by law, or done with the consent of the person who has control of the place where the deposit occurred, then there is no offence.

Note that a fixed penalty notice, according to s88 EPA 1990 is an alternative means of discharging liability in respect of litter.

An alternative regulatory procedure is found at s91 EPA 1990. It is open to an 'aggrieved' person to make a complaint to the Magistrates Court, complaining of the defacement by litter or refuse of a relevant highway, trunk road, the land of a PLA, Crown land, the land of a designated statutory undertaker, the land of a designated educational institution, or land within the litter-control area of a LA. If the Court decides that there is substance in the complaint, it may make a litter abatement order (LAO) requiring the defendant to clear the litter or refuse away.

10.9.3 Offence

> A person who, without reasonable excuse, fails to comply with a litter abatement order shall be guilty of an offence and liable on summary conviction to a fine not exceeding level four on the standard scale together with a further fine of an amount equal to one-twentieth of that level for each day on which the offence continues, after the conviction.

The LAO may specify not only the nature of the litter but also the period during which the litter must be cleaned up. Note that clean-up costs may in certain circumstances be recouped from a defendant.

It will be a defence to prove that the defendant has complied with his duty under s89(1) or (2) EPA 1990 (the duties of a LA). The Code of Practice will be admissible in evidence and may be taken into account by the Court.

A LAO may also be served by a PLA, containing the requirements that the litter or refuse be cleared and a prohibition on the land becoming defaced thus further. Failure to comply with the notice is an offence for which the punishment is set out above 8.9.5. (It will be a defence to show that the defendant has complied with his duty of care in respect of the land, and the Code of Practice will be admissible as above at 8.9.7).

The Appeals procedure may be operated within 21 days of service of the abatement notice.

10.9.10

By s93 EPA 1990, the LA may serve, on the occupiers of premises, a street-litter control notice (SLCN). The authority must inform the person that it is its intention to serve the notice, and give the person an opportunity to make representations about the notice, for 21 days from the point when he was informed.

If it appears to the authority that the notice is not being complied with, then it may apply to the Magistrates Court for an order requiring compliance on the part of the person on whom the notice was served.

10.9.5 Offence

> A person who, without reasonable excuse, fails to comply with an order [under this section], shall be guilty of an offence and liable on summary conviction to a fine not exceeding level four on the standard scale.

It is the duty of the PLAs to keep a public register containing copies of all orders made, including SLCNs. The register must be both secure and accessible to the public.

CHAPTER 11

NOISE POLLUTION

CONTENTS

CHAPTER 11

NOISE POLLUTION

11.1 Introduction

The main statutory provision for noise pollution is contained in Environmental Protection Act 1990 (EPA 1990), under the law of statutory nuisance (see Chapter 10). Noise, for the purposes of statutory nuisance provisions, is defined at s79(1)(g) and s79(1)(ga) EPA 1990. Other statutory controls which relate to noise pollution are found within the Control of Pollution Act 1974 (COPA1974), the Noise and Statutory Nuisance Act 1993 (NSNA 1993) and the Noise Act 1996 (NA 1996). In addition, various regulations implement EC directives in respect of the limiting of noise levels in construction equipment and machinery, domestic appliances and lawnmowers.

In recent years, there has been a marked increase in complaints about noise to local authorities (LAs). The majority of the complaints are dealt with at an informal level but if the nuisance *is* found to exist, an abatement notice is served.

Noise measurement is a complex technical process which involves comparisons between various noise levels over certain periods, according to statutory criteria. Sleep disturbance is one of the most frequent features of a complaint and it is the subject of WHO guidelines. A framework Directive on environmental noise measurement, mapping and control will be proposed by the European Commission in 1999, with the expectation that it will enter into force in 2002. The main issue will be determining whether ambient noise standards and targets will be a matter for domestic legislation. It is not yet clear whether harmonisation of these standards will be achievable.

11.2 Control of Pollution Act 1974 (COPA 1974)

s57 COPA 1974 imposes a duty upon a LA to inspect its area from time to time, 'to decide how to exercise its powers concerning noise-abatement zones (NAZs). NAZs have not generally been established at the time of writing.

11.2.1 Construction sites

The control of noise on construction sites is a matter for the LA. A person who intends to carry out works on a construction site may apply to the LA for a consent under s61 COPA 1974. The application must be made at the same time, or later than, applications for approval under building regulations. The application should contain details of the works to be carried out, the methods which are intended to be used and details of the steps which will be taken to minimise the noise pollution which will ensue. If the LA is satisfied by the content of the application, it may grant a consent, with such attendant conditions or limitations which it judges to be appropriate in the circumstances.

The definition of *'construction'* encompasses the erection, construction, alteration, repair or maintenance of buildings or roads, road works, demolition and any engineering works. Having established that 'construction' is being or is going to be carried out, the LA may serve an notice, under s60 COPA 1974 on the person who is responsible for or has control over the construction.

The notice may contain requirements concerning the ways in which the 'construction' may be carried out. The list of requirements (at s60[3] COPA 1974) is wide-ranging: the notice may address the means by which the works shall be effected, time-limits within which 'construction' may take place, and the measurable levels of noise which may be permitted during 'construction'.

When setting these requirements, the LA is obliged to consider:

(1) The appropriate codes of practice[1] and the need to ensure that the best practice means (BPM) will be used to minimise the noise.

'Best practical means' is defined at s72 COPA 1974: 'practical' should be construed having regard to local conditions and circumstances, as well as to the current state of technical knowledge and the financial implications. Note that the test for 'best practical means' is its compatibility with any duty imposed by the law, that duty being statutorily defined for statutory undertakers.

(2) Specifications of preferable methods and of machinery which will reduce noise-pollution levels, and the need to protect nearby people from the effects of the noise. The notice may specify a time limit for compliance.

An appeal may be made against the notice, to a Magistrates Court, within 21 days from the service of the notice.

11.2.2 Offences

> s60(8) COPA 1974: If a person on whom a notice is served under this section without reasonable excuse contravenes any requirement of the notice he shall be guilty of an offence against this Part of the Act.
>
> s61(5) . . . any person who knowingly carries out the works, or permits the works to be carried out, in contravention of any conditions attached to a consent under this section shall be guilty of an offence against this Part of the Act.

This is an important sub-section: it addresses the liability of the main contractor where the sub-contractor has breached a condition of the consent for which the main contractor applied. The state of knowledge of the subcontractor will be a matter of evidence.

In *Tower Hamlets London Borough v London Docklands Development Corporation* (1992) (unreported), Lloyd J stated that the contravention has been allowed to take place where a person "abstains from taking reasonable steps to prevent an act where it is within that person's power to prevent it."

s61(10) COPA 1974: Where a consent has been obtained and works then carried out by a person who is not the applicant, then the applicant is under a duty to 'take all reasonable steps to bring the consent to the notice of that other person'. Failure to do so will amount to an offence against this part of the Act.

Note that where a persistent flouting of the s60 COPA 1974 notice occurs, the Court of Appeal has decided, in *City of London Corporation v Bovis Construction Ltd* [1992] 3 All ER 697, CA, that an injunction may be granted in support of the notice. The injunction will contain the same 'without reasonable excuse' proviso as the notice, in line with the criminal offence which flows from the breach of a requirement under the notice.

11.2.3 Defence

It will a defence to prove that the alleged contravention complied with the requirements within the consent which had been obtained.

11.2.4 Noise in the streets

11.2.4.1 Loudspeakers

s62 EPA 1990 is amended by the NSNA 1993. The LA may decide that Schedule 2 to that Act may apply to its area, in which case it may make different provisions from those set out below.

> s62(1) EPA 1990 . . . a loud-speaker in a street shall not be operated
>
> (a) between the hours of nine in the evening and eight in the following morning, for any purpose;
>
> (b) at any other time, for the purpose of advertising any entertainment, trade or business.
>
> and any person who operates or permits the operation of a loudspeaker in contravention of this subsection shall be guilty of an offence against this Part of the Act.

The exceptions to this law are contained in s62(2) and (3) EPA 1990.

NAZs may be designated by the LA, who will then be entitled to make noise abatement orders (NAOs), where the noise level has been measured to be in excess of the limits which have been imposed in the zone. Where a zone has been defined, the LA will be obliged to keep a register of the measurements of premises within the zone. Note that the validity of the measurement itself will not be an issue in any court proceedings.

Consents for noise exceeding the registered levels may be made by the LA, and subject to conditions. At present, LA have not generally used this route to regulate noise pollution.

The LA may also serve a noise-reduction order (NRO) which overrides the order served under s65 EPA 1990. It may be served where levels of noise emanating from a premises are not acceptable in respect of the purposes for which the order was originally made. The issue is one of public benefit. The particulars of the NRO must be entered into the register. The order may require the person to reduce the level of noise, to prevent any subsequent increases in the noise level and to take any such steps as may be required in the order. That person may appeal against the NRO, within three months, to the Magistrates Court.

11.2.4.2 Offences

> s65(5) EPA 1990: If noise emitted from any premises constitutes a contravention of subsection(1)[the registered noise level] . . . or of a condition attached to a consent under this section, the person responsible shall be guilty of an offence against this Part of the Act.
>
> s65(6) EPA 1990: A further offence will be committed against this Part of the Act if, after conviction and after the magistrates have ordered a thing to be done to prevent the occurrence or recurrence of the offence, it is not done. The LA may then be directed to do what the convicted person had been required to do.
>
> s66(8) EPA 1990: A person who without reasonable excuse contravenes a NRO shall be guilty of an offence against this Part of this Act.

11.2.4.3 Noise from plant or machinery

s68 EPA 1990 makes provision for the regulation of noise reduction devices, and limitation of noise levels caused by plant or machinery. The Secretary of State has a duty to consult producers and users of plant or machinery before regulating. Different regulations may be made for different areas.

11.2.4.4 Offence

> s68(3) EPA 1990: Any person who contravenes or causes or permits another person to contravene regulations under this section shall be guilty of an offence against this Part of the Act.

11.2.4.5 Defence

It will be a defence to prove that the means used for noise reduction were not less effective than those specified in the regulations

Note that the LA may recoup the costs of executing works in a case where the convicted offender has not complied with the terms of an order of the Court.

11.2.4.6 Appeals

s70 EPA 1990 provides for the form and grounds of appeal. These are dealt with in the various Regulations which have been listed below.

11.2.4.7 Sentencing

S74(1) EPA 1990

> A person guilty of an offence against this Part of this Act shall be liable on summary conviction [to a fine not exceeding level five on the standard scale] together, in any case, with a further fine not exceeding £50 for each day on which the offence continues after the conviction.

11.3 Motor Cycle Noise Act 1987 (MCNA 1987)

This act requires compliance on the part of dealers in motorcycle-exhaust systems or silencers with regulations made by the Secretary of State. Where the offence has been committed with the consent or connivance of an officer or manager of the company or corporation, then that officer or manager may be similarly charged.

The Schedule to the Act creates the offence:

11.3.1 Offence

> s1(1) Any person who contravenes [a regulation] . . . shall be guilty of an offence and liable on summary conviction to imprisonment for a term not exceeding three months or to a fine not exceeding level five on the standard scale.

Third parties may be charged, without prejudice to the charging or not of the first person.

11.3.2 Defence

It will be a defence to prove that the defendant took all reasonable steps and exercised all due diligence to avoid committing the offence

11.4 Noise and Statutory Nuisance Act 1993 (NSNA 1993): audible intruders alarms

This Act has made provision for the regulation of *audible intruder alarms*. By s9 NSNA 1993, a LA may apply Schedule 3 to its area. This schedule will require the person who installs an audible intruder alarm on his premises, *inter alia*, to notify the LA and the police of that installation, together with the names and addresses of current key holders.

11.4.1 Offence

> If the person contravenes any of the regulations under this Schedule, then he shall be guilty of an offence and liable to a fine not exceeding level five [in the case of any prescribed requirements for the alarm], level four [in the case when the alarm is operated in breach of the regulations] or level two [in any other case].

11.5 Noise Act 1996 (NA 1996)

This Act provides a summary procedure for dealing with noise emanating from a dwelling during the night. It first empowers the LA to apply this Act to its area. The LA becomes obliged to investigate a complaint about noise coming from a dwelling during night hours (which, for the purposes of this Act, are between 11pm and 7am). If the noise exceeds the permitted level, then by s3 NA 1996 the authority may serve a warning notice. s3 NA 1996 provides for the conditions of service of the warning notice and for its contents. The warning issued to the person is that they may be guilty of an offence.

11.5.1 Offence

> s4(1) NA 1996: If a warning notice has been served in respect of noise emitted from a dwelling, any person who is responsible for noise which
>
> (a) is emitted form the dwelling in the period specified in the notice, and
> (b) exceeds the permitted level, as measured from within the complainant's dwelling,
>
> is guilty of an offence.

In proceedings for the offence, documentary evidence of the noise measurement (made by an approved device) may be produced. That evidence must be served upon the person in advance. (See s8 NA 1996 below.)

11.5.2 Defence

It is a defence for a person thus charged to show that he had a reasonable excuse for emitting the noise.

11.5.3 Sentence

A person who is guilty of an offence under this section is liable on summary conviction to a fine not exceeding level three on the standard scale.

Note that this offence may initially be dealt with by means of a fixed penalty notice.

The local authority may apply for a warrant, giving it powers of entry and seizure of equipment at premises from where the noise is emanating. Schedule 10 to the Act determines the LA's powers of retention and forfeiture over seized equipment, as well as the regulations governing the consequences of forfeiture and the return of the equipment.

11.5.4 Offences

s(8)NA 1996: It is an offence to obstruct a person exercising these powers. Conviction for such an offence may lead to a fine not exceeding level three on the standard scale.

11.6 Other offences

There are a number of sets of regulations which implement EC Directives in respect of noise pollution, each containing provision for measurement, the providing of information and the determination of limits. Each set of regulations creates offences, whereby breach of those regulations amounts to a summary offence and a person who is convicted will incur a fine.

11.7 Codes of practice which may be relevant

Control of Noise (Code of Practice for Construction and Open Sites) SI 1984/1992
Control of Noise (Code of Practice on Noise from Audible Intruder Alarms) SI 1981/1829
Control of Noise (Code of Practice on Noise from Ice-Cream Van Chimes, etc) SI 1981/1828
Control of Noise (Code of Practice on Noise from Model Aircraft) SI 1981/1830
Control of Noise (Code of Practice for Construction and Open Sites) SI 1987/1730

CHAPTER 12

OFFENCES UNDER THE TOWN AND COUNTRY PLANNING ACT 1990

CONTENTS

CHAPTER 12

OFFENCES UNDER THE TOWN AND COUNTRY PLANNING ACT 1990

12.1 Introduction

Offences created by the Town and Country Planning Act 1990 (TCPA 1990) fall into three categories. Firstly, offences designed to provide the criminal sanction to give effect to the development-control system. These are offences of failing to comply with a notice served, usually by the local planning authority (LPA), requiring some action to have been taken by a set date. The best example is failure to comply with requirements of a s179 TCPA 1990 enforcement notice.

Second, offences providing for the enforcement of a discrete regime, such as tree protection, under tree-preservation orders, or advertisement-display provisions.

Third, offences created to ensure that the planning system's proper working is not obstructed at any stage by the unscrupulous or the dishonest. Such offences are the wilful obstruction of a planning officer exercising a right of entry, contrary to s196C (3) or 325(2) TCPA 1990, or dishonestly providing false evidence to gain a certificate of lawful use under s194 TCPA 1990.

12.2 'Failing to comply with' offences

Discussion of these offences concentrates on notices issued, mostly by the LPA. However, there may be prosecutions in which other public bodies, such as English Heritage or the Secretary of State for the Environment, have exercised their power to issue a notice. Different considerations may also apply to Crown land. These special cases are not covered in detail and the general principles and decided authorities will usually apply. Reference may have to be made to the specific provisions where a prosecution is being considered to which these considerations may apply. The provisions in relation to Crown land, for instance, are found in Part XIII, TCPA 1990.

12.2.1 Enforcing provisions of Enforcement Notices: s179 and 181(5) TCPA 1990

Where there has been a breach of planning control, such as development of land without planning permission or failure to comply with a condition attached to a planning permission, then the LPA may serve an enforcement notice. This is a notice which, in effect, requires the breach of planning control to be put right. Once the appeal procedure, if invoked, has been exhausted, the notice becomes effective and criminal liability can be incurred for failing to comply with it.

Where an enforcement notice is not complied with voluntarily, the LPA can either seek a civil injunction under s187B TCPA 1990 or prosecute under s179 TCPA 1990.

s179 TCPA 1990 creates two separate offences. The 'owner' and the 'occupier/person in control' offence.

s179 (1) and (2) TCPA 1990 read:

> (1) Where at any time after the end of the period for compliance with an enforcement notice, any step required by the notice to be taken has not been taken or any activity required by the notice to cease is being carried on, the person who is then the owner of the land is in breach of an enforcement notice.
>
> (2) Where the owner of land is in breach of an enforcement notice he shall be guilty of an offence.

s179(4) and (5) TCPA 1990 read:

> (4) A person who has control of or an interest in the land to which an enforcement notice relates (other than the owner) must not carry on any activity which is required by the notice to cease or cause or permit such an activity to be carried on.
>
> (5) A person who, at any time, after the end of the period compliance with the notice contravenes subsection (4) shall be guilty of an offence.

Thus the elements the prosecution must prove to make out the offence - whether prosecuting the owner under subsection (1) or the person having an interest in land or in control of it under subsection (5) - are that:

(1) an enforcement notice was in force in relation to the relevant piece of land;
(2) the period allowed for compliance with that notice has expired;
(3) the provisions of the enforcement notice have been breached.

And then - depending on whether the owner is being prosecuted under s179(2) TCPA 1990 or the person in control under s179(5) TCPA 1990 - that the defendant either:

(4A) owned the land in the period covered by the prosecution; or
(4B) had control of, or an interest in, the land and either himself carried on an activity which was required by the notice to cease or caused or permitted such an activity to be carried on.

12.2.2 Common elements

12.2.2.1 That an enforcement notice was in force in relation to the relevant piece of land

Proof of the issue of the notice

Enforcement notices can be issued by LPAs only (s172[1] TCPA 1990) or in certain circumstances by the Secretary of State for the Environment in which case it has the same effect as an enforcement notice issued by the LPA. (s182[3] TCPA 1990). Although there is a rebuttal presumption in public law that what ought to have been done has been done, clear evidence that the notice was issued by the LPA will avoid a submission of no case to answer. Proof is usually in the form of a certified copy of the report to and minute of the committee or subcommittee which authorised the issue of the notice. Where the notice has been issued under some other procedure (typically a procedure for dealing with urgent items), the relevant standing orders should be produced to show how it is that the issue of the notice was authorised in the particular circumstances.

Where there is a complicated planning history or more than one notice, the prosecution will need to ensure that the authorisation does specifically relate to the notice in front of the court. When precise resolution numbers and so forth are checked, it has not been unknown for the authority produced to be found to relate to a previous notice subsequently withdrawn, to a notice covering the same site but different issues, or to the same issues but a slightly but crucially different area of land.

There is usually no need to call a witness specifically to produce the enforcement notice. By s234 (2) of the Local Government Act 1972 (LGA 1972) any document purporting to bear the signature of the authority's proper officer shall be deemed, until the contrary is proved, to have been duly given, made or issued by the LA's authority. In this subsection, 'signature' includes a facsimile of a signature by whatever process reproduced.

This authorises LAs' not uncommon practice of using a rubber stamp of the local-authority solicitor's signature. It also authorises documents signed on behalf of, or *per procurationem*, the specifically authorised officer, although the person actually signing must be able show that they had authority to sign documents in that fashion on behalf of the senior officer. This authority need not be in writing - for instance a legal executive employed by the LA is likely to be authorised to sign documents on behalf of their superior, the local-authority solicitor. See *Swishbrook Limited v Secretary of State for the Environment* [1990] COD 293 and, an authority relating specifically to enforcement notices, *Fitzpatrick v Secretary of State for the Environment, The Times*, December 29th, 1988.

The prosecution may wish to include a line of evidence confirming that the enforcement notice has not been withdrawn but this is not strictly necessary.

12.2.2.2 Crown land

If the relevant breach of planning control is on Crown land, the provisions of s294 and s296 TCPA 1990 apply. These may either prevent the service of an enforcement notice or, under s296 TCPA 1990, require the Crown's consent for the issue of a notice in respect of land owned by the Crown but occupied, typically under a lease, by a private person. Where the requirements of s296(2) TCPA 1990 require the Crown's consent to the issue of an enforcement notice, the prosecution should prove that the relevant consent has been obtained as part of its case. Failure to do so could be the subject of a successful submission of no case to answer. Without consent, no notice shall be served and therefore the prosecution would not be proceeding on an enforcement notice within the terms of the Act.

12.2.2.3 That the period for compliance with the Enforcement Notice had expired

The prosecution must allege and prove that the requirements of the enforcement notice were breached after the period for compliance with it had expired. (See *Maltedge Ltd and Frost v Wokingham DC* [1992] 3 PLR 136.) If an appeal has been entered against the notice it is, for the purposes of the criminal law at least, suspended and the determination of the appeal will redefine the date for compliance with the notice as upheld.

12.2.2.4 That the requirements of the Enforcement Notice have been breached

This is simply a matter of fact. The offence is of strict liability (*R v Collett and others* [1994] 2 All ER 372). There is no requirement for the prosecution to prove any intention on behalf of the owner in relation to the enforcement notice, nor, subject to the defence in s7 TCPA 1990, that the owner was ever served with or knew of the existence of the notice. However, as set out below, an owner who is genuinely and not unreasonably ignorant of the notice may raise certain arguments in his defence which would otherwise be closed to him. For the s4 TCPA 1990 offence it is necessary to prove that the defendant carried on an activity prohibited by the enforcement notice, or caused or permitted such an activity to be carried on, but not that the defendant had any intention that the enforcement should not be complied with.

There are two issues:

(1) What can the prosecution prove has been happening on the land?

This will be a factual issue. The prosecution's evidence will have to be gathered and presented as in any other criminal trial where there may be a factual dispute. As always, contemporaneous notes of visits and dated photographs are likely to produce the most reliable evidence.

(2) Does what the prosecution can prove has occurred contravene the wording of the enforcement notice? Is there an argument as to what the enforcement notice actually means?

Although the enforcement-notice author may not appreciate it at the time, he is also defining the offence's *actus reus*. Whoever drafts the steps required to be taken or the activities that the enforcement notice is to prohibit under s173(3) TCPA 1990, should bear in mind that the words may come under intense scrutiny at contested trial. Any uncertainty or ambiguity will not be resolved in favour of the LPA but, in accordance with the general rule in criminal proceedings, in favour of the defendant. If this principle needed any confirmation, this is provided by a reported decision of the Crown Court (*Warrington District Council v Garvey* [1988] JPL752.)

The defendant will have to point to a genuine ambiguity, such as whether a requirement that a restaurant should not be open to the public after 12 midnight means that all customers have to leave by midnight, coffee finished or not, or whether no fresh customers should be admitted to the restaurant after 12 midnight. Applying *Warrington District Council v Garvey*, the Court would have to apply the alternative most favourable to the defendant leading to a ruling that allowing customers to finish their meals after midnight would not involve a breach of the enforcement notice leading to criminal liability. (This was the interpretation given to the words in *Miah v Secretary of State for the Environment and Hillingdon BC* 1986 JPL 756 although the Court was not considering criminal liability directly.)

Where, however, on careful reading in the light of other provisions such as the General Development Order, the meaning of an enforcement notice is clear, its provisions will be applied. (See *Attorney Generals Reference No. 1 of 1996* [1997] JPL 749.)

Even where the words are clear, any proper doubt as to whether the words, on the face of the enforcement notice, have been breached will be in favour of the defendant. For instance, where the prosecution's case is that there has been 'use' of the land in a way prohibited by the enforcement notice, the *de minimis* rule must be considered. It may not be a 'use of land' for the prosecution to be able to prove only that the prohibited activity has taken place on three or four days in an 18-month or two-year period. Careful drafting of the enforcement notice can help minimise difficulties later. For instance, in a notice prohibiting use of land for the repair of motor vehicles, it is often appropriate to include a step requiring all plant, machinery and materials associated with the repairuse to be removed from the site and not returned. This lessens the need to catch car mechanics redhanded because the evidence of hydraulic jacks, compressors, paint-sprayers and so forth remaining on land after the date for compliance in breach of the notice may be easier to obtain.

Reading the enforcement notice so as to resolve any ambiguity in the notice in favour of the defendant leads to the notice being read so as to exclude from criminal liability any rights which the defendant may have, under other principles of planning law, to use his land even if at first glance they appear prohibited by the wording. This is applying the planning law doctrine set out in *Mansi v Elstree Rural District Council (1964)* 16 P&CR 154 into the criminal law. For example, the parking of a car ancillary to the use of a dwelling house has been held not to be covered by an enforcement notice prohibiting the use of the area of land for car parking *R v Harfield* [1993] 2 PLR 23.

Where the offence alleged is under s179(1), the prosecution must also prove:

12.2.3 That the defendant owns the land

The prosecution must allege and prove that the defendant owned the land during the period covered by the charge.

The definition of 'owner' is given in s336 TCPA 1990:

> owner in relation to any land, means [exceptions not relevant to the offences] a person, other than a mortgagee not in possession, who, whether in his own right or as trustee for any other person, is entitled to receive the rack rent of the land, or, where the land is not let at a rack rent, would be so entitled if it were so let

The most straightforward method of proving this is office-copy entries of the Land Register which prove themselves under s113 of the Land Registration Act 1925 (LRA 1925).

Other sources of evidence are any replies to a notice issued under s171C TCPA 1990 requiring an individual to state what interest he holds in a piece of land. However, it is important to note that the use of evidence which has itself been obtained under threat of prosecution is often challenged in subsequent criminal proceedings on the basis that the use of such evidence is in breach of the European Convention on Human Rights. There is no decided authority on the point in planning law and the authorities are not all one way in relation to the other similar statutory requirements for the answers to be produced and verified.

Although an Inspector's finding that a particular person owned land would be hearsay, any statement by the defendant themselves during the process of entering or conducting an appeal would be admissible as tending to show ownership. Many enforcement notices on which prosecutions under this section are brought will have been appealed. During this process the defendant, whether by entering the appeal, or by making a statement, at the inquiry or in written representations, may make an admission on which the prosecution would wish to rely (such as that he owned the land having bought it on a certain date). There is no reason why, subject to the normal rules governing the admission of evidence, the prosecution cannot do so. However, evidence of the admission cannot be gained from the Inspector's decision-letter determining the appeal. It must come directly from the defendant so as to avoid the hearsay rule. Hence, the defendant may have told the Inspector that he owned the land and the Inspector may have correctly recorded this. However, the prosecution will only be able to adduce that fact by calling a witness who was at the inquiry and who can say that he himself heard the defendant say that he had bought the land, or by producing the defendant's written evidence to this effect. (This is simply the application of basic rules of evidence in criminal proceedings - this particular example was given by Glidewell LJ in the *Ruttle ex p Marshall* case - see below.)

Whilst it is for the prosecution to prove that the defendant owned the land during the period covered by the charge (*R v Ruttle ex p Marshall* [1989] JPL 681) it need not do so right up until the relevant day. In the absence of contradictory evidence, there is a presumption that, once proved, ownership will not have changed (*Whitefield v Gowling* [1974] 28 P&CR 386.)

Complications can be caused by the Act's definition of 'owner' where there has been a bankruptcy in the relevant period. In addition, the prosecution should be cautious to check the exact position where long leaseholders are involved.

It would not be appropriate for the prosecution to proceed under both s179(2) and (5) TCPA 1990 as alternatives.

Where the prosecution is brought under s179(5), the prosecution must also prove:

12.2.4 That the defendant has control of, or an interest in, the land and either carried on an activity which was required by the notice to cease or caused or permitted such an activity to be carried on

'Carried on an activity which was required by the notice to cease'

An enforcement notice's requirements are permitted to be either positive or negative. Positive, in the sense that they may require specific physical steps to be taken to remedy the breach of planning control at which the enforcement notice is aimed. The breach may be the use of the land without planning permission for vehicle repairs and, as part and parcel of that use, an area of the land which was previously grass has been concreted over and plant and material, such as spare body parts and paint-spraying equipment, have been brought onto the land.

As positive steps, the enforcement notice may require that, by the date for compliance, the concrete be broken up and the area it had covered be reseeded with grass; and that all material and plant brought onto the land in connection with the vehicle-repair use be removed and not returned.

As negative steps, the enforcement notice may require that the use of the land for vehicle repairs cease before the date for compliance. Only the landowner can be prosecuted under s179(1) TCPA 1990 if any of the positive steps have not been taken. Under s179(5) TCPA 1990, the person in control of the land, or having an interest in the land, can be prosecuted only if a negative step is not complied with, in the sense that an activity prohibited by the notice, such as vehicle repair, has been carried on.

Acute questions may arise as to whether an isolated number of incidents can be said to be carrying on an activity.

'control of'

Whether the individual or company has control of the land will be a question of fact in each case. Relevant factors are likely to be whether the individual or company determined who could or could not come onto the land and whether that person determined what activities took place on the land and where they were to take place.

'an interest in the land'

The Act's interpretation section does not qualify 'interest'. It is usually taken to be anything more than an informal arrangement. Informal arrangements which, in fact, give control of the land will be covered by that limb of the subsection, although the prosecutor should elect which category it says covers the defendant.

'caused or permitted'

See the consideration of these definitions in the Criminal Proceedings Section of this book (Chapter 16). Evidence of payment is often a strong indication of permitting.

12.2.5 Defences

s179(3) TCPA 1990 reads:

> In proceedings against any person for an offence under subsection (2) it shall be a defence for him to show that he did everything he could be expected to do to secure compliance with the notice.

This applies only to the owner offence under s179(1) TCPA 1990 which is of strict liability and is drafted so that, on its face, the landowner could commit the offence wholly unwittingly and unknowingly. The offence is not available to a defendant under s179(5) TCPA 1990, corresponding with the fact that that offence requires the defendant to have carried on an activity themselves or to have caused or permitted that activity to have been carried on.

This statutory defence appears designed to protect the owner who is not directly in control of the land and is prohibited in some way from dealing with it so as to secure compliance with the notice. The formulation 'did everything he could be expected to do' lessens the scope of the defence, in semantic if not practical terms, compared with the more common 'without reasonable excuse' used to dilute strict liability elsewhere in regulatory offences.

It is difficult to suggest general rules as to what will constitute 'doing everything that could be expected.' It is clear that although the test is objective, judged by society's reasonable expectations, the defendant's personal circumstances, including financial circumstances, are relevant. (See Buckley J, in *Kent County Council v Brockman* 1996 1 PLR 1.)

> The vital words are: 'did everything he could be expected to do to secure compliance with the notice.' If one asks 'expected by whom?', in my judgement the only answer can be 'by the Court as representing the reasonable expectations of society.' If one asks 'well, what could any individual be expected to do?', the answer must come back 'well, tell me the circumstances of the case, including his own circumstances, and I will answer your question.'
>
> It seems to me that the plain meaning of those words does indeed permit a defendant's personal circumstances to be taken into account. I bear in mind, in reaching that conclusion, that this section creates a criminal offence. To hold someone guilty of a criminal offence for not doing something which they are genuinely incapable of doing would be quite contrary to any tenets of criminal law known to me at least.

The onus is on the defendant to make out the defence on the balance of probabilities. In practice, the Court will be considering what other steps the prosecution can point to which the defendant could theoretically have taken and determine whether the reasons for not taking it are credible and reasonable. The Court in *Brockman* has, in fact, brought the defence to this offence closer to the more common 'without reasonable excuse.' The defence would apply where, for instance, the land is occupied by squatters who are breaching the enforcement notice and the owner has asked them to leave and instigated possession proceedings but the prohibited use continues. A defendant is more likely to succeed where the prosecution relies on a failure to carry out a positive step which will involve significant expenditure rather than seeking to suggest why a use of land has continued in breach of the criminal law.

The Courts have warned against accepting readily what in effect is an argument that there are financial reasons for breaking the law. The prosecution is not usually in a position, without a great deal of detective work and persistence, to make an effective challenge to a defendant's assertions of poverty. There is no requirement for the defendant to give notice of this defence to the prosecution who may learn it is being run only when the defendant gives his evidence.

As was pointed out in *Brockman* -

> ... The scheme of s179 and its provisions makes no provision for any discovery or inquiry as to the financial means of the defendant, that is the nature of the incapacity that he is relying on ... The prosecution will have no notice of this defence and not really be able vigorously or satisfactorily to challenge him. ... This section does not make any such provision, but, in my judgement, it is a matter for the Magistrates Court or Crown Court, whichever it may be, to take a sensible but reasonable attitude to a defendant who raises this defence. The onus is upon him and I would ... be very surprised if they were satisfied simply by a defendant waving a bank statement in front of them showing an overdraft or with a mere assertion by him that he was impecunious ...
>
> ... I would expect the Court to be fairly rigorous in the proof which it expects or demands of a defendant and not allow itself to be hoodwinked by protestations of impecuniosity on behalf of any individual.

A specific example of the defence is that of Gypsies who claim they would not be able to comply with the enforcement notice requiring them to remove caravans from land or stop using land for the stationing of a mobile home. Whilst this is not a defence in itself (See *R v Beard* 1997 1 PLR 64), the LPA in such cases may wish to demonstrate that housing can be provided elsewhere - usually with its housing department prepared to treat the family as unintentionally homeless if they comply with the enforcement notice with nowhere else to go.

s179(7) TCPA 1990 reads:

> Where -
>
> (a) a person charged with an offence under this section has not been served with a copy of the enforcement notice; and
> (b) the notice is not contained in the appropriate register kept under Sec.188, it shall be a defence for him to show that he was not aware of the existence of the notice.

Under s188 TCPA 1990 and regulations under that section, the LA is required to keep a public register of enforcement notices. This will allow anybody acquiring or moving to property to check whether or not there are any outstanding enforcement notices requiring compliance. The precise details required to be entered on the register are set by the Town and Country Planning (General Development Procedure) Order 1995 and include a summary of the requirements of the notice and the date for compliance.

12.2.6 Attacking the notice itself during criminal proceedings

Under s174 TCPA 1990, there is a right of appeal to the Secretary of State for the Environment against an enforcement notice, on a wide range of grounds including lack of service and the planning merits. The s285(1) TCPA 1990 prohibits a challenge to the enforcement notice on any of the grounds under which an appeal could have been made under s174 TCPA 1990 in any other proceedings which includes criminal proceedings. (*R v Smith 1984* 48 P&CR 392.)

The exception to this rule is set out in s285(2) TCPA 1990:

> (2) Subsection (1) shall not apply to proceedings brought under s179 against a person who -
> (a) has held an interest in the land since before the enforcement notice was issued under that Part [VII of the Act] ; and
> (b) did not have a copy of the enforcement notice served on him under that Part; and
> (c) satisfies the Court -

i) that he did not know and could not reasonably be expected to know that the enforcement notice had been issued; and
ii) that his interests have been substantially prejudiced by the failure to serve him with a copy of it.

Any defendant who can satisfy the Court that he passes each of these cumulative tests would then, in theory, be able to turn the criminal trial into a planning inquiry. In practice, a prosecution is unlikely to be instigated or continued where s285(2) TCPA 1990 applies.

s285(1) TCPA 1990 only removes the right to challenge the enforcement notice in respect of any point that could have constituted a ground of appeal under s174 TCPA 1990. The extent to which there might be other grounds of challenge which remained available to a defendant in a criminal trial was considered by the House of Lords in *R v Wicks* 1997 2 All ER 801.

In *Wicks* , the defendant accepted that he was in breach of an enforcement, served by the LA, which appeared regular. He wished to allege as a defence at trial that the enforcement notice was not valid because, in issuing it, the LA had acted in bad faith and been motivated by immaterial considerations. The House of Lords held that whether such arguments challenging a notice demanding compliance could be raised in criminal proceedings depended on the relevant statute's particular wording. Whilst the law should be slow to shut out defences, here s179 TCPA 1990 was embedded in an elaborate statutory code for service of the notice and appeal that the prosecution merely had to prove that the notice was one "issued by the planning authority which on its face complies with the requirements of the Act and has not been quashed on appeal or by judicial review", per Lord Hoffman at page 820 g.

Elsewhere in the judgement the point is put as the prosecution having to prove that the notice was issued by the authority, is formally valid and has not been set aside. Per Lord Nicholls at p808 f.

It may be open to a potential defendant to challenge the issue of an enforcement notice alleging bad faith by way of an application for judicial review. However,in criminal proceedings it would appear that effectively only three points can be taken on validity:

(1) That the notice was not issued by the LPA.

Hypothetically, this could be because it is a clever forgery issued by a vindictive neighbour. However, in practice this will involve the defendant showing that the enforcement notice has not been properly authorised and thus cannot be said to be issued by the authority. The defendant would be entitled to call evidence on this point. For example, to show that an apparently valid notice was in fact issued by a planning officer on a frolic of his own. This point is discussed above under what the prosecution must prove.

(2) That the notice is valid on its face or appears formally valid.

Although there is no explicit definition of 'formally valid' within *Wicks*, this appears to mean that the enforcement notice complies with the requirements of s173 TCPA 1990 and the Town and Country Planning (Enforcement Notice and Appeal) Regulations 1992 as to what information it should contain. A notice which does not comply with these requirements would not be 'formally valid,' hence a nullity, and the defendant would have succeeded in showing that there was no notice on which to found the prosecution. A document will be regarded as a nullity on its face, if it can be shown to be so by consideration simply of the notice under attack and of the statutory provisions or legislation governing its contents, without the need to consider any further evidence. Thus a notice would be a nullity if it failed to comply with the requirement of s174(8) TCPA 1990 by not specifying a date on which the notice took effect. A notice would not be 'formally valid' if it required the impossible, such as all vehicles to be removed from the 'blue land' without any definition of which area comprised the 'blue land.'

A notice will not fail the 'formal validity' test if the defendant needs to go beyond its wording and introduce other evidence, for instance of bad faith on behalf of the planning authority, in order to mount an attack.

(3) That the notice has not been quashed on appeal or by way of judicial review.

This will be a question of fact.

12.2.7 Sentencing

The sentence available to the Court is that of a fine or any lower sentencing option such as a conditional discharge. The level of the fine is unlimited on indictment, or £20,000 in the Magistrates Court. Under s179(9) TCPA 1990, the Court is specifically required "in particular to have regard to any financial benefit which has accrued or appears likely to accrue to the defendant in consequence of the offence."

Determining the benefit which has accrued or appears likely to accrue is notoriously difficult. The prosecutor is unlikely to have access to the records of any business which may have been operating in breach of the enforcement notice. However, without some indication the sentencing Court is likely to be in difficulty. The prosecutor should thus be prepared to adduce evidence of the financial benefit accruing under the offence even if this is inevitably an educated estimate.

One reliable indicator may be to consider land values. Thus, if the evidence shows the defendant used land as a hotfood café in breach of an enforcement notice for six months where the lawful use of the land was as a shop, the Court may wish to know the rental value for land that could be properly used as a shop (perhaps £500 per month) compared to land elsewhere that has planning permission or could otherwise be properly used as a hotfood café. If this is a higher figure (perhaps £800 per month) then the Court would have at least some indication that the value to the defendant of operating as a hotfood café was some £300 per month. This is obviously a rough guide and detailed, empirical figures will always be preferable.

12.2.7.1 Cases on sentence in the Court of Appeal

The specific requirement to consider the financial benefit in each case means that there are no guideline-cases as such. The cases do indicate some aggravating and mitigating features and when sentencing should take place.

12.2.7.2 When sentencing should take place

Under Section 1 of the Power of Criminal Courts Act 1973 (PCCA 1973), with the defendant's consent sentence can be deferred for a maximum of six months. This can occur where the offender indicates that, whilst at the moment in breach of the notice's requirements, he intends to comply in the near future. The Court is then able to give him a chance to prove his word and add to the mitigation available to him should he comply with the notice as he has indicated.

If, after the enforcement notice's issue, a planning application has sought permission for matters prohibited by the notice and an appeal result is imminent, it may be appropriate to adjourn sentence to await the appeal's outcome, provided it is weeks not months. If planning permission is, in fact, then granted, meaning the activity covered by the enforcement notice is no longer prohibited, that may be a relevant factor in assessing the gravity of the offence.
R v Polly Newland [1987] JPL 851.

12.2.7.3 Aggravating features

- Environmental harm or harm to amenity.
- Local concern.
- Continued failure to comply with notices
- Previous convictions - especially for the same land and the same breach of planning control

12.2.7.4 Mitigating features

- The notice has been complied with by the time sentence comes to be passed.
- Lack of effect on the general public.
- Belated willingness to conform to the planning system, for instance where the offender has taken steps which mean planning permission was subsequently granted for the matters enforced against.
- Lack of means.

Some examples:

12.2.7.5 1985 - *R v Kevin Fehily* (1985) 7 Cr App Rep S 82

Kevin Fehily carried out work to his bungalow which required planning permission. He failed to comply with enforcement notices and was convicted. Sentence was deferred to give him an opportunity to comply with the notice but this was not taken because of an outstanding planning appeal in respect of the work. Fined £300 with £100 costs, the Crown Court judge specifically taking into account Mr Fehily's poor health and appalling financial circumstances. Between imposition of the fine and appearing before the Court of Appeal, the appellant's persistence paid off and his fourth appeal against the refusal of planning permission was granted, legitimising the works he had done. The Court of Appeal upheld the fine, noting that the enforcement notice had been valid at the time of the commission of the offence and that although permission had finally been granted, Mr Fehily had, in effect, gained a temporary permission in the years beforehand by ignoring planning control.

12.2.7.6 1987 - *R v Polly Newland* (1987) JPL 851

The appellant moved with her family into mobile homes in the Green Belt. She was fined £1,500 on each of two counts of failing to comply with an enforcement notice requiring removal of the mobile homes and ordered to pay

£250 towards prosecution costs. At the Crown Court hearing, the Judge refused to defer sentence until the result of a planning appeal which had been heard, was known. The decision was expected within weeks. The appellant hoped to win the appeal as her Gypsy status would be a relevant factor. The appellant had told the Crown Court she was of very limited means.

The Court of Appeal heard that the result of the planning appeal had indeed arrived shortly after the Crown Court judge had refused to adjourn and had been in the appellant's favour. The Court of Appeal found that the appellant had not been dragging her feet in order to avoid the consequences of the planning legislation.

The Court of Appeal took into account the appellant's previous good character, the history of the matter and her limited means. It reduced the fines to £100 on each count with no order as to costs.

12.2.7.7 1990 - *R v Leslie Tucker Dunn* (1990) 12 Cr App Rep S 225

Fines totalling £3,500 with an order to pay costs of £1,000 upheld. The defendant had continued to use land for carbreaking in breach of enforcement notices and then failed to appear when his appeal against sentence was heard by the Court of Appeal. The Court of Appeal commented that although, on the face of it, these fines did seem to have been very stiff, they were entirely merited by the defendant's conduct of which the learned trial judge had to mark his disapproval.

12.2.7.8 1996 - *R v John Ayling* (1996) 2 Cr App R (S) 266

Fines of £2,000 each on two counts of failing to comply with an enforcement notice upheld together with prosecution costs of £2,252. Appellant had failed to comply with an enforcement notice requiring him to discontinue the use of open land for storing building materials and scrap metals. The field was open to public view from an adjoining footpath and next to a conservation area. The unsightly management of the land had caused complaints and Mr Ayling had not complied with the notices even by the time the case came before the Court of Appeal. The appellant had previously been fined £200 for a breach of the same enforcement notice but had still not cleared up the land. The Court of Appeal characterised the offences as serious breaches, persisted in despite every endeavour to persuade the appellant to comply with the enforcement order. An attempt to rely on Dunn to characterise fines in this region as very stiff failed.

12.2.7.9 1997 - *R v Derek Browning* (1997) 1 PLR 61

Fine of £25,000 with an order to pay costs of £1,000 quashed. Fine of £1,000, order for costs of £500 substituted.

The appellant was the owner of a large house converted from a watermill. He constructed a large, part two-storey outbuilding. After construction, when the building came to council's notice, he was told he required planning permission but made no application. An enforcement notice followed, requiring the building's removal. The defendant's appeal against the enforcement notice was refused. On conviction, sentence was deferred but the appellant did not demolish the building which was still standing at time of hearing before the Court of Appeal.

Derek Browning, who supported his family including two very young children, presented details of means to the Crown Court. These included substantial debts and mortgage arrears. The Crown Court judge assessed the gain in value to the property of the outhouse at £25,000. In allowing the appeal, the Court commented:

> . . . the learned judge was in error in two respects. First, it appears from his sentencing remarks that he fixed the amount of the fine solely by reference to accrued benefit under section 179(9) of the Act and did not take the question of ability to pay into account. That subsection requires the Court to have regard *in particular* [our emphasis] to any financial benefit which has accrued or appears likely to accrue; it does not lessen the concurrent obligation of a Court, when imposing a fine, to have regard not only to the seriousness of the offence but also the financial circumstances of the offender.

[This is of course a statutory obligation under section 18(2) and (3) of the Criminal Justice Act 1991 (CJA 1991).]

> Second, this was not a case in which any substantial financial gain has been achieved or is likely to be achieved by activities conducted in the building. Nor is any future benefit to the appellant likely to accrue from the commission of the offence, provided that planning control is duly enforced as we expect that it will be. On the contrary, he will suffer further loss when demolition is carried out (whether by himself or the council).

Subsection (9) is a new provision in the revised s179 TCPA 1990. It is aimed at developers and other property owners who

> erect unauthorised buildings or (more commonly) make unauthorised changes of use of existing buildings and then derive profit from doing so in breach of planning control. In this case, the appellant had made no significant profit from any activity carried on by him in the unauthorised building, nor is he likely to do so in the future.
>
> The learned judge seems to have been led into error by counsel's suggestion that the unauthorised building enhanced the value of the land by the amount it had cost. This was an erroneous approach based purely on the capital position without regard to the expenditure involved in erecting the building.
>
> We have therefore had to consider the appropriate level of fine to impose on the basis that no substantial benefit accrued or is likely to accrue to the appellant. We have considered the undoubted seriousness of the offence and the financial circumstances of the appellant. In our judgment, while allowing for his financial difficulties, a substantial penalty must be imposed to mark the serious view which we take of what the learned judge rightly described as a flagrant breach of the law, and in all the circumstances have decided to impose a fine of £1,000.

Although the level of fines may be regarded as low for persistent breaches of planning control, all the appellants in the cases cited above were individuals with little money available to meet the only sentencing option of a fine. Companies and other clearly commercial enterprises can and do faces fines of tens of thousands of pounds. Nevertheless, a perception remains that prosecution for breach of an enforcement notice can be a lengthy, uncertain and expensive process leading only to a relatively minor punishment which is unlikely to have a deterrent effect on that defendant or others who learn the details of the case. The likelihood of what the LPA may regard as a low penalty is often a factor in choosing injunctive action over instigating criminal proceedings.

12.2.8 Enforcement notices and subsequent development

An enforcement remains in force until quashed or withdrawn. It is not discharged by being complied with once or several times. If the enforcement notice prohibits the use of land for car repairs, it is not open to a landowner or subsequent user to argue that, because the notice was complied with some years ago, it is spent and he can now resume use for car repairs. To do so may create criminal liability under s179 TCPA 1990.

Where an enforcement notice has required the removal or alteration of buildings or works on the land, they cannot be removed and then replaced after a period, even of many years. Where this occurs, a new offence is committed under s181(5) TCPA 1990 which then supersedes any criminal liability which would otherwise appear to arise under s179(2) TCPA 1990. The offence is summary only and the sentence is a fine not exceeding level five on the standard scale.

Sec.181(5) TCPA 1990 reads:

> (5) Where without planning permission a person carries out any development on land by way of reinstating or restoring buildings or works which have been removed or altered in compliance with an enforcement notice -
>
> (a) he shall be guilty of an offence, . . . , and
>
> (c) no person shall be liable under Sec.179(2) for failure to take any steps required by an enforcement notice by way of removal or alteration of what has been so reinstated or restored.

12.3 Failing to comply with the provisions of a stop notice

12.3.1 Introduction

Enforcement notices do not provide an immediate means of preventing or prohibiting a breach of planning control however flagrant. It is not possible for an enforcement notice to come into effect in under 28 days from its date of service and after that date some period for compliance must be allowed.

An appeal against the notice suspends its operation and may take months to be heard and determined. The notice may remain suspended if leave is subsequently granted for a challenge to the Inspector's determination of the appeal against the enforcement notice to be made in the High Court under s289 TCPA 1990.

The Act provides two more immediate remedies whereby a use of land in breach of planning control can be prohibited. The first is an injunction under s187B TCPA 1990 and the second is the service of a stop notice.

12.3.2 Stop notice

A stop notice is served under s183 TCPA 1990. A stop notice can only require activities to cease; it cannot require any positive physical steps to be taken.

A stop notice can only be served to mirror the prohibition on a use served in a concurrent enforcement notice. The stop notice can require an activity to cease within three days of service in a normal case or in any lesser period where the LPA can give reasons why the shorter period is appropriate.

12.3.3 Offence

Failure to comply with the prohibition contained in a stop notice is an offence under s187 TCPA 1990.

s187(1) TCPA 1990 reads: "If any person contravenes a stop notice after a site notice has been displayed or the stop notice has been served on him he shall be guilty of an offence."

The prosecution must prove that:

(1) a site notice has been displayed or that the stop notice has been served on the defendant;
(2) the stop notice has been contravened.

12.3.4 That a site notice has been displayed or that the stop notice has been served on the defendant

The provisions for service are set out in the s329 TCPA 1990. If the LPA anticipates criminal proceedings, personal service is probably the most effective option.

Under s184(6) TCPA 1990 a site notice is one which is displayed on the land to which the stop notice relates. The site notice must state that a stop notice has been served and what its requirements are; give the date when it takes effect and state that any person contravening it may be prosecuted for an offence under the s187 TCPA 1990.

12.3. 5 That the stop notice has been contravened

Proving that the stop notice has been contravened will be a matter of fact. Under subsection 1B, any person contravenes a stop notice if he causes or permits its contravention. If there is ambiguity in the stop notice, it can be interpreted by looking at the terms of the parent enforcement notice. (*Bristol Stadium Limited v Brown* [1980] JPL 107.) This is so even though the interpretation is taking place in criminal proceedings because by definition a stop notice must have a copy of the enforcement notice annexed to it.

The offence can be charged for any day or longer period of time and a person may be convicted of a second or subsequent offence of contravening the same notice.

12.3.6 Defences

There is a statutory defence under subsection (3) where a defendant can show that the stop notice was not served on him, hence the benefit of personal service, and that he did not know, and could not reasonably have been expected to know, of its existence. This leaves it open for a defendant to show that he had good reason to be unaware of the notice even where a site notice has been displayed.

12.3.7 Challenge to validity

In contrast to an enforcement notice, there is no appeal against a stop notice under the Act. There is also no ouster clause the equivalent of s285 TCPA 1990 in relation to stop notices. It is therefore open to a defendant to challenge the stop notice's validity in criminal proceedings. Invalidity on the face of the notice could be raised, as could failure to comply with other procedural requirements such as the direction under s184(1) TCPA 1990 that a stop notice must refer to the parent enforcement notice and have a copy of that notice annexed to it.

However, it would also be open to a defendant to show that any of the prohibitions on the service of a stop notice in ss183 (3)-(5) TCPA 1990 applied. For instance, that the notice was wrongly served because it related to an activity which had been carried out (whether continuously or not) for more than four years prior to service. (See *R v Jenner* 1983 2 All ER 46 CA.)

12.3.8 Sentence

The sentence is consistent with breach of an enforcement notice, namely a fine limited to £20,000 on summary trial with financial benefit required to be taken into account.

12.4 Other offences following service of a notice

12.4.1 Failure to comply with a Breach of Condition Notice

Where planning permission has been granted subject to conditions and they are breached, there are several options for enforcement open to the

LPA including seeking an injunction or serving an enforcement notice. The planning authority may also serve a breach of condition notice under s187A TCPA 1990.

The notice will require that the breach of condition be rectified within a period of not less than 28 days. There is no appeal against the breach of condition notice then to be in breach of it is a criminal offence. In these respects, the breach of condition notice is similar to a stop notice and is likely to be used in clear cases. A breach of condition notice can be served even if complying with the condition will require some positive step by the recipient.

If the notice is not complied with, an offence may be committed under subsection 9.

The prosecution must prove that:

(1) the period for compliance with the notice has expired;
(2) the notice has not been complied with;
(3) the defendant is the person responsible and was served with the notice.

The person responsible is defined by subsections (2) and (3) TCPA 1990 as any person who is carrying out or has carried out the development, or any person having control of the land on whom the notice has been served. The landowner will be presumed to be in control in the absence of other evidence. (*Nourish v Adamson* [1998] JPL 863.) The offence can only be committed by someone who has been served with the notice and thus the prosecution would have to prove service as part of their case. The offence can be charged by reference to any day or longer period of time and a person can be convicted for a subsequent offence.

12.4.1.1 Defences

There are two statutory defences. Under subsection 11(a) a defendant may show that all reasonable measures to secure compliance with the conditions specified in the notice were taken. What constitutes a reasonable step will be a matter of fact and there is nothing in the section's language to suggest that a defence based on lack of means or profitability is ruled out.

Secondly, under subsection 11(b) TCPA 1990, where the defendant is charged because he was served with the notice as the person in control of the land, it will be a defence to show that he no longer had control of the land. It appears that the subsection refers to the defendant no longer having control of the land at the time the notice was served, rather than at the expiry of the period for compliance. Where control of the land has ceased after the service of the notice but prior to the period for compliance, the potential defence would fall under subsection 11(a).

There is no statutory code for appeal against a breach of condition notice.

It is therefore unsurprising that a wide range of validity points can be raised as defences to prosecution. These include not only the validity of the notice, whether it has been served within time under s171B TCPA 1990 and the vires of the decision to serve it but also questions as to the validity and interpretation of the condition on which it is based. (See *Dilieto v Ealing London Borough Council* [1998] 2 All ER 885.) This decision opens a wide range of issues to the defence, because the validity of a condition is a question on which there is a wide body of case law, the principal authority being *Newbury DC v Secretary of State for the Environment* HL [1981] AC 578.

Issues are also raised by the provisions of s73 and 79(4) TCPA 1990 which allow for applications to be made for a condition to be lifted or varied and for appeal to an Inspector if such an application is not granted by the LPA. These provisions are not suspended or bypassed by the service of a breach of condition notice. Although the outcome of such an application may be crucially relevant to sentence, the subsequent lifting or varying of the condition would not provide a defence for any period when the breach of condition notice had not been complied with before there was any variation or lifting of the condition. Nevertheless, there may well be a defence application that any criminal proceedings be adjourned until the outcome of any such application and appeal is known.

12.4.1.2 Sentence

The offence is summary only and the fine set at level three on the standard scale.

12.4.2 s189 TCPA 1990: Failure to comply with a Discontinuance Notice

Under s102 TCPA 1990, the LA may determine that what it believes to be an undesirable use of land should be discontinued or made the subject of conditions. The LA may equally determine that any buildings or works should be altered or removed. This power is subject to provisions for the payment of compensation. There are related powers for the discontinuance of mineral working under s9 TCPA 1990.
Where an order has been made and served under these provisions, it is an

offence under s189 TCPA 1990 either to continue with or resume the use or to fail to comply with any condition placed on the continuing use of the land under these powers. Criminal liability is incurred by any person who himself fails to comply with the order or causes or permits the use of land in contravention of it.

It is a defence to show that all reasonable measures were taken and all due diligence exercised in order to avoid commission of the offence (subsection 4 TCPA 1990). Where part of this defence is that the offence was committed due to the act or default of another then details of the identity of the other person must be supplied to the prosecution at least seven days before trial. If this information is not supplied, this defence can only be run with the Court's leave. Leave is unlikely to be refused where the only prejudice to the prosecution of a sevenday adjournment will be in costs.

Sentence is a fine, to the statutory maximum, not enhanced to £20,000, in the Magistrates Court and unlimited on indictment.

12.4.3 s216 TCPA 1990: Failure to comply with a Tidy Site Notice

Where land is in such a state that it adversely affects the area's amenity, the LPA may serve a notice under s215 TCPA 1990 requiring steps to be taken to remedy the condition of the land within a specified period. These notices are often referred to as tidy site notices. There are provisions for appeal, not to an Inspector but to the Magistrates Court and further to the Crown Court against the service of the notice or the terms of the notice on specified grounds. Appeal suspends the notice's operation - s217(3) TCPA 1990).

Failure to comply with a notice is an offence under s216 TCPA 1990. s216(2) TCPA 1990 reads:

> If any owner or occupier of land on whom the notice was served fails to take steps required by the notice within the period specified in it for compliance with it, he shall be guilty of an offence and liable on summary conviction to a fine not exceeding level three on the standard scale.

Where a person was served with the notice but ceased to be the owner or occupier of the land before the notice was due to be complied with, there is provision for passing the duty to comply with the notice on to the subsequent owner or occupier. If the original owner or occupier is charged, they may under subsections (3) and (4) TCPA 1990 give notice to the prosecution and have the current owner or occupier brought before the Court, in effect to be charged in their place. However, the original owner or occupier will still have to prove that he took all reasonable steps to ensure compliance with the notice before he can be acquitted under subsection (5) TCPA 1990.

12.4.3.1 Challenging the notice as a defence to criminal proceedings

There is a partial ouster clause under s285(3) TCPA 1990. Under s217 (1)(a) and (b) TCPA 1990, two grounds for appeal against a tidy site notice are that the land's condition does not in fact adversely affect the area's amenity or that the land's condition results from use of the land for which planning permission has been granted or is otherwise lawful as being immune from enforcement proceedings. These grounds of appeal cannot be relied on as defences to prosecution unless the defendant can show that he has owned an interest in the land since before the notice was served on the owner and occupier but not on him, provided he did not appeal against the notice.

There are, however, still the grounds of appeal under s217 (1)(c) and (d) TCPA 1990 that the requirements of the notice exceed what is necessary or that the period for compliance is too short - which are not affected by the ouster clause and can therefore also be run as defences in criminal proceedings. A challenge to the formal validity or vires of the notice can be raised as a defence. (*R v Oxford Crown Court ex p Smith*, *The Times*, December 27th, 1989).

12.4.3.2 Sentence

The offence is summary only. The fine is set at level three on the standard scale.

This is low in comparison to the raised limit of £20,000 for some other offences under the Act. However, under subsection 6, where a person has been convicted of the offence once, he is liable to further prosecution and a daily fine on level three for each day, following his first conviction, on which any of the requirements of the notice remain unfulfilled. For a conviction under this subsection, the prosecution would have to prove that the defendant had been convicted once and he had not, as soon as practicable, done everything in his power to secure compliance with the notice.

12.5 Trees and hedgerows

12.5.1 Introduction

In addition to the system of development control, the TCPA 1990 has provisions covering two discrete areas:
(a) trees and hedgerows;
(b) advertisements (see 12.6).

12.5.2 Tree Preservation Orders (TPOs)

s198 TCPA 1990 gives the LPA power to make a tree preservation order (TPO) in respect of any tree, group of trees or woodlands. The order is made where it appears that the trees or woodland should be preserved for their contribution to the area's amenity. Under s201 TCPA 1990, the authority may make a direction that any TPO which it proposes to make and which would not be effective until confirmed shall take effect immediately. Such orders provide instant protection and are usually made to avoid the tree being lawfully destroyed or lopped before the provisional order is made final. Breach of an order which has come into effect immediately under s201 TCPA 1990 provisions will be equivalent to a breach of the confirmed order in relation to any question of criminal liability.

A TPO may prohibit any cutting down, topping, lopping, uprooting, wilful damage or wilful destruction of the specified trees. The order may, as the model order does, make provision for works to the tree to be carried out with the consent of the LPA which may be given with conditions attached.

12.5.3 Offence

TPOs are ultimately enforced by the offence of contravening a TPO created by s210 TCPA 1990. s210 (1) reads:

If any person, in contravention of a tree preservation order -

> (a) cuts down, uproots or wilfully destroys a tree, or
> (b) wilfully damages, tops or lops a tree in such a manner as to be likely to destroy it he shall be guilty of an offence.

The nature and elements of the offence were considered in *R v Alath Construction Limited* [1991] 1PLR 25.

The prosecution has to prove that:
(1) a TPO was in force;
(2) the defendant contravened the order by cutting the tree down or some other action such as lopping prohibited by the subsection;
(3) the cutting down or other prohibited action was done without the planning authority's permission.

The offence is of absolute liability. (*Maidstone Borough Council v Mortimer* 1981 JPL 112; *R v Alath Construction Limited* - where *Mortimer* was not cited to the Court of Appeal.) Vicarious liability will only arise where the defendant can be shown to have caused the tree to be damaged. A landowner will not be vicariously liable for damage caused by a building contractor carrying out work for him who has been told of the TPO and told not to touch or damage the tree in any way. (*Groveside Homes v Elmbridge Borough Council* [1988] JPL 395.)

Where the prosecution allegation is one of destruction, the Court will have to consider not whether the tree has been physically obliterated but whether it has been altered to such an extent that it no longer has any amenity value. In *Barnet London Borough Council v Eastern Electricity Board* [1973] 2 All ER 319, cable laying had damaged roadside trees' roots so that their life expectancy had been reduced from 20 years to between two and five years. They were also unstable. Before the justices, a submission of no case succeeded on the basis that the trees were still there and alive and that the prosecution had not proved that they were destroyed.

The Divisional Court took a middle course, holding that mere reduction in life expectancy or stability could not amount to destruction but that

> ... one must bear in mind ... that the underlying purpose of the relevant legislation is the preservation of trees and woodlands as amenities, as living creatures providing pleasure, protection and shade; it is their use as such that is sought to be preserved and a tree the subject of a tree preservation order is destroyed in the present context when as a result of that which is done to it, it ceases to have any use as an amenity or something worth preserving. For example, if a person intentionally inflicts on a tree so radical an injury that in all the circumstances any reasonably competent forester would in consequence decide that it ought to be felled, then in our opinion that person wilfully destroys the tree within the meaning of that word in the relevant legislation and order ..., we think that one of the relevant circumstances which a forester could or should take into account in deciding

> whether a given injured tree should be felled is its situation: a tree adjoining a highway, for instance, needs greater stability and more vigorous life than a similar tree in a country field and the former may thus, by reason of its position alone, be destroyed ... by a lesser injury than would be needed to destroy the latter.

(*Barnet LBC v Eastern Electricity* [1973] 2 All ER 319, per May J, p323.)

12.5.4 Defences

There are no statutory defences. The Courts have allowed a variety of points to be taken as a defence to criminal proceedings.

12.5.4.1 That the works damaging the tree were carried out because the tree was dying, dead or dangerous or that the works were to comply with an obligation imposed by an Act of Parliament or for the prevention or abatement of a nuisance

Under s198(6) TCPA 1990, a TPO cannot apply to trees which are dying or dead or have become dangerous. It is therefore open to the defendant to show that, at the time the prosecution rely on, the tree was dying, dead or dangerous. Because it is usually the defendant who will be in the best position to prove the state of the tree at any particular time, it has been held that it is not for the prosecution to prove during their case that the tree was safe and healthy:

R v Alath Construction concerned a beech tree which had proved inconvenient to the construction company. Two applications to fell it had been refused. The day after the great gale of October, 1987, the company had the tree felled. The company was prosecuted and at the end of the prosecution case made a submission of no case, on the basis that the prosecution had not proved that the beech tree had remained in a safe and healthy condition following the gale. The Court of Appeal held that it was for the defendants to show that the tree was dangerous or dying. The prosecution were not therefore put in what would have been a difficult position of visiting the tree in the few hours between the end of the hurricane and the tree being cut down so as to assess its health and determine whether or not it was dangerous. Although it is not clear from the report, it appears that either the defendant company had no evidence as to the tree's state immediately following the gale or that the jury was not convinced by any evidence that the defendant did produce that the tree was dangerous.

Whether or not a tree is in a dangerous condition for the purposes of s198(6) TCPA 1990 is a question of fact. In *Smith v Oliver* [1989] 2 PLR 1, the Divisional Court considered trees in the defendant's front garden. The trees stood against the fence and were not diseased but swayed against the fence in high winds. As the trees grew, they were likely to damage the fence further and roots would have broken the pavement's surface. Mr Justice Farquharson held that whether a tree is dying or dead or has become dangerous

> ... must be a question of fact for the justices. The approach which they should take is the everyday sensible approach of the prudent citizen looking at the trees in question and deciding in his own mind whether he can properly say those trees are dangerous. The existence of the danger must be a present danger. He must be able to say that the existing condition is one of danger in relation to the tree or trees which he is examining. Of course that does not mean that the danger which has been threatened has actually occurred. It is not necessary to show that the tree has fallen or that its roots have disturbed the foundation of the house, fence or pavement nearby. The justices must be in a position to say to themselves that having regard to the state of the tree, its size its position and such effect as any of those factors have so far had, we can properly come to the conclusion that the tree has now become dangerous. It may be that the condition of the tree itself is perfectly healthy, but because of those other factors the magistrates may be able none the less to say that the tree is in the condition described by the subsection, that is to say it has become dangerous.
>
> In deciding that question, the magistrates are entitled to look at what is likely to happen. If the tree has already shown signs of disturbing a fence or a pavement or indeed the house itself, it does not need the justices or indeed anyone concerned with the treatment of the tree to wait for those events actually to occur, namely for the fence to fall down on some passing pedestrian or the condition of the pavement to be such that somebody falls and is injured or that the house begins to subside. The present danger is one that is constituted by the conditions at the time the tree is being examined, and the fact that these other matters may shortly arise is something that can properly be taken into account when the justices come to their decision.
>
> Of course it does not mean that any individual who owns trees and wishes to remove them can say to himself, having regard to

> their position, the way they have been planted and their unsuitability, 'I can see that in a number of years they are going to constitute a danger' and then cut them down. One has to look at the position at the time. If such damage is far off and remote and not immediate in the sense that I have just described, the trees do not come within the meaning of the exemption.

It was also said, by Mr Justice Tudor Price, that:

> A tree has become dangerous at the moment when it constitutes a present danger to persons or property. That may be not only as a result of disease or damage, it may be by reason of its size and location. For example, a tree planted at a roadside may by reason of its very size be judged to have become dangerous in the sense that in a high wind it, or part of it, may fall across the road to the danger of traffic. A common case is that of a forest tree planted in a suburban garden which begins to dominate and tower over the house roof so that in high wind it might fall and hole the roof or its roots begin to undermine the foundation. In each case, it is a question of fact for the justices to see whether or not the person who has felled or lopped without the necessary permission is able to bring himself within the exemption of the Act. (*Smith v Oliver* [1989] 2 PLR 1, per Tudor Price J, p. 4.)

Although the authorities have concentrated on the question of danger, it would be equally open to a defendant to show that the works were carried out in accordance with any of the other exceptions under s198(6) TCPA 1990, namely to comply with an Act of Parliament or to prevent or abate a nuisance.

12.5.4.2 That the correct procedure had not been followed in making the order

In making a TPO, the LA must comply with a procedure set by the Town and Country Planning (Tree Preservation Orders) Regulations 1969. In *Vale of Glamorgan Borough Council v Palmer and Bowles* (1984) JPL 334, the Divisional Court held that a defendant was entitled to raise in his defence a failure to comply with procedure which meant that the TPO under which he was prosecuted was void. On the facts, it was a serious breach of the regulations in that copies of the order had not been deposited as required by the regulations or registered as land charges, meaning that the defendant had no way of knowing that the TPOs had been made. The magistrates' acquittal on the basis that this breach of the regulations rendered the purported order void was upheld.

In deciding *Vale of Glamorgan v Palmer and Bowles*, the Court was considering TPOs made under 1950 regulations. It appears the question of ouster clauses was not considered. s284 (2) (c) TCPA 1990 provides that the validity of any TPO shall only be challenged in the High Court under the provisions of s288 TCPA 1990. It remains to be seen whether on similar facts the point could be taken in quite the same way today.

In *Knowles v Secretary of State for the Environment and Chorley Borough Council* [1988] JPL 593, the borough council made a TPO under s198 TCPA 1990 and simultaneously resolved that it should have immediate effect. However, the land ownership position was complex and the council failed to serve the order on the landowner before he carried out prohibited works to the tree a few days later. Once the order was confirmed, prosecution proceedings were started but adjourned pending a challenge to the validity of the order under s284 and 288 TCPA 1990 in the High Court. Crucially, the landowner could show that he had not learnt about the order from any other source and had thus been in ignorance of it when ordering the works to the tree. The TPO was quashed and the prosecution, presumably, discontinued.

Clearly, asking for criminal proceedings to be adjourned and making a challenge in the High Court is the most appropriate course for a defendant within the six-week time limit. Where a procedural requirement has been breached but the offence not committed until after the six-week time limit, s284 and 288 TCPA 1990 would appear to be clear evidence of Parliament's intention to preclude the validity of the order being raised in criminal proceedings. The statutory framework surrounding the offence is closer to that considered in *R v Wicks* [1997] 2 All ER 801 than in *Boddington v British Transport Police* [1998] 2 All ER 203.

12.5.4.3 That what was damaged was not a tree

The Act contains no definition of tree. Where the TPO protects groups of trees or woodland without specifying individual specimens, it may be necessary to consider whether what has been felled or damaged was in fact a tree. In *Kent County Council and another v Batchelor* (1976) 75 LGR 151, a TPO covered trees in a large area of woodland. Kent County Council and Maidstone Borough Council obtained an injunction preventing cutting down, uprooting, topping, lopping, or otherwise in way damaging or destroying any tree within land covered by the TPO.

Mr Batchelor arranged for an area of land to be cleared by bulldozer. In considering his appeal against a finding that he was in breach of the injunction, Lord Denning commented 'I should have thought that in woodland it [a tree] ought to be something over seven or eight inches in diameter.' This observation was *obiter* since Mr Batchelor's appeal was allowed on the basis that there was not sufficient evidence that the land cleared fell within the area covered by the TPO.

In the later case of *Bullock v SSE* (1980) 40 P&CR 246, the dictum of Lord Denning in *Batchelor* was not followed. In *Bullock* the TPO covered half-an-acre of woodland which was a coppice of ash. The TPO described it as woodlands and as mixed hardwoods consisting mainly of ash. In upholding the TPO, 'tree' was given its dictionary definition meaning without reference to any trunk diameter or other dimensions. It was accepted that this would mean that consent may be required for thinning or management of the coppice but it was noted that the order made provision for such consent to be granted.

Whichever of the two approaches is preferred, it remains open to a defendant to claim that, on the facts of the particular prosecution, it was not a tree within the woodland but bushes, scrub or shrubs that were damaged or lopped. This would be a question of fact in each case with any ambiguity being in the defendant's favour.

12.5.5 Sentence

The sentence is a fine, unlimited on indictment and to the extended maximum of £20,000 in the Magistrates Court. The sentence is required to take into account any financial benefit gained from the offence.

The Court of Appeal has considered the appropriate parameters for sentence on at least two occasions:-

R v Peter Ernest Razzell (1990) 12 Cr App Rep (S) 142:

Peter Razzell was a property developer. He owned a development site on which stood a horse chestnut tree covered by a TPO and an ailanthus, tree of heaven, protected because it stood within a conservation area.

Negotiations with the LPA failed. The land was poisoned and the trees were lopped and had wedges cut out of their trunks. The appellant pleaded guilty on rearraignment after the third day of a trial. The Court of Appeal heard that had the development gone ahead, the profit to the appellant would have been at least £50,000. Fines of £10,000 for each tree and costs of £12,000, a total of £32,000 were upheld in the light of the potential profit.

R v Carlyle Churchill Palmer (1989) 11 Cr App R (S) 407:

Mr Palmer had a cedar tree in the garden of his house which was covered by a TPO. There was some evidence that he was concerned about the effects of the trees roots on the foundations of his house and he had applied for planning permission to instal a root barrier. The application was made in September, 1987, and had not been determined by the time of the great storm of November 16th, 1987. On November 28th, Mr Palmer had the tree cut down, claiming it had become dangerous. This explanation was rejected by the jury.

The prosecution put forward no evidence of financial gain from the offence save for the cost of the installation of the root barrier which would have cost under £1,000. The sentencing judge was also told that the tree's replacement would require the planting of two semimature trees at a cost of £2,500 to £3,460. The Crown Court judge imposed a £6,000 fine.

The Court of Appeal determined that the appropriate starting point was the financial benefit of saving the cost of the root barrier. It was then appropriate to work up, to reflect the deliberate defiance of the order. It was also appropriate to take into account good character, the fact that the tree had been replaced for a cost of just over £1,000 and the appellant's co-operation in relation to other trees in his garden covered by preservation orders.

The Court of Appeal reduced the fine to £3,000.

12.5.6 Summary-only offence under subsection (4) TCPA 1990

Under s210 (4) TCPA 1990, if any person contravenes the provisions of a TPO otherwise than as mentioned in subsection (1) TCPA 1990, he shall be guilty of an offence and liable on summary conviction to a fine not exceeding level four on the standard scale.

This offence covers any breach of the order other than in the specific ways as set out under subsection 1 TCPA 1990. The defences and case-law considered in relation to subsection (1) TCPA 1990 would equally apply to this offence where relevant. Given the very much lower sentence for this offence, a prosecution would usually be brought under subsection (1) TCPA 1990 for any material contravention of a TPO.

12.5.7 Protecting trees in conservation areas

Under s211 TCPA 1990, trees in conservation areas are treated as if they were the subject of a TPO made under s198(3) TCPA 1990. Therefore, any cutting down, topping, lopping, uprooting, wilful damage, or wilful destruction of a tree in a conservation area is prohibited and the carrying out of such work will prima facie constitute an offence.

12.5.7.1 Giving notice under s211(3) TCPA 1990

Anybody contemplating carrying out any works to a tree is entitled to serve on the LPA a notice giving the works' details. The LPA can react in three ways. It can grant consent for the works; it can make a specific TPO or it can make no reply within six weeks. If six weeks passes without any action from the LPA, then the trees covered by the notice are outside the protection given to trees in conservation areas for the two years following the service of the notice. It remains open to the LA to make a specific TPO after the six-week period has ended. (*R v North Hertfordshire District Council ex p Hyde* [1989] 3 PLR 89.)

The Secretary of State has power, under s212 TCPA 1990, to cut the scope of s211 TCPA 1990 and has done so in the *Trees in Conservation Areas - Excepted Cases Regulations SI No. 148/1975*. These regulations include permission for the felling of dangerous trees. They also mean that the controls do not apply to trees of less than 75mm diameter (measured over the bark 1.5 meters above ground level) or slightly larger trees if they are removed to help the growth of other trees.

These regulations mean that there will be few cases in which there is an argument over whether what has been damaged is a tree, because prosecutions will not be brought unless the tree exceeds or exceeded 75mm in diameter 1.5 meters above ground level.

The details of the offence and the sentencing powers are provided by s210 TCPA 1990, as in the case of TPOs.

12.5.8 Hedgerows

Hedgerows are protected not under the TCPA 1990 but under s97 EA 1995.

This section gives power for regulations to be made for the protection of important hedgerows in England and Wales and for those regulations to incorporate criminal offences.

The Regulations under this section are the *Hedgerow Regulations 1997 (SI 1997/1160)*. These have been criticised for limiting the lengths of hedgerow to which they apply. In essence, they have only created blanket protection for rural hedgerows which are more than 20 metres in length or which form part of a network of hedges and are more than 30 years old. A hedgerow may also be protected because it has specific importance historically or in conservation terms.

The system of protection, then, has much in common with the protection of trees in a conservation area. Regulations prohibit the removal of the hedgerow without serving notice on the LPA. The LPA then has 42 days in which either to consent or to require the hedgerow 's retention or fail to reply, in which case protection for the hedgerow is removed for two years from the date of the notice.

If the LPA requires the removal of the hedgerow, there are provisions for appeal against the notice to the Secretary of State.

Reg.7 creates offences under s97(4) EA1995. The principal offence is the removal of a hedgerow contrary to the regulations. Reg.7(1) reads:

> A person who intentionally or recklessly removes or causes or permits another to remove a hedgerow in contravention of (the relevant regulations) . . . is guilty of an offence.

The sentence for this offence is a fine unlimited on indictment and up to the statutory maximum in the Magistrates Court. In determining the sentence, the Court is required to take into account the financial benefit which has accrued or appears likely to accrue as a consequence of the offence.

Reg.2 creates the lesser offence of failing to replant a hedgerow that has been partially removed under general permission for making a new access through the hedge in substitution for an existing access. (Reg.6[2]) This is summary only and punishable with a fine on level three of the standard scale. The regulations also incorporate the provisions from the

TCPA 1990 for the prosecution of culpable directors where a company is found guilty and on offence of obstructing an official of the LPA who has a right of entry on to land under the regulations.

12.6 Advertisement Control

12.6.1 Introduction

s220 to 225 TCPA 1990 and regulations made under this part of the Act provide a complex and comprehensive regime controlling the display of advertisements. There are provisions both for express consent to display advertisements, with the right to appeal should consent be refused, and for deemed consent where regulations prescribe circumstances in which advertisements of maximum dimensions may be displayed without express consent. It is not intended to explore the details of the regulations.

12.6.2 Offence

The criminal sanction is provided by s224(3) TCPA 1990 which creates immediate criminal liability in relation to any advertisement displayed in breach of the regulations. The section determines that if any person displays an advertisement in contravention of the regulations, he shall be guilty of an offence

'Displays' is further defined by subsection (4) TCPA 1990. A person will be deemed to display an advertisement if he is the owner or occupier of the land on which the advertisement is displayed or if the advertisement gives publicity to his goods, trade, business or other concerns.

These provisions, which are most relevant to temporary makeshift sites rather than to a full commercial hoarding, have removed from the prosecution the virtually impossible task of catching the flyposter actually at work in order to have any realistic prospect of conviction.

The wording of the offence indicates that it is an essential ingredient that the advertisement is displayed in contravention of the regulations. However, once it is shown that the advertisement was displayed, it is for the defendant to demonstrate that it had either deemed or express consent.

In *R v O'Brien and Hertsmere District Council* (1997) 74 P&CR 264, it was held that the defendant who asserts that the advertisement has consent is the person most likely to have the facts within his own knowledge and the onus of proof fell on him to demonstrate that consent had been granted or that the advertisement was covered by deemed consent. The defendant displaying the poster claiming to have consent was equivalent to the driver claiming to have insurance.

12.6.3 Defences

There is a statutory defence to the deemed-display provisions. If a person can show that the advertisement was displayed without their knowledge or consent, then they shall not be deemed to display it even though it is on their land or advertises their business. The defence will be made out where it can be shown that either knowledge or consent was absent. Even though a person has or has acquired knowledge of the advertisement, it is open to them to show that they did not consent to it.

In *Edmonds and Tyndall v Merton London Borough Council* (*The Times*, July 6th, 1993), it was held that the chairman and regional organiser of the British National Party could not be responsible for the unauthorised display of advertisements on behalf of the BNP even though they had been made aware of them by letters from the LPA. The prosecution was unable to prove that the defendants had consented to the unauthorised display and the conviction was quashed.

Mr Justice Buckley said that for someone to become guilty of a criminal offence simply on acquiring knowledge of a state of affairs for which he was not responsible was quite contrary to the fundamental principles of criminal law.

This approach was followed in *Wycombe DC v Michael Shanly Group* (1994) 67 P&CR 374. Here, the Court also found that evidence the landowner removed advertisements as soon as he knew they were unauthorised was capable of making out the defence that he had not consented to their display.

On the other side of the line, where the defendant has issued posters which are displayed as advertisements and has learnt of the unauthorised display but has then taken no steps to remove it, he will not have made out the defence.

This was the case even though the posters had been issued by the head office of the British Union for the Abolition of Vivisection (BUAV) with the instruction that they were for legal display only. (*Preston v British Union for the Abolition of Vivisection* , 149 JP 740.)

12.6.4 Sentence

The offence is summary only and the maximum sentence is a fine limited to level three on the standard scale.

12.6.5 Continuing offence

Where there has been a conviction in relation to the display of an advertisement, then the defendant is also liable to a daily fine of one tenth of level three on the standard scale for each day following conviction on which the advertisement remains displayed.

The offence is the display of the advertisement, not the use of an advertisement hoarding. Thus putting up 11 different advertisements on the same hoarding will constitute 11 different offences, not a single continuing offence even though the advertisements may have been identical in size. (*Royal Borough of Kingston Upon Thames v National Solus Sites* [1994] 1 JPL 251.)

This approach has been treated with caution in *O'Brien v London Borough of Croydon* Co/1280/98 (*The Times*, July 27th, 1998) but has not been overruled.

Where there has been a conviction for the display of an advertisement, a fresh offence, not the continuing offence, is committed if the advertisement is removed and then replaced (*Royal Borough of Kensington and Chelsea v Elmton Ltd* 246 EG 1011).

12.7 Offences concerned with operating the planning system

12.7.1 Introduction

The Act contains a small number of offences necessary to enforce the mechanics of operating the planning system, such as the need for planning officers to gain access to land. These provisions are incorporated in the Listed Buildings Act (LBA) and the Hazardous Substances Act 1990 (HSA 1990).

12.7.2 Offences relating to the exercise of rights of entry under the Act

The Act gives authorised officers of the LPA the right to enter private land in order to carry out some of their functions under the planning system.

These rights of entry can be enforced by warrant if necessary and are also made enforceable by a provision that the wilful obstruction of an authorised officer exercising the right of entry is an offence.

Rights of entry are given under s196 A and B TCPA 1990 for enforcement purposes with the corresponding obstruction offence under s196C (2) TCPA 1990; under s214 B and C TCPA 1990 in relation to tree preservation orders with the corresponding obstruction offence under s214D(2) TCPA 1990 and the majority of rights of entry for survey and consideration of planning applications under s324 TCPA 1990 with the corresponding obstruction offence under s325(2) TCPA 1990.

The obstruction should be wilful, which probably means intentional or reckless, and it would be a defence to show that the LPA officer was not duly authorised or accompanying an authorised person, or was otherwise acting outside the scope of their powers.

The offence is summary only. The maximum sentence is a level-three fine.

12.7.3 Unauthorised disclosure of confidential information

The rights of entry under the Act may lead planning officers into areas where confidential business information, or details of trade secrets, become available to them. Each right of entry, save that to look at trees under s214D TCPA 1990, is accompanied by a duty not to disclose confidential information except in the course of performing the duty for which the right of entry was taken. Thus it would be an offence to disclose details of the manufacturing process carried out in a factory unless it were necessary to do so in order to comment on the process's noise implications in assessing an application for planning permission for expansion of use, for instance.

The offence is triable either way. On indictment, it carries an unlimited fine or a maximum two-year prison sentence. Sentence in the Magistrates Court is a fine to the statutory maximum.

This offence of the unlawful disclosure of trade secrets is under s196C(5) - (7) and s325 (3) - (5) TCPA 1990

12.7.4 Obstructing a local planning authority officer exercising powers to execute works

As an alternative to prosecution, the Act often gives the LPA the parallel power of taking steps itself. Under s178 TCPA 1990, where the requirements of an enforcement notice have not been complied with, the LA itself may enter the land, carry out the steps required by the notice and then charge the costs to the landowner or in some cases to the occupier. Wilfully obstructing an authorised officer of the LPA carrying out these or similar powers is an offence triable summarily only. The maximum sentence is a fine up to level three on the standard scale.

This offence is contained in two sections:

s178(6) TCPA 1990 - obstructing the direct action of the LA in executing works in compliance with an enforcement notice.

s209(6) TCPA 1990 - obstructing the LPA in planting trees in replacement for those removed or destroyed in breach of a tree preservation order.

12.7.5 Giving false information in relation to an application for a Certificate of Lawful Use or Development under s191 or 192 TCPA 1990

s191 and 192 TCPA 1990 provide a procedure whereby a certificate can be granted, by the LPA or by the Secretary of State on appeal, which will be conclusive as to the lawfulness of a use of land or a proposed use of land. The grant of a certificate can clearly make an enormous difference to the value of the land which it covers.

The issues which have to be determined in considering an application for a certificate are essentially factual. Often the controversial point will be the date on which a use of land commenced or the date on which a building was erected.

12.7.5.1 s194 (1) TCPA 1990 reads:

If any person, for the purposes of procuring a particular decision on an application (whether by himself or another) for the issue of a certificate under Sec. 191 or 192 -

> (a) knowingly or recklessly makes a statement which is false or misleading in a material particular;
> (b) with intent to deceive uses any document which is false or misleading in a material particular; or
> (c) with intent to deceive, withholds any material information

he shall be guilty of an offence.

The section applies whether the defendant is seeking to have the application granted or refused and whether the defendant has made the application himself or not. The authorities from mainstream criminal law will determine, on any given set of facts, the exact meaning of 'recklessly' or 'intention.'

Subsection (3) TCPA 1990 removes the six-month time limit on the laying of an information in the Magistrates Court although it is arguable that this did not apply in any event since the section creates an 'either way ' offence.

12.7.5.2 Sentence

The offence is triable either way. It is punishable on summary conviction, by a fine not exceeding the statutory maximum; or on indictment by an unlimited fine or a maximum prison sentence of two years.

12.7.6 Failing to respond to a requisition for information under s171C or 330 TCPA 1990

Under s171C TCPA 1990, a notice may be served by the LPA on the owner or occupier of land where it believes there may have been a breach of planning control. The notice can require the recipient to give to the LPA information in writing as to the uses to which the land is being put and has been put and details of ownership and occupation.

12.7.6.1 Failure to respond to the notice or any part of it within 21 days is an offence contrary to s171D TCPA 1990

Although s171D(2) TCPA 1990 suggests that the offence may be charged by reference to single-day or longer periods, this provision does not sit with the nature of the offence. Failure to comply within 21 days is an offence. It is therefore difficult to see the necessity for charging for a specific period of time or for a provision of second and subsequent offences.

12.7.6.2 Defences

It is a statutory defence for the defendant to show that he had a reasonable excuse for failing to comply with a requirement of the notice. The notice in any event can only require the recipient to provide information as far as he is able. There would not appear to be any obligation on the recipient to make any inquiries of their own.

There is no appeal against the service of a notice and all the public law defences and challenges to validity are open to the defendant.

12.7.6.3 Sentence

For an offence of failing to comply with the notice under subsection (1) TCPA 1990, the maximum penalty is a fine on level three of the standard scale.

Under subsection (5) TCPA 1990 it is an offence knowingly or recklessly to make a false or misleading statement in purporting to comply with the notice. The penalty is a fine on level five of the standard scale.

12.7.6.3 Requisition for information under s330 TCPA 1990

s330 TCPA 1990 allows the LPA or the Secretary of Sate to serve a notice on the occupier of premises or any person who directly or indirectly receives rent from the premises. The notice may require information necessary for the LPA to make any order or issue any notice in the carrying out the full range of its function, not simply those concerned with breaches of planning control which trigger the ability to serve a notice under s171C TCPA 1990.

There is no positive duty on the recipient of the notice to make their own inquiries but they can be required to give information as to the nature of their interest in the premises and the name and address of others known to them as having an interest in the premises. They can only be asked about the current use of the land as opposed to the power under s171C TCPA 1990 to ask about any specified use.

Failure to comply with a s330 TCPA 1990 requisition for information within the period specified on the notice, which must be a minimum 21 days, is an offence unless the defendant can show reasonable excuse for not doing so. The offence is summary only. Sentence is a level-three fine.

It is an offence under subsection 330(5) TCPA 1990 knowingly to make any misstatement in answer to a requisition served under the section. The offence is triable either way. In the Crown Court, the offence carries an unlimited fine or a maximum sentence of two years in prison. In the Magistrates Court, the fine is up to the statutory maximum.

12.7.7 Offences by corporations

s331 TCPA 1990 is the director's culpability section. Where any offence under the Act is proved to have been committed by a corporation and with the consent or connivance of, or to be attributable to any neglect on the part of, the company's officers, then officers as well as body corporate shall be guilty of the offence and liable to be proceeded against accordingly.

The officers of a company to whom the section applies are:

> a director, manager, secretary or other similar officer of the body corporate, or
> any person who was purporting to act in any such capacity.

'Director' is given a further definition, as a member of any body corporate established by or under an enactment for the purpose of carrying on under national ownership an industry, part of an industry or undertaking whose affairs are managed by its members.

This provision may be useful where the offence has been committed by a small company in which one or two directors will have a large stake and will benefit unfairly if only the company is punished; especially where a company's assets have been run down approaching sentence. For an example of company directors being fined significantly more than the company itself, see *R v Chambers* (1989) JPL 229, discussed in the section dealing with sentence under the LBA.

CHAPTER 13

PLANNING AND THE HAZARDOUS SUBSTANCES ACT 1990

CONTENTS

CHAPTER 13

PLANNING AND THE HAZARDOUS SUBSTANCES ACT 1990

13.1 Introduction

Under the main TCPA 1990 umbrella, the Hazardous Substances Act 1990 (HSA 1990) sets out a regime separate to that of planning control for regulating hazardous substances' presence on land. The Act's scheme is to avoid or minimise the risk of environmental harm by seeking to ensure that hazardous substances are kept on land only in regulated quantities and conditions. The main requirement, imposed by s4 HSA 1990, is that consent should be obtained for a hazardous substance to be present on, over or under land in quantities greater than prescribed limits. Bringing a hazardous substance on to land will not necessarily constitute a breach of planning control, hence the additional controls.

The criminal sanction for being in breach of the Act's provisions is provided by s23 HSA 1990. This creates an offence where there is contravention of hazardous substance control. s4(1) HSA 1990 creates what appears to be a strict liability offence, *if there is a contravention of hazardous substance control, the appropriate person shall be guilty of an offence.* However, defences are available relating to knowledge.

13.2 What the prosecution must prove

Initially, the prosecution must prove only that:

(1) there has been a contravention of hazardous substance control, and
(2) the defendant is the appropriate person.

13.3 Contravention of hazardous substance control

Under subsection (2) HSA 1990, a contravention can occur in three ways. These are where:

(1) a controlled quantity (or more) of hazardous substance is on land with no consent; or,
(2) the amount of hazardous substance on land exceeds the amount permitted by an extant consent under the Act for allowing the substance to be on land; or
(3) the hazardous substance is on the land in circumstances breaching a condition of an extant consent.

The Planning (Hazardous Substances) Regulations SI 656/92 define which substances are hazardous for the purposes of the Act and the controlled quantity for each. The controlled quantity is the level at which control under the Act is triggered.

For instance, arsine (arsenic hydride) is a toxic hazardous substance whose controlled quantity is one tonne; liquid oxygen and chlorine are explosive hazardous substances whose respective controlled quantities are 500 tonnes and 10 tonnes.

Certain categories of hazardous substance are excluded from control under this Act, to avoid duplication of controls under other statutes. Examples are explosives, controlled by the Health and Safety Executive (HSE) under Explosives Act (EA 1875); controlled waste under the EPA 1990; and radioactive waste.

s4(2) HSA 1990 does not specify the area of land within which the maximum quantities for the substance apply. However, quantities of the hazardous substance are to be aggregated if they are on any land or structure within 500 metres of each other and under the control of the same person. Nor does the section specify to what extent separating the hazardous substance into smaller portions will prevent the Act's provisions applying.

It is an element of the offence that there is no extant consent or that the condition of an extant consent has not been complied with. Consent under the Act can either be specific consent, granted after consideration of an application, or deemed consent, where the Secretary of State has by regulations granted general consent

13.4 The defendant is the appropriate person for the Act's purposes

For the purposes of the offence, the identity of the 'appropriate person' varies depending on which form of the offence is charged. For the 'no consent' subsection 2(a)(i) HSA 1990 and 'quantity in excess of offence' subsection 2(a)(ii) HSA 1990, the appropriate person is either any person knowingly causing the substance to be present on, over or under the land, or any person allowing the substance to be present on, over or under the land, or the person in control of the land.

For the offence of 'failing to comply with a condition on a consent' issued under subsection 2(b) HSA 1990 the appropriate person is simply the person in control of the land. Although the issue does not appear to have been specifically considered, 'knowing' and 'allowing ' are likely to be interpreted in accordance with the usual authorities.

13.5 Defences

Subsections 5,6,7 of s23 HSA 1990 provide defences which in effect require deliberate breaches of the control regime before an offence can be proved. Subsection 5 HSA 1990 provides a defence to all the offences created by the section. It is a defence for the accused to prove that he took all reasonable precautions and exercised all due diligence to avoid commission of the offence, or that the commission of the offence could be avoided only by taking action which would in itself amount to a breach of statutory duty. This provision would provide a defence where the only option open to the defendant would be to remove the hazardous substance in an unsuitable vehicle or similar situations.

Subsection 6 HSA 1990 provides a defence to those facing charges under ss2(a) HSA 1990, the 'no consent' and 'quantity in excess of consent' offences. Where the accused can show that he did not know and had no reason to believe that the substance was present, either at all or in an excess quantity, he shall have a defence. Similarly, ss23(7) HSA 1990 provides the same defence where the accused can show he did not know and had no reason to believe that there was a failure to comply with a condition on the hazardous substances consent.

Given s23 HSA 1990's wording, prosecution is most likely where breaches of control are flagrant. In such cases, a more immediate remedy may be the injunction specifically provided for by s26AA HSA 1990. There are as yet no reported cases on the offence.

13.6 Temporary decriminalisation

Under s27 HSA 1990, the Secretary of State can lift criminal liability under s23 HSA 1990 for a short period, if it is essential that a hazardous substance be on land in what would otherwise be excessive quantities in order to maintain an essential service to a community.

13.7 Sentencing

Subsections 23(4) and 4A HSA 1990 provide the same sentencing options as in other offences under the Planning Acts, namely a fine, limited to £20,000 at summary trial. There is also the provision of the specific duty on the sentencing Court to take into account any financial benefit which has accrued or is likely to accrue from the commission of the offence.

13.8 Failure to comply with a Hazardous Substances Contravention Notice

Where hazardous substance control is breached, the appropriate authority may issue a hazardous substance contravention notice. This would be in the alternative, or in addition to immediate prosecution under s23 HSA 1990. Procedure for implementing and enforcing such notices is imported directly from the Planning Act via regulations made under s25(1)(c) HSA 1990. This means that failing to comply with a hazardous substance notice is an offence governed by provisions of s179 HSA 1990, as modified.

The modifications (set out in Schedule 4 to the 1992 Planning [Hazardous Substances] Regulations) roll the 'owner and person in control' offences together by modifying subsection (1) to read:

> (1) Where at any time after the end of the period for compliance with a hazardous substances contravention notice, any steps required by the notice to be taken have not been taken, the person who is then the owner of the land and any person other than the owner who is in control of the land is in breach of the notice.

Subsections 4 and 5 are omitted. The enforcement notice reads as a hazardous substances contravention notice where necessary elsewhere in the section.

Sentence under s23 HSA 1990 is a fine limited to £20,000 on summary trial.

13.9 Other offences under the Act

s36B HSA 1990 mirrors equivalent sections in the other Planning Acts, as to wilfully obstructing anyone seeking to exercise a legal right of entry and, equally, unlawfully disclosing information obtained pursuant to a right of entry. Further, s37 HSA 1990 incorporates the provisions of s331 HSA 1990 of the principal Act as to prosecuting culpable directors or officers where the offence is committed by their company.

CHAPTER 14

OFFENCES UNDER THE PLANNING (LISTED BUILDINGS AND CONSERVATION AREAS) ACT 1990 - THE 'LISTED BUILDINGS ACT' 1990

CONTENTS

CHAPTER 14

OFFENCES UNDER THE PLANNING (LISTED BUILDINGS AND CONSERVATION AREAS) ACT 1990 - THE 'LISTED BUILDINGS ACT'

14.1 Introduction

In providing the sanction to allow enforcement of the statutory scheme for the protection of listed buildings, the Planning (Listed Buildings and Conservation Areas) Act 1990 - the 'Listed Buildings Act' (LBA 1990) - creates three offences protecting listed buildings and two offences in relation to unlisted buildings standing in a conservation area. The Act also incorporates the offences common to the Town and Country Planning Acts (TCPAs) arising from rights of entry and has the common provision in relation to offences committed by corporations.

14.2 Unauthorised demolition, extension or alteration of a listed building

The principal offence under s7 and s9 LBA 1990 punishes the carrying out of any works whether of demolition, alteration or extension of a listed building which would affect its character as a building of special architectural or historical interest unless prior authorisation has been obtained. This principal offence is necessarily more proactive than any concerned with development control under the Planning Act, because it is not a prerequisite that a notice of some sort has been served and breached before criminal liability is incurred. It is also unusual in that there is scope for magistrates or a jury to have to exercise their own judgement on what may be a subjective issue: that is whether or not there has been an affect on the character of the building as one of special architectural or historical interest. Elsewhere, the Planning Acts appear carefully drafted to keep such questions of architectural or historical judgement out of the arena of the criminal courts.

14.3 Offence under s9 LBA 1990

s7 LBA 1990 reads:

> . . . no person shall execute or cause to be executed any works for the demolition of a listed building or for its alteration or extension in any manner which would affect its character as a building of special architectural or historic interest, unless the works are authorised.
>
> s9 (1) LBA 1990 reads: If a person contravenes Sec.7 he shall be guilty of an offence.

The offence is of absolute liability. (*R v Wells Street Metropolitan Stipendiary Magistrate ex p Westminster City Council [1986] 3 All ER .)* This means that only evidence strictly relevant to the issues that the prosecution has to prove can be adduced. Hence, prejudicial evidence showing that a defendant ignored warnings that he was about to commit the offence or otherwise flouted the controls will be inadmissible and if admitted will lead to the conviction being quashed. (*R v Sandhu [1998 [1 PLR 170 Court of Appeal]*) However, this also means that it is not open to a defendant to show that steps had been taken in an attempt to avoid causing damage and that, in fact, it occurred inadvertently although, of course, such steps would provide mitigation.

14.4 What the prosecution must prove

14.4.1 That the building is listed

A *'listed building'* is one which is for the time being included in the list compiled or approved by the Secretary of State. Proof is usually by way of a certified copy. The list itself only includes the address of the building. There is also a listing description but strictly this does not form part of the list and is, if objected to, arguably inadmissible for the purposes of criminal proceedings.

The exact extent to which a building or group of buildings is listed may not always be clear. s1(5) LBA 1990 makes clear that any object or structure fixed to the building is covered by the listing, as is any object or structure within the curtilage of the building which, although not fixed to the building, forms part of the land and has done so since before July, 1948.

Questions can arise as to whether a particular outhouse, wall or adjoining stable block is covered by the listing of the principal building. There is no simple procedure for determining whether or not a particular adjoining building or extension is listed by application of s1(5) LBA 1990.

This means that in any case where the extent of listing is not clear, it would be open to a defendant to raise by way of defence that as a matter of law no listed building had been affected. It would be a matter of law as to whether the structure or part of the building which was alleged to have been damaged was, in fact, listed by being included in the address on the list.

Also, some buildings are specifically taken out of the listed-building control regime, such as ecclesiastical buildings, scheduled ancient monuments (which have their own protection) and buildings owned by the Crown. Where a building may fall into one of these categories, the relevant provisions and exemption orders should be considered at an early stage.

14.4.2 Temporary listing: Building Preservation Notices (BPNs)

The s3 LBA 1990 provides a procedure for spot-listing or emergency-listing where a building which is not yet listed but thought worthy of listing is about to be altered or demolished. In such circumstances, the LPA serves a Building Preservation Notice (BPN). While such a notice is in force, the building is listed for the purposes, inter alia, of the offence under s9 LBA 1990.

14.4.3 That the defendant executed works or caused works to be executed

'*Works*' has been given a meaning wider than might be expected were a magistrate or jury asked to apply it simply as an ordinary English word. It was held in *Windsor and Maidenhead Borough Council v Secretary of State for the Environment (1988) 2 PLR 17* that repainting a building constituted works amounting to an alteration. Whether or not the alteration affected the special interest of the building would be a separate question. In this case, repainting houses within a listed crescent in pink with black detailing, where all other buildings were white or a pastel colour, was held to require listed building consent. It appears that almost all building or maintenance operations, however minor, will constitute works of alteration. The more controversial question is likely to be whether the historical character or special interest of the building is affected.

'Executed' does not have any defined meaning. It is probably a synonym for 'carried out.'

The Courts will apply the usual authorities in considering whether or not any particular defendant can be said to have caused the works where there is no allegation of them having been directly carried out by the defendant.

14.4.4 That the works of demolition, alteration or extension have affected the building's character as a building of special architectural or historical interest

It is clear from *R v Sandhu* that this is an issue which is to be decided either by the magistrates as a matter of fact or by the jury. The Court of Appeal approved a direction by the trial judge that the jury "must be sure that the [work of] alteration . . . had affected the character of the building as a whole."

Where the defence challenges the allegation that the works have affected its character as a building of special architectural or historical interest, it would be open to both sides to call expert witnesses to give their views to the jury subject to the usual rules as to the scope of expert evidence. This could produce a wide-ranging debate.

14.4.5 That the works were not authorised

This requirement, stemming from the final words of s7 LBA 1990, was endorsed by the Court in *R v Sandhu*. Lack of authorisation is an element of the offence and it would appear that if this negative is not proved, it would be open to the defence to make a submission at the close of the prosecution case. The prosecution should therefore produce evidence that there is no consent for the works, either express, as the result of an application being granted, or in any other form.

14.5 Defences

14.5.1 The 'urgent-works' defence

s9(2)LBA 1990 seeks to provide for the urgent repair of a listed building in the interests of preventing further damage. It also seeks to constrain this defence tightly to avoid providing a loophole allowing the need for listed building consent to be avoided with a claim of urgent repair. The subsection provides a list of criteria each one of which must be established for the defence to succeed. It is for the defendant to make out the defence on the balance of probabilities. The cumulative requirements are that:

> (a) works to the building were urgently necessary in the interests of safety or health or for the preservation of the building;
> (b) it was not practicable to secure safety or health or, as the case may be, the preservation of the building, by works of repair or works for affording temporary support or shelter;
> (c) works carried out were limited to the minimum measures immediately necessary; and
> (d) notice in writing justifying in detail the carrying out of the works was given to the LPA as soon as reasonably practicable.

The requirement under (b), that works of temporary support or shelter was not practicable, may well be the hardest for a defendant to overcome. There is no guidance yet as to whether the cost of works and the defendant's means can be considered in determining what was or was not practicable at any particular time.

Applying the case of *R v Brockman* (decided in relation to the offence under s179 TCPA 1990), financial circumstances may be relevant albeit that the Courts will be slow to accept lack of finance as a complete defence.

14.6 Failing to comply with a condition of Listed Building Consent

s9(2) LBA 1990 reads:

> Without prejudice to subsection (1) if a person executing or causing to be executed any works in relation to a listed building under a listed building consent fails to comply with any condition attached to the consent he shall be guilty of an offence.

The issues in this offence are much narrower. Although not specifically decided by authority, there can be little doubt that the offence is equally one of absolute liability. The prosecution must prove that the consent covered the works and that a condition was breached.

The wording here would cover cases where a condition required works to be done which would not themselves constitute the main offence - e.g. that works to the listed building were to be carried out using certain materials, such as reclaimed bricks contemporary with the erection of the building, or that an extension was to be finished and painted to match the original parts of a listed house.

The 'urgency' defence under subsection (3) applies equally to this offence of breaching a condition.

14.7 Sentencing

This offence is punishable by imprisonment: a two-year maximum on indictment, six months in the Magistrates Court. Short terms of custody have been imposed where wilful breach of listed building control has been shown, although the Court of Appeal commented in *R v Robert Duckworth (1994) 16 Cr App Rep (S) 529* that it would rarely be appropriate to impose a custodial sentence unless the offence was blatant and serious (see below).

The alternative is a fine (or any lesser sentence). The fine is unlimited on indictment and the extended maximum common to other planning offences of £20,000 in the Magistrates Court. Under s9(5) LBA 1990, the sentence is required to take into account any financial benefit which has accrued or appears likely to accrue to the offender. It would also be correct for the sentencer to take into account any financial benefit which evidence shows the defendant intended to gain from the offence even if this has not ultimately materialised.

The appropriate level of fine was considered by the Court of Appeal in *R v Robert Duckworth (1994) 16 Cr App Rep (S) 529*. The Court held that factors relevant to sentence must include the degree of the following:-

(1) *The damage done to the historic structure.* This legislation's purpose is to preserve historic monuments and other similar structures protected by the legislation. The offence is an offence of damaging or altering those structures without appropriate consent or permission. Therefore, the first factor in considering the offence's seriousness is the degree of damage done.

(2) *The financial gain the defendant attempted to achieve.* In nearly all cases, financial gain will have been the defendant's motive. If he disregards the Act's provisions, it will almost certainly have been with a view to saving himself money or to gaining profit for himself. A financial penalty must take into account the financial advantage which the defendant was attempting to achieve, otherwise the sentence's deterrent and punitive effect may be lost.

(3) *The defendant's culpability.* This is in many respects the most important factor. These offences can be committed in a number of circumstances. They are sometimes described as offences of strict liability, whether or not that term is wholly accurate. But the offence may be committed through the defendant's lack of care or, indeed, through ignorance of his proper responsibilities. On the other hand, a defendant may have acted wilfully, in disregard of the need to obtain consent, or even with intent to damage or destroy a historic structure.

On the specific facts of that case, the Court of Appeal reduced a £15,000 fine to £7,500 and a £10,000 costs order to £5,000. The defendant, a chartered surveyor and valuer, had demolished and reconstructed the ground floor of a Grade II listed Elizabethan manor house, although it had previously been damaged by fire which had led to its listing being reduced from Grade II*. The Court of Appeal took into account Mr Duckworth's means but noted that a defendant had destroyed an important part of the historical structure.

Two earlier cases referred to in *Duckworth* were:-

14.7.1 *R v J O Sims Ltd (1993) 14 Cr App Rep (S) 213*

This involved negligent damage to a scheduled ancient monument consisting of the buried remains of a medieval palace. A £75,000 fine was varied to one of £15,000. (See section on ancient monuments.)

14.7.2 *Charles Barclay Simpson (1993) 14 Cr App Rep (S) 602*

Again, an ancient monument case, involving the remains of a Roman fort and settlement at Bishop Auckland, County Durham. Fines totalling £33,000 and costs of £10,000 were reduced to £15,000 and £10,000 respectively, for negligent damage. (See section on ancient monuments.)

14.7.3 *M and G Contractors (1986) 8 Cr App Rep (S) 474* :

A £6,000 fine and an order for £500 costs was upheld for the demolition of a Grade II listed 17th-century barn where planning permission had been obtained to convert it into dwellings. The fine was specifically based on the fact that no profit could be shown to have resulted from the demolition. The Court of Appeal commented: "Had it indeed been shown that this company had made a profit from their breach of the regulations, the fine would have been a very substantial one indeed."

The highest fines tend to have been imposed on property-development companies who, knowing the law, have ignored listed building control in carrying out commercial development or conversion of buildings. In such cases, fines of tens of thousands of pounds with substantial awards of costs have been imposed, especially if there is any suggestion of original fabric having been removed or destroyed.

In 1988, at Cambridge Crown Court, fines totalling £70,000 and costs of £3,2000 were imposed on a property company and two directors where a pair of mid19th-century cottages was demolished. Two applications for listed building consent to demolish the buildings had been turned down. The buildings were demolished whilst the Inspector's decision was awaited on a third application. The Crown Court judge heard evidence on the cleared site's development value. The company was fined a total £2,000 but two of its directors were fined a total £34,000 each with 12 months' imprisonment in default. The case was reported in the press and as *R v Chambers* (1989) JPL 229.

14.8 Other offences in relation to listed buildings

14.8.1 Failure to comply with provisions of a Listed Building Enforcement Notice (LBEN)

s38 LBA 1990 provides for the issue of a Listed Building Enforcement Notice (LBEN). A notice can be issued in an attempt to have put right any works which have affected the building's special historical interest or character. In fact, by virtue of s38(1)(b) LBA 1990, this amounts to any works which would be covered by initial criminal liability of the main offence under the s9 LBA 1990. However, the issuing authority may choose to issue a LBEN rather than proceed straight to a prosecution if, for instance it is believed that the most important objective is to have any damage put right at the expense of the owner of the building, or that for some other reason immediate prosecution would be counterproductive. However, there is nothing in the legislation to prevent the service of a LBEN whilst at the same time prosecuting under s9 LBA 1990 in respect of the same works.

The procedural pattern for issuing a LBEN, appeal against it and prosecution for breach mirrors that under the TCPA 1990. Many decided authorities on the s179 LBA 1990 provisions of the TCPA 1990, on matters such as the availability of challenge to the validity of the notice as a defence and interpretation of the wording of the notice at trial, will be relevant and persuasive to issues arising in connection with this parallel offence. The

LBEN must specify alleged works to which it relates, steps required for compliance, the date on which it takes effect and the period thereafter within which it is to be complied with.

If there has been no appeal against the LBEN, or an appeal has been refused or withdrawn, then failure to comply with the notice will constitute an offence.

14.8.2 What the prosecution must prove

The prosecution must prove that:

(a) the LBEN was issued by the appropriate LPA;
(b) the period for compliance with the notice has expired;
(c) the steps, or a step, required by the LBEN has not been taken; and
(d) the defendant has been the owner of the land to which the building relates at any time after the period for compliance when the notice has not been complied with.

Under this offence, liability attaches to the owner of the land at any time when the steps have not been carried out irrespective of whether or not the owner owned the land at the time the notice was served and the time for compliance expired. By analogy to s179 TCPA 1990, the offence is one of strict liability. Certainly absolute liability was assumed by the Divisional Court when this section's direct predecessor was considered in *Mid - Devon District Council v Avery* (1992) 65 P& CR 47. The definition of owner will be that set out in the principal Act - s91(2) LBA 1990.

s43(3) LBA 1990 simplifies any question of time. The offence can be charged by reference to any day or longer period. A person can be guilty of a second offence or subsequent offence again by reference to any period following the preceding conviction for the offence.

14.8.3 Defences

Under s43(4) LBA 1990 it shall be a defence for the defendant to show that he:

(a) did everything that he could be expected to do to secure that all the steps required by the notice were taken; or
(b) was not served with a copy of the notice and was unaware of its existence.

The defence under s43(4)(a) LBA 1990 mirrors that in s179(3) LBA 1990. A LBEN will always require some positive action to be taken. The issues raised in *Kent County Council v Brockman,* as to the extent to which lack of means will be a defence, may arise more frequently in prosecutions under this section. LBENs may reasonably specify works for the restoration of a building which will cost many thousands of pounds and in some cases hundreds of thousands of pounds.

The defence under s43(4)(b) LBA 1990 requires the defendant to show not only that he was not served but was also unaware of the notice's existence. A purchaser of land who has made the usual precontract enquiries and so forth may find it difficult to show he did not know of the notice, which the planning authority should have registered as a local land charge. However, the defendant will not be deemed to have knowledge of the notice, because either it has been recorded on any register or he ought reasonably to have been aware of it. The requirements of service are those set out in s329 of the main Act. (See s89[1].)

14.8.4 Sentencing

The sentence provided by the section is a fine. This is at the normal level for regulatory offences of £20,000 in the Magistrates Court and unlimited on indictment. In line with similar offences, s43(6) LBA 1990 specifically requires the Court to have regard in particular to any financial benefit which has accrued or appears likely to accrue to the defendant as a consequence of the offence.

In practice, in determining the appropriate level of sentence much may turn on whether or not it was the defendant before the Court who allowed the works to be carried out in the first place, or whether the defendant has been required by the notice to make good another's works. The Court will usually wish to know whether the bringing of a prosecution has itself had an effect and therefore whether or not the remedial works have been carried out at the date of sentence.

14.9 s59 LBA 1990: Damage by an owner

s59(1) LBA 1990 reads:

> If, with the intention of causing damage to a listed building, any relevant person does or permits the doing of any act which causes or is likely to result in damage to the building, he shall be guilty of an offence.

Like any other building or property, a listed building is protected from vandalism by the Criminal Damage Act 1971 (CDA 1971). Intentional or reckless damage to a listed building would be an offence, provided that the perpetrator was not the owner. However, the offence of criminal damage only applies to property belonging to another. Once a building is listed, the purpose of the Act is to protect it and preserve its special architectural or historical interest for the public at large. Without this offence, there would be a loophole because an owner would commit no offence by vandalising his own building. This offence provides an alternative to the offence under s9 LBA 1990 where the prosecutor is faced with architectural theft. This is where the owner of a listed building removes or consents to the removal of original and valuable architectural features, such as fireplaces or panelling, for sale, often for large sums, for insertion into other buildings. Prosecuting under this section will expose the defendant to lower penalties but may avoid difficulties of proving affect on special character or over the definition of 'works'.

The wording of the section creates criminal liability where the *'relevant person'* damages the building. The relevant person is defined by subsection (2) LBA 1990 which reads:

> A person is a relevant person for the purpose of subsection (1) if apart from that subsection he would be entitled to do or permit the act in question

In practice, this will mean the freehold owner or anybody else, such as a leaseholder who would have the right, under the terms of the lease or other arrangement, to damage the property perhaps by the removal of fixtures or fittings.

14.9.1 What the prosecution must prove

The prosecution must prove that:

(a) the building was listed;
(b) the defendant is a relevant person for the purposes of s59(1) LBA 1990;
(c) the defendant intentionally carried out or permitted an act to be done;
(d) the act caused damage to the listed building or was likely to result in damage to the listed building.

s59 LBA 1990 applies only to buildings listed under s1 LBA 1990, not to buildings which are to be treated as listed only by virtue of the urgent step of serving a building preservation notice under s3 LBA 1990.

Questions as to the meaning of 'intention', 'permitted' and 'caused' will be interpreted in line with the authorities interpreting these words where they appear elsewhere in statutes creating regulatory offences. Even if a company is convicted under the 'directing mind and will' principles, the normal provisions for the prosecution of directors do not apply.

14.9.2 Continuing offence

Where a defendant has been convicted of the offence, s59(4) LBA 1990 comes into play:

> If a person convicted of an offence under this section fails to take such reasonable steps as may be necessary to prevent any damage or further damage resulting from the offence, he shall be guilty of a further offence...

There may be cases where the question of what would amount to reasonable steps necessary to prevent further damage becomes an issue for magistrates. The Court, however, will be considering a case in which the defendant has already been convicted of intentional damage to the building. It may be helpful on this issue for the prosecution to write to the defendant before trial, or immediately upon conviction for the offence, for the first time setting out what the prosecution would consider reasonable steps for the purposes of this subsection.

14.9.3 Defences

Under s59(3) LBA 1990 it is a defence to show that the damage resulted from works authorised by planning permission under the Planning Act or by listed building consent. As with all offences under the LBA 1990, it is necessary to check that the exceptions, meaning that the offence does not apply, such as ecclesiastical buildings, church land or Crown property, are not relevant.

14.9.4 Mode of trial and sentence

The offence is triable summarily only and punishable on conviction with a fine on level three of the standard scale. The fine for the continuing offence shall not exceed one tenth of the fine on level three of the standard scale for each day on which the failure continues.

It is not clear why this offence, which involves intentional damage or risk of damage to the listed building, should have attached to it a lesser maximum sentence than the offence of strict liability under s9 LBA 1990. The equivalent section protecting ancient monuments carries a short term of imprisonment as the maximum sentence.

14.10 Offences relating to buildings in Conservation Areas

Under s74 LBA 1990, a building in a conservation area shall not be demolished without the appropriate authority's consent. To integrate this provision into the legislation, many LBA 1990 sections are to have effect in relation to buildings in conservation areas as they have effect in relation to listed buildings, subject to such exceptions and modifications prescribed by regulations

The wording of s7 and 9 LBA 1990 has been modified, to create an offence of executing or causing to be executed works for the demolition of a building in a conservation area unless the works are authorised.

It is similarly an offence under s9(2) LBA 1990, where conservation area consent has been granted for the demolition of an unlisted building with conditions, to carry out the demolition without complying with the conditions of the consent.

The prosecution must prove the designation of the conservation area and that the building stood within it. The offence relates only to demolition, not alteration or extension.

14.10.1 Demolition

In *Shimizu (UK) Limited v Westminster City Council* (1997) 1 All ER 481, the House of Lords held that whether demolition had occurred was a question of fact. For works to amount to demolition, they would have to lead to the pulling down of a building so that it is destroyed completely and broken up. Works leading to the destruction or removal of part of a building, such as the roof or a top floor, were held to constitute alteration rather than demolition. This interpretation of demolition narrows the scope of the offence from that which had been applied by many planning authorities and planning professionals until that date. (See, for instance, para. 4.28 of the 1994 version of Planning Policy Guidance Note 15 [PPG 15].) However, in the context of criminal proceedings, where any ambiguities are to be resolved in favour of the defendant it seems clear that the offence will not be committed unless there is no substantial part of the building left.

s9 provisions of the LBA 1990, as to defences and sentence, apply without change to the offence of demolition of an unlisted building within a conservation area without consent.

14.11 Conservation Area Enforcement Notices

s38 LBA 1990, as modified by the Secretary of State, empowers to issue a Conservation Area Enforcement Notice (CAEN) where demolition works have been carried out without consent. Given the degree to which a building has to be pulled down for demolition to have taken place under *Shimuzu*, the works required by a CAEN are likely to be substantial and could amount to a virtual rebuilding. Under s43 LBA 1990, breach of a CAEN is an offence in the same way as breach of a LBEN. The same provisions and relevant case-law apply.

The exceptions to listed building control also apply within a conservation area. Ecclesiastical buildings and scheduled ancient monuments, for instance, fall outside the scope of the offences.

14.12 Offences related to administration of listed building and conservation area control

Under s88B LBA 1990, the provisions creating offences relating to rights of entry under the Planning Act are reproduced. These are the obstruction of authorised entry under s88B(3) LBA 1990, triable summarily only and punishable by a fine not exceeding level three; and, the unauthorised disclosure of a trade secret by a person who has acquired the information whilst on the land. This, as under the main Act, is an offence carrying in the Magistrates Court a fine to the statutory maximum (currently £5,000), or on indictment an unlimited fine or a maximum two years in prison.

s89 LBA 1990 incorporates the provisions in s331 of the main Act in relation to the conviction of culpable directors where a company has been convicted of any of the offences under the Act, save for that of intentional damage created by s59 LBA 1990.

CHAPTER 15

OFFENCES UNDER THE ANCIENT MONUMENTS AND ARCHAEOLOGICAL AREAS ACT 1979 (AMAAA 1979)

CONTENTS

CHAPTER 15

OFFENCES UNDER THE ANCIENT MONUMENTS AND ARCHAEOLOGICAL AREAS ACT 1979

15.1 Introduction

The Ancient Monuments and Archaeological Areas Act 1979 (AMAAA 1979) is the statute under which ancient monuments and the sites of ancient monuments are identified and protected. The Secretary of State compiles a schedule of ancient monuments which can be a building, structure, work, cave or excavation whether buried or still above ground. Monuments scheduled range from Stonehenge (the first monument to be scheduled under the Ancient Monuments Protection Act 1882 (AMPA 1882), still very much standing above ground, to inaccessible, buried archaeology, such as the site of the Palace of the Roman Governor of London, parts of which lie under Lower Thames Street and the railway arches of Cannon Street station.

15.2 Offences

15.2.1 s1 AMAAA 1979

Once a monument is scheduled under s1 AMAAA 1979, it becomes an offence under s2 AMAAA 1979 to carry out any works without written authorisation from the Secretary of State, known as Scheduled Monument Consent (SMC).

15.2.2 s2 AMAAA 1979

s2 AMAAA 1979 reads:-

> Control of works affecting scheduled monuments:
>
> 2 - (1) If any person executes or causes or permits to be executed any works to which this section applies he shall be guilty of an offence unless the works are authorised under this Part of this Act.

(2)(a) This section applies to any of the following works, that is to say:

(a) any works resulting in the demolition or destruction of or any damage to a scheduled monument;
(b) any works for the purpose of removing or repairing a scheduled monument or any part of it or of making any alterations or additions thereto; and
(c) any flooding or tipping operations on land in, on or under which there is a scheduled monument.

15.3 What the prosecution must prove

The prosecution must prove that:

(a) the building or site is scheduled as an ancient monument;
(b) the defendant executed or caused or permitted to be executed any of the works in subsection 2.

'Works' as well as a having a general meaning is defined in s58 AMAAA 1979 as including any operations undertaken for the purposes of agriculture (within the meaning of the TCPA 1990) or forestry (including afforestation).

The proof of scheduling will be either an authorised copy of the schedule which is administered by English Heritage or by a witness from that organisation producing the scheduling documentation which will normally include a plan.

The specific provisions of this section were considered by the Court of Appeal in *R v Bovis Construction Ltd [1994]* Criminal LR 938.

It was confirmed that the offence was of strict liability.

The *Bovis* case concerned the site of the Palace of the Roman Governor of London. The ancient monument was described as "Roman Governor's Palace (site of), City of London, Greater London, . . . , situated on or under the land as shown outlined in red on the enclosed map . . ." The case concerned the excavation of a manhole shaft into the area and to a depth where the archaeologists believed artefacts would be found. The manhole cover was to be part of works for the redevelopment of Cannon Street railway station. However, the prosecution could not prove specifically that any particular artefact or remain had been lost or damaged. The case was put on the basis that by digging into the site, without allowing the proper opportunity for archaeological investigation, the ancient monument had been damaged. The site of an ancient palace was less valuable in archaeological terms after there had been unrecorded excavation. Ultimately, even if no remains at all were there to be found, this negative information would itself have been of value in the context of other detailed information known about the site.

The prosecution suggested that it was highly likely that Roman remains had, in fact, been destroyed but could not prove this to the required standard without speculation as to the precise area the palace and associated wharves would have occupied.

The appellant construction company claimed that the jury should have been left to decide as a matter of fact whether any actual physical part of the palace's remains had been damaged; and that it was not open to the Secretary of State to designate an area as the site of an ancient monument within which there would be remains but also some areas of soil in which no remains would be found

The Court of Appeal determined that the practice of designating a monument as the site of a palace, castle, or other building or monument was lawful and that within that site the prosecution did not have to prove that an actual remain had been hit. This would cause impossible uncertainty for the owner or developer of land scheduled as the site of a monument. If criminal liability were to turn upon whether or the not the excavator's bucket brought up a Roman jug, or missed it by an inch, the developer would be digging in a minefield, as the trial judge put it at first instance.

It was also clear that the site of the scheduled monument could be damaged through excavation with no opportunity for archaeological research. The rulings of the trial judge were upheld.

15.4 Failure to comply with a condition attached to Scheduled Monument Consent (SMC)

Scheduled Monument Consent (SMC) may be given with conditions attached. Failure to comply with any condition is an offence under subsection 6, although it will be a defence to show that all reasonable precautions were taken and all due diligence exercised in an attempt to avoid contravening the condition. The sentence prescribed is the same as for the offence under subsection 2 AMAAA 1979.

15.5 Defences

s2 AMAAA 1979 provides for several defences which leave a little more room for culpability to be considered than the absolute-liability nature of the offence would at first suggest.

15.5.1 s2(7) AMAAA 1979

In relation to works resulting in demolition, destruction or damage covered by ss(2)(a), ss (7) AMAAA 1979 provides a defence

"for the accused to show that he took all reasonable precautions and exercised all due diligence to avoid or prevent any damage to the monument."

15.5.2 s2(8) AMAAA 1979

In relation to works resulting in demolition, destruction or damage covered by ss (2)(a) and in relation to works of flooding or tipping covered by ss (2)(c), subsection (8) AMAAA 1979 provides a defence "for the accused to prove that he did not know and had no reason to believe that the monument was within the area affected by the works or (as the case may be) that it was a scheduled monument."

Landowners are generally made aware by English Heritage that their property includes a monument or the site of a monument and Ancient Monument Inspectors may visit from time to time. Nevertheless, genuine ignorance will still provide a defence.

The two defences do not apply to works for alteration, removal or repair of a monument under subsection 2(b).

15.5.3 s2(9) AMAAA 1979

All the works within ss (2) are covered by an 'urgent-works' defence in subsection (9) which provides:

> In any proceedings for an offence under this section it shall be a defence to prove that the works were urgently necessary in the interests of safety or health and that notice in writing of the need for works was given to the Secretary of State as soon as reasonably practicable.

The notice to be given to the Secretary of State is that of the need for the works rather than notification that works have been carried out. It may be an interesting question as to how urgent works were, if written notice of the need for them could be given to the Secretary of State.

15.6 Sentencing

Under ss (10) AMAAA 1979, the sentence is a fine, to the level of the statutory maximum on summary trial and unlimited on indictment. The appropriate level of fine has been considered by the Court of Appeal in a small number of cases.

15.6.1 *R v Hugh Edward Conway Seymour (1987) 9 Cr App R(S) 395*

The appellant owned farmland covering about a fifth of the site of a Roman town. Because the site had been scheduled as an ancient monument, he had been paid £127,000 compensation in respect of a planning permission which the scheduling prevented him from implementing.

The defendant was clearly aware that the two fields in question were scheduled as the site of the Roman town. He had been told that he would not need to apply for scheduled monument consent in respect of normal agricultural works but he had also been told that ploughing to a greater depth than normal would require consent.

The defendant as landowner arranged for the land to be ploughed to a depth of 10 to 12 inches. This destroyed a layer of Roman remains which began six inches beneath the surface.

The Crown Court's £10,000 fine was reduced to £3,000. The Court of Appeal noted that much of the town's archaeology remained under adjoining land. It appeared that the Crown Court judge had inadvertently been led to believe that the town's whole site had been ploughed over. It was also important that a letter from English Heritage setting out what could and could not be done on the land was capable of being read ambiguously. The appellant was of good character and had indicated a plea of guilty in writing at a very early stage prior to committal proceedings.

The Court indicated that whilst there could have been confusion over to what depth ploughing would be appropriate "in a situation of importance such as this, it would have been prudent (and indeed, in our view, the duty) of the appellant if he had any doubts at all about the matter to seek adequate and accurate advice."

The fine was reduced from £10,000 to £3,000 on the basis that the offence had been committed through negligence rather than flouting the law. A fine in the region of £10,000 was, the Court said, "a sum more appropriate to a flagrant disregard of an ancient monument for the purposes of personal gain."

However, the level of fines upheld in later cases of negligent damages has risen, although the Court of Appeal has still substantially reduced fines imposed in the Crown Court.

15.6. 2 *R v J O Sims Limited (1993) 14 Cr App R (S)*

The defendant company owned a warehouse which needed underpinning. The warehouse stood over the site of the London palace of the Bishops of Winchester which was a Scheduled Ancient Monument (SAM). The company was aware of the need to gain scheduled monument consent but no consent was sought for the underpinning works. Parts of the buried walls of the palace were damaged and destroyed without the chance for archaeological recording or study of the artefacts.

The company had pleaded guilty and, upon being told of the damage caused, had stopped the building works immediately, leading to direct financial loss to them. The Court, to which *R v Seymour* was cited, regarded the case as one in which the degree of negligence was by no means small. It reduced the £75,000 fine to £15,000.

15.6. 3 *R v Charles Barclay Simpson (1993) 14 Cr App R(S) 602*

Some six months after the case of *R v J O Sims Limited,* £ 15,000 was again the level of fine for damage accepted by the prosecution to be negligent, although it is not clear whether or not *R v J O Sims Limited* or *R v Seymour* were cited.

Mr Simpson owned the site of a Roman fort and settlement in Bishop Auckland, County Durham. The fort was one of several supporting Hadrian's Wall and survived relatively undamaged.

The appellant intended to renovate modern buildings on the site for use as a nursing home and was aware of its Roman associations which he intended to make use of as an advertising feature.

Despite some discussions with the County Archaeology Department, works were commenced without SMC. As a result, at least one building within the fort complex was destroyed and the complete layer of archaeological deposits associated with it destroyed without any form of recording. A trench which formed a separate count on the indictment had also destroyed archaeological deposits.

The appellant had a practically unblemished reputation had entered an early written guilty plea. There was evidence before the Court of the appellant's personal financial difficulties.

The Court said the offences clearly demanded a heavy fine and [had involved] a substantial destruction of part of this country's archaeological heritage.

The total level of fines was reduced from £33,000 to £15,000.

15.7 s28 AMAAA 1979

15.7.1 Deliberate or reckless damage

A more serious offence of damaging an ancient monument deliberately or recklessly is created by the Act's s28. Such damage potentially carries a maximum two-year prison sentence. The prosecuting authorities have often accepted pleas to the lesser offence under s2 AMAAA 1979, even where there has been a count under this section on the indictment. However, there has been at least one successful prosecution under this section. This was where damage was caused by hurried excavation, with no recording, of a section of what had been the moat surrounding a mediaeval priory. The defendant, who had misled officials from English Heritage in order to allow works to continue uninterrupted, pleaded not guilty but was convicted before a jury at Luton Crown Court and fined

s28 AMAAA 1979 reads:

> 28(1) - A person who without lawful excuse destroys or damages any protected monument -
>
> (a) knowing that it is a protected monument: and
> (b) intending to destroy or damage the monument or being reckless as to whether the monument would be destroyed or damaged;
>
> shall be guilty of an offence.

ss(2) AMAAA 1979 makes clear that authority from the owner of the monument is not a defence and the only exception is works for which scheduled monument consent has been obtained. There are no statutory defences.

15.7.2 Sentencing

Under s28(4) AMAAA 1979, in the Magistrates Court the maximum sentence on summary conviction is a fine up to the normal maximum and a maximum six months' imprisonment, or both. In the Crown Court, the fine is unlimited and the maximum period of imprisonment is one of two years.

15.8 Excavating, flooding or tipping in an Area of Archaeological Importance (AAI)

Under Part II of the Act, the Secretary of State has power to designate areas of archaeological importance (AAIs). This power has been used sparingly to designate the historic core of the cities of Canterbury, Exeter, York, Hereford and Chester. These areas are being monitored and it is understood that there are no immediate plans to designate any further areas under AMAAA 1979.

Once an area is designated, it becomes an offence under the s35 AMAAA 1979 to carry out any operations which disturb the ground, and flooding or tipping operations, without first serving a specific notice on the relevant authority. The notice's purpose is to allow the authority to carry out any rescue archaeology considered appropriate. The notice must be served to give six weeks' notice of works. If a precursor to the works is to be clearance of modern buildings on the site, giving information as to when the clearance works will be completed is required. The developer is also required to notify the relevant authority once the site is cleared.

15.9 Metal detectors

15.9.1 Offences

Many historical sites have been damaged by treasure seekers' unofficial and hence unrecorded use of metal detectors. This activity could constitute several different criminal offences:

• Theft: if the land does not belong to the seeker. (See an example considered by the Court of Appeal: *R v Kidd* [1995] Crim LR 406.)

• Under s2 or s28 AMAAA 1979, though both offencesrequire proof of actual damage.

• Under s42 AMAAA 1979, which makes it an offence to use a metal detector within the site of a SAM; within the site of a monument owned by or under the guardianship of English Heritage or the Secretary of State, or within an area designated an AAI. The section creates an offence where there is no need to catch the accused in the act of digging a hole.

The s42 AMAAA 1979 offence is made out if any person uses a metal detector in a protected place without the appropriate authority's written consent.

A *'metal detector'* is defined as any device designed or adapted for detecting or locating any metal or mineral in the ground

The offence is triable summarily only. The prescribed sentence is a £200 fine.

Where the prosecution can show that an artefact has been removed they may prosecute under s42(3) AMAAA 1979 which reads:

> If a person without [written consent] removes any object of archaeological or historic interest which he has discovered by use of a metal detector in a protected place, he shall be guilty of an offence.

This offence is triable either way. In the Magistrates Court, the fine is set at the statutory maximum .

The offence under subsections 42(1) and 42(3) AMAAA 1979 is committed if the metal detector is used with no written consent only. However, where that consent is given but has conditions attached to it, then under subsection 42(5) AMAAA 1979 it is an offence to breach those conditions. Again, the distinction is maintained between simply using the metal detector in breach of a condition, in which case the using offence under subsection (1) applies; and removing an object in breach of a condition, in which case subsection 42(3) AMAAA 1979 applies.

15.9.2 Defences: s42(6) AMAAA 1979

Under subsection (6), it is a defence, to the offence of using a metal detector under subsection (1) AMAAA 1979, for the accused to show that he used the metal detector for a purpose other than detecting or locating objects of archaeological or historical interest.

Under subsection (7) AMAAA 1979, it is a defence, to both the using and the removing offences, for the defendant to prove that he had taken all reasonable precautions to find out whether the place where he used the metal detector was a protected place and did not believe it was.

15.10 Miscellaneous offences

15.10.1 Failure to comply with a requisition for information

s57 AMAAA 1979 includes the provision whereby the relevant authority may require

> the occupier of any land and any person who, either directly or indirectly, receives rent in respect of any land to state in writing the nature of his interest therein and the name and address of any other person known to him as having an interest therein, whether as freeholder, . . . mortgagee, lessee or otherwise.

It is an offence, summary only, to fail without reasonable excuse to give the required information. The maximum sentence is a £200 fine.

Knowingly making a misstatement in reply to such a request is an offence under subsection (3) AMAAA 1979. The offence is triable either way with the fine at the statutory maximum in the Magistrates Court.

15.11 Directors' liability

s58 AMAAA 1979 provides for the prosecution of the directors or other similar officers, where a company is proved to have committed one of the other offences under the Act. Where the offence can be shown to have been committed with the consent or connivance of, or to be attributable to the neglect of, any of the company's officers, then they, as well as the company, shall be guilty of the offence and liable to sentence accordingly.

CHAPTER 16

CRIMINAL PROCEEDINGS: INTRODUCTION AND COMMON TERMS DEFENCES

CONTENTS

CHAPTER 16

CRIMINAL PROCEEDINGS: INTRODUCTION AND COMMON TERMS DEFENCES

16.1 Introduction

Once in the criminal courts, environmental offences are subject to the same procedure and rules of evidence as proceedings for any other criminal offence. This section of the book is designed to give an introduction to some of the principles of criminal law and procedure which are most likely to occur during consideration of an environmental offence. Some points which may occur more frequently in considering regulatory offences will be covered in more detail.

Firstly, this section considers the interpretation likely to be given to some of the words and phrases which regularly arise during consideration of environmental crimes. Second, companies' criminal liability is considered. Third, there is commentary on the criminal process from investigation through to trial.

16.2 Interpretation of words and phrases regularly occurring in consideration of environmental offences (EOs)

All but one environmental crime covered in this book are created by Parliament. The only common-law environmental crime is public nuisance (see Chapter 9 of this book). In the wording of statutes creating the offences, a number of words or phrases are used regularly. Where the Courts have considered their meaning, they will be interpreted consistently, even if used in a different statute to that first considered. For instance, the meaning of 'causes' has been extensively considered by Courts and will be given the same meaning in the light of those authorities whether it relates to a water-pollution offence or to a TCPA 1990 offence.

16.2.1 Damage or damages

Where the law prohibits damage to a tree, ancient monument or other object, the relevant question will be whether what the prosecution can show happened has diminished the value or benefit of what is protected even temporarily. An ancient monument, such as an ancient stone circle, is damaged by having graffiti sprayed on it even assuming this can be harmlessly cleaned off with no permanent effect. A tree will be damaged, even if in time it will recover completely, from losing a branch or having bark stripped. The meaning of 'damage' when considering the offence of criminal damage (vandalism) has been held to have a wide interpretation "so as to include not only permanent or temporary physical harm but also permanent or temporary impairment of value or usefulness." (*Morphitis v Salmon* [1990] Crim LR 48 DC; *R v Whitely* [1993] Cr.App.R. 25 CA.)

The acts alleged to constitute damage may be very shortlived and will still constitute damage even if their effects will disappear without any need for a clear up or other remedial action. In *Hardman v Chief Constable of Somerset* [1986] Crim LR 330 DC, the use of water-soluble paint on pavements as part of an antinuclear protest constituted damage even though rain would have washed the paint away eventually.

16.2.2 Strict or absolute liability

Many environmental crimes are those of strict or absolute liability. They will not be described as such in the statute but the description means that the prosecution do not have to prove that the defendant acted with any particular state of mind. What the defendant meant or did not mean to do is irrelevant. Provided the prosecution can prove that the factual ingredients of the offence have occurred, then there will be no distinction, except on sentence, between whether the defendant, acting or failing to act in breach of law, did so entirely deliberately in a calculated manner or wholly inadvertently in fact whilst doing his best to stay within the law. Evidence will not be allowed to be introduced into a trial of a strict-liability offence which is designed to prove either deliberate intent or that the defendant was taking great care to act within the law. If such evidence is introduced by the prosecution, it will provide a ground for quashing the conviction. (*R v Sandhu* [1998] 1PLR 170.)

In determining whether or not a particular offence is to be one of strict or absolute liability the Courts look to the wording of the statute, to the type of offence and to the statutory framework which surrounds it. In general, the Courts have been prepared to hold that Parliament intended to create offences of strict liability in regulatory-type offences covered in this book, unless the statute specifically mentions a state of mind, such as 'knowingly.'

16.2.3 'Causing or causes'

Despite consistent pleas to avoid overcomplicating the application of 'causing' and for juries to be directed to give it a commonsense meaning, the Appellate Courts have had to define and redefine 'causing' on several different occasions.

It is clear that no specific mental element is required and the use of 'causes' or 'causing' without more creates an offence of strict liability. One frequent issue has been the extent to which a defendant is said to have caused an event where, although it was his actions which made it possible, those actions cannot be said to have been the most immediate or the only cause.

***NRA v Yorkshire Water Services Ltd* [1995] 1 All ER 225**

Yorkshire Water Services owned and maintained sewerage which discharged sewage with consent into waters protected by the National Rivers Authority (NRA). Yorkshire Water was forbidden to discharge many substances into the rivers. One of these substances was a pollutant chemical known as isooctanol. During the night, isooctanol was discharged into a Yorkshire Waters sewer. It was accepted that this discharge was by an unidentified third party and had apparently been surreptitious. It was inevitable that the isooctanol, once in the sewer, would pass through the sewerage system into the River Spen.

The House of Lords held on these facts that Yorkshire Water had caused the discharge of isooctanol:

> I am of the opinion that Yorkshire Water Services having set up a system for gathering effluent into their sewers and thence into their sewage works there to be treated, with an arrangement deliberately intended to carry the results of that treatment into [the river], the special circumstances surrounding the entry of isooctanol into their sewers and works do not preclude the conclusion that Yorkshire Water Services caused the resulting poisonous, noxious and polluting matter to enter the controlled waters, . . .

NRA v Yorkshire Water Services Ltd [1995] 1 All ER225 per Lord Mackay, LC 231.

Lord Mackay in reaching this interpretation specifically applied the words of Lord Wilberforce in *Alphacell v Wooward* [1972] AC 824, namely:

> In my opinion, 'causing' here must be given a commonsense meaning and I deprecate the introduction of refinements, such as *causa causans*, effective cause or *novus actus* . . .
>
> Yorkshire Water were ultimately able to rely on a statutory defence but the decision indicated that whilst each case must be considered on its own facts it *may* not be necessary to show a positive act on the part of the accused to prove that they caused the offence to occur.

***Empress Car Company (Abertillery) Ltd v National Rivers Authority* (1998) Env LR 396**

This approach was confirmed in the most recent case in the House of Lords. *Empress Car Company (Abertillery) Ltd v National Rivers Authority* (1998) Env LR 396. (This case is also considered in the analysis of s85[1] of the WRA 1991.)

On March 20th, 1995, somebody opened the tap on the diesel-oil storage tank belonging to the Empress Car Company in Abertillery. As the tank emptied, oil flowed out on to the surface of the company's yard, into the surface drains and then into the nearby River Ebbw Fach, polluting it. The tank may have been deliberately drained by a person with a grudge against the company.

The House of Lords held that despite the fact that the oil may have been let out of the tank as a malicious act of vandalism, Empress Cars had caused the pollution of the river for the purposes of the offence under s85(i) of the WRA 1991: "A person contravenes this section if he causes . . . any polluting matter to enter any controlled waters" [controlled waters are, in effect, any river or stream].

This decision clarifies the approach to be adopted in cases where there are acts of third parties without which the pollution would not have occurred. The House of Lords held that semantic arguments were distracting and that where there was evidence consistent with the act of a third party, then a two-stage approach should be adopted:

(1) The Court should determine whether the defendant had done anything which caused the pollution, even if it were not the immediate cause. This could be as little as bringing on to their land polluting material such as fuel oil, or operating a manufacturing process which used potential pollutants. The prosecution need only prove something more than absolute passivity.

(2) Assuming the prosecution could show the defendant to have done something, then, Lord Hoffman suggested:

> if the defendant did something which produced a situation in which the polluting matter could escape but a necessary condition of the actual escape which happened was also the act of a third party or a natural event then the justices should consider whether that act or event should be regarded as a normal fact of life or something extraordinary. If it was in the general run of things a matter of ordinary occurrence, it will not negative the causal effect of the defendant's acts even if it was not foreseeable that it would happen to that particular defendant or take that particular form. If it can be regarded as something extraordinary, it will be open to the justices to hold that the defendant did not cause the pollution.
>
> The distinction between ordinary and extraordinary is one of fact and degree to which the justices must apply their common sense and knowledge of what happens in the area.

This formulation of the law as it relates to the acts of third parties or natural events followed the trend of decisions concerning that particular offence and which narrowed the scope for blaming others in order to show that a defendant had not caused an event. For instance, *CPC (UK) Ltd v National Rivers Authority* [1994] Env LR 131 confirmed that a company had caused pollution where the escape occurred as a result of a leaky pipe badly installed by reputable contractors on behalf of the previous owners of a factory.

The focus on ordinary or extraordinary events introduced a new element. It is now clear that only extraordinary intervening events will provide a defence. The only example of an extraordinary intervening event given in the judgement was a terrorist attack. This suggests that the range of events capable of being extraordinary is likely to be very small. The intervening act of a third party will not prevent a conviction even if it was not foreseeable that it would happen to that particular defendant or take that particular form. The judgement gives few examples of ordinary and extraordinary acts other than to confirm that regrettably there is nothing unusual about ordinary vandalism. Empress Cars had not put a lock on the oil-tap, preventing it being turned on by vandals, but even if the defendant had and it had been maliciously broken off, it appears the conviction would still have been upheld.

As a rule of thumb, where there is a twisted chain of events and potential liability for several parties, it may be appropriate to ask how the final criminal state of affairs occurred. The defendant will have caused the event even if he is only part of the cause. If it is not possible to describe how the state of affairs came about without including reference to the defendant, then they can usually be said to come within what has become a wide definition of 'causing.'

16.2.4 Permitting or knowingly permitting

'Permitting' is often coupled with *'knowingly.'* Although this avoids doubt, it is probably unnecessary because it has been held that one cannot permit a state of affairs without knowledge of it. However, Nelson-like blindness or shutting one's eyes to the obvious would constitute sufficient knowledge to permit the state of affairs. (*Ross Hillman v Bond* [1974] QB 435.) Any evidence of payment or reward for allowing something to happen will usually provide conclusive proof of permitting.

Even with knowledge, a defendant cannot permit unless he has some means of preventing the occurrence. Where a defendant had the power to prevent an act occurring and failed to take reasonable steps to do so, he will have permitted that act. For instance, a farmer who allows his land to be used for dumping waste in contravention of the EPA 1990 will have permitted this, even though he may be unaware of the precise time or location of the dumping.

'Permitting' is interpreted as being wider than *'causing'* and often argued to be a less serious offence when it comes to considering sentence.

16.2.5 Intentionally

Questions of intent are relatively rare in consideration of environmental offences. In general, the word is to be given its ordinary meaning without elaboration. For offences of this nature, a defendant will be taken to have intended those consequences of their actions which they foresaw or ought reasonably to have foreseen.

16.2.6 Recklessly

Where *'recklessly'* does occur in these offences, it is often linked in the wording with 'intentionally.' Nevertheless, the prosecution ought to be clear which state of mind it seeks to prove. As a general rule, where someone ignores an obvious risk, that what they are about to do could cause the harm prohibited by the offence, they will have acted recklessly. For instance, knowing that an area is an ancient monument by virtue of it being the site of a medieval village, to dig foundations in it for a new building without first ascertaining exactly where any remains or artefacts are creates an obvious risk of damage, such that the excavation is carried out recklessly as to whether or not the ancient monument will be damaged.

However, *'reckless'* has generated much debate as to its meaning beyond the scope of this general consideration of terms used. Detailed consideration of the relevant case-law may become necessary if a prosecution is brought on this basis.

16.2.7 Knowingly

Where it is a specific element of an offence to show that a defendant knew of something, such as the listing of a building, the scheduling of a monument or the terms of a waste-disposal consent, it is for the prosecution to prove this as part of its case. Clearly, the best evidence will be an admission in interview or some action of the defendant consistent only with knowledge of the appropriate facts. Proof of suspicion is not proof of knowledge but it may be possible to infer knowledge from surrounding circumstances. In effect, the defendant cannot close his eyes to what is clearly before him:

> . . . it is always open to the tribunal of fact, when knowledge on the part of a defendant is required to be proved, to base a finding of knowledge on evidence that the defendant had deliberately shut his eyes to the obvious or refrained from inquiry because he suspected the truth but did not want to have his suspicion confirmed.

(*Westminster CC v Croyalgrange Ltd* (1986) 83 Cr App R 155, per Lord Bridge, p.164.)

This case also confirmed (per Lord Brightman, p.165) that where the prosecution must prove knowledge then:

> although the onus of establishing all the ingredients of the offence must lie on the prosecution, this does not impose an undue burden: if (1) all the other ingredients of the offence are proved, and (2) the defendant (or the responsible officer of a corporate defendant) chooses not to give evidence of his absence of knowledge, and (3) there are no circumstances which sufficiently suggest absence of knowledge,

the Court may properly infer without direct evidence that the defendant did indeed possess the requisite knowledge.

16.2.8 Negligently

The formulation *'negligently'* is relatively rarely used in the drafting of environmental offences. This aspect of a defendant's behaviour will more often be made relevant by a statutory defence. Where 'negligently' occurs, usually in summary-only offences, it is likely to be interpreted according to civil law and the law as to the interpretation of 'careless' in driving cases. The usual definition is 'did the defendant's behaviour, actions or omissions fall below the standard of that of a reasonable man in the same situation.' The issue then becomes one to be determined in the facts and circumstances of the individual case.

16.2.9 Wilfully (as in wilful obstruction)

'Wilfully' is likely to be interpreted as 'deliberately' or 'recklessly.' However, this is deliberately or recklessly as to obstruction. The defendant must intend to do an action, such as to destroy computer records of discharges, and intend or be reckless as to whether this would obstruct officials in their investigation of potential offences.

16.2.10 Consideration of words contained in a notice or order which themselves define the offence

Environmental crimes which involve breach of a notice or consent issued by a regulatory authority involve the factual element of the offence being uniquely defined in each case by the draftsman of that notice. An offence of failing to comply with an Enforcement Notice or a Stop Notice under the TCPAs will involve consideration of precisely what it is that the planning authority has chosen the notice to require or prohibit. Similarly, an offence of failing to comply with the terms of an abatement notice under s80(4) or s82(8) of the EPA 1990 will involve careful scrutiny of the notice's terms.

The words chosen may legitimately be attacked from every possible angle by defendants should prosecution prove necessary. Ultimately, the words used may have to be interpreted and applied several years after being written. This will be by magistrates, jurors or a judge wholly unfamiliar with the circumstances of the case, however protracted its history. In criminal proceedings, the tribunal will examine the words chosen and it will not be relevant to assert, or necessarily even to prove, that the regulatory authority and the defendant really knew all along what was meant. Notices are not to be interpreted so as to give them practical effect and any ambiguity will be interpreted in the defendant's favour. (*Warrington Borough Council v Garvey* [1988] JPL 752.)

16.3 Defences

The statutory provisions creating an offence may also define defences to the charge. Defences are for the defendant to prove and only become relevant on the assumption that the prosecution can prove every other element of the offence to the required standard.

Placing the burden of proof on the defendant is logical because the defences usually rely on matters of which it would be unlikely the prosecution had any knowledge. Placing the burden on the defence also prevents the prosecution having to leap the enormous hurdle of proving a negative beyond reasonable doubt. See s101 Magistrates Court Act 1980 (MCA 1980)

For instance, it is a defence under s179(3) TCPA 1990 for a defendant-owner of land to show that he had done everything that he had been expected to comply with in the enforcement notice which he had nevertheless failed to comply with. This is obviously more logical than placing the reverse burden on the prosecution, of proving a negative beyond reasonable doubt.

The defendant is only required to make out a defence on the balance of probabilities. This is that something is more likely than not, or the 51 per cent test.

CHAPTER 17

CRIMINAL LIABILITY OF COMPANIES

CONTENTS

Chapter 17

CRIMINAL LIABILITY OF COMPANIES

17.1 Introduction

A company can be convicted of criminal acts carried out on its behalf by servants, agents or employees. This general rule can only apply to criminal acts which need not by definition be committed by a human person. Thus a company can be convicted of manslaughter, because a grossly negligent act leading to death can be carried out on its behalf, but not of bigamy because companies cannot get married once let alone twice!

The other prerequisite for corporate liability is that the punishment available is suitable to a company, i.e. that a monetary penalty can be imposed. These rules relate to common law as well as to statutory offences.

17.2 Commission of a crime by a company

Companies commit crimes via human agents or employees. Assuming that a human employee or agent has acted so as to commit the offence, there are two routes by which the company may be held criminally liable:

(1) For crimes of strict liability, a company may be held vicariously liable for the physical acts carried out on its behalf. (*R v British Steel plc* [1995] 1 WLR 1356; *Tesco Supermarkets Limited v Nattrass* [1972] AC 153; *NRA v Alfred McAlpine Homes East*; 'The Independent,' February 3rd, 1994.)

(2) Where a specific state of mind is an element of the offence - such as knowingly permitting a polluting substance to enter a controlled river under s85 of WRA 1991 - the company will be found guilty if the prosecution can prove that the crime was committed with the requisite state of mind by an individual sufficiently close to the control of the company that he can be said to have acted as part of the controlling mind of the company at the time.

17.3 Vicarious liability

An example of vicarious liability would be under s85 WRA 1991, where it is an offence to cause polluting material to enter a controlled river. This is an offence of strict liability. As the authorities on the definition of 'causing' demonstrate, the offence is committed whether pollution occurred inadvertently or deliberately. If an employee is proved to have caused the pollution, perhaps by inadvertently opening the wrong valve at the wrong time, then providing he was acting on the company's behalf, the company will be vicariously liable for his act. The company cannot be said to be liable for his state of mind but this will not avail them, because the state of mind with which the pollution occurred is not part of the offence. (*NRA v Alfred McAlpine Homes East.*)

This liability will only be for employees' acts within the terms of their employment. No employee will be contracted to commit offences but there is a line to be drawn between working in an irregular and unauthorised manner but still essentially on the employer's behalf and acting wholly outside the scope of the employment. In borderline cases, principles drawn from authorities on vicarious liability in civil law may be applied. Old authorities are sometimes relied on to suggest that the principle of vicarious liability may stretch slightly further than offences for which no particular state of mind is required at all. However, these authorities were decided before cases such as the House of Lords decision in *Tesco v Nattras* which considered the controlling mind principle. The demarcation now established is between vicarious liability and controlling mind rather than seeking to stretch the concept of vicarious liability further.

17.4 Company's controlling mind

Although a company exists as a separate entity and person in law, it can obviously only act through the human beings involved with it. It is clear that there are circumstances in which the individuals involved can be said to be so closely concerned with the running of the company that they, their acts and motivation are to be that of the company itself. Where this applies, if they have committed an offence then the company itself will also have done so. Whether an individual can be said to fall into this category will be a matter of mixed fact and law in each case. Thus, on indictment, a judge will determine what facts it is necessary for the prosecution to prove before the principle applies and then leave it to the jury to ask themselves if they can be sure that those facts have been proved. If the jury is sure then the company will also be guilty of the offence.

Three areas:

Each case will turn on its own facts but some categories can be drawn up:

Definitely: Anyone whom the articles and memorandum of association allow to act directly for the company would have to show particular circumstances why they could not be said to be within the principle. In this category are directors, the company secretary and so forth.

Definitely not: The equivalent of a store manager, somebody who although he may have discretion as to how to do so, is charged with carrying out predetermined policy or instructions. They will not have the power to make decisions which will affect the company as a whole (e.g. the store manager in *Tesco v Nattrass; R v Boal* [1992] QB 591.)

Perhaps, perhaps not: Obviously, some positions fall in between. No single test can be determinative. Relevant factors may be whether the individual:

- can act without referring major decisions up the hierarchy;
- is determining company strategy, or implementing a strategy which he has had little say in or control over.

In a company of any size, a position below board level is unlikely to be regarded as the controlling mind and will. (*Woodhouse v Walsall Metropolitan Borough Council* [1994] Env LR 30.)

17.5 Statutory extension of criminal liability

Other person at fault

Some statutes contain provisions designed to cover situations which may arise within the web of strict liability offences where A commits an offence but the person really at fault is B. (Hence, A may have a statutory 'some other person' defence available.) Some statutes have sections creating statutory principles which allow the enforcing authority to bypass A (who may, for instance, have unwittingly been obeying an instruction to carry out the physical acts which constitute the offence) and prosecute B (who may well be more at fault for having given the instruction). An example is s217(3) of WRA 1991 which reads:

> Where the commission by any person of an offence under . . . is due to the act or default of some other person, that other person may be charged with and convicted of the offence by virtue of this section whether or not proceedings for the offence are taken against the first mentioned person.

17.6 Offences by bodies corporate: sections imposing criminal liability for culpable directors, managers and similar employees

Many statutes creating the offences contain sections worded virtually identically to s157 EPA 1990:

> (1) Where an offence under any provision of this Act committed by a body corporate is proved to have been committed with the consent or connivance of, or to have been attributable to any neglect on the part of any director, manager, secretary or other similar officer of the body corporate or a person who was purporting to act in any such capacity, he as well as the body corporate shall be guilty of that offence and shall be liable to be proceeded against and punished accordingly.
>
> (2) Where the affairs of a body corporate are managed by its members, subsection (1) above shall apply in relation to the acts or defaults of a member in connection with his functions of management as if he were a director of the body corporate.

See also examples at s331 TCPA 1990 and s217(1) WRA 1991.

17.6.1 Conniving

These sections introduce the concept of *'conniving'* as an offence. It is generally thought that this would be regarded as acquiescing in offences; giving tacit consent, even if not actively encouraging; allowing a state of affairs to continue and saying nothing about it. (*Huckerby v Elliot* [1970] 1 All ER 189.)

17.6.2 Purporting to act

The inclusion of *'purporting to act'* means that there will be no defence available to someone acting temporarily or for whom there turns out to be some irregularity in their appointment.

This is beyond the general duty on a citizen who is under no general duty to take action personally to prevent crime occurring.

The question of how senior within a company the manager or other officer has to be was considered in *Woodhouse v Walsall MBC* [1994] Env LR 30. A waste-disposal site manager was prosecuted under the corporate liability section of COPA 1974. He was held not to be in a position of real authority with power and responsibility to decide corporate policy and strategy. This was an application of the test in *R v Boal* [1992] QB 591. The defendant managed one of the company's waste-disposal sites but it was the largest and most significant. The defendant was employed as the general manager of the 'special waste' position and had been head-hunted to fill that position. However, he did not sit on the board and was not a director. It was held that the defendant was not sufficiently senior within the company to be caught by the section. He could not be said to have the power and responsibility to decide corporate policy and strategy.

This decision indicates that it will be rare for an employee in a position below board level in a company of any size to be held to come within the 'culpable officers of the company' provisions which employ the standard formula.

The decision leaves open to a company the option of deploying the 'default or act of another' provisions which are often included within the same part of the Act, to shift criminal liability from themselves to the site-manager or other employee. This may not be an attractive option, particularly if the offence is one of strict liability.

CHAPTER 18

PROSECUTORS

CONTENTS

CHAPTER 18

PROSECUTORS

18.1 Local Authorities (LAs)

Under s222 LGA 1972, local authorities (LAs) are entitled to bring criminal prosecutions on behalf of the inhabitants of their area. In practice, the most likely prosecutor for many of the environmental offences will be the local district council, metropolitan borough council, county council or unitary authority. Proceedings are normally brought in the name of the council's solicitor and it may be necessary to consider the question of authorisation to prosecute. Many authorities will have staff and resources specifically devoted to investigating complaints and prosecuting where appropriate. The codes of practice under the Police and Criminal Evidence Act (PCEA) apply where relevant to LA officers, for instance where they are conducting an interview with a potential defendant.

18.2 Crown Prosecution Service (CPS)

The Crown Prosecution Service (CPS) deals with cases begun by the police. If the initial complaint of an environmental offence is made to or investigated by police, the CPS may conduct the prosecution under the provisions of the Prosecution of Offences Act 1985 (POA 1985) in the same way as any other criminal offence. It is also possible for the prosecution, once initiated, to be taken over by another prosecuting authority which deals more regularly with the particular offence, such as a LA.

18.3 Private individuals and nonincorporated associations such as angling societies (NIAs)

It is open to an individual to bring a private prosecution although instances are rare and there is power for the Attorney-General to take over the prosecution once begun. A nonincorporated association (NIA), such as an angling society or local residents' association, has no legal personality and could only act where individual members were prepared to take up the cudgels on its behalf. Prosecutions have been successfully brought by angling societies, pressure groups such as Greenpeace and societies protecting historic buildings.

18.4 Environment Agency (EA)

18.4.1 Introduction

The Environment Agency (EA) and the Scottish Environmental Protection Agency (SEPA) were established by the EA 1995 and came into being on April 1st, 1996.

The EA, on its establishment as a nondepartmental public body (NDPB), took over the functions of Her Majesty's Inspector of Pollution (HMIP), the National Rivers Authority (NRA), the Waste Regulation Authorities (WRAs) and other bodies. The EA's principal aim, expressed at s4 EA 1995, is to protect and enhance the environment taken as a whole, in line with the objective of sustainable development.

'Sustainable development' first appeared as an overarching objective in the 1990 White Paper *This Common Inheritance* and subsequently in the 1994 *UK Strategy for Sustainable Development*.

Statutory Guidance followed, in the form of the document produced by the Secretary of State entitled *The Environment Agency and Sustainable Development*.

The guidance states that in creating the EA, it was not the Government's objective to create new functions, although some inevitably arose. The underlying purpose behind creating the EA was to coordinate the existing functions in environmental regulation and management, thereby bringing a more organised and efficient approach both to management of the environment and to the regulatory controls to which it is subject. The principal aim is seen to be threefold:

(1) to build on the work of the existing bodies in protecting and enhancing the environment; but

(2) to lay greater emphasis on the need to look at the environment as a whole, through an integrated approach, rather than at individual media in isolation; and

(3) to place the EA's activities more firmly in the context of sustainable development.

The most common and widely-used definition of sustainable development is found in *Our Common Future*, the Brundtland report. It is: "development that meets the needs of the present without compromising the ability of future generations to meet their own needs."

The integrated approach is to be used by the EA. This means, in practice, that management and regulation involve taking account of the impacts of pollutants from different sources across the different media, as well as within one particular medium, as well as the trans-medium interaction of different pollutants from different sources. The guidelines suggest that the EA, in performing its functions in an integrated way, should use integrated catchment management planning and other geographic tools where appropriate.

The guidelines set out the Government's statutory objectives for the EA which should:

(i) adopt, across all its functions, an integrated approach to environmental protection and enhancement which considers impacts of substances and activities on all environmental media and on natural resources;

(ii) work with all relevant sectors of society, including regulated organisations, to develop approaches which deliver environmental requirements and goals without imposing excessive costs (in relation to benefits gained) on regulated organisations or society as a whole;

(iii) adopt clear and effective procedures for serving its customers, including by developing single points of contact through which regulated organisations can deal with the EA;

(iv) operate to high professional standards, based on sound science, information and analysis of the environment and of processes which affect it;

(v) organise its activities in ways which reflect good environmental and management practice and provide value for money for those paying its charges and taxpayers as a whole;

(vi) provide clear and readily available advice and information on its work; and

(vii) develop a close and responsive relationship with the public, LAs and other representatives of local communities, regulated organisations and public bodies with environmental responsibilities.

The EA itself is expected to add to this list of objectives and to develop its own targets which relate to international environmental obligations, such as the Montreal Protocol, the Biodiversity Convention and the Climate Change Convention.

18.4.2 EA's structure

The EA is run by a board of directors and a chairman. The directors, with their respective heads of department, have responsibility for the following: national and international relations, science and environmental strategy, finance, personnel, environmental protection, water management, operations, corporate affairs and legal services.

The EA's head office is in Bristol, Avon. Issues concerning IPC and Judicial Review are dealt with there. The EA's work divides over eight regions which cover 26 areas in operational units of three or four areas each. In each region, there are between four and six qualified lawyers dealing with litigation, *inter alia*. Some 9,500 staff work in the 26 areas. Each region has a regional manager and three regional committees covering fisheries, flood defence and environmental protection. The EA has a budget of some £592m which is expected to increase.

Detailed analysis of the EA's enforcement record lies outside this work's ambit but it is right generally to say that the EA was criticised in its earliest years because its prosecution rate was too low and there was substantial inconsistency between regional prosecution policies. These problems' roots lay partly in the juxtaposition, under one new organisation's umbrella, of the functions of the former regulatory bodies - the NRA and HMIP. Over the past year, internal restructuring has taken place. As the organisation matures, it is to be hoped that the problems of consistency, particularly in waste regulation, will diminish. A new *Enforcement Code* has been produced after a consultation period (see below).

Fines have been increasing but both the EA and the Government have clearly indicated they wish to see an increase in some fines imposed on offenders. Fines for waste offences remain markedly lower than fines imposed in the other regimes. For major corporate offending there is an arguable case to be made for fines to be more proportionate to the damage caused by the offence, or to be more punitive for a repeating offender. Recently, the EA said a fine expressed as a minute proportion of a company's budget sent an inadequate message to the boardroom, possibly having a less punitive effect than it might have.

At present, most offences are dealt with in the Magistrates Court where technically complex matters arise before a bench which has not been given *Magistrates Courts Guidelines* on environmental offences. There can be little doubt specialist environmental training for stipendiary magistrates will help in understanding complexities of particular cases where an offence's technical implications do not at present carry their full import.

18.4.3 EA's functions

The EA is responsible for the management and regulation of the water environment, waste and industrial pollution. Its functions, listed in *Environment Agency: Management Statement* are to:

(1) regulate industrial processes with the greatest pollution potential so as to ensure that best-available techniques not entailing excessive cost (BATNEEC) are used to prevent or minimise pollution to the environment as a whole;

(2) regulate the disposal of radioactive waste and (except on nuclear licensed sites) the keeping and use of radioactive material and accumulation of radioactive waste;

(3) regulate the treating, keeping, movement and disposal of controlled waste so as to prevent pollution of the environment or harm to human health, in a manner proportionate to the threat posed;

(4) preserve or improve the quality of rivers, estuaries and coastal waters through its powers to regulate, prevent, mitigate or remedy pollution to water;

(5) take any necessary action to conserve, redistribute, augment and secure proper use of water resources;

(6) exercise a general supervision over all matters relating to flood defence (it also has powers to take certain flood-defence measures as approved by Regional Flood Defence Committees [RFDCs]);

(7) maintain, improve and develop salmon, trout, freshwater and eel fisheries;

(8) promote the conservation and enhancement of inland and coastal waters and their use for recreation;

(9) maintain or improve nonmarine navigation;

(10) regulate the remediation of contaminated land designated as special sites;

(11) administer, in accordance with regulations on producer-responsibility, the registration of businesses and exemption schemes, and the monitoring and enforcement of associated obligations.

The EA is also charged with a duty to obtain environmental information and promote an understanding of methods for environmental protection and management. This is set out in the *Management Statement* as being the responsibility to:

(1) assemble environmental data, from its own monitoring and other sources, so that it can carry out its functions and also form an overview of the general state of environmental pollution;

(2) survey waste-disposal needs and priorities and advise the Secretary of State on his national waste strategy;

(3) report on the state of contaminated land and, as necessary, produce site-specific guidance to local authorities on dealing with contaminated land;

(4) monitor pollution of freshwater, groundwater and the sea (up to three miles from the coast);

(5) publish information about the demand for water and available resources;

(6) survey flood defences and flood-risk areas;

(7) notify the Ministry of outbreaks of notifiable fish disease;

(8) follow technological developments for preventing or reducing pollution;

(9) assess, at the request of Ministers, environmental impacts of pollution or options for avoiding, limiting or cleaning up pollution; and

(10) carry out or promote research related to its activities.

The EA seeks to foster constructive relationships both with other regulatory bodies and with those whom it regulates. It regularly produces specific sets of guidelines aimed at assisting businesses in compliance. For example, in the Environmental Technology Best Practice Programme, launched by the Department of Trade and Industry (DTI) and the Department of the Environment (DoE) in June, 1998, the main themes are waste minimisation and cost-effective cleaner technology. To implement this programme, the EA offers an Environmental Helpline, Environmental Performance Guides and a Good Practice Guide, which includes examples of proven, cost-effective technologies and techniques for New Practice and Future Practice. Funds may be available for these projects.

On May 1st, 1998, the EA began to establish an assessment scheme for pollution-monitoring equipment in line with international standards. This scheme, the Monitoring Certification Scheme (MCERTS), is designed to focus on continuous monitoring systems.

The EA seeks to promote Government-issued codes of practice. For example, in October, 1998, updated Codes of Good Agricultural Practice were issued by the Ministry of Agriculture, Fisheries and Food (MAFF) after consultation with the EA. These offer comprehensive guidance and advice to farmers, to assist them in protecting their environmental resources and in complying with the law. This particular set of codes now pays especial attention to the more complex question of diffuse pollution. This attention marks expansion from point-source pollution which was the regulator's primary concern previously.

The EA is responsible for maintaining public registers. The main ones are the:

(1) Integrated Pollution Control Register;
(2) Radioactive Substances Register;
(3) Water Quality and Pollution Control Register;
(4) Water Abstraction and Impounding Register;
(5) Waste Management Licence Register;
(6) Carriers and Brokers of Controlled Waste Register;
(7) Genetically-Modified Organisms Register;
(8) Chemical Release Inventory.

The EA will refuse to give out information where (i) the information is part of a *sub judice* case, (ii) national security would be compromised, (iii) commercial confidentiality would be breached, (iv) data is not yet completely compiled or (v) release could lead to environmental damage. Written reasons will be given where the EA refuses to divulge information.

The EA holds maps of the main rivers covered by RFDCs and of EA waterworks.

The EA charges if information costs more than £50.00, according to the Code of Practice on Access to Government Information. A recent consultation exercise with the Law Society was done to clarify the issues of the cost of the information and the grounds on which access to it is refused, in the light of the *EC Directive on Access to Information on the Environment* and the UK's *Freedom of Information on the Environment Regulations* 1992.

A *notice* will now be contained in all information given out by the EA (other than the standard information given out by the EA in the form of leaflets, consultation documents, etc). The notice contains:

(i) provisions on the intellectual property rights in the data provided, which remain the property of the respective parties who supplied it (either the EA itself or third parties);

(ii) disclaimers in respect of the accuracy and validity of the information, which it undertakes to use reasonable care to ensure.

The person receiving the information may use EA data for private or own-business purposes but must gain permission from the EA if he intends to use the information for other purposes, such as commercial gain, ensuring that the EA's intellectual property rights are uninfringed. Solicitors, surveyors and other professionals may use the information in accordance with Professional Body Arrangements (PBAs) made between the relevant professional body and the EA.

In respect of solicitors, where formerly an individual data-agreement was required between a firm and the EA, the following general waiver is now agreed as between the EA and solicitors:

(1) A general waiver is given to the Law Society for all solicitors in respect of th EA's intellectual property rights and under s47 of the Copyright, Designs and Patents Act 1988 (as amended) (CDPA 1988), subject to the following paragraphs.

Permission is given to copy any information obtained from the EA (or to use such information in reports or letters) to a client on whose behalf the information was obtained and to copy such information or reports to third parties where necessary as part of the service to that client.

(2) Solicitors using this waiver should make no representations to the clients or others that might suggest that this waiver extends to any other person or that the EA has granted any intellectual property permission to any other person, expressly or by implication, other than as provided for in this waiver.

(3) If solicitors pass on, in accordance with the above waiver, any information obtained from the EA to persons other than clients, they should use every endeavour to attach a copy of the EA's standard notice (copy attached) or otherwise ensure that the notice's contents have been brought to the attention of that other person in the course of regular dealings.

(4) The wording of the EA's standard notice has been approved by the Law Society. It will be deemed to apply to all supplies of information to solicitors although it will still normally be sent by the EA. This is so as to avoid the need to check the status of the person requesting information, to provide an *aide-mémoir* to solicitors and to enable copies of information to be passed to third parties under para. 3.

This notice applies to a far wider class of recipients than just solicitors and represents a substantial improvement and clarification in the requirements for information of litigators and transactional lawyers.

18.4.4 EA's enforcement and prosecution policy

New *Guidelines* for enforcement and prosecution were issued by the EA in November, 1998. They outline the purpose of enforcement as being to protect the environment or to secure compliance with a regulatory system.

They state that where a criminal offence has been committed, then the EA will consider instituting criminal proceedings *in addition* to any other enforcement action.

The EA's enforcement principles are expressed as proportionality, consistency, transparency and targeting.

The new guidelines say that the purpose of the criminal process is to punish wrongdoing, to avoid recurrence and to act as a deterrent to others. Decisions to prosecute are only to be taken after full consideration of the implications and consequences. Decisions on prosecution will take account of the *Code for Crown Prosecutors*.

The following factors will be taken into account when the EA is deciding whether or not to prosecute.

18.4.4.1 Sufficiency of evidence

The EA must be satisfied that there is "sufficient, admissible and reliable evidence that the offence has been committed and that there is a realistic prospect of conviction."

18.4.4.2 Public interest

The public interest factors which affect the decision to prosecute will generally depend on the seriousness of the offence or the circumstances of the offender. These are detailed as being the:

(1) offence's environmental effect;
(2) offence's foreseeability or the circumstances leading to it;
(3) offender's intent, individually and/or corporately;
(4) history of his offending;
(5) offender's attitude;
(6) deterrent effect of a prosecution on the offender and others; and
(7) the offender's personal circumstances.

When deciding whom to prosecute, the EA will proceed against those responsible for the offence. Where a company is responsible for a violation, the company itself will be prosecuted but if officers of the company have played any part in the commission of the offence, then the EA may also proceed against any of those officers. If the officers have connived in the commission of the offence, or been negligent, then they may be proceeded against. There are circumstances in which the EA will apply for the director's disqualification under the Companies Act (CA).

There is a presumption of a prosecution, if sufficient evidence is available, in these circumstances:

(1) incidents or breaches which have significant consequences for the environment, particularly those with potential for significant consequences;

(2) carrying out operations without a relevant licence;
(3) excessive or persistent breaches of regulatory requirements;
(4) failure to comply, or to comply adequately, with formal remedial requirements;
(5) reckless disregard for management or quality standards;
(6) failure to supply information without reasonable excuse, or knowingly or recklessly supplying false or misleading information;
(7) obstruction of EA staff;
(8) impersonating EA staff.

If prosecution is not thought to be the most appropriate course of action, the EA will use the alternatives of a:

- *caution*, i.e. a written acknowledgment that the offender committed the offence, which may be brought to the Court's attention in a future prosecution; or

- *warning*, i.e. a written notification that, in the EA's view, an offence has been committed, which may be recorded and referred to in a future prosecution.

The EA will liaise with any other body having the power to prosecute, to avoid inconsistency and to ensure the most appropriate charges are brought for the offence in question.

18.4.5 The Court

Most offences are dealt with in the Magistrates Court but in certain circumstances the case will be referred to the Crown Court where sentencing powers are greater.

In a successful prosecution in either court, the EA will seek to recover its costs.

CHAPTER 19

INVESTIGATION OF OFFENCES

CONTENTS

Chapter 19

INVESTIGATION OF OFFENCES

19.1 Introduction

In considering the criminal process, from investigation of a possible offence through to trial, this section covers procedural rules and rules of evidence. Practical issues and difficulties encountered in presenting the prosecution or defence of an environmental offence to the Criminal Courts are also considered.

19.2 Power to investigate

It is within the remit of most statutory bodies charged with the regulation of the environment to investigate and prosecute offences where they think fit. Investigation is often also a statutory function and duty. The most obvious additional power that such authorities require from statute is to enter private land to investigate whether offences have occurred and if necessary to gather evidence.

There is no common-law power for an investigator to go on to private land or premises. Relevant statutes frequently provide the power to do so and they make it an offence for anyone to obstruct investigators carrying out their investigations. Recent statutes also regulate the power, so as to limit the infringement of civil liberties to the minimum necessary consistent with effective regulation of the specific area of the law. Thus, in relation to planning law, where time may not be of the essence, power of entry to occupied premises can only be exercised after 24 hours' notice, whereas under s169 WRA 1991 power of entry can be exercised immediately in an emergency and by warrant if necessary.

It is also usually an offence for an investigator to divulge trade secrets or other information gained whilst exercising a power of entry, unless it is necessary to divulge such information in the course of the investigating authority's functions. Examples are s206(7) WIA 1991 and the offences coupled to each right of entry under the TCPA 1990. Some statutes, such as s174 WRA 1991, create an offence of impersonating the official, in this case a water inspector, in order to gain entry to land.

Where access to land is likely to be denied, the investigator seeking to exercise entry should ensure he is aware of precise statutory provisions (e.g. s20 WRA 1991 allows the authorised officer to be accompanied). Contentious issues are often the number of people allowed to come on to the land and what equipment they can bring on with them. Powers-of-entry provisions are usually specific as to the purposes for which entry can be exercised (e.g. to take samples). Entry will be unlawful if these powers are exceeded.

Almost all sections giving access to land will apply to persons authorised in writing by the appropriate authority only. This requirement is normally satisfied by some form of photo-identification card, with a certified copy of the officer's authorisation. Whether or not these are produced, even without being asked for, will probably depend on the nature of the visit and the likely relationship between the investigators and those on the land.

Where a statute qualifies the right of entry, the provisions for doing so should be carefully observed, not only to avoid any civil liability but because breach of the conditions may lead to any evidence gained at a visit being ruled inadmissible in subsequent criminal proceedings.

Minimum force to gain entry may be appropriate. Police forces may also be persuaded to assist if obstruction is anticipated.

See *R v Chief Constable of Devon and Cornwall* (1981) 3 All ER 826.

19.3 Investigators' duties

The conduct of those investigating offences on behalf of public authorities is regulated in two ways:

(1) *By general principles of public law and good administration.* This is particularly true where the investigators may or may not decide to prosecute but their findings may lead to some other action such as the terms of a condition being reviewed. (Re *Pergamon Press Ltd* [1971] 1 Ch 388.) Investigators' promises, indications or assurances will bind the prosecuting authority and may lead to any subsequent criminal proceedings being stayed as an abuse of process if they are ignored. (*Postermobile v Brent LBC, The Times,* December 8th, 1997.)

(2) *By every criminal tribunal being under a duty to exclude evidence which in all the circumstances would have such an adverse effect on the proceedings' fairness*

that the Court ought not to admit it. The duty is at common law and via s78 of the Police and Criminal Evidence Act 1984 (PCEA 1984). Crown Court judges, in particular, will not be slow to exclude evidence gained in a manner which is unfair, or of which they otherwise disapprove.

19.4 Gathering evidence

If a prosecution is to succeed, evidence will be needed to prove each element of the offence and to be in a position to rebut any defence if raised. To this end, it is obviously ideal if somebody directing the investigation has a clear idea of what the possible offences may be for any category of pollution incident and thus what areas the evidence should cover.

19.5 Photographs

A picture can speak a thousand words but not if the photograph finally presented to the jury is a single copy of an unspecified scene at an unspecified time. Photographs cannot normally be produced except by the photographer.

Effective presentation of photographic evidence, whether by the prosecution or defence, can be very persuasive. This is normally helped by the:

use of a *date-stamped camera;*

creation of a *site plan.*

For the site plan, for each photograph taken, the photographer should contemporaneously note the spot where he is standing and the direction in which the camera is pointing. This will allow presentation to a Court of a *numbered list of photographs*, giving the time and date, accompanied by a *plan* on which each photograph's site is ringed together with an arrow showing the direction in which the camera was pointing.

This should help to avoid the impact of the evidence becoming lost. Confusion can set in where a single set of apparently the most obvious, but unmarked, photographs is handed around a jury. This confusion has to be seen to be believed!

Proof of development

Photographs to be used in evidence must be accompanied by proof that the negatives have been correctly developed. This proof can exist in two forms:

(1) *Photographic development within the organisation.* If development is to be done within an organisation, all that is needed is a simple statement from the developer. It should say (a) he received the film marked 'XYZ' and (b) the prints from the untampered negatives are here presented.

(2) *Photographic development by a High Street developer.* Evidence of the film being taken into and collected from the shop will be sufficient to prove the film's development. If this course is followed, then, strictly, the photographer should be called to give evidence that the photographs appear to be views of what he pointed the camera at. In practice, the photographs are likely to be ruled admissible provided the prosecution can show that the film taken to the shop to be developed was the correct one.

19.6 Samples

The water statutes set out a specific procedure to be followed in sampling. For example, s209 WRA 1991 is designed to ensure there is a fair chance for the potential defendant to carry out its own analysis of any evidence the prosecution will adduce.

Failure to comply with the sampling provisions will normally mean that evidence is inadmissible as being unfair under s78 PCEA 1984.

19.7 Evidence obtained under threat of criminal sanction

Many statutes allow the regulatory authority to require information to be provided by a potential defendant. This will often be on key issues (e.g. land ownership, responsibility for activities) and may also require the potential or actual defendant to produce documents and records. Failure to comply with the request within a set time is itself an offence (e.g. s217, TCPA 1990, s203 and 204 WIA 1991.)

Evidence obtained under such provisions, including documents, is incompatible with the right to a fair trial and the presumption of innocence under Art.6 of the European Convention on Human Rights and will be inadmissible in criminal proceedings. (*Saunders v UK* [1996] 23 EHRR 313.)

19.8 Contemporaneous notes

Those called to investigate environmental offences do not always have criminal investigation as a major part of their normal duties. For instance, field wardens for ancient monuments may be called on in their whole career to deal with one potential offence only. Often they will not take contemporaneous notes of incidents; or will take rough notes and destroy them once made into a neat copy later; or come to Court seeking to rely on a typed version of a file note. These documents may be looked at as frequently as possible outside the Court but only the original, contemporaneous notes can be used by a witness once he is giving evidence.

Investigating officers should take notes of their visits and observations. This should be done:

(1) at the time, ideally; or
(2) at the first practicable opportunity, where notes are made of events fresh in the memory.

In practice, notes made on returning to the office, provided the delay is of no more than two or three hours, will be acceptable.

Only *original notes* can be used in the witness box and these points should be kept in mind:

(1) Copies or typed versions are not permissible.

(2) Any defendant is entitled to see the original notes. If these are unavailable, (a) it will be difficult for the prosecution to avoid giving an impression at best of incompetence and at worst of concealment; and (b) the Court may also refuse to admit, or to give any weight to, the witness's evidence without having original notes available for scrutiny.

(3) Photocopied or typed versions of notes can be used as working copies but the original notes must be those which are relied on in the witness box and should be available if called for.

(4) The practice of taking rough, trigger notes on site during the investigation and writing a fuller note a short while after is permissible, provided the originals of both sets of notes are available.

(5) Contemporaneous notes in the witness box invariably improve the quality of the evidence, provided the witness does not simply

read them out rapidly. An example of how not to use notes is provided where an inexperienced police officer gives evidence in a speeding case to a bench of lay magistrates.

(6) In many environmental offences, particularly where breach of the terms of a licence or consent is alleged, the evidence may be of several visits to a site, made sometimes weeks or months apart. Without separate notes of each visit, witnesses usually find it difficult to keep a clear and logical flow in giving their own evidence-in-chief, let alone during cross-examination.

19.9 Gathering evidence for potential defendants

Potential defendants will also do well to take contemporaneous notes of any visit by investigating officers and of surrounding circumstances. Certainly, at site, managers should keep a note of the time of any visit and the names of any regulatory personnel, as well as their own contemporaneous notes of what may or may not have been obvious (e.g. whether foam on a stream at a certain time was visible or not). This will add weight to evidence which may need to be given for the defence and would otherwise be unsupported recollection being recounted months later.

19.10 Investigators' duties and the Codes under the Police and Criminal Evidence Act 1984 (PCEA 1984)

Codes have been drawn up under the Police and Criminal Evidence Act 1984 (PCEA 1984). They govern the conduct of the police in their investigation of criminal offences. The codes and accompanying Home Office circulars provide detailed guidance as to the conduct of interviews, searches and so forth.

s67 (9) PCEA 1984 reads:

> Persons other than police officers who are charged with the duty of investigating offences or charging offenders shall in the discharge of that duty have regard to any relevant provision of . . . a code

- this being one of the codes of practice issued by the Secretary of State.

The codes will apply to any investigator acting on behalf of a regulatory body, LA or central government department (e.g. English Heritage) who has as part of his job the collection of evidence in contemplation of criminal proceedings. Even if, on the facts of a particular case, the codes do not apply, their provisions may still be relevant in setting the principles by which an application to exclude evidence under s78 PCEA 1984 should be assessed.

In *RSPCA v Eager* (1995) Crim LR 59 DC, it was assumed by all parties that the codes bound an RSPCA Inspector. His position would appear indistinguishable from that of a LA's planning-enforcement or environmental health officer. In *R v Wallace Duncan Smith* (1994) 99 Cr App rep 233, the codes were held not to apply where an official of the Bank of England was not required to *investigate* but to *supervise*. Nevertheless, s78 PCEA 1984 was applied so as to exclude evidence of an interview.

19.11 Role of the Codes

s78(1) PCEA 1984 reads:

> In any proceedings the Court may refuse to allow evidence on which the prosecution propose to rely to be given if it appears to the Court that, having regard to all the circumstances, including the circumstances in which the evidence was obtained, the admission of the evidence would have such an adverse effect on the fairness of the proceedings that the Court ought not to admit it.

s76 PCEA 1984 governs circumstances in which confessions can be relied on by the prosecution. Where a confession is challenged, the prosecution must show that it was not obtained by oppression and that it was not obtained in circumstances which may make it unreliable.

If at any time during a trial a bench of magistrates or a Crown Court judge is asked to rule prosecution evidence inadmissible, the codes will form much of the background to that decision. Each case will turn on its own facts and circumstances but a breach of the code will, generally, at least be sufficient to trigger a doubt over the evidence's admissibility, although breach per se does not render evidence inadmissible.

The more significant and substantial the breach, the more likely that the evidence is to be excluded. A breach is more likely to lead to exclusion if it occurs in bad faith or flagrant disregard of the codes' provisions.

In the considering of any breach's seriousness, the particular provision's rationale will be applied. This may be significant in the environmental law field, because it is unlikely that the prosecution would be able to show that a code's rationale had been applied where the investigator was not even aware of it.

The Codes

The five codes are:

A - Stop and search
B - Search and seizure
C - Detention and questioning
D - Identification
E - Tape recording of interviews

Codes C and *E* are the most likely to occur when considering environmental crimes.

19.12 Interviews

Code C is the *Code of Practice for the Detention, Treatment and Questioning of Persons by Police Officers*. This code will apply to interviews conducted by investigators into environmental offences.

19.12.1 Who to interview

In deciding who to interview, it is important to ensure that they are able to give answers relevant to the final defendant. What is said in interview by one individual defendant will not in itself be evidence against any other. If individuals are to be prosecuted, only their answers in interview will be evidence against them, however closely the prosecution alleges they are involved with any codefendants. Where interview evidence is to be used against a company, admissible evidence will be only that from an authorised company spokesman or someone who can be said to be the company's directing mind and will.

There are three potential occasions when investigators are likely to ask questions and want to rely on the answers in criminal proceedings. Different provisions of the code may be relevant to each. The three are:

(1) informal questions on site;
(2) questions after caution at site;
(3) interviews following a request to attend.

19.12.2 Informal questions on site

In general, answers to questions asked before a caution is given will be inadmissible in subsequent criminal proceedings unless the questions are asked for the purposes of identification, etc.

When, following the report of something which may constitute a crime, an investigating officer arrives at the site, it is proper to ask very few questions only (e.g. to determine the role of the person being spoken to, or to ask whether there is a leak or problem which that person is aware of, or perhaps to ask who owns the land.)

These questions will often be part of introductory remarks in which the investigating officer is introducing himself and perhaps showing his identity card and so forth. They will probably also be part of establishing whether or not the person being spoken to can, in fact, give any relevant information, or is likely to be authorised to speak for the company.

Questions after caution at site

As soon as the investigator wishes to ask questions to gain evidence, *the caution* should be given. The caution's current wording is:

> You do not have to say anything. But it may harm your defence if you do not mention when questioned something which you later rely on in Court. Anything you do say may be given in evidence.

In practice, giving the caution is, in the minds of those involved at least, a Rubicon which, at the least, puts the person being questioned on notice of their answers' significance.

Once the caution has been given, the visit's purpose should be made clear to the person being questioned, if it has not been spelt out during the investigators' introducing themselves. The person being spoken to should also be informed that he is not under arrest and may choose to go. The visit's purpose should be made clear so that the person being asked questions is aware of the context behind them. For the questioning to be fair, the person being asked the questions should understand their significance. For example:

> 'We are here on behalf of the borough council to see if this land is being used for spray painting and welding, in breach of an enforcement notice;' or

> 'We are here on behalf of the National Rivers Authority, because foam is polluting the river and we think it may be coming from this factory.'

Questions which go directly to the offence may then be put. For example:

> 'You have told us you are the farmer here and that these are your cows. Is it right that this slurry pool is yours and that you are letting it overflow into the river?'

The answer to such a question would probably be inadmissible without the caution.

It should be noted that police officers would normally arrest the suspect and take him to be interviewed at a police station. Investigating officers will not have a power of arrest and so this may be the only chance to get answers to questions they would like to put.

For the evidence to be admissible, compliance with the provisions for recording an interview, set out at *Code C* (paras 11.5 to 11.13), will also be necessary.

In practice, this means writing out each question and answer and then offering it to the person being asked questions, for him to sign as a correct record (*Code* C, 11.10). This is obviously a cumbersome process if more than a few questions are going to be asked but is necessary if the evidence is to be properly admitted.

Some enforcement officers are reluctant to offer their note of questions and answers to an individual, in case the interviewee rips the document up. The fear is that the investigators would then be left with no evidence. In practice, this may be overcautious, especially because a Court will be concerned by the breach of the code inherent in any failure to offer notes for signature.

This difficulty can be avoided by the accompanying officer also taking notes.

If the notes are ripped up, the investigator should as soon as possible write down as much of the interview as he can remember and on this subsequent record endorse that (a) the defendant ripped the previous one when asked to sign and (b) this is the reason for the delay in making the notes and why they were not offered for signature a second time. A set of ripped notes may have evidential value in themselves!

19.12.3 Prearranged interviews to which the defendant is invited

The investigating officers will not be exercising any powers of arrest and so formal taped interviews can generally take place only where the potential defendant agrees.

Where a large company is the potential defendant, the acceptance of an interview may be the only chance to ask any questions of someone in the appropriate position. To this extent, an attempt to clarify the appropriate person to invite for interview will avoid a wasted appointment.

Code E covers taped interviews but, strictly, applies only to interviews in police stations. It is therefore open to investigators to record the interview by way of contemporaneous notes in accordance with *Code C*. However, any authority involved in more than the minimal number of interviews may find the use of tape-recorded interviews efficient and effective. If tapes are to be used, *Code E* should be studied and followed.

Home Office guidance indicates that the interviewer will want to have planned the interview, to ensure all the offence's elements are covered. In many environmental offences, there may be documents to consider (e.g. a copy of any consent where conditions have been breached). If questions about them are to be asked, interview copies should be available and the document should be identified for the interviewee and the tape.

A common formula for the interview is:

(1) Introductions and caution, etc., in accordance with *Code E*, para.4.3.

If the potential defendant is a company, it is particularly important to clarify that the person being interviewed is able to speak on behalf of the company.

(2) Confirmation of any noncontroversial information (e.g. site ownership, the fact that a company has been operating that site under an appropriate consent for some time and is aware of the terms and conditions).

(3) If, earlier, the interviewee was spoken to on site, getting him to repeat any information or answers he may have given at that time. If any such answers are confirmed now, any earlier breach of the codes may be rectified.

(4) Questions relating to the offence.

(5) Giving a specific opportunity for the interviewee to add or clarify anything.

(6) Close the interview.

19.12.4 Defendants

Defendants can refuse to attend interview or to answer any particular question. However, many defendants will want to maintain a working relationship with those who may continue to monitor and regulate them in any event. Further, they may wish to avoid the inference of recent fabrication which, as the caution points out, can be drawn from failing to attend an interview and then producing an account of events at Court for the first time.

Attendance at interview may therefore be advisable. A corporate defendant may wish to seek clarification of any documents which will be put to them in interview and ensure that the person attending the interview has as detailed knowledge as possible of the allegations and is able to speak for the company.

19.13 Right to legal advice

It is open to a potential defendant to seek legal advice at any time. There is a right to have a legal adviser present during tape-recorded interviews under *Code E*. Where a request for a delay in order to seek legal advice has not been allowed, any admission made in an interview is unlikely to survive as admissible evidence.

Investigating officers arriving at a site are entitled to insist on immediate entry. Delaying the visit whilst legal advice is sought cannot be insisted on, especially where the visit is urgent.

Once a company or individual discovers that investigations are being carried out to determine whether or not they have committed an offence, they are entitled to:

(i) instigate their own investigations;

(ii) if appropriate, take their own samples and

(iii) contact any potential witnesses themselves.

However, they will have no power to enter any land, or to force anyone to speak to them or their representatives.

19.14 End of the investigation

Once investigations are complete, the decision will have to be taken on whether or not to prosecute. If proceedings are to be instituted, the process begins at the Magistrates Court.

CHAPTER 20

DECISION TO PROSECUTE

CONTENTS

CHAPTER 20

DECISION TO PROSECUTE

20.1 Introduction

The criteria for determining whether or not to proceed to prosecution, assuming evidence is available suggesting that an environmental offence has been committed, may involve factors additional to the simple consideration of whether or not the evidence is available to provide a reasonable prospect of success.

In addition to the usual criteria, the environmental prosecutor/regulator will also be considering the best way to rectify, prevent or avoid the recurrence of the environmental harm that has been created.

These officers are also likely to take account of the fact that they will have to continue to enforce the environmental-control regime in the future and that this may be done most effectively through maintaining a working relationship with the relevant landowners or business operators.

20.2 Criteria considered by regulatory authorities

Guidance to prosecuting authorities is published. They are advised to take into account objective and open criteria when deciding whether or not to prosecute.

Criteria used by the EA to determine whether or not to take criminal proceedings are considered in Chapter 18 where the EA's role and functions are considered in detail.

Similar issues are covered in the guidance to planning authorities, in deciding whether or not to prosecute where there is evidence of the offence of 'failing to comply with the terms of an enforcement notice.'

The *Good Practice Guide* to enforcing planning control, published by central Government in 1997, gives the following advice:

Enforcing Planning Control, Good Practice Guide, 1997

> Chapter 11:
>
> 11.1 . . . Whether prosecution in the Court is the most appropriate way to achieve compliance with an effective enforcement notice is for the LPA to decide. In some cases, it may suffice for the LPA to warn of their intention to prosecute if, during the compliance period, someone is seen to make no serious effort to take the steps an enforcement notice requires.
>
> 11.2 The LPA should consider carefully what is likely to be the most efficient and cost-effective way of compelling someone who is contravening an enforcement notice to comply with its requirements. If it is known that prosecution proceedings will result in substantial delay in remedying the effects of a breach of control, the LPA may prefer the alternative course of taking default action under s178 of the 1990 Act. Or it may be expedient simultaneously to initiate prosecution proceedings and take default action, especially if the offence is blatant and causes serious environmental harm.

There is often concern that the levels of fine likely to be imposed by the Courts following conviction are not high enough to provide an effective deterrent. However, some statutory provisions specifically require the sentencer to consider the level of benefit which has accrued or could have accrued to the offender.

In contrast, the advice in relation to what is usually seen as the more serious step - issuing a stop notice - is more bullish:

> Para.7.15 - to emphasise the seriousness of contravening a stop notice, the LPA should always consider a possible prosecution as soon as they have evidence of an offence.

20.3 Criteria considered by the Crown Prosecution Service (CPS)

Where the initial investigation of a complaint that an environmental crime has been committed is conducted by the police, then the prosecuting authority will be the Crown Prosecution Service (CPS). The papers may be taken over by another agency dealing more regularly with the specific category of offences. However, there are occasions when the investigation and prosecution of the offence have been conducted by the police and CPS (e.g. prosecutions of offences relating to ancient monuments conducted by the police and CPS following initial complaints from English Heritage).

Criteria applied by the CPS to determine whether or not a prosecution should proceed are contained in the *Code for Crown Prosecutors*.

The code applies two tests:

(1) *The evidential test.* This is an initial hurdle. It asks whether there is evidence sufficient to provide a realistic prospect of conviction.

(2) *The public interest test.* The code introduces this test:

> 6.2 The public interest must be considered in each case where there is enough evidence to provide a realistic prospect of conviction. In cases of any seriousness, a prosecution will usually take place unless there are public interest factors tending against prosecution which clearly outweigh those tending in favour. Although there may be public interest factors against prosecution in a particular case, often the prosecution should go ahead and those factors should be put to the Court for consideration when sentence is being passed.
>
> 6.3 Crown Prosecutors must balance the factors for and against conviction carefully and fairly. Public interest factors that can affect the decision to prosecute usually depend on the seriousness of the offence or the circumstances of the offender. Some factors may increase the need to prosecute but others may suggest that another course of action would be better.

The code then lists factors which may tend to weigh in favour of or against prosecution. Unsurprisingly, these are not especially relevant to environmental crimes. Factors such as repeated offences, premeditation, scale of harm, whether the harm done by the offence has been put right are also likely to be taken into account by the regulatory bodies in deciding whether to prosecute.

20.4 Alternatives to prosecution

The ultimate aim of the regulatory regimes and the offences which give them teeth may not always be best served by prosecution. Where, as is frequently the case, the harm caused by the pollution leak or the tipping of rubbish has occurred over a period, is still not remedied and may recur, the one-off prosecution may well be relatively ineffective. Criminal Courts have no power to require pollution to be cleared up or for burning of refuse to stop immediately. The Courts can only impose the penalty provided by the words of the relevant statute. For many of the offences this is a fine and there is no option of imposing a prison sentence, however severe the case's circumstances. Regulators sometimes perceive the fines imposed by the Courts to be relatively low, especially where the defendant is an established company. Therefore, even when there is sufficient evidence to bring proceedings, the prosecutor may consider other options or remedies.

The most comprehensive alternative remedy is the *injunction*. In comparison to prosecution, an injunction can force a company or individual to take specific action within a short timescale. Where pollution or environmental harm is continuing, the injunction can provide immediate, specific relief. The injunction also has teeth, because to fail to comply with it can lead to *proceedings for contempt of court*, with imprisonment one of the options available to punish the contemner should breach of an injunction be proved. Punishment for breach of injunction is the only way that even the most serious and flagrant breach of planning control can be marked with a period in custody.

Whilst there has always been the power to grant an injunction to prevent persistent or threatened breach of the criminal law, some statutes now give a *specific power to grant injunctions* which it may be possible to apply at an early stage (e.g. s187B of the TCPA 1990 allows for the granting of an injunction even before the issue of an enforcement notice; s24 EPA 1990 gives a specific alternative of civil proceedings to prosecution for breach of a prohibition or enforcement notice under Part I of that Act).

20.5 Default action

In cases where prosecution is being considered because the defendant has failed to take steps required by a notice, or failed to remedy a state of affairs, there are often parallel powers for the enforcing authority to take direct remedial action (e.g. under s178 TCPA 1990 or s78N or 78P EPA 1990). There is usually provision for recovering the costs of the works from the landowner or occupier.

Default action can ensure that action is taken reasonably quickly. However, default action will not have the deterrent affect of a prosecution where the landowner or occupier:

(i) has no money and cannot be made to pay for the cost of taking the steps; or
(ii) the costs which the LA is able to recover do not outweigh the profit made from the failure to comply with the notice.

Nonetheless, there is usually no reason in principle why a regulatory authority should not both take default action and prosecute for the offence. An important factor is likely to be the regulatory authority's view as to which step is most conducive to continuing compliance and the avoidance of future environmental harm.

There may be cases in which a prosecution would be counterproductive. Equally, the advice given to LPAs when considering enforcement action may be apposite - avoid being strong with the weak and weak with the strong.

CHAPTER 21

COMMENCING CRIMINAL PROCEEDINGS

CONTENTS

CHAPTER 21

COMMENCING CRIMINAL PROCEEDINGS

21.1 Who can start criminal proceedings?

Normally, anyone can bring a prosecution before the Courts to prove that an offence has been committed s6, Prosecution of Offences Act 1985 (POA 1985). The Director of Public Prosecutions (DPP) may take over a prosecution begun by an individual. Prosecutions cannot be brought by unincorporated associations (e.g. angling clubs) although one or two leading members can bring the prosecution on behalf of the other members. Private prosecutions have been brought successfully by representatives of pressure groups (e.g. Greenpeace in relation to a breach involving effluent discharge; the Society for the Protection of Ancient Buildings (SPAB) for a listed-building offence).

In environmental crime, however, there are exceptions to and practical restrictions on this general entitlement to bring prosecutions.

21.2 Statutory limits on who may prosecute

Many of the relevant statutes specifically limit those entitled to bring prosecutions, or require the consent of a certain official or body before prosecution can be brought. Examples:

(i) s216 WRA 1991 prevents prosecutions for offences under the Act being brought, under the Act's Chapter II, Part II, for water-abstraction and drought offences, except by the EA, or by or with the DPP's consent;

(ii) s118(10) EPA 1990 prevents prosecutions being brought under that section, which deals with genetically-modified (GM) organisms, except by the Secretary of State or by or with the DPP's consent;

(iii) s211 WIA 1991, for offences under sewerage provisions, prevents prosecution being brought other than with the Attorney-General's consent, except by a party aggrieved, a sewerage undertaker, or a body whose function is to enforce the provisions.

21.3 Practical restrictions

The powers to investigate (e.g. to enter private land and take samples of water) are given to certain authorised personnel only. Thus the practical difficulties of gathering the evidence and thoroughly investigating offences mean it is usually the authorised bodies (e.g. LAs or the EA) who investigate complaints and bring prosecutions, even if any other organisations or individuals are equally concerned to see incidents of environmental harm lead to prosecution.

Under s42(1)(c) of the Supreme Court Act 1981 (SCA 1981), the Attorney-General may seek an order preventing a vexatious litigant from instituting criminal proceedings.

21.4 Authority to prosecute

The prosecutor should be sure, before commencing proceedings, that he is entitled to bring proceedings for the offence. Where the EA or LA only are entitled to prosecute a particular offence, it will be necessary to show that those actually appearing in Court are specifically authorised or have delegated powers to do so. (See, for example, *Bob Keats v F arrant* [1951] 1 ALL ER 899; *Oberst v Coombs* [1955] 53 LGR 316.)

In a prosecution by a LA, this will normally involve the relevant committee (e.g. the planning committee where offences under the Planning or Listed Buildings Acts are concerned) passing a resolution to authorise criminal proceedings subject to the Council's relevant officers being satisfied as to the evidence and propriety of doing so.

Where a notice (e.g. an enforcement notice) has been served and offences will only be committed if it is not complied with, authorisation can be given at the time of the notice covering any future breaches of its terms. It is more usual, however, to consider the matter once the enforcement notices are live and offences are actually in the offing, if not occurring already.

Alternatively, the LA's standing orders can give general authorisation to the borough solicitor, or some other appropriate officer, to initiate and prosecute criminal proceedings on their behalf. Statutory agencies (e.g. the EA) can delegate their prosecution function to employees, who should be able to prove their authority to:

(i) appear; and
(ii) prosecute the specific case.

21.5 Proving authority to prosecute

The simplest way to prove authority to prosecute is to present a certified copy of the appropriate:

(1) *minute* of the resolution giving authority to prosecute; and

(2) *standing order*, with a certified copy of the *minute* of the council's resolution adopting those minutes.

Sworn oral evidence from the appropriate officer that he has the required authority may well be sufficient but appropriate documentation will be preferable. (*Dee and Clwyd River Authority v Parry* [1967] 65 LGR 488.)

21.6 Issues arising if there is no apparent authority to prosecute

21.6.1 What a defendant should do where specific authority to prosecute is required but there appears to be no evidence of it

If specific authority is required to prosecute and such authorisation has not been obtained, then the criminal proceedings are a nullity. A nullity does not found a plea of *autrefois acquit*. This means the prosecution could start the proceedings again. Apart from receiving their costs thrown away, the defendant may therefore only achieve a phyrric victory. That is unless the case's circumstances mean delay is itself desirable (e.g. where the offence charged is summary only and a time limit has expired).

Later ratification of the prosecution by the appropriate authority would appear impossible, because the consent is needed to the proceedings being instituted. This is likely to have occurred by the time the point is taken. It is therefore worth taking the point as a knockout at an early stage, rather than incurring the costs, etc., of allowing a trial to proceed.

21.6.2 Where no specific consent is required for prosecution but there is no evidence that the public authority for whom the prosecution is purportedly conducted has consented to it

This is more of a problem in theory than in fact. In theory, the prosecution is being conducted by the relevant officer personally and any costs, etc., would be borne by him. In practice, this will obviously make no difference to the evidence and the substantive issues. Ratification will be possible in this instance. Any public authority is entitled to go back and ratify acts done on its behalf. Thus, if the prosecution realises at any stage, it should inform the defence and seek ratification as quickly as possible. (Probably under urgency powers, if necessary!)

What if the prosecution fails to prove it has authority to prosecute?

Authority to prosecute is not a specific element of any offence. It is not entirely clear but it appears that if the point is taken at the close of the prosecution case, the Court could either (i) allow the prosecution to reopen its case under the slip rule or, (ii) if, in fact, no authority has been gained, declare the proceedings a nullity and force the prosecution to start again.

21.7 Issuing criminal proceedings

Proceedings for environmental crime will normally begin by the *laying of an information* to and the *issuing of a summons* by the Magistrates Court (unless police are involved, e.g. arresting a demonstrator who obstructs an official).

21.8 Laying an information

The *information* is the document which tells the Court system that a prosecution is intended and sets out the proposed charge. *The information should:*

21.8.1 Contents

Specify the defendant's name and address. Care may need to be taken, where a company is being charged, to ensure the right defendant is proceeded against. There is power to amend a defendant's details (e.g. correcting the spelling of a name) but at a later stage there is no power to substitute one defendant for another.

21.8.2 Details of offence

Set out the offence alleged to have been committed and give sufficient information for the accused to understand what he is alleged to have done, when and where. This should include any statutory provision alleged to have been contravened.

21.8.3 Specify the prosecutor's name and address

The information need not be in writing or on oath (unless in extreme cases it is hoped to persuade the Justices to issue an arrest warrant) but, in practice, informations are made in writing and sent to the Clerk to the Justices of the local Magistrates Court.

Regular prosecutors will usually have a prescribed form and probably a rubber-stamp signature. These will not invalidate the information. The wording of the information is usually a lengthy paragraph.

The Clerk to the Justices will then consider the information, checking that it:

(i) alleges an offence known to law (hence the value of including the specific statutory provision);
(ii) alleges an offence committed within the jurisdiction of his bench of Magistrates (hence the practice of adding 'within the County of . . . ' when saying where the offence is alleged to have been committed);
(iii) has been laid within any relevant time limit; and
(iv) any necessary consents to prosecution have been obtained.

Once the Clerk to the Justices is satisfied that an information is properly laid, he will arrange for a *summons* requiring the defendant to attend Court to answer the information to be served.

21.9 Time limits

Informations for summary-only offences must be laid within six months of the offence being committed. The six months starts on the day *after* the offence is alleged to have been committed and ends with the day the Justices' Clerk *receives* the summons. The Clerk is deemed to have received the summons on the day it is delivered at the office, whether or not it is actually read and considered that day.

Some statutes also specifically set time limits for commencing criminal proceedings which *extend* the six-month period for laying an information even in relation to summary-only offences. Example: s101 WRA 1991 extends the limit to 12 months for many summary-only offences created by the Act. Extended time limits are calculated in the same way.

Where an information is laid *out of time*, a summons will not be issued and no criminal proceedings can be brought for the specific offence alleged.

21.10 Continuing offences

Some offences are continuing. These usually involve breach of a prohibitory notice (e.g. an enforcement notice (TCPA 1990) or an abatement notice [EPA 1990]). An offence will be committed throughout the period (i) the notice is breached or (ii) some other state of affairs which has become criminal exists. Hence, once these offences occur, they continue to be committed until remedied or stopped. These offences can be considered in relation to any period once the offence (e.g. failing to comply with the notice) has occurred and has not been put right. In effect, this means no time limits will expire unless the breach is remedied.

21.11 Information should specify only one offence

21.11.1 Duplicity

Each information can only allege one offence. If several offences are to be alleged, perhaps several incidents of pollution, even if on the same day, corresponding separate informations must be laid. To allege more than one offence in an information is duplicitous. The prosecutor will be required to elect one of the offences to on which proceed. Having to start again on the other will at best be awkward and at worst impossible if a time limit has expired.

21.11.2 More than one defendant

It is possible for more than one defendant to be accused by the same information. (Although they will be individually summonsed.) Thus a company, its employees and a director could all be accused of the same offence in the one information. Whether or not all the cases are heard together will be considered before any trial that may become necessary.

21.12 Answering a summons

The summons will be sent out with a form for acknowledgement of service and instructions as to how the case will proceed. Any queries should be addressed to the Clerk to the Justices rather than to the prosecutor.

There are certain circumstances in which pleas of guilty by post can be entered to most summary-only offences. However, this procedure is best suited to offences such as minor road-traffic matters with which Magistrates deal frequently and will be familiar. Prosecutors of environmental offences may prefer to ensure both parties are present when the case is dealt with.

CHAPTER 22

PROCEEDING IN THE MAGISTRATES COURT

CONTENTS

CHAPTER 22

PROCEEDINGS IN THE MAGISTRATES COURT

22.1 First appearance before the Court

The summons sent by the Magistrates Court will specify the day on which the defendant is to appear. This first appearance is often not the date on which a trial takes place or a guilty plea is heard and sentence passed. The first appearance is a *preliminary hearing* at which the Court may consider several issues. An individual can appear in person or be represented by a barrister or solicitor. A company must be represented.

22.2 Company representation

A company can appear through a legal representative in all Courts. It is not possible for a company to appear without legal representation in the Crown Court.

In the Magistrates Court, a company may appear without legal representation for limited purposes. These are:

(1) entering a plea of guilty or not guilty;
(2) consenting to summary trial or electing for trial by jury; and
(3) applying to have the charge dismissed.

Otherwise, a company will normally have a barrister or solicitor to act for it. Magistrates have discretion to regulate their own procedure and could be persuaded to hear a company without legal representation for some matters (e.g. mitigation). This would be exceptional, however.

Where a company is to appear without a barrister or a solicitor, it can only do so through:

(1) the company secretary;
(2) a director of the company; or
(3) some other representative.

In all three instances, it is essential that the person appearing for the company can show his authority to act and speak for the company. It would be unusual for this to be accepted without documentary evidence. If the magistrates cannot be sure that the representative before them can properly speak for the company, proceedings are likely to be adjourned for clarification.

22.3 Classification of offences

Environmental offences (EOs) fall into two categories:

(i) those triable either way, in either the Magistrates or the Crown Court; and

(ii) those triable summarily only, in the Magistrates Court.

The main difference between the two categories is the offence's gravity. This is reflected in that the maximum fine for summary-only offences is fixed at £5,000 (or less on the standard scale) unless specifically raised by statute when the specific offence was created. This occurs frequently for either-way offences created under environmental legislation where maximum fines in Magistrates Courts are raised to £20,000. The limit was raised because persistent defaulters often regarded the maximum fine as a tax, or running expense, rather than as a penalty. However, the maximum fine has not normally been raised if the offence remains triable only by magistrates.

The statute's words determine which category an offence falls into. Unless the statute makes clear that the offence can be tried on indictment, it will be summary only. Contrast s90(3) with 90B(3) WRA 1991.

22.4 Summary trial

For summary-only offences, the Court will immediately proceed to hear whether the defendant pleads guilty or not guilty and to consider the arrangements for (i) trial or (ii) hearing the facts of the case and considering sentence.

The rules of evidence applied to a summary trial are no different to those applied in a Crown Court trial. However, there are some differences in procedure, largely resulting from the different tribunals hearing the case. The separation of functions between a judge and a jury in the Crown Court is not present in the Magistrates Court. The magistrates are the judges of issues of fact and law. On points of law, they are advised by their Clerk. Decided cases, in relation to the law of evidence or the interpretation of a particular offence, will apply whether the trial is before magistrates or in the Crown Court before a judge and jury.

22.5 Magistrates Court procedure for either-way offences

22.5.1 Plea before venue

A recent change to Magistrates Court procedure now makes it possible for a defendant charged with an either-way offence to indicate whether or not he intends to plead guilty before a decision is taken on whether the case will be heard in the Magistrates Court or the Crown Court. A defendant pleading at the earliest opportunity will receive maximum credit but any scope for negotiation with the prosecution as to the exact factual basis on which the plea is offered is then immediately lost.

The Clerk to the Magistrates will explain and conduct procedure. The defendant will be identified, then the charge will be read. The defendant will then be asked whether, if the case were to proceed to trial, he would plead guilty or not guilty. Before the defendant answers, the Clerk will explain the consequences of indicating a plea of guilty or not guilty.

If the defendant indicates a *not guilty plea* or makes no indication, then the case proceeds to mode of trial. If the defendant indicates a *guilty plea*, then the magistrates will formally find him guilty and enter a conviction. The magistrates will then hear the facts of the case and any mitigation. They will either proceed to sentence or commit the defendant to the Crown Court for sentence, if they consider their sentencing powers insufficient.

22.6 Advance information for either-way offences

Where the alleged offence is triable either way, then under the *Magistrates Court Advance Information Rules* 1985 the defence can request and the prosecution must supply advance information of the prosecution case before the decision is taken as to mode of trial. The application of these rules is considered with the general and continuing prosecution duty of disclosure.

At this specific stage, many prosecutors serve a 'summary of the facts for the purposes of advance information' either by (i) including it with the information, so that it can be served with the summons, or (ii) sending it to the defendant shortly after service of the summons. This avoids a fruitless Court appearance where the defendant requests advance information and the case is adjourned (i) for this to be supplied, or (ii) for it to be considered where it can be handed over straight away.

22.7 Mode of trial

22.7.1 Place of trial

The Magistrates Court must first decide whether the seriousness of the facts alleged in the case mean their powers of punishment would be insufficient to reflect the seriousness of the offence if the defendant were found guilty. For these purposes, the prosecution's allegations are taken as accurate.

If the prosecution believes that the case is sufficiently serious to go to the Crown Court, it will make a short statement in open court setting out its view and the reasons for it.

22.7.2 Prosecution presentation

Because the offence may not be one with which the magistrates deal regularly, the prosecution should:

(1) Outline what the offence involves as far as the statute is concerned, suggesting what the mischief appears to have been that Parliament was seeking to avoid. Photocopies of the relevant section are usually appreciated, especially by the Magistrates' Clerk.

(2) Briefly give a summary of what the prosecution says happened.

(3) Indicate where the prosecution (who are likely to have more experience of the offence than the magistrates) say the offence fits in the scale of things. *Several factors will determine the seriousness of the offence*:

Environmental harm

What was the damage caused and the length of time over which the offence was committed? Is a stretch of water which has been polluted one which had a valuable diversity of flora and fauna which has been seriously affected, or is it of average or below-average interest? Was pollutant allowed to leak into a river for a few hours only and then stopped by the offender himself, or did pollution occur over a long period and was halted only when discovered by the investigating authority or another third party?

Motivation for offence

Deliberate breach of the law, having weighed up the likely penalty against the financial advantages of committing the offence, is obviously at the other end of the scale to inadvertent commission of an offence of strict liability.

Was it an offence where warning letters and requests to prevent or discontinue problems were ignored leading to prosecution as a last resort, or did the events happen quickly, without warning, albeit that they could have been prevented?

The clerk and the magistrates may also want an indication of the complexity of the issues and the estimated length of the trial. These factors do not in law determine the place of trial but (i) there are often practical difficulties in lay benches sitting for more than a couple of consecutive days and (ii) a stipendiary magistrate may be more comfortable with complex issues of law or be able to sit for a longer continuous period.

Having heard the prosecution, the magistrates then determine the *mode of trial*. Under s19 of the Magistrates Courts Act 1980 (MCA 1980), the magistrates are required to consider the following factors in reaching their own decision:

(1) the nature of the case;
(2) whether the circumstances make the offence one of serious character;
(3) whether the punishment which a Magistrates Court would have power to inflict would be adequate;
(4) any other circumstances which appear to the Court to make it more suitable for the offence to be tried in one way rather than the other;
(5) any representations made by the prosecution or the defence.

The *National Mode of Trial Guidelines*, issued to all magistrates in 1995, do not deal with environmental offences. The general guidance they give is:

(a) the Court should never make its decisions on grounds of convenience or expedition;
(b) the Court should assume for the purpose of deciding mode of trial that the prosecution's version of the facts is correct;
(c) if the offences are alleged to be specimens, that is a relevant consideration: the fact that the defendant if convicted will be asking for other offences to be taken into consideration is not;
(d) where cases involve complex questions of fact, or difficult questions of law, including difficult issues of the disclosure of sensitive material, the Court should consider committing for trial;
(e) where two or more defendants are jointly charged with an offence, each has an individual right to elect his mode of trial;
(f) in general, either-way offences should be tried summarily unless the Court considers that the particular case has one or more of the features (indicating Crown Court trial) **and** that its sentencing powers are insufficient;
(g) the Court should also consider its power to commit an offender for sentence under the MCA 1980 (s38) if, in course of the hearing, information emerges which leads it to conclude that the offence is so serious, or the offender such a risk to the public, that its sentencing powers are inadequate.

Magistrates are also told that, where the amount of damage being considered is more than £10,000, they can regard it as high and consider committing for trial. This may obviously be relevant where, for instance, the cost of a clean-up operation is more than £10,000.

At this mode-of-trial stage, the offender's persistence cannot be taken into account, because this would prejudice a fair trial by revealing previous convictions. However, should the defendant plead or be found guilty, the previous record becomes relevant; and should magistrates consider it alters their view of the offence, to such a degree that their powers of punishment are no longer sufficient, they may commit for sentence to the Crown Court.

If the magistrates consider the matter is not suitable for summary trial, matters proceed to a committal to the Crown Court. If the case is considered suitable for summary trial, the defendant is then asked to elect where he wishes to be tried.

22.8 Defendant's right to elect trial by judge and jury

The defendant has an absolute right to elect trial for either-way offences. Several factors may influence his choice as to whether he wishes to appear in the Magistrates Court or the Crown Court:

(1) Crown Court trial will increase defendant and prosecution costs. A convicted defendant will almost certainly face an application that he be made to pay prosecution costs. A private prosecutor's costs will far exceed amounts normally sought by the CPS following conviction. It is not uncommon for a party convicted of an EO to be ordered to pay a relatively modest fine but costs running into tens of thousands of pounds following Crown Court trial.

(2) A trial before a jury will almost certainly take longer to consider the same evidence than a trial before magistrates but it is not this alone which increases costs.

Accepted wisdom and lawyers' gossip usually suggest that juries are more likely than magistrates to acquit. This is on the basis that a jury has come along expecting a robbery or murder. Indeed, papers sent to jurors, before jury service, indicate that they will probably be dealing with the more serious crimes and they will find a lengthy consideration of an EO tedious. This, however, may not be as true as is usually assumed.

Provided the prosecution keeps the case's presentation digestible and is carefully prepared, with documents and bundles, to present a case that is easy to follow and without innumerable delays (e.g. while one unnumbered photograph is passed to the witness, then to the judge and then hand-to-hand along 12 jurors), then experience suggests both sides will get a fair and considered hearing. Anecdotal experience suggests environmental prosecutions in the Crown Court fail more through something going wrong with proving each element of the offence, or other legal points, than through perverse verdicts from bored juries.

If a guilty plea is to be entered, at some stage, the publicity and cost will probably be far less in the Magistrates Court than in the Crown Court and appeal against sentence is as of right.

If the defendant elects summary trial, the magistrates proceed to trial and sentence. If the defendant elects for Crown Court trial, committal proceedings commence.

22.9 Committal proceedings

22.9.1 Proceedings

In cases where magistrates have declined jurisdiction, or the defendant has elected trial in the Crown Court, the next stage is committal proceedings.

Committal proceedings are the first opportunity for the defence to test the prosecution's evidence. Before magistrates can commit a case to the Crown Court for trial, they must be satisfied there is a case to answer in relation to the offence. This is often also described as a *prima facie case*. When magistrates undertake the function of deciding whether there is a case to answer, they are known as *Examining Justices.*

The procedure for the conduct of committal proceedings was altered by the Criminal Proceedings and Investigations Act 1996 (CPIA 1996). The relevant changes considered in this chapter apply to all cases where no criminal investigation into the offence began before April 1st, 1997. It will now be rare in EO's that criminal investigations into a specific offence will have started before that date.

The changes include abolition of the defence's right to:

(1) test the prosecution's case by requiring attendance of prosecution witnesses before the Examining Justices to give oral evidence and to be cross-examined;

(2) call evidence at committal proceedings.

These two changes' effect is that all committal proceedings are now undertaken using documentary evidence alone.

There have also been changes to the *nature and scope of documentary evidence* admissible for the purposes of committal proceedings. The changes are in the MCA 1980 (s5A to 5F). Put simply, to be admissible for the purposes of committal proceedings, evidence must satisfy two criteria. It must:-

(a) be tendered by the prosecution; and
(b) fall within a specific category listed in the MCA 1980 (s5B to 5F).

Categories of evidence listed in the MCA 1980 are witness statements; the documents and other exhibits referred to in those witness statements, if any; depositions taken before a magistrate; the documents and other exhibits referred to in those depositions, if any; and other witness statements and documents which comply with s5D (witness statements) and s5E (documents) of the MCA 1980.

All evidence on which the prosecution intends to rely at committal proceedings must comply with the detailed requirements in the MCA 1980 (s5A to 5F). Regard should be had to the requirements of those sections of the MCA 1980 in any given case.

Other, incidental, changes concern such matters as witness orders and alibi warnings.

22.9.2 Committal papers

If the prosecution has not already done so under the advance-information rules, it will have to prepare and serve on the defendant a *bundle* of the statements of witnesses and documentary exhibits on which it intends to rely, to show that there is a case for the defendant to answer that the alleged offence has been committed.

The committal bundle is served on the defence for it to consider whether it wishes (i) to contest the proposed committal, arguing that there is no case to answer, or (ii) to accept that a prima facie case exists and consent to the case being committed to the Crown Court using a shortened, formalised procedure.

Committal proceedings can therefore be divided into two types:

(1) with consideration of the evidence; or

(2) without consideration of the evidence.

22.9.3 Committal proceedings with consideration of the evidence

Contested committals are held under the provisions of s6(1) MCA 1980 . They have been colloquially known as 'Section 6(1)' or 'old-style' committals. Now, however, because oral or live evidence has been abolished, they are often also referred to as a 'readthrough'. A defendant should ordinarily be present in Court during a committal with consideration of the evidence.

Under the new procedure, the prosecution opens the committal proceedings by outlining the case, usually drawing attention to the most important aspects of the evidence, and by explaining relevant points of law. The prosecution then tenders the documentary evidence contained in the committal bundle. This is done by the prosecutor reading the statements aloud and referring the Examining Justices to any relevant exhibits. In certain circumstances and with the leave of the Court an oral account or summary of the evidence can be given by the prosecutor upon the Court's direction.

Examining Justices are empowered to take possession of documentary exhibits produced by witness statements. This, however, is not mandatory and, in practice, can cause problems, because the prosecution will not normally see the exhibits again until the trial.

Therefore, in practice, it may well be best for the prosecution to keep the original documentary exhibits. This will facilitate the preparation of *jury bundles* for trial and avoids problems at trial where there are many documents with which the Clerk to the Court may not be familiar. In practice, a bundle of the original documentary exhibits is best kept by the representative of the prosecution sitting behind counsel for the prosecution. The original of any document can then be found quickly should it be needed.

The defence then has the opportunity to make a *submission of no case to answer.* If the defence exercises its right to make a submission, the prosecution is then entitled to make a submission in reply. Where the defence, unusually, does not make a submission of no case to answer, the prosecution may only make a submission after tendering the evidence if the Examining Justices indicate that they are not minded to commit the defendant for trial.

The Justices will then determine whether there is a prima facie case. If they find that there is, they will cause the charge to be written down, if this has not already been done. In practice, the charge will have been reduced to writing by the prosecution in the form of a draft indictment. If the defendant is not represented by counsel or a solicitor, the Court must then read the charge to the defendant and explain the charge in ordinary language. The defendant is then committed to the Crown Court for trial.

If the Examining Justices find that there is not sufficient evidence to justify a committal to the Crown Court, the Justices will refuse to commit the defendant. The defendant will then be discharged by the Court. In those circumstances, the prosecution must choose whether to abandon the case or seek further evidence and lay a fresh information.

22.9.4 Committal proceedings without consideration of the evidence

Noncontested committals are held under the provisions of s6(2) MCA 1980 and are known as 'Section 6(2)' or 'paper committals'. However, a 's6(2)' cannot be held where the defendant is not legally represented. A defendant who is legally represented does not have to be present in Court for a committal without consideration of the evidence.

In a s6(2) committal, the prosecution tenders to the Examining Justices the documentary evidence (which, to be admissible for the purpose of committal, must comply with the provisions of s5A[2] MCA 1980). The evidence is tendered by the prosecution by handing to the Clerk to the Justices the original witness statements and documentary exhibits (together with a copy bundle to be sent to the Crown Court). The documentary exhibits need not be the originals which should be retained by the prosecution for the preparation of jury bundles. Copies of the witness statements and documentary exhibits should already have been served on the defence as the committal papers.

The Examining Justices then confirm with the defendant's counsel or solicitor that they do not want to make a submission of no case to answer. In practice, this usually takes the form of the Examining Justices asking the defendant's legal representative whether the defendant consents to a s6(2) committal. On the Justices being satisfied that the defendant is legally represented and that the defence consents to a s6(2) committal, the case is then committed to the Crown Court for trial.

Whether the committal is under s6(1) or s6(2), the Court will also consider the following questions:-

Bail: usually granted unconditionally in environmental cases.

Alibi: alibi warnings formerly given by the Clerk to the Justices have now been abolished by CPIA 1996. The issue of alibis is now dealt with in the defence statement prepared for the purposes of disclosure in Crown Court trials. (See alibis in the Crown Court chapter on disclosure.)

Witnesses: witness orders have also now been abolished at the committal stage by CPIA 1996. Under the new procedure, all witness statements and depositions tendered by the prosecution for the purposes of committal may be read as evidence at trial in the Crown Court, unless the defendant objects to them being read and requires the witnesses' attendance. The objection must be made in writing to the prosecution and the Crown Court within 14 days of committal. In practice, witness requirements will be reconsidered at the Crown Court hearing for pleas and directions.

Legal Aid: where a defendant is represented on Legal Aid at the committal stage, the Justices should be asked to continue the Legal Aid Order for trial in the Crown Court.

Reporting Restrictions: the defence may ask for the restrictions on what may be reported to be lifted. Reporting restrictions are assumed to remain unless this application is made.

Once committal proceedings have been completed, the defendant will be required to attend at the Crown Court nominated by the Justices, at a date usually specified by the Justices and which is usually about six weeks after committal. Attendance on this date is for the purposes of a preliminary hearing known as a *Plea and Directions Hearing.*

22.10 Magistrates Courts: sentencing and committal for sentence

Following a guilty plea, or conviction after trial, the magistrates proceed to sentence. In EOs other than public nuisance, their powers are limited by the statute creating the offence, or by the general limits on the maximum sentence they can pass.

Some of the more minor offences have sentences limited by reference to a fine at a level (one to five) on the standard scale. The standard scale currently sets fines at:

Level 1 £200
Level 2 £500
Level 3 £1,000
Level 4 £2,500
Level 5 £5,000.

Other summary-only offences refer to the statutory maximum which is £5,000. If the magistrates are sentencing for an either-way offence, the maximum fine they can impose is £5,000, unless the statute specifies an uplift, invariably to £20,000.

Where magistrates are sentencing the defendant for an either-way offence, because either (i) there was indication of plea before venue or (ii) the magistrates ruled the case suitable for summary trial and the defendant did not elect for Crown Court trial, then there is power to commit to the Crown Court for sentence. This occurs where the magistrates, having heard more about the case or the defendant (e.g. the level of profit made, a previous record of offences), consider their powers of sentence insufficient to reflect the offence's gravity.

They can then commit the defendant to the Crown Court for sentence. The Crown Court sits with a judge and magistrates to hear the facts and to sentence, without the Magistrates Court limit on maximum imposable sentence.

Where the defendant is an individual, there may be a Presentence Report by the Probation Service (PS), on motivation, remorse, financial circumstances, etc. The PS arranges to interview the defendant and report.

22.11 Appeal from the Magistrates Court

Where the case is summary only, or has stayed in the Magistrates Court following mode of trial, the magistrates may hear the case. If the defendant is found guilty or has pleaded guilty, they pass sentence.

There are three avenues of appeal from the Magistrates Court:

22.11.1 Appeal as of right to the Crown Court

If the defendant gives notice in writing to the prosecutor and the Clerk to the Justices, he may appeal to the Crown Court against conviction, sentence or both. The appeal will be an entirely fresh hearing. It will be heard by a Crown Court judge and two magistrates from a different area to that of the magistrates who first heard the case. Notice of appeal has to be given within 21 days but the Crown Court is empowered to allow an appeal out of time.

Appeal to the Crown Court is open to a defendant only. It is the only route of appeal which provides for an unfettered second attempt by the defence.

The Crown Court's determination on appeal can itself be challenged by way of case stated, or by an appeal to the Court of Criminal Appeal.

22.11.2 Appeal to the Divisional Court by way of case stated

If a defendant believes that the magistrates have erred in law or acted in breach of procedure, or there are any other grounds for appeal other than that the defendant is dissatisfied with the view the magistrates took of the facts, then an appeal to the High Court can be entered by way of case stated. This procedure is also open to a prosecutor who wishes to have the magistrates' legal reasoning reviewed. Much of the case-law relevant to environmental crime results from magistrates' decisions being challenged by way of case stated. The Divisional Court will only consider the magistrates' decision. The Court will not hear the case again.

22.11.3 Application for Judicial Review

Magistrates Courts are also susceptible to Judicial Review under the provisions of *Order 53 of the Rules of the Supreme Court*. Again, this does not provide a rehearing but is a review of the magistrates' decisionmaking process rather than of the merits of the decision itself.

The detailed provisions as to the procedure for appealing to the Crown Court, applying for the Justices to state a case, or making an application for Judicial Review are found primarily in MCA 1980 and the Rules of the Supreme Court.

References to the European Court and applications to the European Court of Human Rights are considered under appeal from the Crown Court.

CHAPTER 23

PROCEEDINGS IN THE CROWN COURT

CONTENTS

CHAPTER 23

PROCEEDINGS IN THE CROWN COURT

23.1 Introduction

Proceedings in the Crown Court with trial taking place before a judge and jury are covered by a large number of Acts of Parliament, procedural rules and decided cases. This section can do no more than consider those aspects of Crown Court proceedings most likely to be encountered where an environmental offence (EO) is being considered. The aim is to provide an introduction rather than comprehensive and detailed guidance on every point which may come up during a Crown Court trial.

23.2 Indictment

Once a case is committed to the Crown Court, the wording of the charge on the information must be converted into that of the indictment. The indictment is the formal document which sets out the allegations the defendant faces. It is these allegations which if proved will form the factual basis for sentence.

All prosecutions in the Crown Court are technically on behalf of the Queen and so the indictment will be drafted and the case known as *Regina versus* . . . even though for all practical purposes the prosecution is brought by others (e.g. a LA or a regulatory agency).

It is for the prosecution, not the Crown Court, to draft the indictment. The indictment need not set out the same charges as at committal, providing the evidence at committal supports the offence now alleged. If there has been an old-style committal and it appears that a slightly different offence is appropriate, or that the dates, or other details, need to be changed, this can be done, provided there is evidence to support the new allegations already on the papers.

The draft indictment (known as *the bill*) should be drafted and lodged with the Crown Court within 28 days of committal, although it is possible for this period to be extended initially by 28 days within the Crown Court Office and thereafter by a Crown Court Judge.

Opposition to the *late preferring* of a bill is unlikely to succeed unless the defence can show that it is in some way taken by surprise. This is unlikely unless the indictment is significantly different from the committal charges.

The drafting of indictments is governed by the *Indictment Rules* 1971 which will determine any objection to the form of the indictment. It is not unusual for counsel to draft indictments. In drafting indictments for EOs, some issues may occur fairly regularly:

> The indictment will probably be the first document a jury sees and the jury will be referred to it by the judge in summing up. EOs may be difficult to encapsulate in a few words but a jury will appreciate a simple rather than an intimidating wording when it is the first contact with the issues that the jury is to face.
>
> Each count of the indictment should only allege one offence.
>
> Rule 6 of the Indictment Rules requires that where an offence is created by statute, the relevant provision should be set out in the statement of offence.
>
> The particulars of the offence should set out all those elements of the offence which the prosecution needs to have covered by the close of its case. It is not necessary to deal with any defences which may be raised by a defendant.
>
> Where the prosecution are alleging more than one offence, or prosecuting more than one defendant, consideration should be given to whether it is appropriate for all matters to be tried at the same time in front of the same jury.

23.3 Plea and directions hearing

The next stage in the process - and the first time the prosecution and defendant will meet since committal - is at the hearing for plea and directions. At this stage, defendants may have more to consider than prosecutors.

When considering sentence, credit will be given for a guilty plea. The earlier in the process that plea is tendered, the better. The degree of credit reduces as time goes on. However, even a plea on the morning of a trial will bring some credit and probably reduce any award for costs. The plea and directions hearing will usually include arraignment. It is therefore the earliest opportunity to enter a guilty plea, since the defence has had the chance to consider the detailed evidence presented at the committal hearing. Significant credit can be claimed for a plea entered at this first stage of Crown Court proceedings as well as avoiding liability for prosecution costs incurred in preparing for trial

Where a plea is entered, practice varies from Court to Court as to what happens next. The prosecution may wish to clarify beforehand what will happen in the event of a guilty plea being entered at plea and directions. Namely, whether the judge will then want to go on, hear the prosecution case and mitigation and sentence that day, or whether the hearing of an effective plea will be put off until later.

This may be particularly important if there is to be a dispute to be determined before sentence, or if the defence wishes to call any character witnesses or other evidence in mitigation. In most Courts, there are many pleas and directions heard on the same day, meaning there will not be time for full presentation of the case by the prosecution followed by mitigation and sentence.

If the case is to proceed to trial then the primary purpose of the plea and directions hearing is to assist as much as possible in the smooth running of the trial. There is a standard form to be filled in which details of witness requirements, bundles of papers and so forth are to be confirmed.

The prosecution will open the case to the jury so there is a need (i) to know what the issues in the trial are likely to be and (ii) to have some indication of the course the trial is likely to follow, a need to give an opening speech that is relevant and does not cover evidence which may be successfully objected to later.

Defence counsel often give an informal indication such as 'you can open on everything but not the verbals of the lorry driver.' This means that any of the current prosecution evidence can be mentioned in opening save the alleged damaging remarks of the company lorry drivers. These, the defence will argue, for instance, cannot be confessions on behalf of the company and should be kept from the jury.

One direction which may help in an EO case more than usual is the defence notifying the prosecution of points of law, with relevant authorities which are to be taken, before the case is opened to the jury, at least 14 days before trial.

23.4 Trial documents

In most EO cases, juries will be considering documents and perhaps maps and photographs. It will also be helpful for the prosecution to know which documents it is agreed that they can put in front of the jury in opening. At the plea and directions hearing, if not, ideally, before, the prosecution should offer to serve a draft jury bundle within a short period and seek to be notified of any defence objections thereafter. It is also good practice to serve a copy of this bundle on the Court, for the trial judge to use, and also to check that the documentation with the Court is in order. The judge should at least have the indictment; a full set of witness statements (including any notices of additional evidence) and copy exhibits.

23.5 Original documents

The prosecution should retain the original exhibits in a file. These should have been retained at committal. Loss of original documents which have been properly authenticated where necessary is probably the single largest cause of hiccups in the prosecution case - although not necessarily fatal (see *R v Wayte* 1976 Cr App Rep 110 CA).

23.6 Expert evidence

Any outstanding issues as to service of experts' reports and background calculations will also normally be determined at the hearing for plea and directions.

23.7 Admissions

In any criminal trial, points which are agreed can be put before the jury as admissions under s10 Criminal Justice Act 1967 (CJA 1967). Admissions can considerably reduce a trial's length and cost. The defence will only make an admission of a point which the prosecution has to prove where there is no doubt that the point can be proved if the prosecution is required to do so. Potential points for admission may cover areas of the case which the prosecution needs to prove but which are not controversial, such as that:

- the defendant owned a relevant piece of land between xxxxx dates;
- an enforcement notice or consent to discharge was lawfully issued;
- xxxxx river was controlled waters for the purposes of the WRA 1991;
- the proceedings are properly brought on behalf of xxxxx prosecuting authority.

23.8 Set down for trial

If the case is to be contested, the Plea and Directions may also cover appropriate dates for the case to be heard, depending on witness availability, Court time, etc.

23.9 Trial

As indicated, the trial will follow the same procedure and be governed by the same rules of evidence as any other criminal trial. Some of the following points may occur in relation to EOs :

23.10 Jury selection

If the prosecutor is a LA, the judge may be prepared to ask each juror if they live within the area of xxxxx district or borough council, or if they or any member of their family have ever worked for xxxxx borough council, and exclude from the panel any potential jurors to whom this applies. If the defence is going to make this request, it should be mentioned at plea and directions, so that, if possible, jurors can be called from an area outside the council boundary. On at least one occasion, a trial has had to be adjourned when most of the panel of potential jurors turned out to live in the council area.

There may be other considerations for the jury panel to be canvassed, at plea and directions or with the trial judge. (Example: where a prosecution was brought under the Ancient Monuments Act 1979 [AMA 1979]4, jurors were asked whether they were members of English Heritage.)

23.11 Disclosure

23.11.1 Material gathered during investigation

In all cases where it is suspected that an offence has been committed, an investigation will be undertaken, by police or an investigating authority, to ascertain whether there is sufficient evidence to secure a conviction for an offence justifying bringing a prosecution. In certain circumstances, the material which as a result of that investigation comes into the control and possession of the police, the investigating authority or the prosecution must be disclosed to the defence.

The material gathered on investigation of an alleged offence can be divided into two distinct categories, on which the prosecution, to secure a conviction at trial:-

(a) intends to rely; and

(b) does not intend to rely.

23.11.2 Disclosure of material on which the prosecution intends to rely at trial

This is commonly referred to as the prosecution case. The nature of the alleged offence will determine whether the defence is entitled to disclosure of the prosecution case. For offences which may be tried by magistrates only (commonly known as *summary offences*), the defence is not entitled to disclosure of the material on which the prosecution intends to rely.

In practice, however, especially in prosecutions of summary offences where there is technical evidence, the prosecution often gives to the defence notice of its case by disclosing the witness statements and other evidence on which the prosecution intends to rely before the trial.

In all cases of offences which may be tried on indictment, the prosecution is required to disclose to the defence the material on which it intends to rely at trial. This will most certainly be disclosed to the defence before committal proceedings in the form of the committal bundle. After committal for trial on indictment, any further material on which the prosecution intends to rely must be disclosed to the defence by way of a *Notice of Additional Evidence.*

In cases of offences which are triable either way, the prosecution must provide to the defence copies of its witness statements or a summary of the evidence on which it intends to rely, if the defence requests such information, before the mode of trial hearing takes place, pursuant to the *Magistrates Court (Advance Information) Rules* 1985. In practice, the prosecution usually provides the defence with copies of prosecution witness statements. However, it must be remembered that the defence is not entitled to statements; a summary of the prosecution evidence is sufficient. The provision of advance disclosure is designed to facilitate mode of trial, giving the defendant the chance to make an informed choice for the mode of trial.

23.11.3 Disclosure of material on which the prosecution does not intend to rely at trial

Material which is within the custody or control of the prosecution on which the prosecution does not intend to rely at trial is commonly known as *unused material.*

Common-law rules on disclosure of unused material to the defence have been superseded by the statutory framework for disclosure of unused material in the CPIA 1996.

CPIA (Part I) creates a three-stage procedure for the purpose of disclosure of unused material which is supplemented by a *Code of Practice* issued pursuant to Part II of the same Act. The Code of Practice applies to criminal investigations undertaken by police officers. The CPIA also provides that those other than police officers charged with the duty of conducting criminal investigations must have regard to the Code's provisions.

The Code contains detailed rules for the conduct of the investigation. It creates a regime whereby the investigator is given responsibility for ensuring that information relevant to the investigation is retained and recorded. Information relevant to the investigation can include information (i) gathered in course of the investigation and (ii) information generated by the investigation.

The Code also creates the role of a *disclosure officer* (DO) whose functions are distinct from those of the investigator. The DO is responsible for examining material retained by the police during the investigation; revealing that material to the prosecutor during the investigation and during any criminal proceedings resulting from it and certifying that he has done this. The DO also has the role of disclosing material to the defence at the prosecutor's request.

Under the Code, the DO is charged with the responsibility of preparing a schedule of all the information that has been retained and recorded as a result of the investigation, including that which does not form part of the prosecution case. The DO is also required to keep a *schedule of sensitive material* which, in the investigator's opinion, is material, disclosure of which is not in the public interest.

The DO will then give the schedules to the prosecutor, preferably at the same time as he provides the material which makes up the prosecution case. Detailed provisions in the Code require the DO to provide certain information to the prosecutor. It may be, however, that not all the material on the schedules is provided to the prosecutor. As such, the Code requires the DO to allow the prosecutor to inspect such material on request and to copy such material to the prosecutor if requested.

The Code requires the DO to draw to the prosecutor's attention material which might undermine the prosecution case. The DO must also certify that the Code's requirements were complied with to the best of his knowledge and belief.

Once the defence has served its defence statement in compliance with the procedure, the DO must reconsider the material retained in light of the contents of the defence statement and draw the prosecutor's attention to any material which might reasonably be expected to assist the defence if it were disclosed. At this stage, the DO must again certify that the Code's requirements were complied with to the best of his knowledge and belief.

The new procedure for disclosure of unused material applies to all cases where no criminal investigations into the offence had begun before April 1st, 1997 and is mandatory in all cases which are tried in the Crown Court on indictment. The procedure can be used voluntarily in summary trials, including trials in the *Youth Court.*

23.11.4 Three-stage statutory procedure

The statutory procedure for disclosure of unused material can be divided into three stages:-

(a) primary disclosure by the prosecution;
(b) disclosure of the defence case; and
(c) secondary disclosure by the prosecution.

23.11.4.1 Primary prosecution disclosure

The prosecution must effect primary disclosure of unused material which has previously been undisclosed to the defence if, in the prosecutor's opinion, the unused material could undermine the prosecution case. The prosecution must effect primary disclosure as soon as is reasonably practicable after a defendant is committed for trial to the Crown Court.

If, in the prosecutor's opinion, there is no unused material which could undermine the prosecution case against the defendant then the defence must be given a written statement indicating that opinion.

Material for these purposes includes material which is in the prosecutor's possession and came into his possession in connection with the case for the prosecution against the defendant or, material which the prosecutor has inspected in connection with the case for the prosecution against the defendant pursuant to the terms of the Code of Practice. Put simply, the latter type of material not in the possession of the prosecutor is material which has been gathered and recorded by the investigating officers in the case which the prosecutor has inspected but which is not in the prosecutor's possession.

Unused material is disclosed to the defence either by providing them with a copy of it, or, if in the prosecutor's opinion that is not practicable or desirable, by allowing the defence to inspect it at a reasonable time and location and by taking steps to secure that the defence be allowed to do so.

23.11.4.2 Disclosure of defence case

On the prosecution complying with the requirements of primary disclosure, or purporting to do so, the next step in the procedure is the requirement for the defence to provide the Court and the prosecution with a *defence statement*. A defence statement, however, is only required after the defendant has been committed to the Crown Court for trial.

A defence statement is a written statement which (i) sets out, in general terms, the nature of the defendant's defence, (ii) indicates which matters the defendant takes in issue with the prosecution and (iii) sets out, in the case of each of those matters, the reason why the defendant takes issue with the prosecution.

If the defence statement discloses an *alibi*, particulars of the alibi must be given in the statement, including the name and address of any alibi witness if these are known to the defendant at the time of making the defence statement. If the defendant does not know the name and address of an alibi witness at the time of making the defence statement, then the defendant must include in the statement any information in his possession which could be of material assistance in finding the alibi witness.

The defence statement must be given to the Court and the prosecution within 14 days of the prosecution complying, or purporting to comply, with the requirements of primary disclosure. The period for service of the defence statement may be extended at the discretion of the Court, as long as the application for an extension is made in writing to the Court, within the initial time period for service, stating that the defendant believes, on reasonable grounds, that it is not possible for him to provide a defence statement within the stipulated period. The application must also state the defendant's grounds for believing that it is not possible to comply with the time limits and must specify the number of days by which the defendant wished the period extended.

The Court may only grant an extension of the time limit for serving the defence statement if it is satisfied that the defendant could not reasonably provide, or could not reasonably have provided, the defence statement within the 14-day period. The period by which the Court extends the time for compliance is entirely at the Court's own discretion and the period for compliance will be extended by so many days as the Court so specifies.

The Court may further extend the time for compliance by so many days as the Court may specify and there is no limit on the number of applications for an extension that can be made. However, on each application, the Court must be satisfied that the defendant could not reasonably provide, or could not reasonably have provided, the defence statement within the extended time period.

Failure by the defence to comply with its obligations to disclose the defence case means that the prosecution is under no obligation to effect *secondary disclosure*. However, the CPIA specifically empower the Court, or a party with the Court's leave, to comment on deficiencies in the defence disclosure. Further, in deciding the defendant's guilt, the Court or jury may draw inferences from the defendant's failure to fulfil his obligations. However, the defendant may not be convicted solely on the basis of such an inference being drawn.

23.11.4.3 Secondary prosecution disclosure

On receipt of the defence statement, the next stage in the procedure is for the prosecution to effect secondary disclosure. At this stage of the procedure, the prosecution must disclose any material previously undisclosed to the defence which could reasonably be expected to assist the defence case as disclosed in the defence statement.

The prosecution must effect secondary disclosure as soon as is reasonably practicable after the defence has served its defence statement. If, in the prosecutor's opinion, there is no such material, then the prosecution must give the defence a written statement to that effect.

Material for purposes of secondary disclosure has the same meaning as for the purpose of primary disclosure. Similarly, the prosecutor can disclose the material to the defence in the same manner as for primary disclosure.

23.11.4.4 Review of disclosure obligations by the Court

In cases where the defence has served a defence statement and the prosecution has effected, purported to effect, or failed to effect secondary disclosure, the defence may apply to the Court for an order requiring the prosecution to disclose material. The defence may only seek such an order in these circumstances where, at any time, it has reasonable cause to believe that there is prosecution material which could reasonably be expected to assist the defence, as disclosed in the defence statement, and the material has not been disclosed.

The review procedure applies to material either in the prosecutor's possession or which the prosecutor has inspected. Also, and in contrast with the definition of material for the purposes of primary and secondary disclosure, it applies to any material which the DO must either supply to the prosecutor or allow the prosecutor to inspect if requested.

Throughout the procedure and up and until the defendant is acquitted or convicted, the prosecution is under a continuing duty to review questions of disclosure.

In all circumstances, material must not be disclosed to the extent that the Court, on an application by the prosecutor, concludes that it is not in the public interest to disclose it and orders accordingly. Similarly, material intercepted in obedience to a warrant issued under the Interception and Communications Act 1985 (ICA 1985), or material which indicates that such a warrant has been issued, or that material has been intercepted in obedience to such a warrant, must not be disclosed.

23.12 Expert evidence

Expert evidence, whether to be called for the defence or the prosecution, is subject to a requirement of advance notice in the Crown Court. See *Crown Court (Advance Notice of Expert Evidence) Rules* 1987 which require the expert's report of either side to be served on the other party or parties as soon as practicable after committal. Once the report is served, the other party may by notice in writing seek copies of the materials such as calculations or samples on which the expert evidence is based.

If advance notice is not given, the expert evidence may only be adduced with leave of the Court which may well only be given after allowing an adjournment the costs of which are to be borne by the party in breach of the rules.

There is no such requirement in the Magistrates Court. In practice, expert evidence is sometimes served either in an attempt to persuade the prosecution to discontinue, or to avoid an application for an adjournment which may cause delay and extra cost if successful.

23.13 Preservation of exhibits

The prosecution is not under a strict duty to preserve exhibits but it should clearly make efforts to do so, especially where samples are involved. Indeed, in most cases where an environmental prosecutor wishes to rely on samples there is a requirement, in the legislation creating the offence, to ensure that samples taken are split and the defence given its own. If the prosecution is going to conduct tests on any exhibit which will permanently alter or destroy it, best practice is to give the defence a chance to examine the exhibit for itself first (unless this is a split-sample case). Failure to give such an opportunity will not render the results of the subsequent destructive test inadmissible but may lead to justified adverse comment from opposing parties and perhaps the Court.

23.14 Verdict

After a not guilty verdict, the defendant will be discharged and seek his costs.

After a guilty verdict, or following a plea of guilty, the Court proceeds to sentence.

23.15 Sentence

The procedure for sentence will be essentially the same whether sentence is being passed by the Magistrates Court or the Crown Court.

After a conviction, the Court will have heard the facts during the trial. On a plea of guilty, the prosecution outlines the facts of the case. If there is any dispute as to these facts, the Court must either accept the defence version or determine the factual position through a procedure known as a *Newton hearing*.

Where the Court is required to take into account the financial benefit accruing from the offence, the prosecution should be in a position to say what the figure or approximate figure is. If the prosecution makes a mere assertion as to financial benefit which is challenged by the defence, sentence will be passed on the defence figures unless they are clearly untenable.

The prosecution will also bring to the Court's attention any relevant previous convictions or cautions and be able to tell the Court what the sentencing powers under the relevant statutory provisions are. If there are any recognised guideline cases, the prosecution should also be able to refer the Court to them.

Factors relevant to sentence for EOs, which the Court may wish to know about from the prosecution, could be:

- the degree of damage and remediation costs;
- any warnings which preceded prosecution or attempts to resolve any problems without bringing criminal proceedings;
- any evidence of premeditation or calculation;
- in offences of strict liability, whether the prosecution says the offence was committed negligently or not; and
- details of relevant previous convictions.

23.16 Mitigation

Mitigation will then be put forward on behalf of the defendant. This may include the presentation of a Presentence Report prepared by the Probation Service. The prosecution is entitled to correct any matter put forward in mitigation which is untrue or unfair. Mitigating factors likely to be relevant to EOs would include:

- a guilty plea (for which the Court will indicate what credit has been given);
- efforts to rectify the harm;
- precautions taken to prevent the harm, even though these were unsuccessful;
- evidence of a review of procedure in an effort to prevent offences occurring again; and
- financial circumstances.

The defence may also want to cite any reported cases of sentence in relation to a particular offence.

Having heard the mitigation, the Court will pass sentence and, if appropriate, make an order that the defence pay the prosecution's costs.

23.17 Costs

Provisions for the award of costs in criminal proceedings are made by Prosecution of Defences Act 1985 (POA 1985) and are the subject of a practice direction reported at 93 Cr App R 89.

23.17.1 Defendant's costs orders

Where a defendant is acquitted, or the prosecution is not proceeded with, the Court has power to order that the costs of the defence shall be paid out of central funds (s16 POA 1985). This is the usual order, unless (i) the defendant can be said to have brought suspicion on himself and has misled the prosecution into thinking the case against him was stronger than it was or (ii) there was ample evidence to support a conviction but the defendant was acquitted on a meritless technicality (1991 Practice Direction, para. 2.2)

It may be that the advice of the practice direction will have to be amended as the European Convention on Human Rights gains influence. *Minelli v*

Switzerland 5 EHRR 554 and *Leutscher v The Netherlands* (1997) 24 EHRR 181 suggest that to refuse to award costs on the basis that the acquittal was a meritless technicality is inconsistent with the presumption of innocence.

The Court may order the prosecution to pay all or part of the defendant's costs but only where the costs have been incurred as the result of an unnecessary or improper act or omission by the prosecutor.

23.17.2 Prosecution costs

s17 POA 1985 provides for the costs of proceedings in the Crown Court or the Divisional Court to be paid to the prosecutor out of central funds. However, this only applies to a private prosecutor. Costs will not be paid out of central funds to a public authority, including a LA or the EA.

If a defendant is found guilty, or loses an appeal against sentence or conviction, s18 POA 1985 empowers to order that he pays part or all of the prosecution costs.

The amount of any such award of costs is to be fixed by the sentencing Court. There is no power of taxation. Where the application for prosecution costs is to be substantial, details of the claim should be served on the defence to give it the opportunity to challenge any items claimed that it regards as unreasonable. The Court will then have to make a summary determination as to what costs it would be reasonable to award. If the case is being prosecuted by a public authority, it will be entitled to claim for time spent by its officers in preparing for the proceedings and in investigating the offences. (*Neville v Gardner Merchant* [1983] 5 Cr App Rep S 349.)

The Court, having arrived at a figure, will also have to take into account the defendant's ability to pay. It is for this reason that many awards of costs do not reflect the true cost to the prosecution of bringing the proceedings. There are conflicting authorities but there appears to be no requirement that costs should bear any proportion to the sentence awarded. If the prosecution's costs are thousands of pounds, the prosecution is still prima facie entitled to them even if the fine imposed for the offence is hundreds of pounds.

23.18 Legal Aid

Subject to means, personal defendants to criminal charges are entitled to Legal Aid. The grant of Legal Aid is governed by the Legal Aid Act 1988

(LAA 1988) and by regulations made under that Act, currently the *Legal Aid in Criminal and Care Proceedings Regulations* 1989 which are regularly updated and amended. There are two sets of regulations: the General Regulations SI 1989/344 and the Costs Regulations SI 1989/343.

Legal Aid will cover not only representation but preparation of the case and, if appropriate, the costs of instructing expert witnesses.

23.19 Appeal from the Crown Court

Appeal from the Crown Court lies to the Court of Criminal Appeal. Appeal against conviction is broadly on the grounds that the conviction was unsafe, which covers both misdirection on the law and procedural irregularity. Appeal against sentence is on the grounds that the sentence passed was on the wrong factual basis, took into account irrelevant matters or that there are now fresh matters to be taken into account, or that it was manifestly excessive or wrong in law or principle. For the purposes of an appeal, a sentence includes an order to pay costs. (*R v Hayden* 60 Cr App R 304.) The procedure for appealing to the Court of Appeal Criminal Division is governed by the Criminal Appeal Act 1968 (CAA 1968), the *Criminal Appeal Rules* 1968, the Practice Direction at 1988 1 WLR 34, the Criminal Appeal Act 1995, and the guide issued by the Registrar of Criminal Appeals at 77 Cr App R 138.

There is provision for further appeal to the House of Lords under CAA 1968 and rules.

23.20 European Court of Justice (ECJ) and European Court of Human Rights (ECHR)

There is also provision for a party to ask the Court to exercise its power, under the EC Treaty (Art.177), to refer a question of Community Law for preliminary determination by the European Court of Justice (ECJ). This power is, in fact, also available to a Court of first instance but is more likely to arise at the appellate level - *Criminal Appeal (References to European Court) Rules* SI 1972/1786 and the *Crown Court Rules* 1982 (Rule 29).

The European Court of Human Rights (ECHR) also has jurisdiction to consider a complaint that an individual's rights under the the European Convention for the Protection of Human Rights and Fundamental Freedoms and process. This is not an appeal as such and the ECHR will not consider an application until the aggrieved party has exhausted the appellate process within his own country.

The ECHR 1953 is not yet part of domestic law but is increasingly used as an aid to the interpretation of statutes and statutory instruments.

CHAPTER 24

INTERNATIONAL ENVIRONMENTAL CRIME

CONTENTS

CHAPTER 24

INTERNATIONAL ENVIRONMENTAL CRIME

24.1 Introduction

The international community is increasingly aware of the necessity for committed transboundary environmental regulations which take account of environmental crime. Some instances of transboundary environmental violations are so severe that they are now viewed and prosecuted as crimes. The will of the international community has expressed itself in a number of international agreements which have binding legal status for the states which are parties to the agreements. Such agreements are thus being implemented in national law, in compliance with the terms of the treaties.

24.2 Basel Convention on the Control of Transboundary Movements of Hazardous Wastes and their Disposal

The clearest and best developed reflection of this growth in the understanding of international environmental crime is to be seen in the *Basel Convention on the Control of Transboundary Movements of Hazardous Wastes and their Disposal*. Within this Convention the illegal or unauthorised movement of transboundary waste is criminalised. Waste itself is defined by reference to Annexes 1-3 of the Convention which distinguish between different types. Radioactive waste (subject to specific controls in other international instruments), and waste which derives from the normal operations of a ship (likewise dealt with through other international instruments) are excluded from the Convention. There are reporting requirements for parties and comprehensive requirements for the management of hazardous waste. There are prohibitions in respect of the export of hazardous waste to countries which forbid imports of the substance and requirements for notification and regulation of a transboundary movement of hazardous waste in accordance with Annex V A. Where a transboundary movement cannot be completed in accordance with the terms of the contract, the waste must be returned to the State of export.

Art. 4 of the Convention says "Each Party shall take appropriate legal, administrative and other measures to implement and enforce the provisions of this Convention, including measures to prevent and punish conduct in contravention of the Convention."

Art. 9 of the Convention sets out, *inter alia*, the illegality of transboundary movement (i) of hazardous waste without notification, without prior consent, with consent obtained upon the basis of falsification, misrepresentation or fraud, (ii) of waste which does not conform in a material way with its documentation, or which results in the deliberate disposal of that waste in contravention of the Convention or general principles of international law.

Art. 10 sets out the objectives of cooperation between the parties, which includes cooperation over (i) the provision of information, on either a bilateral or multilateral basis, and (ii) monitoring, technological developments, technology transfer and technical capacity.

Art. 12 foresees the establishment of a protocol which sets out rules and procedures in respect of liability and compensation for damage.

States have now begun to subject the movement of hazardous waste to regulatory controls by enacting measures which will gradually implement the terms of the Convention.

24.3 Convention on International Trade in Endangered Species of Wild Fauna and Flora (CITES)

The Endangered Species (Import and Export) Act was passed in the UK, for the purpose of implementing the Convention on International Trade in Endangered Species of Wild Fauna and Flora 1973 (CITES). The regulations in CITES are designed to protect endangered species of flora and fauna by regulating or prohibiting their international trade. Appended to CITES are three lists of species:

(i) trade in Appendix I species is prohibited, other than in a restricted group of categories which must be subject to a permit and certification system;
(ii) Appendix II species are still regarded as at risk, although restricted trade is permitted;
(iii) Appendix III lists species which are rare if not endangered and therefore must be subject to regulation.

Sections of this Act deal with the restriction by a licensing system of importation and exportation of certain animals and plants, which are set out in a Schedule to the Act, which may be modified by the Secretary of State. The Act creates the offence of dealing in illegally imported 'things ', and gives power to the Secretary of State to restrict the places of import, and the movement of certain live animals after importation. The Act includes potential direct criminal liability for the directors or managers of a corporation where the corporation is alleged to have committed an offence under the Act.

Note also the *Control of Trade in Endangered Species (Enforcement) Regulations* 1997: these regulations were made in pursuance of Council Regulation (EEC) No 3626/82 (OJ No L384, 31.12.82. These regulations create, *inter alia*, criminal offences relating to breach of requirements under the Principal Regulation: the offences arise out of the making of false statements or giving false information; the misuse of permits or certificates; the contravention of a term of a permit or certificate; the moving of a live specimen from the address specified in the permit to another address without prior authorisation and other offences relating to dealing in Annex A or Annex B specimens.

24.4 Developments

There is an increasing impetus within the international community to find new and improved levels of international cooperation, upon which transboundary environmental regulation and enforcement will heavily depend, with the proliferation of waste and the increased volume of trade in the global economy. For example, in May, 1997, the environmental leaders of the Group of Eight (G8) met for the first time, specifically to address issues of enforcement at a global level. A statement issued after this meeting gave strong support both to goals of enforcement at an international level and to the value of access to information for the citizen. In January, 1998, a further meeting was held, between the enforcement officials of the same group of states, to reinforce their efforts to coordinate enforcement regimes. Environmental law enforcement remained a high priority for discussion at the recent G8 summit in the UK. There is still a great distance between the goals and the means for achieving them internationally and a dearth of technical capacity and investigative resources available to investigate potential violations. What seems clear is that coordination between states is likely to improve as the need for enforcement of environmental laws proliferates.

24.5 Other conventions

International cooperation can be distinguished in two different ways: primary international cooperation (transfer of proceedings and transfer of execution) and secondary cooperation (extradition and legal assistance). In Europe, the *Strasbourg Convention* (1957) deals with extradition, on which a new Convention will come into effect which will abolish a number of the traditional exceptions. The *European Convention* on the transfer of proceedings in criminal matters (Strasbourg 1972) has been ratified by few states. It does not provide for the physical transfer of the subject and in fact extradition may be used where appropriate. The *European Convention on the International Validity of Criminal Judgments* (The Hague 1970) has also received scant support from states, probably because the assumption on which it is based is that the original sentence will be converted by the requested state. By contrast, the *Convention on the Transfer of Sentenced Prisoners* (Strasbourg 1983) has international application, has been ratified by 33 states and gives states the options of choosing between continued enforcement and conversion of sentence. The convention has no application where a convicted person has already returned to his home state. Thus a convicted person may evade punishment where he cannot be extradited. Also, the *Schengen Agreement* (in force since March, 1995) provides for the regulation of interstate cooperation, the right to hot pursuit across the border and the informal exchange of information.

A general analysis of international criminal law lies outside the scope of this work. There can be no doubt that if environmental legislation proliferates at the international level, as it seems likely to, then to the extent that enforcement requires international cooperation, domestic legislation will increasingly reflect that requirement, both through provisions for the acquisition of information and through the detailed regulation of enforcement procedures.

24.6 Conclusion

International environmental cooperation at the level of criminal enforcement could be described as being still in a state of infancy. Definitional terms and customary norms in respect of conditions necessary for prosecution are beginning to emerge from the Treaties and Conventions which specifically address environmental crime. States are beginning to create a climate which will foster the cooperation at a transboundary level which is essential to deal with the global environmental challenges which are presented by the global trading community. At the investigative level, Interpol instituted a working party on Environmental Crime in 1992 which promotes international cooperation in criminal environmental investigation, as does the International Network for Environmental Compliance and Enforcement (INECE). The ultimate objective is to render international compliance with established and safe environmental regulation and management. Criminal sanctions are the final and most powerful instruments for use in achieving that objective: these instruments have been little used in the recent past but it is clear that the international community is now beginning to appreciate their potential.

CHAPTER 25

EUROPEAN ENVIRONMENTAL CRIME

CONTENTS

CHAPTER 25

EUROPEAN ENVIRONMENTAL CRIME

25.1 Introduction

Over the past thirty to forty years, to varying extents, individual states have begun to develop criminal enforcement procedures which naturally reflect the legislative norms of the individual state legislature. The measures have to meet the challenges which environmental regulation and enforcement now present, both at a technical level and at the important level of public growth of awareness. At the level of state cooperation, a draft convention being produced by the Council of Europe on the protection of the environment through criminal law indicates the emergence of some common principles in the law.

Unsurprisingly, there is considerable discrepancy between individual states over issues of liability, particularly at the corporate level. For example, in the UK, the Netherlands and Denmark, corporate criminal liability is a well established legal notion. In Germany and Spain, it has yet to be established at all. The draft convention emphasises the importance of establishing corporate criminal liability which currently barely exists. Another area where there are contrasting regimes within the EC is in the notion of confiscating illegal benefits gained by corporations in committing an offence: it seems that a tendency to broaden the general scope of corporate criminal liability is emerging which counters the prevailing tendency in a number of countries to prosecute the individual but neglect the issue of corporate liability. Criminal procedures are normally used only as a last resort in enforcing environmental regulation but they generally contain sanctions which outstrip the powers available to administrative authorities, as well as significant deterrent properties. Paradoxically, these criminal sanctions are generally underused: the more serious types of environmental offences are committed by corporations, and prosecutions against successful businessmen, with the attendant risks of unemployment flowing from punitive fines or a shutdown of the operation, contain their own deterrent. The prosecution of individual officers of a corporation has been infrequent but appears to be a means of enforcement which is increasingly used. A readjustment is occurring of the balance between the responsibility of the individual with the liability of legal persons. For example, there is a broader way in which the *mens rea* of a corporation may be construed, according to its inferred knowledge and technical capacity. EC antitrust law has produced clarification of the principles and categories of the liability of enterprises and this may come to be reflected in EC law reform in environmental management and regulation.

The relationship between administrative and criminal sanctions varies considerably throughout the EC. It appears that where an administrative system is strong and efficient, and the administrative authority has powers to levy fines and impose other sanctions, then criminal provisions are less frequently resorted to. The intrinsic weakness in this type of system is the established working relationship which is likely to exist between the authority and the corporation. In some European countries, a system of administrative penal law operates, where fines may be levied for the contravention of administrative regulations. In Italy, this administrative penal law embraces a wider set of sanctions, including fiscal fines, suspension of activities and compensation or restoration.

An overview of the roles played by the authorities and the police in bringing a criminal prosecution reveals that the UK is the only country where the police have no role to play in a prosecution. In other EC countries, the police will tend to have responsibility for bringing the prosecution on the basis of evidence provided by the enforcing arm of the administrative authority after a preliminary investigation. The technical and often complex nature of the evidence which is required for a criminal prosecution will generally be the basis of cooperation between the police and the administrative authority. Generally, in EC countries the public prosecutor is responsible for conducting the prosecution, although in the UK it is the responsibility of the Environment Agency.

The role of the individual or the nongovernmental organisation (NGO) in a criminal prosecution is normally determined by the rules of criminal procedure of the state in question. The individual has a potentially very powerful role to play in increasing public awareness, although his role, similar to that of the NGO, is largely in a reporting capacity, providing evidence or being a witness. In some EC countries, the individual may bring a prosecution himself and in others he may be joined in the action in his capacity as victim and claim compensatory damages in a successful prosecution.

A variety of different criminal enforcement procedures are used in EC countries where criminal sanctions for environmental violations are a relatively recent phenomenon within the body of legislation. Generally speaking, the criminal enforcement regime will operate in conjunction with the administrative system of regulation, and offences occur when the administrative sanctions have been violated, with more serious and damaging violations attracting heavier penalties.

A brief analysis of the criminal environmental regimes in selected countries follows. It contains an overview of the environmental law enforcement regime of the country, and the types of enforcement which tend to be used in different circumstances:

25.2 Scandinavia

25.2.1 Denmark

Denmark, a unitary state, has been developing an environmental law enforcement regime since the 1970s. The main legislation providing for enforcement of the law is the Environmental Protection Act (EPA), which first entered into force in 1974. Its enforcement regime is based on a permit system. The subsequent Act, which became law in 1992, also operates on a system of licensing. Uniquely, s10 of that Act permits a person to enter into an environmental agreement as an *alternative* to joining the statutory regime. There has been an increased trend towards cooperation within the regulatory system, with great emphasis being placed upon the importance of environmental management, audit schemes and environmental contracts and covenants.

In 1997, the new EPA was passed, containing three new enforcement provisions: (1) The concept of 'environmental responsibility' is introduced, the loss of which may prevent a person or company from acquiring permission for new polluting activities. Loss of 'environmental responsibility' will occur where someone has been formerly convicted of a gross violation of environmental legislation, or been previously disqualified from polluting activities, or is liable for outstanding clean-up costs. (2) Where the loss of environmental responsibility is in respect of a company, this is linked directly to the management of the company and individual members of the board who have authority over decision-making procedures. (3) A register is now compiled, containing a list of persons or companies who have lost environmental responsibility as a consequence of conviction for a previous environmental violation.

25.2.1.1 Enforcement

This takes place primarily at an administrative level where an infringement may result in an injunction or a prohibition, either of which is resorted to only after warnings have been given. Criminal prosecutions in Denmark are mounted by the police, on the basis of a report given to them by the environmental authority. A large number of reports do not get as far as trial and something like a half of all cases are dealt with by means of fines by the Chief Constable, because companies generally wish to avoid the opprobrium of a public trial of the matter. Some 300 to 500 cases are reported to the police annually, these cases falling into two groups:

> (1) is the type of case where a continuing offence occurs, usually involving a repeating breach of an emission authorisation (eg, cases against farmers whose stubble-burning breaches the regulation that there must be a 2-metre wide cultivation-free zone alongside watercourses);
> (2) is where the breach has been so serious that it merits a criminal sanction (eg where there has been a very large unauthorised emission).

25.2.1.2

When a case is brought against a company, it is not necessary to identify the person who actually committed the offence, or to examine the practices of the company. It is sufficient for the prosecutor to establish that the company acted wilfully or negligently. However, in circumstances where the director of a company has authorised the violation, then he may be charged personally.

25.2.1.3

Danish environmental enforcement provisions do not allow immunity from prosecution to the Municipalities or the State. Sewage treatment plants, incineration plants and landfill sites are all administered by the Municipalities, whilst the Ministry of Defence and the Railways are state enterprises and it is perceived to be a necessary adjunct of good environmental management policy that these bodies are as accountable for their actions as any other person or company. Public awareness is an important deterrent factor in enforcement.

25.2.1.4 Legislation

The legislation providing for enforcement is found in the EPA 1992. Sanctions are fines for the conduct of licensed activity without a permit, or in violation of licence conditions. In circumstances where the violation put another person in danger, referred to as *'knowing endangerment'*, or where an economic benefit was obtained by the person who committed the offence, then a term of imprisonment not exceeding two years may be imposed. Where an illegal gain has been made by the offender, then this will be taken into account in the imposition of a fine.

25.2.1.5 Conventions

Denmark is a party to the following conventions:

European Convention on Mutual Assistance.

[Note the Danish reservation that assistance may be refused if proceedings have already been instituted by the Danish State or a third state, if the offence has already been dealt with in the courts in Denmark or a third state, or if judicial authorities in either have waived or discontinued proceedings in the same matter.]

European Convention on Extradition.
European Convention on Transfer of Proceedings.
European Convention on the International Validity of Criminal Judgments.
Convention on the Transfer of Prisoners.

25.2.2 Sweden

25.2.2.1 Introduction

Sweden, a unitary state, legislates for environmental regulation and enforcement at a central level. There three main groups of legislation:

(1) Laws dealing with land regulation, which address issues of land use in agriculture, eg the Maintenance of Fair Farmland Act 1979 (MFFA 1979), the Forestry Conservation Act 1979 (FCA 1979), the Water Act 1983 (WA 1983) and the Nature Conservation Act 1964 (NCA 1964);
(2) Laws dealing with protection of the environment, eg the Environment Protection Act 1969 (EPA 1969), the Health Protection Act 1982 (HPA 1982) and the Act on Chemical Products 1985 (ACP 1985);
(3) Laws dealing with the regulation of natural resources, through the Water Act 1983 (WA 1983), the Forestry Conservation Act 1979 (FCA 1979) and the Natural Resources Act 1987 (NRA 1987).

A radical review of Swedish environmental law has been in progress for some time and a new Bill is currently before the Swedish Parliament reflecting an advanced approach to environmental management and regulation. A new Code has been produced by the Government which contains 15 new national environmental quantity goals, aimed at achieving *sustainable development* in these areas within a generation. The goals reflect an advanced integrated approach, by the Swedish legislature, to the business of environmental management, both at media and administrative levels. Long-term environmental quality goals will constitute a framework for the broad environmental strategy. They will form the basis of three objectives.

(1) the protection of the environment, through the control of emissions and the protection of biodiversity;
(2) the maintenance of sustainable supplies from renewable resources, which will guarantee the long-term survival of the productive capacity of ecosystems;
(3) efficiency of resource utilisation, which amounts to the more efficient use of energy and other natural resources.

Stricter control and special regulatory measures, including prohibitions and prior consent procedures for the management of hazardous substances are envisaged in the Bill.

25.2.2.2 Enforcement

Enforcement of environmental legislation is primarily administrative, with criminal sanctions available for certain particular violations. Conduct of a criminal case is the responsibility of the public prosecutor who makes a decision to prosecute on the basis of preliminary reports. Criminal sanctions appeared for the first time in 1981 in an amendment to the EPA 1969, incorporated in the Criminal Code, where criminal liability attaches to a person who: (i) pollutes the soil water or the atmosphere in a way which causes danger to human or animal life, or vegetation; (ii) stores waste to the same effects; or (iii) who causes 'considerable nuisance' to the environment through noise, vibration or waste.

Criminal liability will not occur where the polluting activity is within the ambit of conditions already imposed upon the person. Provision has been made within the EPA for criminal liability to attach to offences arising out of circumstances where administrative rules have been broken (eg failures to observe a duty of prepermit investigation, to report polluting activities to the government and to comply with licence conditions).

25.2.2.3 Legislation

The EPA is the primary source of criminal sanctions, although some criminal provisions are only to be found in the Criminal Code. Sanctions used are the usual ones, fines and terms of imprisonment. Sanctions contained in certain specific Acts extend only as far as a fine with no imprisonment. The maximum term of imprisonment is usually two years, although in the most serious cases a term not exceeding six years may be imposed. There is also the sanction of an environmental protection fine. This fine is an administrative charge and may be imposed upon a person or company committing an offence where the objective conditions for criminal liability have been established. The charge may reflect the amount of illegal gain which the violation has produced for the offender.

25.2.2.4 Conventions

Sweden is a party to the following conventions:

European Convention on Mutual Assistance.

[Note the Swedish reservation that assistance may be refused when the offence in question is one which is not punishable under Swedish law, or when the offence is already being investigated or tried in Sweden or in a third-party state, or when the Swedish authorities have already investigated the offence and decided not to pursue a prosecution, or when trial of the offence is time-barred. For rogatory letters in respect of seizure or house-visitation to be executed, the offence must be an extraditable one, and the letters must be consistent with Swedish law.]

European Convention on Extradition.
European Convention on the Transfer of Proceedings.
European Convention on the International Validity of Criminal Judgments.
Convention on the Transfer of Prisoners.

25.3 Germany

25.3.1. Introduction

Germany is a federal state and, accordingly, legislative competence exists on two levels, the federal and the Länder. Environmental criminal legislation first appeared formally in the body of federal law in 1980. Three main groups of enforcement procedures have emerged:

(1) in the administrative agencies ranging from agency remediation of damage at the person or company's expense, to a complete shutdown of the activity giving rise to the violation.
(2) An administrative group of procedures arising out of *administrative* penal law: these involve the imposition of fines (*Geldbusse*) upon the manager of the company committing the violation. This fine is not considered to be a criminal sanction and is used because true criminal sanctions may not be imposed upon a legal entity. The violation is described as an 'illegal and reproachable action'. This fine may be extremely high (up to 1 million DM) when it is imposed as a penalty for an intentional criminal offence Criminal sanctions within

the third group of procedures: in 1994, the law was modified to include criminal sanctions within a criminal environmental code for offences resulting in water pollution, soil pollution, and air pollution. Provisions now exist which deal with noise pollution, the illegal deposit of waste and the illegal exploitation of a licensed activity. Note that, specifically, pollution which occurs through the emission of a toxic substance may be an offence even in circumstances where conditions have been complied with. These measures have parallel status in civil and criminal law. The Länder, generally responsible for administrative legislation, may not legislate divergently from the federal legislative, where the federal legislature has already exercised its powers. In practice, environmental enforcement provisions are the province of the Länder, through administrative measures and use of the system of administrative penal law (the *Ordnungswidrigkeitenrecht*).

25.3.2 Sanctions

The *Geldbusse,* mentioned above, is not a criminal penalty. Criminal penalties take the form of fines *or* prison sentences, and the respective penalties are laid out in the provisions of the code which define the offence. Where a fine may be imposed, it is a matter for the court to determine the amount, by reference to the circumstances of the case, because there is no limit marked within the legislation. The length of a term of prison sentence generally reflects whether the defendant acted negligently or intentionally. In cases of water, soil or air pollution, if the defendant acted negligently the maximum term of imprisonment is three years. If he acted intentionally, this tariff rises to a maximum term of five years' imprisonment. Where there has been 'knowing endangerment' as a result of a toxic emission, the sentence may increase to between three and ten years, depending upon the negligence or intent of the offence. Where death occurs as a result of the violation, then a term of ten years will be imposed.

Other sanctions, rarely resorted to, are available under the general German criminal code: (i) debarring an individual from the practice of his profession (which has become particularly important as a sanction for the illegal transport of waste); (ii) means for dealing with the accrual of illegal gains from an offence; (iii) seizure of property (which in an environmental case may result in the confiscation of property used to commit the offence, in effect the confiscation of an entire industrial plant).

Prosecutions are generally brought by the Länder, conducted by the public prosecutor. Environmental bodies perform an important role in providing the technical information which gives rise to the prosecution. Note that there is no immunity from prosecution for civil servants, in particular those who are responsible for the issue of permits for polluting activities.

25.3.3 Conventions

Germany is a party to the following Conventions:
European Convention on Mutual Assistance.

> [Note that the search and seizure of property is only permitted where German conditions in respect of dual criminal liability have been met, and municipal law has been complied with.]
>
> European Convention on Extradition.
> Convention on the Transfer of Prisoners.
> Schengen Convention.

25.4 Netherlands

25.4.1 Introduction

The Netherlands is a unitary state and, until 1993, Dutch environmental laws were substantially an accumulation of statutes passed by central government, some of which reflected a sectoral approach to environmental management and regulation. Specific provision for environmental management and protection first appeared in Dutch national law in the 1960s, with the passage of the Marine Oil Pollution Act 1958 (MOP 1958), the Water Pollution Act 1969 (WPA 1969), the Air Pollution Act 1970 (APA 1979). The sectoral approach was adopted in the Act of Chemical Waste 1976 (ACW 1976), the Act on Waste 1977 (AW 1977), and the Noise Nuisance Act 1979 (NNA 1979). Each Act contained different provisions and permits for environmental management. The integration of these laws and the unification of the regulatory provisions were achieved in the Environment Management Act 1993 (EMA 1993) which is now the main source of environmental regulation. The main criminal sanctions supporting this coordinated regime are to be found in the Economic Offences Act (EOA), which has a correspondingly coordinated effect.

25.4.2 Enforcement

Enforcement is achieved in the Netherlands using administrative, civil and criminal sanctions. Administrative measures, in the EMA, include penalty payments (which may be imposed by the appropriate authority on a continuing basis for the amount of time that the violation continues to occur). It is also open to the authority to effect remediation and then require reimbursement of the costs incurred from the offending party. Other sanctions are also available to the authority, the strongest of which is the ultimate withdrawal of a licence.

25.4.3 Sanctions

Further criminal sanctions are available under the Dutch Penal Code where a person who is negligently or intentionally responsible for the illegal emission of a polluting substance into the air, water or soil, thereby endangering either a person's life or public health, 'knowing endangerment', will be liable to criminal sanctions. Under Dutch law, a victim may intervene in a criminal prosecution, which may give rise to the imposition of a compensation order in favour of the victim.

These sanctions are used infrequently, because most emissions which occur are within the terms of the licence granted and therefore the subject of administrative law.

What appears to be emerging from the growth of Dutch environmental case law is, firstly, an increase in the use of criminal law as an enforcement provision, and, secondly, an increased emphasis on a civil environmental duty of care, combined with deregulation and self-regulation. Nevertheless, some duty of care provisions are supported by the EOA, for example the duty-of-care found in the Soil Protection Act (SPA). The Dutch Criminal Code does provide for the prosecution of offences of a general nature which may have specific application in environmental law, examples of which are the offences of forgery, or participation in an illegal organisation. There is limited immunity from prosecution for public servants who may be liable other then when carrying out a specific governmental task.

25.4.4 Legislation

There are two different sets of sanctions in Dutch legislation: they are to be found for environmental offences under the EOA and in the Criminal Code.

Under the EOA, the amount of a maximum sanction will depend upon whether the offence is an infraction or a crime. If the offence was intentional, it has the status of a crime and may attract a fine of 100,000 guilders or a term of imprisonment not exceeding six years. If the offence was committed negligently, then the fine will not exceed 25,000 guilders or a term of imprisonment not exceeding one year. Where the offence has been committed by a legal entity and the judge perceives that the levels of fine are inappropriately low, then the level of fines may be raised. The fine may also be increased to reflect the amount of illegal gain which was made by the defendant committing the offence. A fine may be imposed under this Act in addition to a criminal penalty, although generally Dutch law does not allow for the imposition of a sentence of imprisonment *and* a fine.

There are further sanctions available under this Act which address the activities of the business where the environmental offence took place. These range from the publication of the judgment after trial to the shutting down of the company altogether. It is open to the judge to order the defendant to comply with the terms of any environmental requirement imposed by the authority. This creates substantial opportunities for remediation.

Under the Criminal Code, fines not exceeding 25,000 guilders may be imposed, if the crime has been committed negligently, rising to 100,000 guilders when the crime has been committed intentionally. If the crime has been committed by a legal entity, then the fine can be increased to 1,000,000 guilders. If criminal liability has been established and the emission was committed negligently, then a term of imprisonment of one year may be imposed. This may be increased to two years, if the offence resulted in a death. In circumstances where the emission was intentional, then a term of imprisonment not exceeding 12 years may be imposed, rising to 15 years where a death has resulted from the offence.

Also contained within Dutch legislation is a regulation which addresses the recoupment of an illegal gain and provisions for cost savings.

25.4.5 Conventions

The Netherlands are a party to the following conventions:

European Convention on Mutual Assistance.

> [Note that assistance may be refused if the Dutch authorities take the view that the issue under inquiry is connected to a person's political convictions, religion, nationality, race or ethnic group. It may also be refused if the impending prosecution is already occurring in the Netherlands, or if the proceedings are incompatible with the principle of *non bis in idem*.
>
> The Government has also issued a declaration in respect of letters rogatory for search and seizure, to the effect that such letters will only be executed for extraditable offences within the meaning of the European Convention on Extradition, and provided that the execution of such letters has been authorised by a Netherlands court in accordance with municipal law.]

European Convention on Extradition.
European Convention on the Transfer of Proceedings.
European Convention on the International Validity of Criminal Judgments.
Convention on the Transfer of Prisoners.
Schengen Convention.

25.5 Convention on the Protection of the Environment through Criminal Law

The *Convention for the Protection of the Environment by Criminal Law*, elaborated by the Council of Europe, illustrates the emergence of a common policy of enforcement procedures among EC countries.

This Convention was signed on November 4th, 1998. There are seven initial signatories, namely Denmark, Finland, France, Germany, Iceland and Sweden. The purpose of the Convention is to establish a regime of criminal liability whereby the commission of certain intentional or negligent acts are rendered criminal offences.

Art. 2 requires a party to the Convention to adopt measures which criminalise the intentional discharge, emission or introduction of substances or ionising radiation into any medium which results in death, injury or the significant risk thereof. Similar measures are to be adopted in repect of any unlawful discharge or emission causing deterioration, death, serious injury or substantial damage. Dealing in hazardous waste, unlawfully operating a plant involving a dangerous activity and manufacturing and dealing generally in hazardous radioactive substances are also to be the subject of such measures.

Art. 3 requires appropriate measures to be taken by parties to criminalise the same groups of offences where they are committed *negligently*.

Art. 4 requires the adoption of appropriate measures to establish criminal or administrative offences where there have been unlawful discharges, emissions or introductions of a quantity of substances or ionising radiation into a medium; the unlawful manufacture of and dealing in nuclear materials, radioactive substances or hazardous chemicals; the unlawful causing of changes detrimental to a national park, nature reserve, water conservation area or other protected area; or the unlawful possession, taking and damaging or killing of or trading in protected wild flora and fauna species.

Art. 5 of the Convention outlines the requirements for establishing a party's jurisdiction, and Arts. 6, 7 and 8 determine the requirement for criminal sanctions for the offences, specifically to include imprisonment, pecuniary sanctions, confiscation measures and the possibility of restoring the environment.

Art. 9 requires a party to enact measures which create criminal corporate liability, which will not exclude criminal proceedings against a natural person. Art. 10 requires measures to be enacted which will enable cooperation between the environmental protection authority, the investigating agency and the prosecuting authority. Art. 11 permits a party to grant any group with an interest in protecting the environment a right to participate in criminal proceedings. Art. 12 advocates the widest possible levels of cooperation in these matters between parties.

The Convention echoes the environmental section in the *Resolutions of the XVth International Congress of Penal Law.*

CHAPTER 26

AMERICAN ENVIRONMENTAL CRIME

CONTENTS

CHAPTER 26

AMERICAN ENVIRONMENTAL CRIME

26.1 Introduction

Nine major statutes govern federal enforcement in the USA:

Resource, Conservation and Recovery Act 1976 (RCRA 1976)
Toxic Substances Control Act 1976 (TSCA 1976)
Federal Insecticide, Fungicide and Rodenticide Act 1947 (FIFRA 1947)
Comprehensive Environmental Response, Compensation and Liability Act 1980 (CERCLA 1980)
Clean Air Act 1963 (CAA 1963)
Safe Drinking Water Act 1974 (SDWA 1974)
Federal Water Pollution Control Act (Clean Water Act 1977) (CWA 1977)
Rivers and Harbours Act 1899 (RHA 1899)
Endangered Species Act 1973 (ESA 1973)

26.2 Resource, Conservation and Recovery Act 19 (RCRA)

This provides a detailed scheme for the federal regulation of hazardous wastes. It legislates for the generation, treatment, storage, transportation and disposal of such substances. '*Hazardous waste*' is defined as 'solid' (garbage, refuse, sludge from a waste-water treatment plant, water supply treatment plant or air-pollution control facility) and either 'listed', (the Environment Protection Agency [EPA] has a long, expanding list), 'discarded' (abandoned, recycled or inherently wastelike) or possessed of one or more of the following characteristics: ignitability, corrosivity, reactivity, or toxicity.

26.2.1 Offences

(i) Criminal penalties may be imposed upon anyone who knowingly treats, stores or disposes of hazardous waste without a permit, or transports it to a site having no permit. It is not a defence for that person to assert that he did not know the waste was hazardous, or that he did not know what the waste was. Some US courts have required the accused to establish the status of the waste, others have not. Corporate officers are increasingly prosecuted under this statute.

ii) A person may also commit the offence of 'knowing endangerment', which amounts to the equivalent of 'recklessness' in British law - that is, a knowing violation of the law, placing another 'in danger of death or serious bodily injury'. For the prosecution to succeed against an individual, it must be proved by evidence that the defendant is aware of the nature of his conduct.

26.2.2 Defences

A belief that the waste in question is being recycled.

Administrative defences have generally not succeeded, such as compliance with closure plans, or the Government's failure to provide test sample results.

Financial constraints also fail.

25.2.3 Penalties

For 'knowingly transporting' the waste substance, etc:

(i) up to five years imprisonment;
(ii) fines of up to $50,000 per day.

For 'knowing endangerment':

(i) up to 15 years' imprisonment;
(ii) Fines of up to $250,000 for individuals, $1,000,000 for companies.

26.3 Toxic Substance Control Act 1976 (TCSA 1976)

This statute legislates for the testing by the EPA of any substance which it assesses as likely to 'present an unreasonable risk of injury to health or the environment'. Prior notice must be given to the EPA of any new and envisaged manufacture of such a substance. The EPA may restrict or attach conditions to such manufacture, or prohibit it altogether. Flouting of such prohibition or conditions is being prosecuted in the criminal courts.

26.3.1 Offence

Knowing or wilful violation of the statute.

26.3.2 Penalties

(i) A fine, not exceeding $25,000;
(ii) imprisonment, for a term not exceeding one year.

26.4 Federal Insecticide, Fungicide and Rodenticide Act 1947 (FIFRA 1947)

This Act requires the registration of pesticides, prohibiting the distribution, the sale and the use of any pesticide not so registered. The EPA may limit the dealing in any pesticide not so registered and prosecute any violation of its requirements.

26.4.1 Offence

It must be proved by the prosecution that the defendant *knowingly* violated the provision. The defendant user's awareness of the registered status of the product is sufficient to establish 'knowledge'. The term 'user' includes adviser, and the adviser may be criminally liable, depending upon the state of his knowledge. The term also includes an employer, although the courts look at the employer's liability in the light of his knowledge as an individual. There is no private right of action under this statute.

26.4.2 Penalties

(i) For commercial violation (ie by dealers, commercial applicators, retailers) of a provision of this Act, offenders may be fined up to $25,000 per violation and/or imprisoned, imprisonment not to exceed one year.
(ii) A producer or registered user found guilty of a violation may be fined up to $50,000 per offence and/or imprisoned, imprisonment not to exceed one year.
(iii) A private user may be fined up to $1,000 per violation, and/or imprisoned, imprisonment not to exceed 30 days.

26.5 Comprehensive Environmental Response, Compensation and Liability Act 1980 (CERCLA 1980)

This statute was enacted for the purpose of dealing comprehensively with the problems arising out of 'abandoned and inactive hazardous waste disposal sites'. The main thrust of the statute is remedial and accordingly liability is imposed upon the following classes of person:

(i) The current owner/operator of the site where the waste is. The test of liability for the owner/operator is twofold: the extent to which actual control is exercised by the owner/operator, and the extent to which that owner/operator has authority over determining the method of disposal of the waste.
(ii) The owner/operator of the site at the time when the disposal was made, the person who arranged for the making of the disposal, and the person who transported the waste. Successive owner/operators may be held liable if the liability was transferred with the contract of ownership.

Note that in *Seminole Tribe of Florida v Florida* [1996] 116 S Ct 1114, the Supreme Court decided that Congress may not enact a statute which authorises a citizen to start proceedings against a State. Accordingly, state liability is precluded under CERCLA.

26.5.1 Offences

(i) Failure to report a release of a hazardous substance to the appropriate federal agency.

The government must prove, beyond reasonable doubt, that there was a hazardous substance; that it was of a reportable quantity; that it was released by a person 'in charge'(which category is defined widely, to include anyone who is in a position of responsibility for or knowledge of the substance); from a site; that the release was outwith the terms of the permit; that the defendant failed to notify the EPA as soon he knew about the release; that the government incurred remediation costs as a consequence of the release, although this last does not have to be proved by the prosecutor.

(ii) Failure to notify the EPA of the existence of a hazardous waste disposal site which has no permit.

The government must prove that the defendant owned or operated a site at which the substance was stored and that he knowingly failed to notify the EPA of its existence.

(iii) The knowing destruction or falsification of records.

The government has to prove that the defendant was the person required to notify, that he knowingly destroyed records and that those records were subject to reporting requirements.

(iv) Submission of false claims for reimbursement from the Superfund.

The government has to prove the defendant's state of knowledge, ie that he gave false information in support of a claim for reimbursement.

26.5.2 Penalties

(i) For failure to notify the EPA of the release of a hazardous substance, or for submitting a claim to the Superfund on the basis of false information in for a first offence, a fine not exceeding $250,000 for an individual ($500,000 for a corporation) and/or imprisonment not exceeding three years. This term may be increased to five years for subsequent offences.
(ii) For failure to notify the EPA of the existence of a waste disposal site: a fine not exceeding $10,000 and/or imprisonment not exceeding one year.
(iii) For the knowing destruction or falsification of records: a fine 'in accordance with Title 18 of the US Code' and /or imprisonment not exceeding three years.

Note that under the Superfund Amendments and Reauthorisation Act 1986 (SARA 1986), the EPA may pay a reward of up to $10,000 to a person who provides information leading to the arrest and conviction of a person for an offence under CERCLA.

26.6 Clean Air Act 1963 (CAA 1963)

This statute provides for the management and regulation of air pollution. It contains administrative and civil sanctions in addition to the criminal ones and these are more frequently used. The CAA, through the EPA, requires the operator of an air pollution source to maintain records, install monitoring equipment, allow sampling of emissions, provide the EPA with relevant information and to submit compliance certifications.

26.6.1 Programmes

The CAA legislates for the EPA to provide a number of different programmes:

(a) National Ambient Air Quality Standards (NAAQS)which regulate the levels of concentration of pollutants in the air. Enforcement is through State or Federal Implementation Plans. State plans must contain standards no lower than those set by the EPA.

(b) National Uniform Emission Standards for Hazardous Air Pollutants (NESHAPs) which regulate emissions of pollutants from existing and new sources. State plans must contain standards no lower than those set by the EPA.

(c) New Source Performance Standards (NSPS) which control emissions of air pollutants from newly-constructed sites. 'Source' is defined by the EPA and these regulations apply to sites which begin construction after the commencement of the regulations. These standards are enforced by State Implementation Plans.

(d) Limits for the emission of sulphur dioxide, by allowance and planned reductions

(e) The gradual phasing out of ozone-damaging substances, using the method of emission allowance.

26.6.2 Offences

i) when a pollutant is knowingly or negligently emitted which exceeds the NAAQS, NESHAPs, NSPS or the emission allowances for sulphur dioxide and ozone-depleting substances.
(ii) Failure to provide reports, or to fail to comply with the terms of an order made by the EPA.
(iii) Making a false statement, or tampering with EPA monitoring devices.
(iv) Failure to pay fees.

Administrative and civil sanctions apply to violations of the CAA or for making a false claim from the Superfund. A person may be prosecuted in the criminal courts as well as in the civil jurisdiction. The offence is committed when the violation occurs *knowingly* or *negligently*. Knowledge here is knowledge of the discharge, rather than knowledge of the legal standards which apply to the substance. The prosecutor does not have to prove the defendant's intention to violate the provision, simply that he was aware of the violation itself. Negligence here is where an emission occurs and the person responsible is aware of the danger of death or serious bodily harm which may ensue to another. The statutory defences pertaining to federal crimes are available to persons charged with *'knowing endangerment of others'*. In addition to these, there is a defence of consent to reasonably foreseeable dangers from substance emissions in the course of the pursuance of certain professions, medical treatment or scientific experimentation. Other defences run include issues of technical or economic considerations but these are more often reflected in the imposition of fines than as a successful defence.

26.6.3 Penalties

Each of the offences under this Act can attract fines under Title 18, or a term of imprisonment not exceeding one year, or both. In the case of NESHAP violations, there is a distinction between individual defendants and the corporate offender, the former liable to a fine under Title 18 and/or imprisonment not exceeding 15 years, the latter subject to a fine not exceeding $1,000,000 per violation. (Note that violations can attract civil penalties of up to $25,000 per day, a temporary or permanent injunction, or both.)

26.7 The Federal Water Pollution Control Act 1977 (FWPCA 1977) (also known as the Clean Water Act [CWA])

26.7.1 Pollutant Regime

The purpose of this Act is to establish the regime by which pollutants are discharged into US waters. They are either prohibited from being discharged (certain pollutants, eg radiological, chemical substances) or regulated in being discharged (eg toxic pollutants must be treated before discharged into publicly-owned treatment works). The instruments of the regime are limitations, water quality standards and permit programmes (National Pollutant Discharge Elimination System - NPDES). There are reporting and monitoring requirements (Discharge Monitoring Reports - DMRs), remediation requirements and the prohibition of dredging, filling or discharge of oil and sewage sludge. Pollution is defined as 'the man-made or man-induced alteration of the chemical, physical, biological and radiological integrity of water'. The Act applies to point sources only.

The enforcement of this Act suffers at present because the Act has not been reauthorised and its funding status remains unclear.

26.7.2 Offences

(i) The discharge of a pollutant into the navigable waters of the USA without the authorisation of a NPDES permit.
(ii) Falsification or misrepresentation of material information required by the CWA.
(iii) Failure to comply with a CWA regulation.

There are three levels of criminal culpability under this Act: negligence, knowing violation and knowing endangerment. A negligent violation may arise from the defendant's ignorance, but for a higher degree of culpability the prosecution must prove that the defendant had actual belief or awareness that the violation put another in danger of death or serious bodily injury. Circumstantial evidence may be used to produce an inference of actual knowledge, as may steps taken by the defendant to avoid being in possession of information.

(iv) Failure to comply with the regulations, or to fail to obtain a permit, or to abide by its terms and conditions.
(v) Failure to notify the EPA of a discharge, failure to keep records and failure to comply with monitoring requirements.

26.7.3 Defences

Of the defences available under this Act, the most consistently successful are:

(i) If the person who is endangered has given his consent, then this is a defence to the charge of knowing endangerment where the offence contained a danger which was reasonably foreseeable(eg occupational hazard or scientific experiment).
(ii) The notification requirement for a discharge of oil or hazardous waste may only be used in a criminal prosecution if the offence alleged is either perjury or giving a false statement, although if the notification is late, the defence may no longer be available.
(iii) The defendant may succeed in avoiding conviction if he can show that he was misled by the Government into thinking that a permit was not necessary. A defendant may also succeed on the grounds that the monitoring process, which forms the basis of the charge, was faulty.

Note that compliance with a permit is not a defence to a charge under this statute where the standard has predated the establishment of federal standards.

26.7.4 Penalties

(1) For a defendant guilty of a first-time *negligent* violation, a fine of between $2,500 and $25,000 per day, per violation, may be imposed, and/or imprisonment of not more than one year.

(2) For a defendant guilty of a knowing violation, a fine of between $5,000 and $50,000 per day, per violation, may be imposed and/or a prison term may be imposed. Subsequent offences carry double penalties.

(3) For being guilty of knowing endangerment, an individual is liable to a fine not exceeding $250,000 and/or years' imprisonment and a corporation may be fined up to $1,000,000. Subsequent offences may carry double penalties.

(4) The offences of providing false information or tampering with monitoring equipment may attract fines of $10,000 and/or imprisonment not exceeding two years. Subsequent offences may attract double penalties.

(5) Failing to notify the appropriate agency of a discharge of oil or hazardous substance may attract a fine not exceeding $10,000 and/or a term of imprisonment not exceeding five years.

26.8 Rivers and Harbours Act 1899 (RHA 1899)

This statute legislates for the management of the navigable waters of the USA in respect of unauthorised obstructions and the deposit of refuse. Consent must be obtained for the construction of any edifice on a navigable water.

26.8.1 Offences

- Deposit of refuse, irrespective of the nature or quantity of the refuse. It is not necessary for the deposit to obstruct the waterway.

- Unauthorised obstruction of the waterway.

26.8.2 Defences

US courts do not consistently construe offences under this Act as being of strict liability. Sabotage and theft, as well as acts of third parties, have succeeded as defences.

Compliance with Federal Water Quality Standards (FWQSs) does not succeed, however. Neither does the argument that the defendant behaved consistently with common practice in his business.

26.8.3 Penalties

Convictions under this statute are classified as misdemeanours and may incur a fine ranging from $500 to $2,500 and/or imprisonment of between 30 days and one year.

26.9 Safe Drinking Water Act 1974 (SDWA 1974)

26.9.1 Introduction

The purpose of this statute is to manage and regulate water quality with reference to the level of contaminants in groundwater and public water systems. By this Act, the EPA has established national primary drinking water regulations (NPDWRs) and a permit system for the discharge of contaminants into underground water (UICs), for which the EPA provides minimum standards. The Act regulates the amount of lead in drinking water coolers (defined as 'any mechanical device affixed to drinking water supply plumbing which actively cools water for human consumption'). This has included the compilation by the EPA of a list of types of water cooler which are not lead-free. The Act also creates the offence of tampering with public water systems.

26.9.2 Offences

Violations of the provisions of this Act, including the interstate sale or manufacture of coolers which are not lead-free. The prosecutor must show that the violation was done knowingly. Tampering with a public water system (or threatening to or attempting to do so) is an offence of specific intent which must be proved by the prosecutor.

26.9.3 Penalties

Violations of the provisions of this Act which have been committed wilfully can attract a fine in accordance with Title 18, or imprisonment not exceeding three years (five years in respect of tampering with the public water system).

26.10 Endangered Species Act 1973 (ESA 1973)

26.10.1 Purpose of Act

This Act was passed to conserve the habitats of endangered species and to legislate for their conservation. It established jurisdiction with two federal agencies: the Department of the Interior delegated its powers to the Fish and Wildlife Service (FWS), dealing with terrestrial species, and to the National Marine Fisheries Service (NMFS) dealing with marine species. The ambit of this work excludes a detailed analysis of the means by which habitats are conserved. Suffice to say that the ESA provides for the prohibition of certain actions which will threaten an endangered species. These prohibitions include the import and export of the species in question, taking the species and dealing in the species at interstate level. Violation of regulations pursuant to the Act is also prohibited. Exceptions and permits may be granted.

26.10.2 Offences

Knowing violations of specific prohibitions of the Act give rise to criminal liability, as well as attracting civil sanctions (up to $25,000 per violation of a prohibition, $12,000 per violation of a regulation pursuant to the Act, $500 per regulation, permit or certificate issued under the Act).

26.10.3 Defences

If the defendant can show that he was acting in self-defence, this will be a defence. A defence is also provided if the person can show that he was in possession of a valid permit or exemption.

26.10.4 Penalties

A conviction for a knowing violation can attract a fine not exceeding $50,000 and/or imprisonment not exceeding one year. Conviction for the violation of any other regulation can attract a fine not exceeding $25,000 and/or imprisonment not exceeding six months. Other penalties may be imposed, such as revocation of permits, forfeiture of equipment and illegally-taken species, as well as injunctions against persons violating the Act.

26.11 Environmental Protection Agency (EPA)

26.11.1 Function of the EPA

The EPA combines with the Department of Justice (DoJ) to enforce criminal convictions under the provisions of these various statutes. There has been an increase in the number of criminal prosecutions in recent years. In 1997, a total 278 criminal cases were referred to the DoJ for prosecution. $169.3m was imposed in criminal fines. The EPA currently employs about 200 prosecutors.

There remains a degree of flexibility in the enforcement policy of the EPA: the central justification for a prosecution appears to be culpable conduct in conjunction with significant environmental harm, although it has been suggested that 'the minimal scienter requirement has resulted in increased significance of prior compliance and degree of harm and decreased focus on culpability.'[1*] Other means of enforcement avoiding criminal litigation include comprehensive settlements (including injunctive relief, self-auditing, pollution prevention and the restoration of the ecosystem). The EPA will not seek the imposition of punitive fines for companies who identify and remedy violations. It will not make a criminal referral if the person or company has acted in good faith, other than in circumstances where to do so would be to condone either the deliberate violation of a condition by a party, or flouting an environmental philosophy. There is an increasing emphasis on self-auditing, which is the more effective since the audit is not treated as privileged information and is therefore not protected from public disclosure. Public awareness is increasingly used successfully as a means for achieving compliance. The Emergency Planning and Community Right to Know Act 19 (EPCRA 19), with its Toxics Release Inventory has proved to be an unexpectedly powerful piece of 'right to know' legislation. Information contained within the register is made increasingly assimilable by the environmentally-aware public.

26.11.2 Decision to prosecute

The basis upon which the EPA decides to prosecute is twofold: whether there has been significant environmental harm and whether there is evidence of culpable conduct.[2]

(1) Significant environmental harm is assessed by reference to actual harm, or the threat of significant harm. Failure to report an actual discharge will generally be an additional factor.

When an Act appears to be part of a growing trend within a particular part of the regulated community, then a prosecution will be considered primarily for its deterrent effect within that branch of the regulated community.

(2) Culpable conduct will be assessed by reference to one of the following:

(a) a history of repeated violations of a similar nature;
(b) deliberate misconduct which results in a violation;
(c) concealment of conduct;
(d) tampering with monitoring or control equipment;
(e) operating a business with pollution-related activities, without a permit, licence, manifest or other required documentation;
(f) corporate conduct where an audit has been made and remediation has not occurred.

* Endnotes, see page 474.

A system of Regional Case Screening operates, to assess enforcement on a continuing basis, both in the light of evidential developments and legal and regulatory interpretation of cases, to ensure that a consistent approach is being maintained as far as possible.

26.12 Department of Justice (DoJ)

The DoJ operates a similarly flexible approach. It will consider a number of factors when deciding whether to bring a criminal prosecution for a violation. In Congress, the Assistant Attorney-General recently expressed the prosecution policy thus:

> We bring environmental criminal cases for the same reasons the Department brings other criminal cases: to promote respect for the law, to achieve adequate deterrence, to provide just punishment, to ensure restitution for victims and to remedy the harm caused by offences. Our environmental crimes program is an essential part of our programme to protect human health, the environment and our natural resources.

Factors the DoJ takes into account when considering prosecution are whether there has been voluntary disclosure, the quality and timeliness of a potential defendant's cooperation, whether a compliance programme is in place, the extent to which it has been observed, and in respect of a corporation, the degree to which employees are punished for non-compliance or violation of the company's environmental policy. The US courts take the view that it is important to consider the effect of a criminal penalty upon the health of the company, although it is essential to bear in mind that without *effective* criminal sanctions, a company may take the view that a penalty for an environmental violation offence amounts to an expense to be factored into the cost of doing business. Nevertheless, the rate of prosecutions in the USA has risen consistently over the past two decades and currently looks to enforcement targets being met through the prosecution of smaller companies for smaller infractions and criminal violations. An important feature of the US system of enforcement is the parallel proceedings which can occur. Discovery through civil proceedings may be protected from use in an impending criminal prosecution and challenges for double jeopardy are not generally successful.

26.13 Corporate liability

The issue of corporate liability threads through all the legislation. A company is included in the definition of a person, and liability for criminal violations extends to the employees or agents of the company. Some statutes include sanctions against company officers in their capacity as operators. The 'responsible corporate officer doctrine' operates to apportion liability to those in authority, rather than to the perpetrator of the violation. Note the Commerce Clause (legislation preventing the placing of an undue burden on interstate commerce) has been successfully raised in an number of cases as a defence to charges of unauthorised waste disposal. Corporate liability is an enormous area of environmental law enforcement and further detailed analysis lies outside the scope of this work.

Notes

1 Criminal Enforcement of Environmental Law: Part I, 25 Envtl L Rep 10,459, 10,466 (September 1995).
2 See 'The Exercise of Investigative Discretion', published by USEPA, effective January, 1994.

About the Authors

Peter Harrison, Barrister

Practising from 6, Pump Court in the Temple

Called to the Bar in 1987, Peter Harrison has more than ten years' experience of prosecuting and defending environmental crimes. He has appeared before magistrates, juries, the Divisional Court and the Court of Appeal. He has prosecuted environmental offences on behalf of the EA, local authorities including County Councils, the Crown Prosecution Service (CPS) and private prosecutors. He has defended cases on behalf of individuals, firms and companies.

He is a member of the Planning and Environmental Bar Association; the Criminal Bar Association and the Environmental Law Foundation.

Fiona Darroch, Barrister

Practising from 10/11 Grays Inn Square

Fiona Darroch has specialised in Environmental law since the beginning of her career as a lawyer. She has prosecuted and defended environmental crime, and practises in all areas of environmental law. She has a Masters Degree in Environmental Law from London University (SOAS) and she is a member of the Environmental Law Foundation.

TABLE OF CASES

1. National Legislation

x. United Kingdom of Great Britain and Northern Ireland

x. United States of America

2. European Cases

TABLE OF STATUTES

1. National Legislation

x. Kingdom of Denmark

x. Kingdom of the Netherlands

x. Kingdom of Sweden.

x. United Kingdom of Great Britain and Northern Ireland

x. United States of America

2. European Legislation.

3. International Legislation

TABLE OF STATUTORY INSTRUMENTS

INDEX